I0807353

Churchyard and cemetery

MANCHESTER
1824
Manchester University Press

Churchyard and cemetery

Tradition and modernity in rural North Yorkshire

Julie Rugg

Manchester University Press

Published by Manchester University Press
Altrincham Street, Manchester M1 7JA, UK
www.manchesteruniversitypress.co.uk

British Library Cataloguing-in-Publication Data is available

Library of Congress Cataloging-in-Publication Data is available

ISBN 978 0 7190 9735 5 *paperback*

First published by Manchester University Press in hardback 2013

This paperback edition first published 2015

Printed by Lightning Source

Contents

List of plates, figures and tables

Plates

Figures

Maps

Tables

Preface

This is not a history of death in the nineteenth and twentieth centuries. Few historians would lay claim to the ability to write on so substantial a subject, and the majority settle down to consider one or two particular aspects of mortality. This study concentrates very specifically on the ownership and management of burial space. Ostensibly, this seems to be a rather marginal aspect of what has in the past been a rather marginal subject. There is little that is immediately appealing about burial management, and this history dwells in the decidedly unglamorous by-waters of vestry minutes, legislative process and the slow and steady grind of administrative functions such as entries in the parish burial register, applications for burial board funds, and *London Gazette* lists of Orders in Council to close churchyards. However, the dryness of these sources belies the strength of the passions evoked by the issue of burial, played out on local and national stages. In the second half of the nineteenth century, few problems frayed tempers faster in either House of Parliament than debate on Dissenters' burial grievances. Locally, representatives of different denominations sometimes declared themselves so intransigently opposed on the issue of burials that government departments were asked to intervene. More importantly, however, a detailed history of burial space offers a steady chronology of measurable indicators, and takes the historian to the very heart of the big questions posited by historians such as Philippe Ariès: when and how did attitudes towards mortality change?

Any history of burial should be rooted firmly in place, and

Preface

North Yorkshire is a very particular place. Now, as ever, the funeral of a farmer fills the church to capacity and until recently the local newspapers listed everyone who attended. This study focuses on a central portion of what used to be termed the North Riding, and covers an area which runs from the northern tip of the Wolds, up through the North York Moors to the edge of industrialised Teesside, and to the west through the Vale of York to the eastern fringe of the Yorkshire Dales. Although early eighteenth-century industries flourished in parts of the area, its small settlements have generally been subject to ongoing depopulation. With the exception of Harrogate, Knaresborough, Ripon and a handful of market towns, the villages have tended to remain largely unchanged in size. Agriculture remains a principal occupation in many areas, although some of the villages are slowly becoming dormitory settlements as access to roads such as the A19 and A64 mimics railways in the nineteenth century, in facilitating easy movement from country to city.

It seems rather perverse to look for change in the heart of such studied rurality, particular where the subject is burial and where the culture is generally deemed to be traditional and conservative. Furthermore, there is in this area no history of radical Dissent to offer substantive challenge to the status quo. In central North Riding both Primitive and Wesleyan Methodism flourished in the nineteenth century, but the Old Dissent was clustered in the market towns, and Quakers tended to be thinly spread. As a consequence, there was never any substantial burial provision that was independent of the Church of England. It could be argued that some churchyards in this study have changed very little since the Anglo-Saxon period: burials continue to take place at a rate of no more than maybe one or two a year. However, rurality notwithstanding, the area has still been subject to the play of national legislation which in the nineteenth century introduced a new regulatory framework. Board of Health inspectors visited even the most remote churchyards, and letters passed with frequency between the Burials Office in Whitehall and many of the Yorkshire villages in the study.

In choosing to study a rural area, the book is able to shift focus from the massed mortality of cities and towns. As a consequence, it becomes possible then to see nuances in the data and to explore themes that might otherwise be lost. This is just one history of burial, and other areas may have a different history in which the play of denominational difference and patterns of landownership might offer another pattern of behaviour. However, whatever area is studied, there will remain the consistent context of changes in national legislation including the passage of the Burial Acts, the Churchyard Consecration Act of 1867, Marten's Act of 1879, the evolution of the Church of England's management of its churchyards, and changes to the structures and responsibilities of local government. Every local history of burial will have to take these elements into account, and here – for the first time – this context is considered in detail.

Any study of such large undertaking will accrue high levels of personal indebtedness. The research was completed with substantial financial support from the ESRC, grant number RES-062-23-0929, 'Death and community in rural settlements: changing burial culture in small towns and villages c. 1850–2007'. A joint application for funding followed conversation with Professor Keith Snell at the Local Studies Department, University of Leicester, and Professor Snell's studies relating to burial in Leicestershire are forthcoming. I am, above all, grateful to Dr Susan Buckham, who allowed me to bend her ear on every aspect of this study. Dr Brian Parsons and Dr Peter Jupp have been exceedingly kind in offering judicious comment on papers, offering references and – in Brian's case – going above and beyond in securing legal material. All three suffered an extended working lunch to consider minute and major aspects of emerging findings, and I benefited enormously from the discussion. I have been extremely fortunate in having a neighbour with high professional standing in the field of historic landscape conservation: Janette Ray has been subjected to too many conversations about churchyards. Professor Edward Royle was also hugely helpful at a crucial stage of the project. Professor David Bebbington continued to educate me on aspects of Victorian Nonconformity, and batted back particular queries with graceful speed. Papers on emerging findings from the research have been presented at the Modern History Conference and at the Cemetery Research Group annual colloquium: comments and questions helped enormously. The research also included a series of interviews with local vicars, churchwardens, funeral directors and town and parish clerks. Detailed findings from those interviews are not reported here, but did contribute an essential context for understanding more contemporary material.

For any true historian, archival work is generally gleeful; staff in various record offices will be used to muffled excitement and convoluted accounts of discovery. I have been grateful for assistance at the Church of England archives at Bermondsey and Lambeth Palace, and at the National Archives at Kew. Thanks are also due to Phillip Andrew and staff at Harrogate's Stonefall Cemetery and Crematorium, for essential access to records held there, and I am grateful for sight of the records held in the cemetery chapel at Malton. The Minster Library's staff are invariably helpful, and it is always satisfying to visit a library with stepladders. Permission has been granted to reproduce documents in the custody of the Borthwick Institute. I am also indebted to the North Yorkshire Record Office for facilitating access to and reproduction of illustrations for this text. Thanks also go to the search room staff of the North Yorkshire Record Office at Northallerton. Their pleasantness and professionalism has always been deeply appreciated. I have benefited immeasurably from working closely with the Institute of Cemetery and Crematorium Managers, members of which have contributed substantially to the creation of the Cemetery Research Group Archive which includes industry conference reports and journals. Members of the Institute have also advised on various aspects of the project, and have commented on papers presented at industry conferences.

I dedicate this book to Chris and Lyra, who are now doggedly resigned to wandering around churchyards and lending me their cameras when mine gets full.

List of abbreviations

BI	Borthwick Institute, University of York
CERC	Church of England Record Centre, Bermondsey
CRGA	Cemetery Research Group Archive, York
HCA	Hull City Archives
LPL	Lambeth Palace Library
NA	National Archive
NYRO	North Yorkshire Record Office
WYAS	West Yorkshire Archive Service

1

'So precisely the invention of a critical period':[1] *theorising cemeteries*

> The secular, explicitly landscaped memorial park – that is, the cemetery, as opposed to the churchyard or other sacred or customary space – is so precisely the invention of a critical period in the history of our times (the late eighteenth and early nineteenth centuries) that thinking about its origins and meaning might allow us to understand what, if anything, is distinctively modern about death.[2]

Thus Thomas Laqueur defined the cemetery as a distinctive space: secular and landscaped, and with origins in a critical period. The cemetery's emergence is deemed to be part of the history of progress, and a 'triumph of modern hygiene'.[3] Indeed, the cemetery stands as a quintessential statement of modern attitudes towards mortality. These contentions constitute useful devices to explore changing burial practices in England through the nineteenth and twentieth centuries. It is certain that, in making his comments, Laqueur had in mind an image of cemeteries such as Kensal Green (1832) or Highgate (1839), both in London. But this study re-angles the lens to review a largely unexplored aspect of burial provision: a combined history of cemeteries and churchyards in rural areas. The research is based on the detailed study of 352 churchyards, cemeteries and burial grounds located in a central portion of what was the North Riding of Yorkshire, in the north of England.[4] This spatial specificity constitutes a particularly useful way to explore change: concentration lends depth of narrative without necessarily compromising the ability to make wider generalisations, as evidenced in other studies. For example, Sarah Tarlow's 'archaeology of bereavement' on emotion and burial derived its source material from a limited number of burial sites on the islands of Orkney.[5] Perhaps more pertinently to this study, David Charles Sloane's history of cemeteries in the United States focused on burials in the New York State to illustrate broader national trends in the United States.[6]

In addition, a concentration on rural areas prompts the reframing of key questions that have generally posited the cemetery in urban space. Hotz claimed that 'in the greater part of rural England, public cemeteries were relatively unknown'.[7] Nevertheless, it is notable that, between 1850 and 2007, 44 cemeteries were laid out in the Yorkshire case study area: indeed, soon after the passage of the first of the Burial Acts, cemeteries were established in the larger market towns of Northallerton (1856) and New Malton (1859) and in the village of Kirby Misperton (1861). Despite the fact that cemeteries were often established in rural areas, a principal conclusion of this book is that continuity may be a better descriptor of burial history, and evidence of profound dislocation is scanty. Indeed the book asks where 'modern' burial practice can be located, both in time and in place. It might be assumed that disjunction was created in the 1850s, when the introduction of the Burial Acts created a framework for the closure of churchyards and the opening of cemeteries, managed by secular authorities. In practice, however, the new kind of burial space that was created was not so radically different.

This introduction begins by reviewing the bundle of theories attached to the creation of cemeteries in the period from around the mid-eighteenth century: first, cemeteries are hegemonic space, and reflect the dominance of professional discourses and social elites; and, second, the introduction of cemeteries comprised a break from traditional practices. Both these developments mean that, third, cemeteries reflect and facilitate the expression of distinctively modern attitudes to mortality. As will be seen, these perspectives at times offer a more cogent commentary on historiography; they are based on artificial paradigms of 'cemetery' and 'churchyard', so constituting a false dichotomy; and they fail to understand the chronology and national specificity of change. Furthermore, there has also been a tendency to give prominence to elite commentary. This includes discussion of exceptional or iconic sites such as Père Lachaise (1804) in Paris or Abney Park (1840), Brompton (1840) or West Norwood (1837) Cemeteries in London: the 'ordinary' or 'typical' site is generally overlooked. The writing of pioneering individuals – for example, Edwin Chadwick or John Claudius Loudon – is often given greater attention than analysis of actual burial practices and how they changed over time. Use of a fuller range of sources allows the creation of richer and more nuanced narratives of burial space, where the local and vernacular might have a central place. Most crucially, these theories generally fail to appreciate the significance of the fact that most cemeteries were at least part if not wholly consecrated. This action placed the consecrated section under the control of the Church of England, creating what was essentially an extension of the existing parish churchyard.

Theorising cemeteries

Hegemonic space

The view that cemeteries constituted a species of hegemonic space constitutes perhaps the most pervasive theory relating to nineteenth-century cemeteries in particular. Historians, archaeologists and sociologists argue that cemeteries demonstrate both scientific and social hegemony. For many writers, cemeteries constitute a reflection of the ascendancy of scientific discourses that re-modelled the urban environment in an attempt to eradicate disease. The belief that emanations or miasmas from decomposing bodies could have a detrimental impact on public health was discussed as a scientific fact by the end of the eighteenth century: indeed, the highly influential French *Encyclopédie*, printed in seventeen volumes between 1751 and 1772, contained an entry by D'Alembert that underlined the dangers of these 'deadly emanations'.[8] Measures to curtail intramural interment – burial in churches and within the city walls, close to dwellings – were introduced in a number of European countries.[9] For example, in France in 1776 a Royal Declaration proposed the closure of inner-city churchyards and subsequent creation of new burial spaces controlled by the municipal authorities on the outskirts of the city. Similarly, Gustavus III of Sweden issued regulations against church burial in 1783 and encouraged extramural burials, again against a backdrop of public health improvement.[10]

In England, there had been sporadic publication on the dangers of intramural interment in the eighteenth century. For example, Sir John Vanbrugh had advocated use of 'cimitarys provided in the Skirts of towne' in 1711, as part of plans to rebuild London.[11] In 1726, Thomas Lewis, a London clergyman, contributed *No Charnel Houses: Being an Enquiry into the Profaneness, Indecency and Pernicious Consequences on the Living of Burying the Dead in Churches and Churchyards*.[12] There was at that time no legislative response. From the 1830s, a much wider audience for burial reform was created by the publication of the remarkably popular *Gatherings from Graveyards* (1839) by the London doctor George Alfred Walker. This book, regarded as an authoritative medical text and cited widely, gave extended and graphic case studies of deaths caused by graveyard miasmas. Further evidence was provided in Edwin Chadwick's report of 1843, *A Supplementary Report on the Results of a Special Enquiry into the Practice of Interment in Towns*. These texts, together with John Claudius Loudon's *On the Laying Out, Planting and Management of Cemeteries* (1843), presented a rationale for the scientific appropriation of burial space and a blueprint for its management. Thus the emergence of the cemetery has been interpreted as the victory of modern hygiene over popular custom. Indeed, the development can be viewed in accordance with the theories of the French philosopher Michel Foucauld, who believed that a primary objective for the State in the eighteenth and nineteenth century was the appropriation of the individuated, unbounded body.[13]

The cemetery evidenced the expression of scientific hegemony, and also – perhaps even more so – facilitated the demonstration of an idealised social order in which bourgeois conceptions of civility defined distinctive funerary behaviours. In their discussion of Bradford's Undercliffe Cemetery (1854), Rawnsley and Reynolds argued that rapid population growth in the city had created social uncertainty: spatial patterning in the cemetery then became a visual representation of the emerging hierarchy.[14] This argument was furthered in 1982 by the archaeologist Parker Pearson, who contended that funerary memorials equated to a ritual communication that expressed not 'reality' but an idealised conception of social order. The funeral was a means by which 'deceased individuals may be manipulated for the purpose of status aggrandisement'.[15] More recent research has reiterated the existence of spatial divisions within cemeteries as expressive of class demarcation. For example, a study comparing the garden cemetery in the UK and in Australia concluded that the garden cemetery 'was a place to inscribe class (especially middle class) literally on and in the ground, to demarcate, to sort and to assert worthiness and importance'.[16] Furthermore, it has been argued that, as the cemetery celebrated the ascendancy of bourgeois ideals, it disempowered poorer communities. Cemeteries were located at a distance from communities, so adding to funeral expense through the time and cost of travel, whilst offering the poor little more than undifferentiated burial in unmarked mass graves. According to Herman, the cemetery alienated the working classes from their 'familial and communitarian roots, separating them from the history of their "species-being"'.[17]

Plate 1.1 Pateley Bridge Cemetery. In the 1870s, 'select' interments were available for £9 8s, and fourth-class graves for 16s 6d.

Modern space

Another theory embedded within a number of studies on cemetery development is that cemeteries constitute an innately modern phenomenon. Two interconnected themes can be distinguished within this discourse. Herman pinpointed 'discontinuity' as being the most salient element of modernity expressed by cemetery establishment.[18] For Giddens, modernity comprised a 'deconstruction of the metanarratives of religious tradition'.[19] The centuries-long hold of the Church on the final resting place had been broken. The cemetery permitted the appropriation of burial space by municipal authorities, and its relocation away from the 'sacred and immortal heart' of the community.[20] The discontinuity appears to be stark: churchyard space inhabited a spiritual realm; cemetery space was clearly secular. Indeed, for Laqueur, the cemetery was not only not spiritual, it operated in consciously capitalist terms, since, in the first half of the nineteenth century in the UK, the majority of cemeteries were established by cemetery companies.[21] A second theme within discussion of the modernity of cemeteries relates to attitudes towards the corpse. In the 'premodern' period, the dead were 'omnipresent' and the corpse decomposed – stinking and messy – in the churchyard at the centre of the settlement and in full view.[22] Cemeteries reflected the desire to sequester the corpse, and with it all reminders of mortality. For example, Ragon commented in 1983:

> The dead are no longer feared but we continue to shut them away in coffins, which have been nailed down or (even more securely) screwed down, and which are then enclosed in sealed, concreted burial vaults, under very heavy stone. And all this further enclosed in a cemetery surrounded by high walls, the gates of which are kept locked. What a mass of precautions to take against an inanimate corpse.[23]

Thus changing burial practice charts a shift from the communal experience of mortality underpinned by a Christian *gemeinschaft* and burial of all alike in the parish churchyard, to an individualised approach with each corpse, interred amongst strangers, placed in 'his little box for his little personal decomposition'.[24]

Problems with existing theory

There are a number of problems with the existing theoretical frameworks, as much of this text will demonstrate. Here, it is worth highlighting some major objections.

Historiographic preoccupations

First, it is worth remembering, as Munslow suggests, that 'the history that we write is . . . an engagement with our own age'.[25] To a large degree, the close association between cemetery establishment and the deployment of the 'dominant ideology' thesis reflects both the left-leaning *zeitgeist* of much of academia in the 1970s and 1980s and the tenor of the three principal studies that have been credited with the introduction of cemeteries as a serious subject for study: Morley's *Death, Heaven and the Victorians*, Curl's *Victorian Celebration of Death* and Brooks's *Mortal Remains.*[26] Each of these studies described in detail an elite material culture of grief, which appeared to be expressed through the conspicuous consumption of funerary goods, grave space and domestic memorials. Brooks's study is particularly unswerving in its understanding that the cemetery represented the play of middle-class ideology. His use of the terms 'bourgeois', 'middling sort' and 'middle class' as descriptors becomes so prolific as to begin to lack sense. For example, erection of a memorial in Kensal Green was 'a badge of belonging, an expression of middle-class membership', joint-stock cemeteries catered for 'a middle-class market' and one cemetery – that of Chorlton Row Cemetery (1820) in Manchester – was simply 'bourgeois'.[27] Similarly, the representation of the cemetery as an innately modern phenomenon has reflected the desire of contemporary sociologists to identify and categorise 'modernity'. As both discourses have gathered momentum, a presumption has arisen that it is the nature of cemeteries to be 'modern' and 'hegemonic' space, and any new study is perforce grounded in that understanding, with some essential questions remaining unasked.

It is arguable that, with the arrival of 'postmodernity' and collapse of the notion that mortality remains a 'taboo' area culturally and academically, alternative thinking on cemeteries has started to emerge.[28] Tarlow's work on monumentation in the islands of Orkney is a new departure: any attempt to appreciate the experience of loss and the ways in which it may affect commemorative practices had been markedly absent from a great deal of earlier cemetery writing. For example, the embarrassment at having to deal with grief is almost palpable in Morley. Indeed, he takes the now unthinkable step of inviting the reader to find amusement in a sentimental gloss on the use of the word 'only' in a memorial to the single child of a bereaved couple.[29] Rawnsley and Reynolds hinted at similar gaps in their interpretation, but curiously noted that an analysis of cemetery usage was 'not the place to examine the emotional and psychological aspects of burial and mourning'.[30] In 1993, Tyson – reviewing the 'self-presentation' she deemed evident in mortuary behaviour in the Candie Cemetery in Guernsey – indicated that the cemetery's visual culture of death 'undoubtedly expresses religious, psychological and even philosophical attitudes', but hurries on to more material concerns.[31] It is clear that existing theories attached to cemeteries have tended to limit the consideration of other issues.

False dichotomies

A second problem with existing theory as it relates to cemeteries is that it rests very heavily on the contradistinction of stereotypes of 'churchyard' and 'cemetery'. These stereotypes posit the churchyard as sacred, eternal, spaces, which 'speak of place' in a way that cemeteries do not. Cemeteries, evidently capitalist, reflect societies in which social status is more important than spirituality. Creating this type of false dichotomy fails to appreciate that the long-established practices of church and churchyard burial were entirely capable of reflecting social hierarchies, and it would be mistaken to presume that the highly organised space afforded by the cemetery somehow presented a new canvas on which to draw social difference. From the earliest times, the history of burial under the aegis of the Church of England indicates the full and widespread understanding of the values that could be attached to different locations for burial. The most desirable places were those closest to the high altar and in the chancel. The nave, aisle and chantries were of lesser value, and status progressed downwards in the western parts of the church. Indeed, Finch notes in his study of intramural interment in Norfolk that church interiors 'present an immediate impression of a parochial elite'.[32] The church porch was held in higher regard than the churchyard, the southern portion of which was, according to folklore, preferred to the northern.[33] Certain practices reinforced this preference: in 1844, the burial records of St Leonard's at New Malton recorded the interment of a suicide in the north side of the churchyard.[34] From the medieval period onwards, interment in the more desirable burial locations was a reflection less of spiritual merit than of the economic worth of the deceased, and those with the means to pay began to secure interment in places that had been reserved for the clergy. Formal commemoration spilled out into the churchyard. Houlbrooke noted the proliferation of memorials from the 1650s, from elaborate chest tombs to small headstones.[35] By the eighteenth century, pressure on space particularly in urban areas meant the increasing use of mass burial for the very poor. The 'evil' of 'parish or poor's graves' was noted in London in 1774: 'these are pits capable of holding three or four coffins abreast and about seven in depth; are always kept open until full'.[36] It is clear that the gradation of options and prices could be detailed. For example, an early nineteenth-century table of charges in All Saints, Bakewell, Derbyshire, indicates fees for a common headstone, a double headstone, a flat stone and a large stone in the churchyard, ranging from 7s to £1; a brick grave in the churchyard at 12s; and either a tomb in the churchyard or a monument in the church itself, each costing £3 3s.[37] Thus, spatial organisation of interment in the church and churchyard could reflect social standing from the most affluent to those suffering abject destitution.

Church and churchyard burial was a profitable business, and had been since the medieval period. Indeed, three different sets of charges were variously applied: the cost of the burial itself which might or might not include the sexton's fee for digging the ground and ringing the bell and a clerk's fee for registering the burial; a 'mortuary fee', charged by the minister for the funeral service; and the fee charged for permission to erect a monument. The loan of a hearse and mortcloth could also augment parish incomes.[38] Law texts often state that, by tradition, interment in the churchyard carried no cost unless it could be demonstrated that local practice was to make such a charge; in practice, a burial fee was invariably paid.[39] In terms of mortuary fees, evidence for what was termed a 'sawelsceatt', or soul-scot, dates from as early as 870: Wulfstan, Archbishop of Canterbury and Church law maker, ordered that the payment be made 'at the open grave'.[40] The heavy reliance of the Church of England on revenues from burial is evident from its earliest history onwards. Daniell indicates that the medieval Church actively opposed the provision of separate burial grounds in institutions such as hospitals and monasteries; often, some form of recompense would be required to the clergy of the 'home' parish of a person interred outside the churchyard.[41] Gittings also discussed this 'double payment' as a feature of Church burial in the early modern period.[42] Thomas Lewis, writing in 1726, castigated church burial as being a consequence of, amongst other things, clerical greed.[43] A year later, Henry Spelman complained that 'no ground in the kingdom is now sold so dear as a grave ... the church-wardens of parishes ... sell graves in the church and churchyard like ware in their shop'.[44] The fact that the management of church and churchyard burial has never been explored in detail perhaps partly explains the overly forthright claims that, in the introduction of the cemetery, death had 'become a visibly commercial institution'[45] or 'but one more aspect of consumer culture'.[46]

In addition, the idealised churchyard – in contradistinction to the model cemetery – is proposed as being rooted in place, with an ancient history: 'their essence lay in their being where they were, and had been, since far back enough to become a hallowed and meaningful part of the landscape'.[47] In actuality, new churchyards were always being created, particularly so in the nineteenth century. For example the Church Building Act, 1818 provided funds for the creation of four new churches and churchyards on the outskirts of Sheffield between 1825 and 1840. Of these, St Philip's and St George's contributed substantially to meeting burial need in the city, and so reducing pressure on the space around the Cathedral. Indeed, these churchyards were established around the same time as the first major cemetery in the city, in 1836.[48] Of the 273 churchyards in the North Yorkshire study, 59 – just over a fifth – were constructed after 1801. In some cases, churchyards reflected population growth. For example, Harrogate emerged from the combination of the villages of High and Low Harrogate in the first half of the nineteenth century. From 1749, the two settlements relied on a chapel of ease to the church of St John the Baptist in Knaresborough. This chapel was rebuilt with a churchyard in 1823, and this burial site pre-dated the local cemetery only by thirty years.[49] New provision was also evident in more rural locations, as was the demolition and relocation of existing sites. For example, the Cholmeley family's remodelling of Brandsby village included demolition of the ancient All Saints church, and its re-erection in the late

Plate 1.2 New Malton Cemetery approach. This cemetery, the grandest in the case study area, contains an intact double chapel with porte-cochère.

1760s, possibly on another site.[50] In the remote settlement of Bilsdale Midcable, St John's was erected with a churchyard in 1896, following the division of the parish. In some areas, the area around a church came into use for burial centuries after the church was opened: this was the case at the chapel of ease at Thornton-le-Beans. Although the church was opened in 1770, the first burial in the churchyard was not until 1959. The fact that churchyards which are still used by the community can be laid out within time-frames deemed to be 'modern' undermines the implicit notion that churchyard history somehow came to a close in the 1850s. As much of this text will demonstrate, settlements often dealt with the need for new burial space by adding land to their churchyards, or creating new churchyards that were detached spatially but still owned by the Church authorities.

Lastly, not all cemeteries were 'explicitly designed memorial parks'.[51] The cemetery laid out at New Malton in 1859 featured double chapels and an impressive, tree-lined drive; overall, the site cost £2,500. The Harrogate Burial Board spent more than £5,000 laying out the cemetery at Grove Road, which contained both Church of England and Nonconformist chapels in 4.5 acres. But these sites were not necessarily typical. The cemetery at Kirby Misperton was laid out for £400, a sum which included £60 in interest payments. Although the site was bounded by a wall, it contained little else in the way of cemetery-specific infrastructure such as a chapel or even a formal road. At Old Malton, the Burial Board's first cemetery constituted an addition to the existing churchyard of St Mary's Abbey in 1883. The Board laid out another cemetery in 1907, but this comprised little more than a fifth of an acre or so of land bounded by a wall. In some locations, the cemetery remains indistinguishable visibly from a churchyard extension, particularly when that extension is not adjacent to the church.

Lack of geographic and chronological specificity

A third problem with existing theory is that the chronology and national specificity of change in burial provision is poorly understood. For example, Herman brings forward a melange of international secondary sources to support contentions on the nature of burial space and her reading of the development and management of Brookwood Cemetery, Woking (1854).[52] However, it is clear that the history of burial in the UK, and even more particularly in England, does not accord with change in Continental Europe or in the United States. In part, difficulty lies with the sheer complexity of English burial legislation, and the need to consider the purport of all the nineteenth-century Burial Acts in their entirety. There is a presumption of 'victory' for the scientific elite in the passage of Edward Chadwick's Metropolitan Interments Act of 1850. This Act was informed by the French *Pompes Funèbres*, in which funerary matters were overseen entirely by the State, following in tone from the codification of burial matters proposed by the *Encyclopédie*. However, the 1850 Act was almost immediately repealed. The subsequent Burial Acts proposed an alternative system which ensured continued Church and vestry control of burial provision. An effective chronological framework has, therefore, to meld not only an understanding of the passage of legislation but also an appreciation of how legislation was implemented and amended.

In addition, the vagueness which is attached to meanings of 'modernity' means that this concept becomes something of a moveable feast. 'Modernity' is applied to cemeteries at a number of junctures. For example, Roach goes so far as to claim that 'the segregation of the dead has some precise historical dates', and posits the first half of the eighteenth century as being particularly important. For Laqueur, the late eighteenth and early nineteenth centuries are 'a critical period'.[53] But, as much of this text will demonstrate, it is not always advisable to generalise about the progress of change or to pinpoint critical moments. It is possible to argue that in the case study area there was no revolution in burial practice, and limited evidence of discontinuity. However, during the 150-year period covered by this study, new funerary habits did evolve, irrespective of whether the location was the cemetery or the churchyard.

The meaning and significance of consecration

On 2 April 1854, the Bishop of London, Charles James Blomfield, commented in a personal letter that 'whatever the ratepayers' opinions of Mr Chadwick', he had performed his duties 'with great consideration for the interests of the clergy, when they came into question'.[54] Edwin Chadwick, often posited as a prime agent in the secularisation of burial practice, in actuality ensured the continuation of Church of England control of burial space.

Blomfield's comment is a reflection on the fact that, in England, the Burial Acts required burial board cemeteries to be wholly or partly consecrated.[55] The Burial Acts applied whether the cemetery was established in the town or in the country. Consecration is so central to an understanding of burial history in England that here it is worth taking some time to explain exactly what this action signified. Church of England canon law does not require burial in consecrated ground, and it is not therefore mandatory for a churchyard to be consecrated. However, the ritual act of consecration had been defined in Anglo-Saxon church law. The act could be performed only by a bishop, and included purification of the ground by sprinkling it with holy water, procession around the site with prayer at each corner and sometimes the middle, and the celebration of mass.[56]

Following the Reformation, Protestant belief eschewed any activity that gave the appearance of trying to influence a soul's final destination following death, such as prayer or burial in 'sacred' soil.[57] However, the ritual became 'a matter of ecclesiastical practice, and indicated that the land had been set aside for Godly purpose and so was, in that regard, sacred'.[58] The consecration of a new churchyard extension at Raskelf, near Easingwold, in 1902 by the Bishop of Beverley, was reported in detail in the local newspaper. The report commented that the service used was a new one recently devised by the Archbishop of York for this purpose. The service began with a processional hymn, 'On resurrection morn'. Inside the church, the Bishop gave an 'impressive address', in which he said that

> We should look upon our churchyard as God's house in the open air, and just as we dedicated our churches to Him, so we did also that part where our loved ones were laid to rest. We are told in God's word our bodies are the temples of the Holy Ghost, so they are laid to rest with reverence, and in the hope of a joyful resurrection, when soul and body will be reunited ... The setting aside of a new burial ground should be the occasion for solemn thought. For whom is it intended? If not for those present it will be for those near and dear to us. So we must look upon it as holy ground and treat it with due reverence.[59]

The Bishop then moved to the churchyard, accompanied by the churchwardens and followed by the clergy and choir and remaining congregation. Dr Preston, the vicar, presented the Bishop with the Petition for Consecration. The bishop then slowly walked around the ground with his retinue, repeating Psalm 90. After this, the vicar presented the 'Sentence of Consecration' to the Bishop, which he read aloud, 'and then dedicated and consecrated the allotted portion of ground'. Everyone returned to the church, where Psalm 103 was repeated. 'Brief life is here our portion' was sung, and an offertory was taken. Thus, the consecration ritual signalled the spiritual and emotional value of the churchyard, and a reminder to treat that land with due respect.

However, during the nineteenth century, the substantial economic connotations of consecration also became paramount. Consecration was in essence a legal action, by which the Church of England appropriated control of the land in question. Indeed, in order for consecration to take place, undoubted proof as to ownership of the land had to be provided to the Diocesan Registrar. Although – as has been seen at Raskelf – consecration included some ritual at the site, consecration itself was actually secured by the signing by the bishop or the archbishop of a document entitled a 'sentence of consecration'. This legal document was lodged with the diocesan registry. The sentence of consecration generally included a map of the site indicating the portion to be consecrated. Indeed, a vestry's application for consecration – termed a 'petition for consecration' – generally included a legal statement on conveyance of the site, and a map indicating that the area to be consecrated had been bounded securely. In the case of churchyard extensions, as at Raskelf, proof had to be provided that the land had been added to the freehold of the incumbent. Consecration brought the land under the authority of the ordinary, or bishop, and was thereafter subject to Church law, through the consistory courts. Any substantive change to the churchyard would require faculty, or specific 'permission', secured from the diocesan authorities; the 'deconsecration' of burial space constituted a substantial legal undertaking.[60] Burial boards were obliged to consecrate at least half their site, which conveyed control of that portion of land to the Church of England, to be regarded thereafter as parish burial space. In the larger cemeteries, the bishop had the authority to appoint cemetery chaplains, who would be responsible for all the funeral services. In the smaller cemeteries, cemetery burial services were usually taken by the existing parish clergy, and burial fees were payable to those clergy as they had been in the parish burial ground. Through the act of consecration, burial board cemeteries *extended* the Church of England's holding of burial space.

Thus, it can be argued that, in England, theories relating to cemetery development have generally overemphasised the dichotomy between churchyard and cemetery space. In actuality, these two types of space were more similar than dissimilar: churchyards could be very new; they contained within themselves the possibility of expressing social status; the pauper dead were not necessarily treated worse in the cemetery than they had been in the churchyard; and cemeteries contained 'sacred', consecrated space that was largely construed as parish burial ground. The history of burial does not, therefore, comprise a simple shift from churchyard to cemetery. As will be seen, changing burial practices were evident across both types of burial space.

A history of rural burial provision: continuity and change

In exploring the social history of burial in rural areas, this book aims to encompass some of the principles underpinning '*l'histoire des mentalités*'. For Darnton, this approach comprised an attempt to understand the mental landscapes of past communities much in the same way that anthropologists study alien cultures.[61] As interpreted by Iggers, the construction of a history of mentalities constituted a rejection of 'any theory-guided questions that ... threaten to deprive the manifestations of the culture of their vitality'.[62] This research has attempted to step away from rather inflexible ideological approaches, to allow individuals and communities to speak for themselves with the minimum of pre- or post-judgement. Kong recognised that, in the field of geography, the study of deathscapes required 'more specific and grounded contributions' that required 'painstaking fieldwork'.[63] This research uses a combination of documentary sources to consider the decisions made about the provision and management of burial space in 277 settlements. The study reviewed administrative records such as parish burial registers and the minutes of vestry meetings, parochial church councils, parish councils and rural district councils. In addition, the research has explored documentation around particular instances of change, including letters sent between diocesan authorities and incumbents. The study has also reviewed some national records including selected records of the Ecclesiastical Commissioners – the Church of England's 'management arm' – relating to churchyard management. In addition, the research has reviewed administrative documents relating to the General Board of Health and, later, the Home Office, dating from around 1850 to 1940 and which relate to central regulation of burial space. Further detail on these sources is given in Appendix Three.

The data are generally handled in two halves, and deal with the history of burial before and after 1894. This year constitutes a useful turning point. The Local Government Act, 1894 provided a new regulatory and administrative framework for the provision of services including the laying out of burial space. The Act dissolved the civic authority of vestries, and increased the possibility that other, higher-tier, local government agencies would become involved in local decision making with regard to burial space. Indeed, it is demonstrated that the end of the nineteenth century rather than its mid-point constitutes the more convincing watershed for change in burial practice. The book asks whether, from this period, it became more likely for strategic decisions on burial space and its management to be made at higher local authority levels, so reducing the degree of very localised control that had been evident until that point.

Chapter 2 carries three principal functions. First, it summarises burial legislation up until 1850, which is the starting point for this study. This early history had introduced a number of essential principles that continued to dominate the provision of burial space including the need to respect religious political difference at the same time as protecting the interests of the Church, and the importance of local control. The public health consequences of churchyard 'miasmas' and overcrowding had been acknowledged in legislation which forbade interments in new churches built under the Church Building Act, 1818.[64] However, the Public Health Act, 1848, introduced regulation on the closure of churchyards that was strengthened by the Burial Acts that followed in the 1850s. This first chapter also describes the area of Yorkshire in which this study is located. Spreading from the Yorkshire Dales to the west, through the Vales of Mowbray and York and bounded by the North York Moors to the north and the Yorkshire Wolds to the east, this area had, by 1850, seen its principal cottage industries collapse in the face of competition from the heavy industrial development of West and South Yorkshire. Some of the area's market towns were able to flourish following the development of improved transport links, but overall the area tended to be subject to depopulation. Harrogate, by far the largest settlement in the study, developed rapidly from the 1820s and in 1911 had a population of 33,703. The remaining towns were much smaller in scale: in the same year Ripon, which is the next settlement in size, had a population of just 8,218.[65] For much of the period in question, the area can be characterised in terms of strong adherence to both Wesleyan and Primitive Methodism, although this did not necessarily preclude active worship at the local parish church. Market towns contained pockets of the 'Old Dissent', principally Independents, although Quaker meeting houses were also in evidence in small and scattered settlements particularly on the North York Moors.

The study aimed to locate all the places in which burial had taken place in the period from 1850 to 2007, and constitutes a series of micro-histories of individual burial places – churchyards, cemeteries, burial grounds and mausolea – and the wider burial history of the settlements in which they were located. Typical places included for example Raskelf,[66] which had through its history only one burial place, St Mary's churchyard, which was extended in 1902 and for which a further extension was secured in the 1950s; and Great Ayton, where All Saints churchyard was closed and a burial board cemetery laid out in the early 1880s, and where interment for the substantial Quaker population continued to be available in the burial ground attached to the meeting house. In 1850, 43 of the 277 settlements in the study had no burial provision at all. However, in the majority of settlements, the local community was continuing to use a churchyard attached to a church often dating from the Anglo-Saxon or Norman period.

Chapter 3 considers the issue of churchyard closure. The cessation of burials in churchyards was effected by the issuing of separate Orders in Council for each churchyard deemed to be insanitary, following inspection by a Board of Health official. A review of the process of closure indicates high levels of local proactivity, since inspection visits were generally invited. Often there was a degree of negotiation on the timescale for closure, and on any conditions that might be attached to the closure order, for example, to allow continued interments in certain types of grave. A total of 25 such orders were issued for churchyards in central North Yorkshire, so calling into question any automatic association between excessive levels of use and the need for closure to take place. Indeed, in some of the churchyards subject to closure orders, the scale of burial amounted to fewer than one or two interments a month. There are indications that the closures reflected an unwillingness to countenance the disturbance of even very old remains. However, in many cases burials continued within closed churchyards, indicating that disturbance would be tolerated in order to achieve burial close to a family member.

Churchyard closure generally signalled that burial space was made available elsewhere, and in most cases before 1894 this meant that the churchyard itself had been extended. Chapter 4 reviews the incidence of churchyard extension, which was commonplace during the nineteenth century. Up until 1867, this process was overseen by the Ecclesiastical Commissioners, since any land added to the churchyard – even glebe land – had to be conveyed formally, via the Commissioners, prior to consecration. The bureaucracy related to this process created substantial difficulty, expense and delay for local vestries that were compelled to use the Commissioners' solicitors, who were based in London.

Bishops were to the fore in criticising the entire procedure, and the Churchyard Consecration Act, 1867 was a consequence. This Act simplified aspects of conveyance and consecration, but also signalled a change in practice: conveyance could be completed by local solicitors, and to a large degree the Commissioners could be bypassed entirely. The need to extend the churchyard reflected the fact that, above ground, churchyards were becoming congested by the proliferation of formal and informal monuments. The laying out of an extension created the opportunity to introduce management practices that had been developed for cemeteries. This style of management fed expectations that more elaborate commemoration would be permitted, but also underlined the assumption that graves in the churchyard were being granted in perpetuity: churchyard space was acquiring features of cemetery space.

The Burial Acts introduced legislation that permitted vestries to establish burial boards, which could raise loans repayable through the rates to fund the laying out of new cemeteries. In central North Riding, a total of eighteen burial boards were in operation before 1894, and Chapter 5 reviews in detail the operation of the ten largest boards in that group. In drawing out the detail of how burial boards set about purchasing and managing a site, the chapter addresses the contention that the Burial Acts were a centralising intervention, by which the State controlled the local provision of burial space through the regulation of technical, financial and administrative aspects of burial board business. In actuality, a great deal of the regulation proposed by the State was permissive, and some essential elements were simply disregarded at a local level. In particular, sanitary requirements that just one body be permitted in each grave, in order to facilitate faster decomposition and so permit the burial board to reuse the grave, ran counter to the emerging preference for burial in perpetuity. The chapter also addresses the contention that a 'specific novelty' attached to cemetery burial, by comparing the costs of burial and opportunities for commemoration in both churchyard and cemetery.

A second contention frequently proposed with regard to the cemetery is its secularising tendency. In actual fact, as Chapter 6 demonstrates, the Burial Acts maintained and even strengthened the hold of the Church of England on burial space, by substantially increasing the amount of consecrated land under its control. The religious-political nature of the provision of burial space was played out nationally in decades-long struggle at parliamentary level to arrive at legislation that was deemed to treat Anglicans and non-Anglicans in an equitable way. These issues also played out at a local level, in the decisions around the ways in which burial boards interpreted their responsibility with regard to consecration, and the apportionment of space within the cemetery. Central North Riding was very strongly Methodist, with relatively limited representation of those denominations that were generally to the fore in politicising burial issues. As a consequence, the supply of alternative burial space was small, prior to the Burial Acts, and – with the exception of a more dispersed Quaker provision – tended to be clustered in the larger market towns. The Burial Acts substantially increased the supply of unconsecrated burial space. In addition, the Burial Laws Amendment Act introduced the possibility that non-Anglican ministers could hold funeral services in consecrated space, including existing churchyards. It is notable that, in central North Riding, the take-up of this option was not particularly enthusiastic. By the end of the nineteenth century, the Church of England was in as strong a position as it had been in 1850.

This situation was to change, as a consequence of a tranche of legislation passed in the final decades of the nineteenth and at the very beginning of the twentieth century. Chapter 7 reviews this new legislative context for burial that substantially undermined the centrality of the Church. It has been noted that this study has posited 1894 as a pivotal point in burial history, and the importance of the Local Government Act is discussed in this chapter. However, its impact was augmented by three other key provisions. First, the passage of the Public Health (Interment) Act, 1879 – a largely overlooked piece of legislation – created a new legal framework for cemeteries, that sat wholly outside the existing Burial Acts. Under this Act, it was possible for local authorities and sanitary authorities to establish cemeteries that had no clear connection to the existing parish structure. The Act adopted the Cemetery Clauses Act, 1847, which meant that authorities were permitted to consecrate all or part of the cemeteries that were created, but there was no obligation so to do. The confusion caused by the creation of this parallel but unconnected legislation was deeply felt at local level. In some instances, local authorities chose to create new cemeteries that were completely unconsecrated, so disadvantaging the local Anglican community. A parliamentary inquiry into the application of the 1879 Act led directly into the framing of new legislation, in 1900.

This penultimate Burial Act took a decisive step away from a key defining principle of the earlier acts. In the 1850s, the Bishop of London had ensured that the Burial Acts had posed no threat to the economic interests of the Church of England. Indeed by the end of the nineteenth century it was generally thought to be the case that the Church was – if anything – profiteering from regulations that allowed the imposition of high monument erection fees in consecrated sections, in addition to receiving fees for all burials in those sections, irrespective of whether the service was taken by an Anglican minister. The Burial Act, 1900, ensured that the Church could no longer receive monument fees in consecrated sections, and would receive burial fees only 'for services rendered'. The Act also contained the presumption that land in the cemetery would remain unconsecrated, unless a case could be made for its consecration. One further, highly symbolic, shift was the transfer of the substantial business of burial from the Home Office to the Local Government Board. Burials were henceforth to be regarded as a wholly sanitary issue, in which the interests of the Church of England would no longer be of concern. A final blow to the position of the Church came with the passage of the Cremation Act 1902. The Church of England had been ambivalent about cremation, and its ambivalence was reflected in clauses within the Act that required new crematoria to be built on unconsecrated ground. The Church of England had essentially disenfranchised itself from a mode of disposal that would come to dominate the twentieth century.

Chapter 8 addresses the contention that this new legislative context for burial in the twentieth century might then introduce the opportunity for a substantial centralisation of burial provision. However, it appears that the legislation was itself one of the key reasons why this centralisation did not materialise. Although patterns of local government in rural areas had altered with the introduction of rural district councils (RDCs), those councils were markedly reluctant to engage with the opportunities presented by the Public Health (Interment) Act, 1879. A handful of cemeteries were indeed laid out under the Act by RDCs, but the sheer complexity of the legislation meant that the RDCs were much more likely to press villages to seek extension to the churchyard when the need for additional space became evident. RDCs were further discouraged by the fact that it was becoming very evident that cemetery provision would always require rate support: it was a loss-making enterprise that few local authorities were eager to embrace.

In these circumstances, in central North Riding, recourse to the extension of the churchyard was as commonplace in the twentieth century as it had been in the nineteenth. Simplification of the legal frameworks for extension had finally become realised, as the Church of England streamlined the associated bureaucracy, underlining the advantages of churchyard extension in comparison with cemetery establishment. However, as Chapter 9 indicates, the nature of the churchyard continued to change. The unwillingness to reuse the ground and the desire for burial in perpetuity, with each grave being marked by a formal monument, meant that – once extended – it was entirely likely that a churchyard would be extended again a second or even third time. In essence, churchyard space was recreated as cemetery space, with graves – ordered by row and plot number – often reserved by faculty or more informally. As land ran out even in extended portions, parochial church councils began to institute more stringent regulations to exclude non-parishioners.

Chapter 10 reviews the changing landscape of the churchyard, and considered rationalisation or 're-ordering', closures and church redundancy, and the growing incidence of cremation. The landscape of burial was subject to revision through much of the twentieth century, as the simpler lawn cemetery replaced its Victorian counterpart. These developments were also evident in the churchyard, which also saw programmes of mound-levelling and stone clearance. This did not mean that village communities had a diminished attachment to the space around the churchyard. As has been seen, investment in monumentation continued within churchyard extensions. Through the middle years of the twentieth century, there was a substantial decrease in the incidence of churchyard closure by Order in Council, although less formal methods might be used to transfer responsibility of maintenance to civic authorities. Substantial encouragement to return to a formal process of closure was given in s. 215 of the Local Government Act, 1972, which allowed the transfer of responsibility for maintenance of closed churchyards from parochial church councils to parish or district councils with only a three-month notice period. In addition, in rural areas, the rationalisation of benefices that followed the Pastoral Measure of 1968 meant that a number of churches were made redundant. However, in almost all these cases the closure and even demolition of the church has not precluded the continued use of the churchyard.

The growing popularity of cremation constitutes a substantial change in English funerary culture during the course of the twentieth century. There is evidence that communities throughout the central North Riding travelled some distance to make use of cremation facilities in the larger settlements on the periphery of the case study area; indeed, the catchment area of Harrogate's crematorium, opened in 1937, extended far into the Yorkshire Dales. The initial ambivalence of the Church of England with regard to cremation was overtaken by an understanding that cremation offered the opportunity for continued use of churchyards that were reaching capacity for full-body interment. There was debate on the appropriate aesthetics for the commemoration of cremated remains within the churchyard but, in arriving at an accommodation on this issue, the Church has ensured that the churchyard retains a focal point for commemorative activity.

The final chapter of the book reviews the pattern of burial provision in 2007 compared with 1850, and concludes that there is evidence of both continuity and change. The Church of England has retained a strong hold on burial provision in many rural villages in central North Riding. Ownership of burial space by secular authorities has created a patchwork of provision, with parish, town and district councils having some level of involvement. This diversity reflects the fact that burial legislation remains largely permissive, and local authorities are in no way obliged to provide burial space. Overall, the notion of an eager and Foucauldian appropriation of burial space by the State has simply failed to materialise in the Yorkshire countryside.

The book draws to a conclusion with some consideration of the wider themes suggested by the study. These are that the study of changing burial culture is served better by a narrative that does not simply presume a shift in practice from churchyard to cemetery; that the study of commemorative practice is perhaps more indicative of continuity than might be supposed; that the desire of family members to be buried close to each other has driven much of the change in burial practice since 1850; that the cemetery is not necessarily an agency of degraded funerary ritual; and that the Church of England has a central place in the history of burial reform. In reviewing this joint history of cemeteries and churchyards, this study finds that these types of burial space are more similar than might have been supposed, but retain distinctive differences that continue to make definition between the two essential.

Conclusion

Cemeteries and churchyards are highly emotional and spiritually charged spaces, and their innate drama means that they are frequently deployed as symbolic representations. These representations can be more or less unfortunate, but are useful in provoking questions which lead to a deeper and more nuanced understanding of burial history. Sociological theorists in particular are generally mistaken in the assumptions they make about cemetery space, in failing to appreciate cultural and chronological specificities which make generalising across time and place innately problematic. In borrowing from sociological theory, historians sometimes contribute to the continuation of rhetoric that artificially stereotypes both the cemetery and the churchyard, and which simply overlooks the realities of burial history.

This study gives a detailed description of change in burial provision in central North Riding. This area is used to trace the passage and implementation of national legislation that framed the provision of burial space, concentrating on the various burial enactments of the nineteenth century, but also considering Church of England measures and wider legislation that altered the pattern of local governance in rural areas. By starting from the 'bottom up' and researching how one region responded to these changes in legislation, it becomes possible to question the meta-narratives that propose a secularisation of funerary practice, and that 'modernity' – in the shape of cemetery provision – undermined ancient traditions of churchyard burial.

Notes

1 T. Laqueur, 'The places of the dead in modernity' in Jones, C. and Wahrman, D. (eds), *The Age of Cultural Revolutions. Britain and France, 1750–1820* (London: University of California Press, 2002), p. 17.
2 *Ibid.*
3 T. Laqueur, 'Cemeteries, religion and the culture of capitalism' in Garnett, J. and Matthew C. (eds), *Revival and Religion since 1700* (London: Hambleton Press, 1993), p. 184.
4 The area included in the study comprises the three modern local authority areas of Ryedale, Hambleton and Harrogate. These three areas together comprise the central belt of what was the North Riding and northern portions of the East and West Ridings. See Map 1.
5 S. Tarlow, *Bereavement and Commemoration: An Archaeology of Mortality* (Oxford: Blackwell, 1999).
6 D. C. Sloane, *The Last Great Necessity: Cemeteries in American History* (Baltimore, MD: Johns Hopkins University Press, 1991).
7 M. E. Hotz, *Literary Remains: Representations of Death and Burial in Victorian England* (Albany, NY: State University of New York Press, 2008), p. 103.
8 'Cimitière' in *Encyclopédie, ou Dictionnaire Raisonné des Sciences, des Arts et des Métiers*, accessed in June 2005 at humanities. uchicago.edul/ARTFL/projects/encyc/. See also R. Etlin, *The Architecture of Death: The Transformation of the Cemetery in Eighteenth-Century Paris* (Cambridge, MA: MIT Press, 1984).
9 See, for example, C. Denk and J. Ziesemer (eds), *Der Bürgerliche Tod: Städtische Bestattungskultur von der Aufklärung bis zum Frühen 20. Jarhundert* (München: ICOMOS, 2007).
10 P. Ariès, trans. H. Weaver, *The Hour of Our Death* (Harmondsworth: Penguin, 1983); T. Andersson, 'Appearances and beyond: time and change in Swedish landscape architecture', *Journal of Garden History*, 17 (1997), 278–94.
11 J. Vanburgh quoted in L. Whistler, *The Imagination of Vanbrugh and His Fellow Artists* (London: B. T. Batsford, 1954).
12 See M. Jenner, 'Death, decomposition and dechristianisation? Public health and Christian burial in eighteenth-century England', *English Historical Studies*, 487:CXX (2005), 615–32.
13 M. Foucault, 'Different spaces', trans. R. Hurley in Faubion, J. D. (ed.), *The Essential Works of Foucault, 1954–1984* (Harmondsworth: Penguin, 2000); P. Johnson, 'The modern cemetery: a design for life', *Social and Cultural Geography*, 9:7 (2008), 777–90.

14 S. Rawnsley and J. Reynolds, 'Undercliffe Cemetery, Bradford', *History Workshop*, 4 (Autumn 1977), 215–21.
15 M. Parker Pearson, 'Mortuary practices, society and ideology: an ethnoarchaeological study' in Hodder, I. (ed.), *Symbolic and Structural Archaeology* (Cambridge: Cambridge University Press, 1982), p. 112.
16 S. K. Martin, 'Monuments in the garden: the garden cemetery in Australia', *Postcolonial Studies*, 3:7 (1994), p. 348.
17 A. Herman, 'Death has a touch of class: society and space in Brookwood Cemetery, 1853–1903', *Journal of Historic Geography*, 36:3 (2010), p. 313.
18 *Ibid.*, p. 306.
19 As quoted by P. A. Meller, 'Death in high modernity: the contemporary presence and absence of death' in Clark, D. (ed.), *The Sociology of Death: Theory, Culture and Practice* (Oxford: Blackwell Publishers, 1993), p. 17.
20 Foucault, 'Different spaces', p. 6.
21 Laqueur, 'Cemeteries, religion and the culture of capitalism'.
22 J. Roach, *Cities of the Dead: Circum-Atlantic Performance* (New York: Columbia University Press, 1996), p. 48.
23 Michel Ragon, *The Space of Death: A Study in Funerary Architecture, Decoration and Urbanism*, trans. A. Sheridan (Charlottesville, VA: University Press of Virginia, 1983), p. 16.
24 Foucault, 'Different spaces', p. 181.
25 A. Munslow, *The Routledge Companion to Historical Studies* (London: Routledge, 2000), p. 17.
26 J. Morley, *Death, Heaven and the Victorians* (Pittsburgh, PA: University of Pittsburgh Press, 1971); James Stevens Curl, *The Victorian Celebration of Death* (Newton Abbot: David & Charles, 1972); Christopher Brooks (ed.) *Mortal Remains: The History and Present State of the Victorian and Edwardian Cemetery* (Exeter: Wheaton Publishers Ltd, 1989).
27 C. Brooks, *Mortal Remains*, pp. 12, 29 and 19.
28 T. Walter, *The Revival of Death* (London: Routledge, 1994).
29 Morley, *Death, Heaven and the Victorians*, p. 43.
30 Rawnsley and Reynolds, 'Undercliffe Cemetery', p. 219.
31 N. Tyson, 'Candie Cemetery and its monuments: death and self-presentation in 19th century St Peter Port, Guernsey', *Société Guernesiaine Report and Transactions*, 23:3 (1993), p. 600.
32 J. Finch, '"According to the qualitie and degree of the person deceased": funeral monuments and the construction of social identities', *Scottish Archaeological Review*, 8:15 (1991), p. 109.

33 R. W. Muncey, *A History of the Consecration of Churches and Churchyards* (Cambridge: W. Heffer & Sons Ltd. 1930), pp. 135ff; C. Daniell, *Death and Burial in Medieval England* (London: Routledge, 1997), p. 99.
34 BI, N/MAL/l/9, Burials, 1813–1885. The interment took place on 22 Nov 1844.
35 R. Houlbrooke, *Death, Religion and the Family in England, 1480–1750* (Oxford: Clarendon Press, 1998), pp. 362ff.
36 C. Gittings, *Death, Burial and the Individual* (London: Croom Helm, 1984), p. 64.
37 L. Knighton, *Bakewell Church* (Derby: Derbyshire Countryside Ltd, 1985), p. 4.
38 M. Smith, 'The Church of Scotland and the funeral industry in nineteenth-century Edinburgh', *The Scottish Historical Review*, 88:1 (2009), p. 111.
39 C. J. Polson, *The Disposal of the Dead* (London: English Universities Press, 1953), p. 162.
40 V. Thompson, *Dying and Death in Later Anglo-Saxon England* (Woodbridge: The Boydell Press, 2004).
41 Daniell, *Death and Burial*, pp. 91ff.
42 Gittings, *Death, Burial and the Individual*, p. 132.
43 Thomas Lewis, *Churches No Charnel Houses: Being an Enquiry into the Profaneness, Indecency and Pernicious Consequences on the Living of Burying the Dead in Churches and Churchyards* (1726), quoted by R. Houlbrooke, 'The age of decency', in Jupp, P. C. and Gittings, C. (eds), *Death in England: An Illustrated History* (Manchester: Manchester University Press, 1999), p. 193.
44 H. Spelman, quoted in Gittings, *Death, Burial and the Individual*, p. 142.
45 G. Nash, 'Pomp and circumstances: archaeology, modernity and the corporatisation of death: early social and political Victorian attitudes towards burial practice' in Graves-Brown, P. M. (ed.), *Matter, Materiality and Culture* (London: Routledge, 2000), p. 113.
46 Laqueur, 'Cemeteries, religion and the culture of capitalism', p. 199.
47 Laqueur, 'The places of the dead', p. 17.
48 F. Stirling, 'Grave re-use: a feasibility study' (PhD dissertation, University of Sheffield, 2009), pp. 34ff.
49 William Grainge, *The History and Topography of Harrogate* (London: Simkins, Marshall and Co., 1882).
50 William Page, *A History of the County of York, North Riding: Volume 2* (London: Victoria County History, 1923), pp. 103–7.
51 Laqueur, 'The places of the dead in modernity', p. 17.
52 Herman, 'Death has a touch of class'.

53 Laqueur, 'The places of the dead in modernity', p. 17; Roach, *Cities of the Dead*, p. 50.

54 LPL: *Papers of C. J. Blomfield, Bishop of London*, Mansell (1977), vol. 55, Sep 1853–Nov 1854, 2 Apr 1854.

55 Legislation differed in Scotland, where on a number of fronts the history of burial differs from that of England. See for example E. McFarland, 'Researching death, mourning and commemoration in modern Scotland', *Journal of Scottish Historical Studies*, 24:1 (2005), 20–44.

56 Helen Gittos, 'Creating the sacred: Anglo-Saxon rituals for consecrating cemeteries', in Lucy, S. and Reynolds, A. (eds), *Burial in Early Medieval England and Wales* (London: Society for Medieval Archaeology, 2002).

57 A. Spicer, '"God will have a house": sacred space and rites of consecration in early seventeenth-century England', in Hamilton, S. and Spicer, A. (eds), *Defining the Holy: Sacred Space in Medieval and Early Modern Europe* (Aldershot: Ashgate, 2005).

58 Norman Doe, *The Legal Framework of the Church of England; A Critical Study in a Comparative Context* (Oxford: Clarendon Press, 1996), p. 412.

59 *Easingwold Advertiser and Weekly News*, 22 Feb 1902.

60 T. Briden and B. Hanson, *Moore's Introduction to English Canon Law* (London: Mowbray, 1992), chapter 11.

61 R. Darnton, *The Great Cat Massacre and Other Episodes in French Cultural History* (London: Allen Lane, 1984), p. 3.

62 G. G. Iggers, *Historiography in the Twentieth Century: From Scientific Objectivity to the Postmodern Challenge* (Hanover, NH: University Press of New England, 1997), p. 124.

63 L. Kong, 'Cemeteries and columbaria, memorials and mausoleums: narrative and interpretation in the study of deathscapes in geography', *Australian Geographical Studies*, 37:1 (2002), p. 8.

64 Church Building Act (1818), s. 80.

65 visionofbritain.org.uk, pages accessed March 2012.

66 Note that the village name is variously spelled 'Raskelfe' and 'Raskelf'; other settlements where names are spelled variably include Kirkbymoorside (Kirkby Moorside) and Thornton-le-Dale (Thornton Dale).

Part One

The churchyard in the cemetery, 1850–1894

2

Burial in 1850: national and local contexts

It is always tempting to view the beginning of any research period as a static point from which substantial change then takes place. No such claim is made here. Even from the 1820s, burial provision was in flux. Early in the decade, the economic viability of the joint-stock cemetery format had been firmly proved by the establishment of cemeteries in Manchester and Liverpool, and from the earliest years of Queen Victoria's reign cemeteries were becoming an increasingly common addition to townscapes throughout England. In addition, growing investment in church building had begun to augment churchyard provision in many of these same cities. From the 1840s, a regulatory framework for burial in England had begun to emerge: burials were not permitted in the new 'Million Act' churches; a clauses act contained provision for the consecration and location of new cemeteries; and the Public Health Act of 1848 granted powers to enforce the closure of churchyards that were deemed insanitary. Despite all these changes in the first half of the nineteenth century, 1850 still remains a suitable time from which to consider a history of burial provision in rural England. The first of the Burial Acts – passed in the 1850s – created a much more formalised structure both for new cemetery provision and for churchyard closure. However, it is important to understand that, by the middle of the nineteenth century, a number of the issues that were to dominate much of the second half of the nineteenth century had already been rehearsed both nationally and locally.

This chapter carries the task of setting three essential contexts. First, it is necessary to consider in a little more detail the history of cemeteries and burial generally prior to the passage of the earliest Burial Acts in the 1850s. A number of authors have characterised this period of cemetery history in terms of capitalist excess, since the majority of cemeteries in the first half of the nineteenth century were laid out by private companies. However, as will be seen, the popularity of the joint-stock format can be explained by factors other than the desire to see a return on investment. Furthermore, this 'first generation' of nineteenth-century cemeteries provided a primer or model for later developments, in establishing the principal of localised control of burial space and the need to respect denominational difference.

Second, the chapter goes on to consider the area chosen for study. Rural North Yorkshire was, in the middle of the nineteenth century, remarkably variable: some market towns were thriving but others were seeing the first stage of their eventual decline. The two small villages of High and Low Harrogate began their rapid development into a major urban centre that eventually overtook both the previously dominant neighbour, Knaresborough, and the cathedral city of Ripon. Large swathes of the study area were sparsely populated and poor economically, with little investment in transport infrastructure and without ratepayers or large landowners able to fund improvements in sanitation, health or welfare. Other areas were more populous, and in some cases benefited from the active estate management of leading families such as the Dawnays, Fevershams, Fitzwilliams and Earls of Carlisle at Castle Howard. Overall, outside the handful of major settlements, the region was beginning the slow process of gradual depopulation.

Third, the chapter gives a snapshot of burial provision in the study area in 1850, based on analysis of the 277 distinct townships and parishes included in the study that had some form of burial provision in the period 1850 to present. In the middle of the century, the majority of these settlements were reliant on 'ancient' churchyards with origins in the Anglo-Saxon or Norman period. Signs of change were already in evidence: in around a tenth of the settlements in the study, a new churchyard was in use which had been laid out after 1801. Although cemetery provision was known in other parts of Yorkshire, the use of cemeteries had not percolated out to more rural locations. Methodism was a marked feature of rural society in this part of the country: even very small villages might have both Primitive and Wesleyan Methodist chapels. However, these denominations generally did not commonly express themselves through separate burial provision in the case study location. There were no more than twenty non-Anglican burial grounds in existence in 1850. Although the Church of England retained a strong hold on burial space, churchyards were not necessarily central to life in every village since not every village had a church. 'Corpse paths', marking the passage of a coffin from one settlement to the churchyard in another, crossed a number of fields. For some places, the second half of the nineteenth century brought new churchyards as a consequence of the Victorian passion for church building.

Cemeteries in the first half of the nineteenth century

The social history of disposal of the dead in the first half of the nineteenth century is under-researched, and existing histories underline gaps more frequently than they elucidate a clear picture. This author's study of cemetery companies from 1819 to 1853 begins to establish a chronological framework of cemetery development, but remains unaccompanied by similar study of change in churchyard provision or of the development of burial space attached to Nonconformist places of worship.[1] However, it is helpful to rehearse what is known about this early history, particularly as it establishes the broader framework of some of the themes that emerge later in the century.

Early cemetery companies

In the 1820s, cemeteries – so often discussed as being principally 'status-obsessed' – were more usually concerned with the expression of religious identity. Indeed it is possible to argue that the very first significant 'cemeteries' in the UK were, strictly speaking, burial grounds since their intention was to meet the needs of particular denominations rather than the population more generally.[2] This group of sites included the Rosary Burial Ground in Norwich (1819), Rushholme Road in Manchester (1820), Liverpool Necropolis (1825) and the Westgate Hill Cemetery in Newcastle (1825). Each of these sites used joint-stock financing to fund the purchase of land and laying out of cemetery space. Joint-stock financing had underpinned the development of canals and other aspects of national and international industrial development and in the realms of urban improvement had come to be regarded as a preferable alternative to a call on the rates.[3] Early reports of favourable returns from the cemetery companies at Manchester and Liverpool were particularly influential in encouraging investor confidence in the format.

The first cemetery companies were distinguished by their adherence to religious independence, and were dominated by representatives from denominations that had particular cause in terms of burial grievance: Congregationalists, Quakers and Baptists.[4] Manchester's Rusholme Road Cemetery was established by the prominent Congregationalist George Hadfield, who was at that time embroiled in a series of campaigns to protect and promote Dissenters' interests. For Hadfield, burial space that was separate from the Church of England was essential in ensuring that Nonconformist families could have the minister of their choice preside at their funerals.[5] As will be seen, this right was not conferred until the passage of the Burial Laws

Amendment Act, 1880 allowed non-Anglican clergy to take funeral services in churchyards or other consecrated burial space. It was perhaps unsurprising that Hadfield's initiative was copied in Liverpool: Thomas Raffles, the leading Congregationalist of the city, had worked with Hadfield on the foundation of the Blackburn Academy, a training college for Congregationalist ministers. John Bruce, who was co-pastor with Raffles of the influential Newington chapel, became registrar of the Liverpool Necropolis at Low Hill.[6] For Nonconformists, ownership of their own burial space also meant that the space would not be consecrated. This practice did not accord with an understanding that personal faith alone could be the only guarantee of a heavenly afterlife, and that what happened to the body after death – such as placing it in specially 'blessed' ground – was immaterial. John Wesley himself had expressed the opinion that consecration was 'a mere relic of Romish superstition', 'wrong in itself, not being authorised either by any law of God, or by any law of the land'.[7]

The issue of consecration

As the joint-stock cemetery format gained in popularity, its use beyond the Nonconformist community meant that some consideration had to be given by company directors to the need to consecrate all or at least some of their site. A failure to do so meant that the cemetery would remain unused by a substantial proportion of the local population. This issue gained particular significance under the Poor Law since in 1844 an amendment to the Poor Law Act, 1834, required that those who died in the workhouse would be interred 'in the churchyard or other consecrated burial ground'; the fees for these burials would be secured for the clergy.[8] The first company to seek consecration for its cemetery was the St James Cemetery, which was established in Liverpool in 1829, soon after Low Hill. The St James Cemetery directors stressed their connection with the Established Church, and – in an open letter written to the Mayor – indicated that 'their sole object is to provide for the Members of the Established Church and for others who prefer burial in *consecrated* ground'.[9] The projectors of the St James Cemetery had originally considered that it would be sufficient to donate their profits to some unspecified church purpose.[10] However, a more formal arrangement was required, and negotiation on the matter was entered into with the Bishop of Chester, Charles James Blomfield.

Blomfield's tenure at the Diocese was short-lived, from 1824 to 1828, but this period and his subsequent appointment as Bishop of London had immeasurable significance in terms of the later history of cemeteries. Blomfield was a church builder, and conscious of any opportunity to improve or extend the reach of the church and promote its financial interests.[11] The Bishop realised that a consecrated cemetery in Liverpool would constitute competition for Church of England churchyards in the city and so reduce clerical income from burial fees. However, if the Trustees of the St James Cemetery were required to apply for an Act of Parliament before consecration would be agreed, then appropriate clerical compensation clauses could be inserted into the act at the Commons or Lords stages. In the event, the act establishing the St James Cemetery specified that compensation be made for loss of burial fees for the churches of St Peter and St Nicholas.[12] Blomfield's transference to London meant that the consecration of St James Cemetery was actually performed by the succeeding Bishop of Chester, John Bird Sumner, in January 1829. However, for Blomfield, the issue of cemetery consecration arose again almost immediately in London, with the establishment of the General Cemetery Company.

Plans for a grand cemetery for the capital had been mooted through much of the 1820s, and the Provisional Committee for the General Cemetery Company was in operation early in 1830.[13] The Company noted that the Bishop of London had sanctioned the building of the St James Cemetery, and it was resolved to ascertain the Bishop's views on a possible site in London. Throughout this period and during later debates on the matter of burial reform, the Bishop of London carefully balanced the objectives of improving public health and protecting clerical incomes. His intervention at Kensal Green ensured that the cemetery was established by Act of Parliament and was entirely consecrated. Furthermore, any incumbent of a parish in the Diocese of London that was noted within the weekly bills of mortality for London would be given a fee corresponding to the cost of interment where burial took place in the cemetery rather than the parish churchyard. Thus, compensation of 1s 6d would be paid where interment in the cemetery was in a common grave, but 5s for interment in a catacomb, vault or bricked grave.[14] After consecration, and on application from the Nonconformist community, an unconsecrated portion was added to the site. The Bishop required the building of a wall demarcating the two sections, a measure which was apparently regretted by the Company's directors as being unnecessarily sectarian.[15]

Around the same time, an innovation of sorts arose in York where the York General Cemetery Company had created a cemetery principally as a response to poor burial conditions in the city. Arrival at a resolution to the problem had been long delayed by the inability of the city's separate parishes to agree a strategy: at one stage, it was even mooted that each parish have its own burial ground on the city's outskirts. However, by 1836, plans were in train to effect a compromise. The Archbishop of York, Edward Venables-Vernon Harcourt, was approached and on hearing an explanation of the planned cemetery 'promised to consecrate the portion of the ground and chapel allotted to the Established Church'.[16] In order to save the cost of two buildings, the line of consecration ran directly through the cemetery chapel. The Archbishop readily agreed to complete what he termed a 'rare and interesting ceremony'.[17] He had perhaps a less keen eye than Bishop Blomfield for the consequences of his action: the site was established by a deed of settlement and local clergy were not compensated for loss of fees. However, the notion of part-consecration quickly became established as a solution to possible tensions between denominations on the allocation of land.

In 1847, the passage of the Cemeteries Clauses Act acknowledged that most communities would have to apply for a private bill in order to secure the agreement of the local bishop to consecrate part of the cemetery. This Act was one of a number of acts which established template clauses that could be incorporated in to private bills, so reducing legal costs.[18] The Cemetery Clauses Act, rarely discussed in literature relating to the development of cemeteries in England, underlined a number of key principles that would become essential components of the later Burial Acts: that a company could apply to the local bishop for consecration of a portion of the cemetery, which would be used 'only for burials according to the rites of the Established Church'; that the company should 'define by suitable marks the consecrated and unconsecrated portions of the cemetery'; that compensatory sums should be paid to each incumbent and clerk of the parish from which a body has been removed for burial in the cemetery; and that the consent of the bishop was required on the appointment of a specific chaplain to officiate in the consecrated section, and the stipend the chaplain would be paid.[19]

Cemeteries and public health prior to the Burial Acts

The need for a clauses act reflected the increased popularity of the joint-stock cemetery format from the mid-1830s. From this period, the religious-political motivations for establishing cemeteries were increasingly overshadowed by a strengthening belief in the adverse public health consequences of burial in the midst of heavily populated areas. According to the dominant miasmatic theory, bad smells were a cause of disease. Putrefaction of vegetable or animal matter produced 'a new compound which when applied to the human body produces a phenomenon constituting fever'.[20] Indeed, Thomas Wakley, Coroner for West Middlesex and editor of the *Lancet*, asserted that 'putrid exhalations from dead bodies, in concentrated degree, produces highly injurious and even fatal effects on the living subject'.[21] Substantial anecdotal evidence was brought forward demonstrating a link between exposure to noxious graveyard 'emanations' and, in some dramatic cases, instantaneous death.[22] The abolition of intramural interment – burial at the heart of the community – attracted strong support from the scientific elite, including the sanitary reformer Thomas Southwood Smith, eminent doctors such as the fever expert John Armstrong, and perhaps most conspicuously by the campaigner Dr George Alfred Walker. Grisly details of local churchyard overcrowding became commonplace reports in local newspapers throughout the United Kingdom. In the majority of large towns and cities, communities adopted the joint-stock format and laid out part-consecrated cemeteries. In many cases, the cemetery companies were linked to the local government structure and directors often included the mayor, aldermen, the clergy and other leading professionals. Close co-operation between companies and the council was often evident: for example, the General Cemetery Company in Newcastle was granted suitable land by the town council, in exchange for ninety shares in the company.[23] All companies expressed themselves satisfied that their endeavours would return a pecuniary reward for investors, but the principal reason for taking action generally reflected a desire to improve local burial provision.[24]

Despite a context of considerable agitation on the subject of intramural interment, the Cemetery Clauses Act offered little regulation in terms of the sanitary aspects of cemetery management. Indeed, the Act simply required cemeteries to be laid out 200 yards from the nearest dwelling place, unless specific consent in writing was obtained from the owner and occupier of such dwelling; companies would be subject to a penalty if 'offensive matter' from the cemetery were to flow into a nearby source of water; and interment was not permitted in any chapel erected in the cemetery.[25] The Act was clearly inadequate as a means of controlling the public health consequences of continued interment in existing churchyards and burial grounds. The weakness of the Act in this regard is perhaps explained by the fact that the issue was addressed more directly by the Public Health Act of 1848. The wider import of this Act has been discussed in many places elsewhere, and here is not the place to explore its recommendations in detail.[26] It is sufficient to note that, as a measure to contain the incidence of intramural interment, the Act was flawed. Its proponent, the sanitary reformer Edwin Chadwick, had originally intended the Act to empower local authorities to own and administer cemeteries but was dissuaded from this action by Sir George Grey, who considered that the proposal would attract Nonconformist opposition.[27] Consequently, the provisions were much less directive. The Act provided the newly established General Board of Health (GBoH) with powers to make unlawful *continued* burial in any existing burial ground or church in which the Act was applied, providing that 'sufficient means of interment exist within a convenient distance from such burial ground, church or place of public worship'.[28] Furthermore – and with long-standing consequences in terms of public administration – no replacement burial ground could be formed without the consent of the GBoH.[29] The cholera epidemic of 1848–9 brought the Act into immediate operation: in September 1849 alone, some nineteen churchyards were affected, with a further 25 subject to 'precautionary measures' in the following month. Throughout the crisis, the General Board of Health advised that all churchyards in the capital be covered with quicklime, to a depth of three inches.[30] There has been very limited study of how local government and the Church nationally engaged with the provisions of the Public Health Act relating to churchyard closure, in part perhaps because of the limited time between this Act and the first of the Burial Acts in the early 1850s. The incidence of a cholera epidemic clearly accelerated the pace of events, but in most localities there was a delay between the passage of burial legislation, the negotiation of agreement between local agencies on the manner of its implementation and a 'countable' outcome such as a definite churchyard closure date. The panicked response in London can be contrasted with York, where A. E. Hargrove's rather visceral 1847 polemic *The Baneful Custom of Interment in Towns and the Present State of York Graveyards* had led to local meetings and petitions to close the city's churchyards. The 1848 legislation gave sufficient powers, and the city did have alternative burial provision in the new general cemetery. However, by 1853, only thirteen of the city's 24 churchyards had closed to further interment, and in all cases the action had been voluntary.[31]

Nationally, further and much more far-reaching burial legislation followed the Public Health Act. The Metropolitan Interments Act of 1850 encompassed Edwin Chadwick's plan to recreate the French *Pompes Funèbres*, and included powers for the State to absorb all burial and funeral directing services in London. The GBoH would be responsible for all funerals – which would be made available on a sliding scale depending on the income of the family involved – and would provide new cemeteries managed on strictly sanitary principles, following the closure of all inner-city churchyards. In the broader history of public enactment on burials, this Act is very much an aberration; indeed, the legislation was repealed in its entirety by the Burial Act of 1852. The 1850 Act had been passed in a fog of hysteria created by the cholera epidemic of 1848–9; after the epidemic passed, the appetite for such radical reform diminished rapidly. The Treasury prevaricated on the economics of the State purchase of existing cemeteries and the impossibility of achieving the monopoly of the funeral industry deemed to be essential to the success of the scheme.[32] By contrast, the Burial Act, 1852 – its geographic reach extended beyond the capital by a further Burial Act in 1853 – built on the principles laid by earlier legislation. Discontinuation of burial in certain churchyards might be enforced by Order in Council, and churchwardens, on the instruction from at least ten ratepayers, might convene a vestry meeting to determine whether a burial ground might be provided and, if so, to appoint a burial board to pursue the matter.[33] It is with this permissive legislation – which very decidedly continued a tradition of localism in burial matters – that a 'second generation' of cemetery establishment emerged.

Rural North Yorkshire in 1850

Pursuing the history of rural burial provision in the second half of the nineteenth century might appear to be a perverse decision, given the substantial investment in cemetery infrastructure which took place in major cities and towns over the same period. In the first twenty years of the Burial Acts, well over five hundred new cemeteries were laid out by burial boards in England and Wales.[34] Many of these boards embarked on spectacular cemetery projects: the majority of cemeteries on the English Heritage list of Parks and Gardens of Special Historic Interest were laid out by these agencies.[35] A national history of burial boards has yet to be written, and is not the principal objective of this book. Rather, this text will focus on changing provision in a rural area of England, where decisions relating to churchyards and cemeteries had a different dynamic and were driven less by exigencies of substantial increases in population.

Geography and population

This study covers the modern local authority districts of Ryedale, Hambleton and Harrogate. These three districts comprise the central portion of the old North Riding, and extend from Pateley Bridge in Nidderdale to the west, to a mid-way point between Malton and the coast, to the east. The study includes the eastern fringe of the Yorkshire

Dales, much of the North York Moors and the northern tranche of the Yorkshire Wolds. The area bounded by the modern unitary authority of York is excluded. Although Harrogate Borough contains by far the largest settlement in the study – Harrogate itself – the borough boundary encompasses a substantial rural hinterland to the north and west of the city. Principal market towns include New Malton, Norton, Pickering, Easingwold, Ripon, Northallerton, Knaresborough, Bedale, Thirsk and Pateley Bridge. The research area comprised warpentakes in North, East and West Riding, which are listed in Table 2.1.

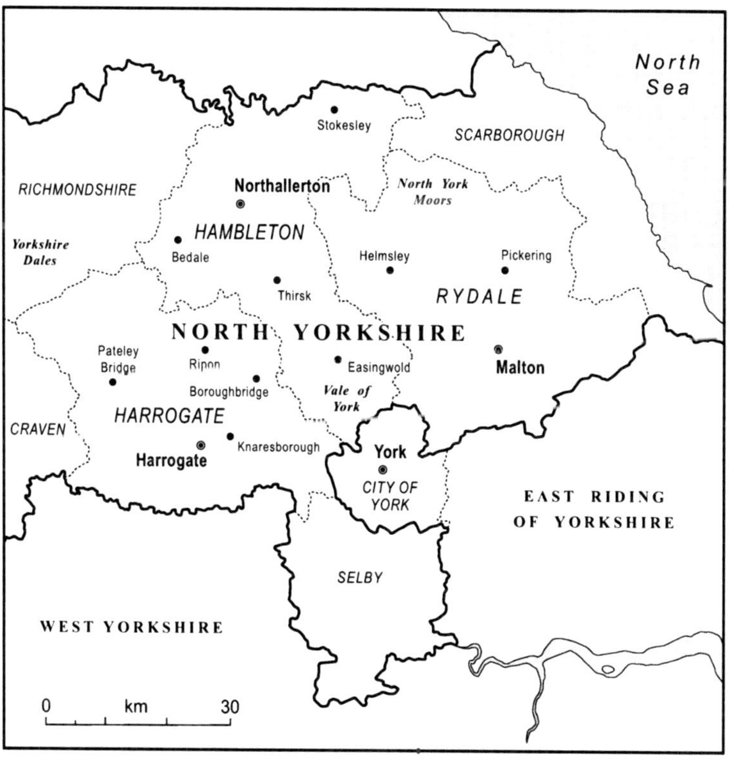

Map 2.1 Central North Riding: Harrogate, Hambleton and Ryedale

Table 2.1 Warpentakes included in the study

East Riding	Buckrose*
North Riding	Allertonshire, Birdforth, Bulmer, Gilling East*, Hallikeld, Hang East*, Langbaurgh Liberty West*, Pickering, Ryedale
West Riding	Claro Lower, Claro Upper*, Ripon Liberty.

Note: An asterisk indicates that part of the warpentake is included.

According to Bateman's calculations in 1876, some 40 per cent of the North Riding was owned by peers and great landowners.[36] Central North Riding included some large landed estates, not least of which was that owned by the Earls of Carlisle at Castle Howard, which encompassed a number of estate villages. Through the nineteenth century, the Earl of Feversham owned much of the area around Helmsley and almost all of Helmsley itself, aside from a couple of properties.[37] The northern edge of the Wolds was under the control of the Sykes family of Sledmere, and Earl Fitzwilliam owned a substantial portion of New Malton, Old Malton and Norton. In addition to estate villages, there were a number of settlements whose development was directly connected to the activity of a single industrial employer. For example, the population around Rosedale quadrupled from 1860 following the opening of new mines by the Rosedale and Ferry Hill Iron Company Ltd, which paid for an extension to the churchyard in 1874.[38] The company failed soon after, and the settlement dwindled substantially.

Population decline tended to be widespread in central North Riding. Raven's analysis of census figures for 1801 and 1851 indicated that even the market towns of the area did not always excel in terms of population growth. Easingwold, Pickering and Stokesley all increased by around 50 per cent; New Malton and Bedale fared less well, increasing by just a fifth; Helmsley grew by just two per cent.[39] Mining and textile development had flourished in some locations in the late eighteenth and early nineteenth century.

Lead mining was one industry that had become well established in Nidderdale by 1850, and quarrying was encouraged by the expansion of the railway in the 1860s.[40] Fewston had, by 1848, five flax mills and a corn mill, and the village itself had 850 inhabitants and could support a number of shops and an inn.[41] However, industrial activity and localised concomitant population growth were overtaken in the process of more intensive urban development to the south and west. The flax-spinning and linen mills that were important in such towns as Great Ayton, Osmotherley, Ampleforth and Appleton Wiske had by the mid-1850s largely disappeared. Overall, by mid-century, much of the area had agriculture as the principal economy. The development of railway links had meant that some market towns thrived, as agricultural products were moved to the urban areas, but for others with poor transport links – such as Coxwold and Hovingham – there was protracted decrease in terms of size. This did not necessarily mean that central North Riding could be characterised as being impoverished. The area was renowned for its expertise in horse breeding, and – as Rider Haggard found in 1902 – parts of the area made a good living from agriculture even during the Depression of the late nineteenth century.[42]

The research included, as its sample, all the settlements in the three districts of Hambleton, Ryedale and Harrogate that had at least one place in which burials took place in the years 1850–2007; 277 such places were located. In general analysis, individual burial places are used as case units, and the place in which the burial sites were located is generally here referred to as a 'settlement'. In some instances the settlements were defined nucleated townships or villages that were originally within larger parishes, and that over time acquired their own separate burial space. In other instances, the settlement constituted a parish that contained one single nucleated settlement with some outlying farms and houses. In all instances, the settlements were and still are distinguishable 'places'. The highly rural nature of the area and its ongoing de-population meant that few of these settlements lost their individual identity as a consequence of urban sprawl, and the generally slower pace of change made it easier to track trends that might have been accelerated in more heavily populated areas. The research also includes as a 'settlement' some remote locations where a churchyard – perhaps once serving a larger population than currently exists – operated, but in the service of a highly dispersed community. As will be seen, some settlements only latterly acquired burial provision, and had none of their own at the start of the research period; these are included. In many other cases, settlements did not acquire burial provision at all, and continued to be reliant on neighbouring provision. These dependent settlements are omitted from the study.[43]

Definitions of rurality are not central to this study, and, in the case of a large area covering an extended period, the nature of the settlements will change over time and parish boundaries will alter. A classification for each settlement has been given according to its population size according to the census in 2001 less as a definitive statement, and more as indicative data characterising the area in question.[44] Comparison with a nineteenth-century source such as Bulmer's *Directory* indicates that, for many of these places, their scale has changed very little. Overall, nearly half the places in the study constituted small villages with populations of between 101 and 500 people. These included villages in the Wolds such as Kirby Grindalythe, Helperthorpe and Weaverthorpe; settlements in the Howardian Hills, for example Coneysthorpe, Terrington and Dalby; Ingleby Greenhow and Carleton in Cleveland, which are Cleveland Hills villages; and the many small villages in the Vale of York itself. To the west, research included communities in Nidderdale, such as Fewston, Dacre Banks and Hampsthwaite. Remote and scattered settlements located in the North York Moors, on the eastern edge of the Yorkshire Dales and the northern edge of the Wolds comprised around a quarter of the places in the study, but even in the Vale of

York there are very small villages, for example, Birdforth or Baldersby St James. The growth of the large towns and cities in North Yorkshire has tended to mask continuing depopulation of these more rural areas, which was certainly in train by the second half of the nineteenth century.[45] Around a fifth of the settlements in the study had a population in excess of 1,500 according to the 2001 census, but even these places were relatively small. With the exception of Harrogate, the remaining towns – Northallerton, Knaresborough, New Malton and Ripon – did not even reach 16,000 inhabitants.

Religion

For the whole of the research period, the area was covered by two Church of England dioceses: Ripon and Leeds, which was created in 1836, and York. The level of rurality was challenging for the clergy. In responding to the Archbishop's visitation return in 1868, the vicar of Kildale, a widespread settlement in the Cleveland Hills, wrote that 'the parish is consisting of widely scattered farms. One is 4 or 5 miles from the church: others a long way off. I have no horse.'[46] Further south, the parish of Helmsley was – in 1870 – spread over 36 square miles.[47] The second half of the century saw the creation of a number of chapels of ease, which aimed to reduce the travel distance of outlying parishioners to the principal 'mother' church. Some, but not all, of these chapels had attached burial space. For example, at Aldwark, a chapel of ease was built between 1846 and 1853 at the request of Lady Frankland-Russell of Thirkleby Park, to serve parishioners who hitherto had to travel to the mother church of St Mary's at Alne. The chapel of ease was dedicated to St Stephen and had a churchyard; burials taking place there were recorded in the burial registers of St Mary's. The size of the parishes meant that many contained separate townships and, as the period progressed, a number of benefices were split. For example, Bilsdale, which lies to the north of Rievaulx Abbey in the North York Moors National Park, was called 'Bilsdale Westside' by Bulmer in 1890.[48] This large parish was served by the church of St Hilda's at Chop Gate until 1896, when the parish was divided: Bilsdale Midcable – the southern portion – became a parish in its own right with a church dedicated to St John built by the Earl of Feversham. Church building and church rebuilding were endemic throughout the period, and, although the Church of England itself was a constant presence, its provision of places of worship and places of burial was by no means static.

The religious census of 1851 indicated that both church-going and chapel-going were strong in North Yorkshire. Indeed, the Index of Attendance for North Riding was 63.9 per cent of the population, compared with 52.9 for the West Riding and 58.8 for the East Riding; the average for England and Wales was 58.1.[49] Church of England attendance was also higher for the North Riding, with 41.6 per cent of attendances at church, compared with 37.0 per cent and 34.2 per cent for the East and West Ridings respectively. Material investment in church infrastructure was substantial in the nineteenth century. Practically every church in the case study area was subject to substantial renovation or in some cases complete demolition and rebuilding in the second half of the nineteenth century.[50] Although the work was often initiated and financed by local aristocracy or leading landowners for the most part, communities themselves contributed both money and in some cases labour and resources. When Harwood Brierley wrote in 1897 about the 'oldest unrestored church in Yorkshire' – St Mary's at Scawton – he was clearly describing an exceptional circumstance. Even in this poor community, with 'no more than two houses that look inhabitable, and one of these is the rectory', a sum of £400 had been raised towards the £600 cost of refurbishment.[51]

Overall in Yorkshire, Methodism remained the strongest religious denomination: both Wesleyan and Primitive Methodism were solidly supported. Attendances at Methodist chapels in North Riding were lower than in East Riding, at 45.4 per cent compared with 47.3 per cent. However, village histories and Bulmer's directories demonstrate the pervasive nature of Methodism throughout the case study area, and not just in the market towns. Many places, such as the tiny dispersed settlement at Chop Gate in the Cleveland Hills, were from the second half of the nineteenth century able to support two Methodist chapels in addition to an Anglican church.[52] Indeed, some villages were renowned for their strong adherence to Nonconformity: Osmotherley is the site of the oldest Wesleyan chapel in the country, built in 1754; other New Methodist communities in the area were established following one or more visits by John Wesley himself, which was the case in Hawby, for example. The Old Dissent prospered principally in the principal market towns: Pickering, New Malton, Kirkbymoorside and Helmsley all had Independent or Congregationalist chapels. Baptists were not strongly represented in the area. They had chapels in a small handful of places – Bedale, New Malton and Masham, for example – but were very limited in number compared with other parts of England.[53] Furthermore, there is no evidence of a Baptist burial ground in the case study area. The influence of the Old Dissent appeared not to extend out of the market towns, with the exception of Quakers. Quaker Meetings were widely dispersed, and there were handfuls of Friends in very small settlements such as Hutton-le-Hole and Huby near Sutton-on-the-Forest. In some places – such as Great Ayton – Quakers constituted a substantial presence in the community, but in others evidence of meeting houses and attached burial grounds had by 1850 begun to disappear from the landscape.

As will be seen, relations between Anglicans and Nonconformists could be remarkably variable across the central belt of North Yorkshire: at Alne the vicar reported in 1865 that although the principal farmers were generally Wesleyans, 'there is no dislike of my ministrations, or political opposition'.[54] Indeed, there appears to be no record of conflict between denominations on the matter of interment in the parish of Alne. In other locations, tensions between the vicar and local Nonconformists could be evident, perhaps particularly where the local clergy were considered to be high-handed. The notoriously prickly vicar of Helmsley, Charles Norris Gray, appears to have provoked more than one burial controversy. Even where the clergy could be conciliatory, the strong expression of denominational principles could mean that burial issues often required careful negotiation and took remarkable tact to resolve.

Burial in North Yorkshire, 1850

As a basis for later discussion, it is useful to consider a 'snapshot' of burial provision in the case study area in the year 1850. Overall, there are 277 settlements in the study where burial took place between 1850 and 2007. Almost all these settlements had burial provision that was well-established by mid-century.

Cemeteries

There were no cemeteries in the case study area in 1850, reflecting its rural character. Nationally, cemetery companies were in operation in almost all major urban areas including, in Yorkshire, Leeds (1835), York (1836), Sheffield (1836), Hull (1845) and Rotherham (1849). Harrogate had developed perhaps a couple of decades too late to have been part of this first generation of cemetery development, and instead established its first major provision under the Burial Acts. This is not to say that there had been no increases in burial space, but need had generally been met through the extension of an existing churchyard. For example, in Knaresborough, additional land was added to the church of St John the Baptist in 1828.[55] However, it is notable that the first cemeteries were established soon after the passage of the first of the Burial Acts, in Northallerton and in New Malton.

Table 2.2 Burial provision in the case study settlements, 1850

	Number	*Percentage*
No burial space as yet in the settlement	43	16
Old churchyard (pre-1800)	186	67
Recent churchyard (1801–50)	30	11
Both Church of England churchyard and one or more denominational burial grounds	15	5
Denominational burial ground only	4	2
TOTAL	277	100

Old and new churchyards

In 1850, just over two-thirds of settlements with burial space were reliant on churchyards with burial space brought into use before 1801. The majority of these can comfortably be described as 'ancient', with origins in the medieval period.[56] Indeed, very many settlements in this part of Yorkshire are of Anglo-Saxon origin: placenames including 'Kirkby' or 'Kirby' indicate tenth-century settlement.[57] Kirkby, Kirkby Overblow, Kirkbymoorside and Kirk Hammerton all had pre-Conquest churches. One of the earliest – St Gregory's Minster in Kirkdale – dates from the seventh century and was rebuilt in the eleventh; a sundial dating from the Anglo-Saxon period remains above the south doorway. Use of this churchyard continues to the present day.[58] The fact that in 1850 these villages were using a churchyard that had been established in the Anglo-Saxon period constitutes an essential indicator of continuity which is integral to the notion of churchyard burial.

However, a further 11 per cent of settlements had a churchyard established in or after 1801, the great majority attached to churches that were built between 1820 and 1850. Nationally, this was a period in which substantial investment was made in the creation of Anglican churches. The Church Building Act of 1818 was the first of a series of measures to support the construction of churches, which took place under the aegis of the Church Building Commission. Generally speaking, early nineteenth-century church building tends to be discussed in terms of limited provision for worship in the rapidly increasing towns and cities, and concern for the morals of the urban poor. In the case study area, at least 24 new churches were built, including St Cuthbert in Pateley Bridge and Holy Trinity in Ripon. However, the majority of new churches were not in market towns but in villages such as North Stainley and Great Fencote. Many of these churches were fairly modest, and tended to be chapels of ease. It was also the case that existing chapels of ease might have churchyards that were only latterly brought into use. So, for example, a chapel dedicated to All Saints had been in existence at Farnley since the seventeenth century, but it is probable that interments in its churchyard began only in the 1840s. Central North Riding was not necessarily exceptional in this regard. Nationally, Hope estimated that the Church Building Commission, in operation between 1818 and 1856, secured eight hundred sites for new churchyards, a figure which challenges the scale of new provision brought by cemetery companies.[59] It could be argued that new church building itself brought substantial dislocation to existing burial practice. Consciousness that this could be the case was evident in Great Ayton, where attempts to improve All Saints had been called into question by the probability of renovation interfering with existing graves: it was planned that the new church would be 'as near as possible to the old burial ground'.[60] These 'new' churchyards lacked ancestral continuity but probably carried the advantage of being close in geographic terms.

Burial grounds

A small number of settlements had what might be termed as a 'mixed economy' of burial provision, in having one or more Nonconformist burial grounds in addition to an Anglican churchyard. As has been seen, Nonconformity was marked in this part of Yorkshire, and although innumerable Wesleyan and Primitive Methodist chapels were created, it was not common for these chapels to have adjacent burial space. Independents often had separate burial space, but even in this case there are no more than a handful of instances in the central North Riding. At Pateley Bridge and Pickering, the Independent chapels had burial space, as did Providence Chapel at Dacre. This chapel was opened in 1827, as a 'mission station' of the Congregationalist church at Pateley Bridge, but the first interment in the burial ground did not take place until 1837.[61] Overall in the case study area in 1850 alternative burial provision more typically comprised the burial ground attached to Quaker meeting houses. This provision spread across a range of settlement types including market towns or larger villages such Great Ayton, Helmsley, Kirkbymoorside, Osmotherley and Stokesley. In Thirsk the Quakers had two burial grounds. Some Quaker burial grounds were located at some distance from the nearest settlement, for example at Lowna in the North Yorkshire Moors and in the fields near Dacre in Nidderdale. Quaker burial grounds tended to have only a small number of interments – perhaps one or two a year. Even though the site at Great Ayton was extended in 1789 and in 1842, its size remained small and interments were few.[62] Roman Catholics also had some burial provision in the case study area. St John the Evangelist at Easingwold and St Joseph's at Bishop Thornton had attached space for interment. The Roman Catholic Ampleforth Abbey had a small burial ground used by the monks; opened in 1841, the site has had only a handful of burials. In summary, although Nonconformity was strong, there was limited provision of burial space outside the aegis of the Church of England. Furthermore, where non-Anglican burial space was in evidence, it was clear that use was confined to very local Nonconformist or Roman Catholic communities: there was little sense that these burial places served a wide geographic area, and burial numbers tended to be low. It is reasonable to conclude that in 1850, in this central belt of North Riding, the Church of England carried a near-monopoly of burial provision.

No local provision

In 42 settlements, communities were reliant on churchyards in other villages and had yet to establish provision that was more local. For example, the parish of Alne contained six townships including Alne, Aldwark, Tollerton, Flawith, Tholthorpe and Youlton: St Mary the Virgin at Alne provided burial space for the whole parish. Residents at Aldwark were perhaps two miles away by road, and a chapel of ease with churchyard was constructed in the early 1850s. Similarly, Copt Hewick, to the east of Ripon, had no church itself until the construction of Holy Innocents in 1876. Until that time, parishioners used the churchyard of St John the Evangelist at Sharow, which was itself a recent construction, having opened in 1825. In the Wolds, the villagers of Helperthorpe did have a chapel of ease but no churchyard until the rebuilding of the church and addition of a churchyard by Sir Tatton Sykes in 1872; up until that time the villagers used the churchyard at Weaverthorpe. At Howsham, just north of Stamford Bridge, the parishioners used the churchyard at Scrayingham, walking along the old 'coffin road' or 'corpse path' across the fields. Similarly, the residents of Thornton-le-Beans used a corpse path to the churchyard at North Otterington. The existence of corpse paths linking settlements across the study area underlines the fact that villages were often at some distance from their nearest burial space. By the end of the research period, each of these settlements had gained its 'own' burial provision, most often in the second half of the nineteenth century.

Conclusion

Thus, burial provision in the central portion of the North Riding of Yorkshire in 1850 can be characterised as being dominated by the Church of England; non-Anglican burial grounds were few and served very localised need which tended to be limited in scale. There were no cemeteries in this part of rural England in 1850. However, the image of a long-standing tradition of local churchyard use must be subject to modification. Even in rural areas, the early nineteenth century saw the building of a number of churches which brought new churchyards into use in many settlements. The churchyard was not always central, spatially, to the village life and many, many settlements had no 'local' churchyard: their traditional place of interment might be some miles distant. The second half of the nineteenth century was a period which, for many rural communities, brought burial closer to home.

The year 1850 is not seminal in the history of burial provision, but is a useful starting point for the consideration of change in rural burial practice. The Burial Acts constituted a new framework which communities could use to change their existing practices. However, this legislation was largely permissive and local communities could decide for themselves which actions they would take. This book studies the ways in which religion, local politics, basic economics and changing commemorative practice framed the decisions that were made.

Hitherto, the social history of burial has tended to be preoccupied by the exceptional. Rural North Yorkshire does not constitute a special or distinctive location in which to undertake this kind of study. Strongly Methodist and gradually depopulating, North Yorkshire is one local context in which burial legislation was played out. As the study will demonstrate, even within this area, outcomes could be markedly diverse. Across England, it is likely that different rural regions will have their own distinctive history of change in burial practice: perhaps in locations where the Old Dissent left a more substantial legacy of independent burial space; or where industrialisation and settlement patterns led to larger population densities; or where the number of ratepayers might more readily support the creation of grander cemeteries. It is unlikely that this portion of rural England is unique in its pattern of experience, but its focus on the typical makes the study no less valid.

Notes

1 J. Rugg, 'The rise of cemetery companies in Britain, 1820–53' (PhD dissertation, University of Stirling, 1992). Much of the following discussion draws on this thesis.
2 J. Rugg, 'Defining the place of burial: what makes a cemetery a cemetery?', *Mortality*, 5:3 (2000), 238–59.
3 K. Grady, *The Georgian Public Buildings of Leeds and the West Riding* (Leeds: Publications of the Thoresby Society, 1989); B. C. Hunt, *The Development of the Business Corporation in England, 1800–1867* (Cambridge, MA: Harvard University Press, 1936); R. C. Mitchie, *Money, Mania and Markets: Investment Company Formation and the Stock Exchange in Nineteenth-Century Scotland* (Edinburgh: John Donald, 1981).
4 Rugg, 'The rise of cemetery companies', chapter 3.
5 Manchester Archive Office, MS923 2 H536, Personal Narrative of George Hadfield, 1860, p. 81.
6 Ian Sellers, 'Liverpool Nonconformity' (PhD dissertation, University of Keele, 1969).
7 John Wesley, quoted by G. Collison, *Cemetery Interment* (London: Orme, Brown, Green and Longman, 1840), p. 192.
8 Poor Law Amendment Act (1844), s. 31.
9 Liverpool Archive Office, 352 CEM/3/7/1, Minute Book of the Trustees of the St James Cemetery, Liverpool, 2 Sep 1825. Underlining original.
10 *Ibid.*
11 P. J. Welch, 'Bishop Blomfield and church extension in London', *Journal of Ecclesiastical History*, 4 (1953), 203–15.
12 An Act for providing an additional cemetery in the parish of Liverpool in the County Palatine of Lancaster (1826), s. 18.
13 R. Richardson and J. S. Curl, 'George Frederick Carden and the genesis of the General Cemetery Company' in Curl, J. S. (ed.), *Kensal Green Cemetery* (Chichester: Phillimore & Co., 2001).
14 Collison, *Cemetery Interment*, p. 158.
15 J. S. Curl, 'The General Cemetery from 1833 to 1842', in Curl, *Kensal Green Cemetery*, p. 28.
16 *York Herald*, 28 Aug 1836.

17 *Yorkshire Gazette*, 9 Sep 1837.
18 J. Prest, *Liberty and Locality: Parliament, Permissive Legislation and Ratepayers' Democracies in the Nineteenth Century* (Oxford: Clarendon Press, 1990).
19 Cemeteries Clauses Act (1847), ss. 23, 24, 27 and 30.
20 T. Southwood Smith, *A Treatise on Fever* (London, 1830), quoted by M. Flinn (ed.), *Report on the Sanitary Condition of the Labouring Classes* (Edinburgh: Edinburgh University Press, 1965), p. 62.
21 *Lancet*, 2 (1839), p. 40.
22 See, for example, 1842 (327) *Report from the Select Committee on Improvement of the Health of Towns: Effect of Interment of Bodies in Towns*, p. x.
23 Tyne and Wear Archives, DX446, Prospectus of the Newcastle-upon-Tyne General Cemetery Company, 1834.
24 J. Rugg, 'A new burial form and its meanings: cemetery establishment in the first half of the nineteenth century' in Cox, M. (ed.), *Grave Concerns: Death and Burial in England, 1700–1850* (York, Council for British Archaeology: 1998).
25 Cemetery Clauses Act (1847), ss. 10, 20, 21 and 39.
26 See for example, S. E. Finer, *The Life and Times of Edwin Chadwick* (London: Methuen, 1952); C. Hamlin, *Public Health and Social Justice in the Age of Chadwick, Britain 1800–1854* (Cambridge: Cambridge University Press, 1998); R. A. Lewis, *Edwin Chadwick and the Public Health Movement* (London: Longmans, Green and Co., 1952).
27 Finer, *Life and Times*, p. 322.
28 Public Health Act (1848), s. 82.
29 *Ibid.*, s. 83.
30 CERC, 11686/2, Church Commissioners: churches, burial grounds and parsonages, conveyance of sites, general file, 1845–65, various documents detailing churchyard closures, as requested by the General Board of Health.
31 H. Murray, *This Garden of Death: The History of York Cemetery, 1837–2007* (York: Friends of York Cemetery, 2008), p. 37.
32 A full account of the passage of the Metropolitan Interment Act is in Finer, *Life and Times*, pp. 355ff.
33 Burial Act (1852), ss. 2, 10 and 12.
34 1873 (116) *Churchyards and Cemeteries. Returns of all parishes in England and Wales in which any new portion of ground has been consecrated to serve as a churchyard during the last ten years, and of the approximate extent in each case of such portion of ground, distinguishing those which have been purchased by the parish and those which have been*

purchased by voluntary subscription or presented as a free gift; and, of the names of all parishes in England and Wales in which cemeteries have been constituted, whether under burial acts or otherwise, containing a portion of unconsecrated ground.

35 english-heritage.org.uk/publications/list-cemeteries/, accessed 23 October 2011.

36 J. Bateman, *The Great Landowners of Great Britain and Ireland* (Leicester: Leicester University Press, 1971 [1876]), p. 511.

37 N. Mant, *Eighteen Years' Work in a Yorkshire Parish* (Scarborough: E. T. W. Dennis, 1889).

38 BI, CD Add. 1874/2, Addition to churchyard.

39 N. Raven, 'De-industrialisation and the urban response: the small towns of the North Riding of Yorkshire c1790–1850', in Weedon, R. and Milne, A. (eds), *Aspects of Small English Towns in the Eighteenth and Nineteenth Centuries* (Leicester: Centre for Urban History, 1993).

40 B. Jennings (ed.), *A History of Nidderdale* (Huddersfield: Advertiser Press, 1967).

41 'Fetcham – Fincham', A Topographical Dictionary of England (1848), pp. 232–5, from www.british-history.ac.uk/report.aspx ?compid=50962&strquery=fewston, accessed 23 September 2010.

42 R. A. Butlin, 'Agriculture' in Butlin, R. A. (ed.), *Historical Atlas of North Yorkshire* (Otley: Westbury, 2003); R. Haggard, *Rural England: Being an Account of Agricultural and Social Researches Carried Out in the Years 1901 and 1902* (London: Longmans, Green and Co., 1906).

43 Appendix Four lists all the sites in the study.

44 This five-part classification included: dispersed settlements and settlements with fewer than 100 individuals; small villages with 101–500 inhabitants; larger villages with 501–1,500 inhabitants; small towns and cities with a population of 15,001+; and areas defined as suburbs.

45 R. Lawton, 'Population change, 1700–1900' in Butlin, R. A. (ed.), *Historical Atlas of North Yorkshire* (Otley: Westbury, 2003).

46 BI, v.1868/Ret 1, Archbishop's Visitation return, 1868.

47 N. Mant, *Eighteen Years' Work.*

48 T. Bulmer, *History, Topography and Directory of North Yorkshire* (Preston: T. Bulmer and Co., 1890), p. 708.

49 J. Wolffe, *The Religious Census of 1851 in Yorkshire* (York: Borthwick Paper 108, 2005).

50 N. Pevsner, *Yorkshire The North Riding* (London: Yale University

Press, 2002 [1966]); N. Pevsner, *Yorkshire The West Riding* (London: Yale University Press, 2003 [1959]); N. Pevsner and D. Neave, *Yorkshire: York and the East Riding* (London: Yale University Press, 2005 [1972]).

51 H. Brierley, 'The oldest unrestored church in Yorkshire, St Mary's Scawton', *Illustrated Church News*, 29 Oct 1897.

52 J. Rushton, *The History of Ryedale: From the Earliest Times to the year 2000* (Trowbridge: Blackthorn Press, 2003); T. Bulmer, *Directory*.

53 K. D. M. Snell and P. S. Ell, *Rival Jerusalems: The Geography of Victorian Religion* (Cambridge: Cambridge University Press, 2000).

54 BI, v.1868/Ret 1, Archbishop's Visitation return, 1868, Alne.

55 NYRO, PR/KN 9/1, Sentence of consecration of additional burial ground, 1828.

56 Pevsner, *Yorkshire*; Bulmer, *Gazette*.

57 A. Jones, *A Thousand Years of the English Parish* (Moreton-in-Marsh: Windrush Press, 2000), p. 94.

58 N. Pevsner, *Yorkshire The North Riding*, p. 216.

59 M. H. Port, *Six Hundred New Churches: A Study of the Church Building Commission, 1818–1856, and Its Church Building Activities* (London: SPCK, 1961), p. 113fn.

60 Quoted in D. O'Sullivan, *Great Ayton: A History of the Village* (Great Ayton: private publication, nd).

61 T. Whitehead, *Illustrated Guide to Nidderdale and a History of Its Congregational Churches* (Keighley: Feather Books, 1932), pp. 168–9.

62 NYRO, R/Q/G 4/1, Durham Quarterly Meeting: Trust Property Book (1886).

3

'Dr Hoffman was good enough to consult me':[1] churchyard closures

The opening of new cemeteries took place in the context of churchyard closures. Although the first of these developments has attracted a great deal of academic attention, nineteenth-century churchyard closures have so far not been subject to scrutiny. Within the broad narratives of burial change, closures have substantial importance. For innumerable communities, interment in the precincts of the church had continued for centuries, and the sudden cessation of this practice from the mid-1800s must have constituted a troubling disruption. Closures are often explained through reference to over-rapid population growth. However, analysis of the incidence of churchyard closures in rural areas brings into question the importance of demographics. As is the case with very many aspects of burial history considered in this study, churchyard closures merit far more detailed and extensive study than is afforded here. Indeed, this chapter considers some aspects of the process, but also provokes further questions for which answers are not yet forthcoming. Here, a start is made by reviewing the incidence of churchyard closure in central North Riding in the period up to 1894.

In the second half of the nineteenth century, 25 Orders in Council were issued relating to churchyards in central North Riding, the earliest order being for All Saints', Northallerton in 1854.[2] The Home Office employed a burial inspector who could recommend immediate closure or an end to interment after a named date, which was often just weeks after the inspection took place. It might be presumed that closures reflected a Foucauldian process, with state-sponsored scientific and professional bodies deposing traditional and pastoral provision in the realms of death. However, the chapter reviews each of the churchyard closures in the case study area and asks how far such an interpretation is an accurate reflection of the process. For example, it is notable that the means of effecting closure through an Order in Council was set in train by the local community, which could request an inspection visit from the specified central agency: the General Board of Health initially or later in the century the Burials Office within the Home Office. Closures were not always absolute, and negotiation could take place to the degree that continued interment in the churchyard could take place. Orders often referred to part of the churchyard only, and specified exemptions or defined circumstances in which burial might continue. Indeed, examination of burial registers indicates that interments could continue for decades in a churchyard after its supposed closure. A more substantial and intriguing question is why closure orders were sought if – as was often the case – continued use was made of the churchyard. In answering this question, it is possible to conclude that contradictory and conflicted attitudes towards the dead body were in evidence.

The legalities of churchyard closure

The legal processes around the decision to discontinue burial in the churchyard in the nineteenth century are not well understood. Vestries might choose to take one of two courses of action. It might simply be decided that no further burials would be allowed in the churchyard. At New Malton, interments in the churchyard around St Michael's at the centre of town had declined substantially, and between 1820 and 1850 just 24 burials took place. The thirteenth-century church of St Leonard – located a little further to the town's periphery – accommodated almost all the town's 70–100 interments a year. However, in 1850 it was decided that burials at St Michael's would entirely cease 'by consent'.[3] Burials at St Leonard's dropped substantially when the cemetery opened in December 1859, to no more than one a year. It is not clear why the New Malton vestries took this option, since there is no relevant documentation in local vestry minutes. It is also difficult to understand why the apparently simple decision to close 'by consent' was not taken more often in preference to the formal and complex process of closure by Order in Council.

Closure by Order in Council

The process of closing a churchyard by Order in Council was defined by the Burial Acts, and had emerged as a consequence of the desire to protect the interests of the Church of England. Through the 1840s in particular, the proliferation of cemetery companies reflected the wish to tackle the public health consequences of burial in the city. However, one measure that was outside the control of town and parish councils was the ability to close inner-city churchyards which had become 'filled with the dead even to heaping up' and 'almost humanised with interment'.[4] Ostensibly, intramural interment comprised simply another nuisance on a list including inadequate sewerage, limited water supply, poor-quality air and ill-maintained or non-existent roads. Progress to introduce public health measures had initially been hindered by the need to counter a substantial range of vested interests. As the century progressed, the benefits of reform generally overcame any case that could be made to retain the status quo. The specific case of burial was another matter entirely, since in this case the 'status quo' comprised Anglican churchyard provision. Even well-intentioned burial reform implied both critique of the Church and a threat to clerical incomes, so attracting the attention of bishops and

Nonconformists alike. Almost immediately, from the early 1840s, the issue of intramural interment carried two religious-political imperatives: that no proposed burial reform would damage the interests of the Church, and the claims of Nonconformists would not be overlooked. As a consequence, the Burial Acts were separate from the general stream of legislative enactment on public health.

The inconsistency of the relationship is made evident in the early years of the General Board of Health (GBoH), which was established by the Public Health Act, 1848. The GBoH oversaw the creation of local boards of health which were made up of local ratepayers and had the authority to oversee improvements to water supply, house drainage, sewerage and roads.[5] The boards could ask the GBoH to send an inspector, who would visit the area and take evidence from interested parties. The subsequent report could be used as a basis for a programme of sanitary measures. The local board of health could undertake reform by applying for loans payable over thirty years and secured against the poor rate, but the loans had to be sanctioned by the GBoH centrally. Hamlin has stressed that the GBoH was not an 'enforcer': rather, its work was to promote public health and act as an external auditor of expenditure to quell local fears of corruption and jobbery.[6] GBoH reports sometimes – but not always – addressed local burial provision, and included description of the churchyard, the reproduction of data on its usage, discussion with the vicar and/or sexton about the pressure on space, and evidence on public health in its vicinity. Inconsistency in dealing with the issue is evident in the reports produced for Northallerton, Ripon and New Malton. In the case of Ripon, the generally high mortality rate of the city provoked a GBoH inspection, and William Ranger reported on the sanitary condition of the town. However, despite the very heavy rate of burial within the Cathedral itself and its precincts, Ranger's report did not include any reference to interment or make any relevant recommendations.[7] Nevertheless, in 1855 the City took the step of securing a closure order for the Cathedral and its nearby sister church, Trinity. The report by Robert Rawlinson for New Malton contained a little more discussion of burial provision, noting the existence of burial grounds in New Malton, Old Malton and Norton but without describing conditions in any of these sites. The fact that the principal churchyards had already been closed and measures to secure further space were in hand perhaps precluded further comment.

The 1850 report on Northallerton by William Ranger contained much more detail on sanitary conditions in the town's burial grounds and indicated that the churchyard of All Saints was under considerable pressure.[8] The churchyard, 'obtained by immemorial occupation' was described as being 1 acre, 1 rood and 10 perches, and enclosed by a wall. The churchyard stood 3 to 5 feet from the level of the street. The vicar, T. Burnett Stewart, did not believe the ground to be overcrowded 'in comparison with many churchyards in towns', and was rather circumspect in his comments:

> I must leave it to those more able than myself to decide as to the expediency of sepulture in town, even under the most favourable circumstances, and will only mention facts: that I have never heard any complaint made of offensive or injurious smells proceeding at any time from any part of the churchyard.[9]

The vicar concluded by hoping that the parishioners would recommend the procurement of burial ground 'removed from the church and houses of the towns'. The sexton, W. Hirbank, also gave evidence, and stated that his predecessor had 'complained of the alluvium [*sic*] arising during the time of digging'. From 1681 to 1837, a total of 7,490 interments had taken place in the churchyard but the soil appeared to be suitable for decomposition: it was 'in most parts black and gravel underneath, but never gets down to water'. Further evidence in the report was presented by a Mr Fowle, who confirmed that graves were being created above the level of the adjacent street.[10] Burial records indicate that accumulated interments in the churchyard were substantial in number: 1,472 interments took place in the twenty years prior to closure.[11] An Order in Council for closure at Northallerton commanded that 'burials in the parish church, and in the churchyard of the same, to be discontinued forthwith' from 1 May 1854.[12] It is clear, therefore, that, even where the GBoH took an active role in assessing sanitary conditions in a particular location, closure by Order in Council was not a necessary consequence.

Local negotiation

In actuality, the process of applying for and securing a closure order relied much more on local initiative than might be supposed. The process was defined under s. 1 of the Burial Act of 1853.[13] Initially, it had been suggested that the Burial Act should remove from the Secretary of State the 'invidious task of closing the churchyard' by setting a fixed date by which burial in all sites would cease.[14] However, this substantial level of central control looked too much like Chadwick's ambitious plan for a single state burial authority. The measure that was finally enacted used Orders in Council: upon the representation of a Secretary of State, the Queen could order the discontinuation of interment in a particular burial ground or place of burial, which ensured that a case was made for each closure. The Order in Council carried the force of legislation and its detail was reproduced in the *London Gazette* and, locally, in a notice on the church door. As with other public health measures, the GBoH or Home Office did not proactively seek out sanitary nuisance and order the necessary reform, although on occasion the report of a nuisance might provoke a visit.[15] Indeed, a small burials inspectorate had been established. In 1852, Dr John Sutherland accepted an appointment to make inspections, but following a move to India 1853 he was replaced by Dr P. H. Holland, who had also worked in the GBoH.[16] Dr Hoffman then took up the post in 1879, and nearly nine years into his appointment reported that he had made fifteen hundred visits.[17] It was possible for any individual or agency to contact Whitehall and request an inspection of the churchyard, and there is evidence that Drs Holland and Hoffman visited towns and even quite remote villages all over central North Riding. Letters requesting an inspection visit are extant for some churchyards, and in these cases it appeared that initiative came from the incumbent. For example in Great Ayton, the Reverend John Collins wrote to the appropriate office in Whitehall in 1880:

> I write with reference to the churchyard of this parish and request that you come and inspect it ... I may add that the churchyard has for some time past been quite full, and we have lately endeavoured to secure more room by pulling down part of the church. This however was only a temporary provision and quite insufficient to meet the requirements of the parish. The churchyard should be closed and a new burial ground provided forthwith.[18]

Similarly, again in 1880, the churchwardens at Helmsley – clearly writing on the instruction of the vicar, the Reverend Charles Norris Gray – also wrote to the Home Office for an Order in Council to close the old churchyard which was deemed 'utterly unfit to be used any longer for burials of the dead'.[19]

The regulation required that the Burials Office was to give ten days' notice to the vicar and vestry clerk or churchwardens that an inspection was to take place. Local notice of the visit had to be posted prominently so that anyone could take the opportunity to present evidence or opinion to the inspector, who met with the vicar and churchwardens at the churchyard itself. After the visit, a recommendation could be made to effect closure. Once in operation, the regulation was subject to some criticism: in the House of Commons in 1854 the complaint was made that 'the peremptory and positive orders of the Home Secretary had often led to great inconvenience' in offering little time for communities to make alternative provision.[20] Furthermore, permission to use family vaults could be refused. However, it is probable that the earliest inspections by the Burials Office included the most egregious cases of insanitary overcrowding, of the type that Walker described in 1839 and that most certainly would not have improved since that time. In those cases, immediate and absolute cessation of interment would have been imperative. The Burial Act, 1855, relaxed the regulation, and permitted the Privy Council to order the postponement of any discontinuation or 'otherwise to vary any Order in Council'.[21] The experience in the Yorkshire area indicated the level of flexibility which then pertained. In Ripon, concern about the continued use of the Trinity churchyard had led to a further inspection in 1880. At that time, a notice was printed by the vicar of Trinity to inform parishioners about the outcome of the visit, which was undertaken by Dr Hoffman. It was clear that Dr Hoffman had discussed a number of possible options with the vicar, who then notified his parishioners that although immediate closure had not been recommended,

> Dr Hoffman was good enough to consult me as to the time when we are likely to be full, and upon my replying that (according to the average of the last three years) eighteen months or, at the most, two years would be the farthest date, he ruled that an order shall be issued to close the churchyard to all new applicants, whether full or no, in June 1883.[22]

No such order was issued for Trinity churchyard, incidentally. It is notable that closure did not always follow an inspection. Dr Holland visited Great Smeaton following a request by the incumbent in 1877, but concluded that, although parts of the ground were indeed full, there was unused ground and so he reported: 'I do not think any interference be recommended, at least at present.'[23]

Postponements and amendments

Even where orders had been issued, alteration could take place. At Gate Helmsley, an order issued in October 1879 was later amended to allow continued burials in vaults and walled graves.[24] Requests for revision could be even more specific. In Middlesmoor, an 1877 order was altered in 1899 to allow for the interment of the Baynes family in their existing walled grave.[25] It was also the case that discontinuance was often delayed. In Kirby Misperton, the initial closure order of 1859 was postponed to later in the same year, to allow the village time to settle the method by which they would pay for and secure new land.[26] Controversy and disagreement about the possible extension of the churchyard delayed the closure of St Mary's at Wath.[27] More time was also needed at Pateley Bridge, which ran into substantial difficulty in its measures to set up a burial board. Here, the initial order required closure – with exceptions – from 31 December 1871, but the Pateley Bridge Burial Board successfully secured postponements every year until 1874.[28] Perhaps the longest postponement related to the closure of St Peter's churchyard at Osmotherley where an Order in Council was issued in 1877 but closure was not effected until 1905. The reasons for this substantial delay are uncertain, but perhaps reflect the complexity of funding arrangements, which were shared between three townships. Thus, although churchyard closures took place within the wider public health framework, their operation sat to one side of more 'mainstream' local sanitary initiatives. Closures were the consequence of local proactivity and, overall, the process can be more readily characterised in terms of local negotiation than by inflexible central imposition.

Reasons for closure

Scale of operation

Change in burial practice often reflects trends in mortality. Crisis can be a spur to the creation of additional burial grounds: for example, in the seventeenth century, plague pits were opened around London, and cholera burial grounds were established in places such as York and Nottingham during the 1832 epidemic.[29] Throughout nineteenth-century Europe, investment in new cemeteries often followed massive expansion of the urban population coupled with heightened concerns brought by recurrent cholera outbreaks. The first half of the nineteenth century saw growth in almost all the market towns in the North Riding. Even though Knaresborough's population had begun to decline from the 1830s, its population in 1851 was still 43 per cent higher than it had been in 1801.[30] Other dramatic increases included Easingwold which grew by 53 per cent between 1801 and 1851, and Pickering which increased by 56 per cent over the same period (see Table 3.1).

Table 3.1 Population change in selected market towns

Town	*1801*	*1851*	*Percentage increase*
New Malton	3047	3841	26
Northallerton	2138	3086	44
Thirsk	2092	3001	43
Pickering	1994	3112	56
Easingwold	1467	2240	53
Helmsley	1449	1481	2
Stokesley	1369	2040	49
Bedale	1005	1200	19

Source: N. Raven, 'De-industrialisation and the urban response: the small towns of the North Riding of Yorkshire c1790–1850' in Weedon, R. and Milne, A. (eds), *Aspects of English Small Towns in the Eighteenth and Nineteenth centuries* (Leicester: Centre for Urban History, 1993).

It is possible therefore that increased mortality overwhelmed the space available in the local churchyards. Of the fourteen largest market towns and villages in the study in 1850 – Ripon, Northallerton, Knaresborough, New Malton,

Pickering, Norton, Bedale, Thirsk, Great Ayton, Easingwold, Boroughbridge, Aldborough, Kirkbymoorside and Pateley Bridge – ten had Orders in Council closing their principal churchyard. New Malton, as has been seen, had closures by consent. In two cases, orders were issued twice for the same town: Knaresborough had its old churchyard and the churchyard extension closed using two separate orders, in 1855 and 1878; and Norton had both the 'church cemetery' and the churchyard of St Nicholas closed in 1885 and 1893 respectively.

Data on the scale of interments prior to closure are readily available in parish burial registers. Table 3.2 summarises the number of interments in each named churchyard in the twenty years before the Order in Council. The churchyard of St John the Baptist at Knaresborough was remarkable, in accommodating 3,472 interments in the twenty years before the first closure order in 1855, and a further 3,172 in the twenty years prior to the second closure order, which applied to the extension laid out in the late 1850s.

In Ripon, pressure on the Cathedral's 1.5-acre burial space was also heavy: the site had been extended in 1829 and interments continued in the Cathedral itself, although space was limited. Indeed, notes in the burial register indicated to the sexton where further interments could be squeezed in, for example: 'small space remains on each side of this vault for two other vaults.'[31] Trinity Church – opened in 1827 – created another churchyard in the west of the city but nevertheless the average annual burial rate at the Cathedral increased.[32] In 1855, an Order in Council restricted interments at both sites.[33]

As shown in Table 3.2, the scale could be startling, as the total numbers of interments prior to a closure order indicate. However, it is very difficult to anticipate how these numbers would be interpreted locally: a 'snapshot' does not reflect ongoing trends, and increasing demand is difficult to identify. Figure 3.1 indicates the total number of burials in the churchyards at Northallerton, Knaresborough and

Table 3.2 Town and large village closures

Settlement	*Churchyard*	*Churchyard size (acres)*	*Order in Council [postponement year]*	*Total interments in 20 years prior to closure*
Northallerton	All Saints	1.310	1852	1472
Knaresborough	St John the Baptist	na	1855	3472
Ripon	Cathedral	1.500	1855	2642
Ripon	Trinity	na	1855	572
Stokesley	St Peter and St Paul	0.856	1869	1012
Pateley Bridge	St Mary the Virgin	0.754	1871 [1874]	1398
Pateley Bridge	St Cuthbert	0.884	1871 [1874]	
Knaresborough	St John the Baptist	na	1878	3174
Helmsley	All Saints	na	1880	1030
Thirsk	St Mary	1.644	1880	1345
Great Ayton	All Saints	0.801	1880 [1882]	679
Aldborough	St Andrew	na	1881	na
Old Malton	St Mary	1.397	1882	c. 777
Norton	St Nicholas detached extension	0.706	1885	na

Sources: churchyard sizes generally taken from OS maps, and relate to the churchyard size at the time of the closure order; dates in brackets indicate that an official postponement was secured; interment numbers taken from parish burial registers.

Ripon Cathedral, from 1813 to 1854 when the first closure order was issued at Northallerton. There is no clear evidence of accelerating pressure on burial space: indeed, use is remarkably 'lumpy'. Ripon Cathedral had 188 interments in 1840, but only 99 in 1845; St John the Baptist at Knaresborough had 140 interments in 1821, 225 in 1848 and 158 in 1851; and All Saints at Northallerton had 54 interments in 1845, 106 in 1847 and 53 in 1850. These figures indicate that it must have been extremely difficult to predict burial numbers year-on-year, and that – on the basis of numbers alone – a closure order was necessary.

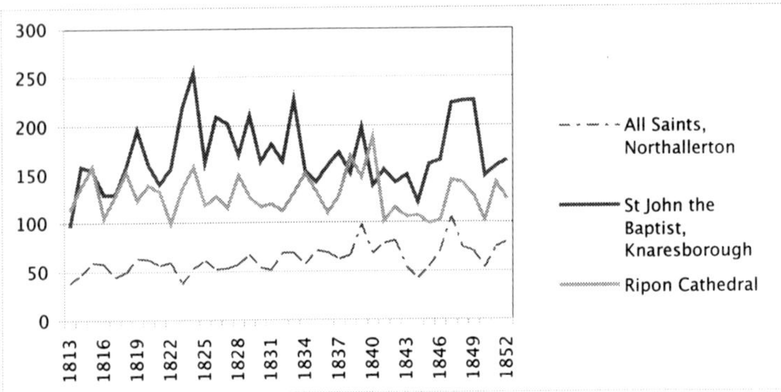

Figure 3.1 Burials in selected churchyards, 1813–1852

However, population change does not appear to be a convincing explanation for settlements in which Orders in Council were issued but where demand for burial space was – at best – limited. For example, St Lawrence's churchyard in Kirby Misperton was closed in 1858. The churchyard was small, being less than half an acre in size, but the village was not a large one and had a population of 270 in 1881.[34] The churchyard was the principal burial location of a larger parish including the townships of Barughs Ambo, Great and Little Habton, and Ryton. Nevertheless, the number of interments at St Lawrence's was low, and averaged at little over one a month. Kirby Misperton was not atypical. In none of these cases in Table 3.3 did interments reach above an average of two a month in the twenty years before closure. The churchyards in the 'village' group were, on average, just under half an acre in size – compared with just over an acre amongst the larger village and town group – but, even so, proportionally the use still remained far below that of the larger settlements.

Table 3.3 Village closures

Settlement	*Churchyard*	*Churchyard size (acres)*	*Closure order [postponement date]*	*Total interments 20 years prior to closure*
Kirby Misperton	St Lawrence	0.443	1858 [1860]	329
Sutton-on-the-Forest	All Hallows	0.798	1866	382
Osmotherley	St Peter	0.512	1877 [1905]	500
Middlesmoor	St Chad	0.653	1877	310
Kirkby Fleetham	St Mary	0.561	1878	234
Gate Helmsley	St Mary	'less than half an acre'	1879	93
Warthill	St Mary	0.286	1879	59
Kirkby Overblow	All Saints	na	1884	na
Wath	St Mary	c. 0.656	1886 [1887]	279
Boroughbridge	St James	0.601	1890	411
Crakehall	St Gregory	0.504	1891 [1892]	245
Appleton Wiske	St Mary	na	1892	132
Nidd	St Paul and St Margaret	0.313	1893	42

Sources: see Table 3.2.

Disturbance of the dead

It remains the case that, even where there was limited demand for burial space, conditions could still develop that were considered to be unacceptable. It is possible to argue that the number of interments was a less salient factor in churchyard closures than alteration in perceptions relating to churchyard conditions. Tarlow posits that, during the nineteenth century, an increased identification of self with body modified attitudes towards corpses.[35] Research on cemetery companies concluded that changing sensibilities around the treatment of the corpse had as much impact as sanitary concerns on the desire to improve burial provision. In urban areas, pressure on burial space was such that previous interments were routinely disturbed by new burials.

The descriptions by George Alfred Walker of London churchyards and burial grounds employed deeply gothic prose, reflecting and directing a shift in the rhetoric used to describe intramural interment. *Gatherings from Graveyards*, published in 1839, took the reader on a protracted tour of metropolitan burial sites, where 'the soil was saturated, absolutely saturated, with human putrescence'.[36] Private chapels, set up as small-scale speculations, also effected burial in their underground 'vaults'. Enon Chapel was perhaps the worst of this type of site, and consequently attracted considerably notoriety. Walker wrote:

> I have several times visited this Golgotha. I was struck with the total disregard of decency exhibited, – numbers of coffins were piled high in confusion – large quantities of bones were mixed with the earth, and lying upon the floor of this cellar (for vault it ought not to be called), lids of *coffins* might be trodden upon almost at every step. My reflections upon leaving the masses of corruption here exposed, were painful in the extreme; I want language to express the intense feelings of pity, contempt and abhorrence I experienced. Can it be, thought I, that in the nineteenth century, in the very centre of the most magnificent city of the universe, such sad, very sad mementos of ignorance, cupidity, and degraded morality still exist? Possibly I am now treading over the mouldering remains of many, once the cherished idols of the heart's best and purest affections, – here, thought I, may repose one who had his cares, his anxieties who, perchance, may have well fulfilled life's duties, and who has tasted its pleasures and its sorrows, – here he sleeps as I must sleep; yet I could not but desire that I might have a better resting place – a *Christian* burial.[37]

The quotation bears lengthy reproduction, since Walker amalgamates a number of rhetorical devices and concerns. The alluring relish with which the confusion of corpses is described gives way to indignation and then a species of melancholic reverie. Walker reflects on the personalities of the people whose bodies were deposited in the vault – 'cherished idols' –

and the loving relationships they enjoyed. Walker's descriptions often included extracts from epitaphs on churchyard monuments, again giving identities to the 'anonymous' corpses. It is perhaps in this text that the Victorian ambiguity with regard to fear of the 'massed' dead and solicitude for the single corpse is most evident. Walker-style rhetoric was commonplace in discussion about the nature of burial conditions outside the capital. For example, George Milner, writing in Hull, reflected at length on the issue in the 1846 publication *On Cemetery Burial; or, Sepulture Ancient and Modern*, stressing that in the overcrowded burial grounds of the city 'scarcely another interment could take place without the grave being desecrated; – the bones of the older tenant are disturbed to make way for the mortal remains of another, which, it is lamentable to state, in the majority of cases, are again dug up by the sexton ... The most shocking mutilations and displacements have been commonly practised'.[38]

The fact that new burials routinely disturbed previous interments was not restricted to urban churchyards. In North Yorkshire, given the ancient nature of many of the sites in question, it would have been unusual indeed for any new interment not to have brought older bones to the surface. For example, in Northallerton, the sexton reported to William Ranger that there was 'no means of ascertaining if there is room for a grave, except by digging down' and that the sexton had at 'no instance lately made a grave without disturbing the remains of previous burials, and removed as many as five skulls in getting down to a single grave. Having once commenced a grave he digs through everything he meets with.'[39] However, there is evidence of a growing unwillingness to countenance this disturbance. For example, the Reverend S. T. Mosse, vicar of Great Smeaton, wrote to the Burials Office in 1877 with details of conditions in St Eloy's churchyard. The site was 'overcrowded 3 skulls and other bones were exhumed in digging a grave last week, and I am well advised it is not possible to find space for another corpse without similar desecration and disturbance of the dead'.[40]

Similarly, in St Andrew's at Aldborough, a parish notebook recorded suggested improvements for the churchyard in 1866, with the terse comment '9 skulls were dug up – 5 another time in making a grave'.[41] Five years later, a circular to local landowners seeking funds to extend the churchyard stated that 'Aldborough churchyard is the only legal burial place; and this churchyard is so crowded that not a single grave can be made in it without disturbing human remains to such an extent as to be neither decent towards the dead, nor healthy for the living'.[42] Burials continued to take place at St Mary the Virgin churchyard in Pateley Bridge, since the Order in Council issued in 1874 had permitted continued interment in walled graves. However, this practice was objected to on the grounds that remains were being disturbed. In 1877, Bentley, the sexton, was questioned on his practices by Mr Metcalfe who was a member of the Pateley Bridge Burial Board. Bentley had been asked about an open grave, and admitted that it had contained the remains of a Mrs Groves who had been buried there 43 years previously. Her remains were being moved in order for her daughter to be buried in the same grave. Metcalfe commented that 'these instances showed that in recent interments the fore elders had literally to give way for their children', and in his view the 'bodies of remains of those buried even 30 or 40 years ago should be allowed to rest peacefully for all time'.[43] Similar concern about the disturbance of the dead was expressed at Helmsley. In their request for an inspection visit, the churchwardens wrote that:

> The last burial that took place caused a great disturbance, as another corpse was cut through – that of a woman whose daughter is still alive – in order to make the grave. Moreover, *not a spadeful of the ground can be turned over in any part* without human bones being exposed: it has constantly been the case that the officiating minister has to take the funeral with bones lying bare on all sides of him, and on one occasion with three skulls lying at his feet, one of them with a quantity of hair upon it. He was hardly able to get through the service.[44]

The example of closures in the smaller churchyards indicates that there were concerns even where the rate of use was extremely limited and there was little probability of disturbing a recent interment or the body of a 'named' individual. For example, interments at West Rounton churchyard averaged at about four burials a year, but in 1891 a report to the Northallerton Rural Sanitary Authority indicated that 'It is too small for the requirements of the parish and also that it is overcrowded in every portion of it, so much so that a grave cannot be dug without exposing often more than one coffin'.[45] Thus it appears that disturbance of even the very 'distant' dead – a practice which had permitted the reuse of churchyards over a period of centuries – was beginning to be regarded with some distaste.

Orders in Council in operation

Notwithstanding the strong presumption in some instances that previous interments in the churchyard should remain undisturbed, the way in which Orders in Council were implemented indicates a degree of 'duality' in attitudes towards the dead body. Although it is clear that interference with earlier burials was regarded with distaste, absolute cessation of continued interment in a churchyard was rarely ordered and indeed was often resisted. The majority of closure orders were partial and applied to churchyards that had further space in an extension, or closure allowed certain types of interment to continue. There were also instances in which communities simply did not comply with an Order in Council, either because of confusion about its exact meaning or because an alternative was not yet available. In addition, there were examples of blatant disregard. As will be seen, there is ample evidence of communities continuing to use churchyards closed by Order in Council but where it is clear that there had been no extension.

Conditional use following closure

Almost all the Orders in Council issued for the case study area in the second half of the nineteenth century specified circumstances in which interments could continue. In some instances, the order applied only to the 'old' section of the churchyard, for example, as at Gate Helmsley, Warthill, Aldborough, Boroughbridge and Ripon. In each of these places, the churchyard in question had had a recent extension: for example, Gate Helmsley had been extended by just 14 perches in 1868,[46] and Warthill had had a small addition three years prior to the order.[47] In Ripon, the closure order exempted interments in the 1829 extension lying 'eastward of the cathedral'. The majority of Orders in Council at this period also ordered the cessation of interments with the exception of burials that were deemed to comply with certain sanitary requirements. The wording of these exemptions differed from place to place, but generally incorporated one or more of the following provisions: burials in existing vaults or walled graves; burials in partly walled graves where there would be no disturbance of remains; and burial in earth graves that could be opened to a depth of 5 feet without disturbing remains. Furthermore, in each case it was specified that, within each of these types of grave, further interments were to be entirely separated from previous burials, and segregated by appropriate stonework or embedded in charcoal. For example, burials in the churchyard of St Gregory's, Crakehall, were to be ended on a specified date, but 'In such walled graves as are now existing in the churchyard burials may be allowed on condition that every coffin therein buried be separately enclosed by stonework or brickwork properly cemented'.[48] However, provisions could be more detailed, such as the Order for St Mary's, Wath, which – in summary – excluded burials in vaults and walled graves where each coffin was to be separated by stonework; in existing partly walled graves that could be opened to a depth of 5 feet and where there would be no disturbance of remains; in existing earth graves that could be opened to 5 feet; and in reserved spaces as yet unused and that when opened were free from water.[49] Thus, it appears, the 'suite' of exceptions was generally amended according to local circumstances. Another type of 'local circumstance' was sensitivity to the desire of particular family members to seek burial close to each other.[50] In some orders, families were named. It was perhaps unsurprising that the vault of the Earl of Feversham would be excluded from the order relating to the closure of All Saints at Helmsley, but a Miss Jane Elizabeth Clarke was excluded from the provision of the Aldborough order.[51] It is possible to argue that 'sensitivity' was more often extended to wealthier members of the community who had invested in the creation of vaults and brick graves in the churchyard. However, some orders were rather more general. For example, at Knaresborough the 1855 order allowed for continued burial in family graves, and the 1878 order allowed for interment in 'earthen graves for the burial of the widowers or widows of those already buried there'.[52] The operation of exceptions is often clearly indicated in the burial registers. Following a closure order issued for St Mary's in Thirsk, interments were allowed only of widows or widowers with their predeceased spouses, and in existing vaults and walled graves. The rate of interments dropped substantially and in the following ten years comprised just 26 in total.[53] At St Gregory's, Crakehall, a closure order was issued in 1892 and after that date there were just seven further burials in the churchyard, and noted in the margin was the comment that these interments had been 'in walled graves', as permitted by the order.[54] However, the scale of burials did not always fall. A closure order issued in 1858 indicated that further burials were permitted in vaults and walled graves at St Lawrence's in Kirby Misperton, but interments had continued to the extent that in 1913 a second closure order was issued, directing that burials be 'discontinued entirely and forthwith'.[55]

Confusion over requirements

A second reason why burials could continue after the issuing of a closure order was, perhaps unsurprisingly, confusion locally as to what an order actually required. In Osmotherley, an exchange of letters between the vicar and the Burials Office attempted to clarify definitions after St Peter's churchyard was closed 'except in graves not less than five feet deep which can be opened without the exposure of coffins, or disturbance of bones'.[56] Amongst extant documentation relating to the closure is a copy of the order itself, on which the Reverend Henry Jones wrote: 'I asked for a clear definition of "entire bones" and remarked that a grave might be opened when no burial has taken place for 20 or more years, and yet one entire bone might be found and the rule in this case be disobeyed.'[57] The response from Whitehall was terse, acknowledging receipt of the letter and commenting obliquely that 'if the bones are at all decayed they cannot be considered entire'.[58] At Pateley Bridge, interments at the churchyard at St Mary the Virgin and in the Independent burial ground had continued after the closure order of 1874. In 1876, the Board had a 'long discussion' on the subject: they had been told by the vicar that 'unoccupied ground was being used, under the plea that the Order in Council did not prohibit the use of such ground'.[59] The Reverend Samuel Gray sent a letter to the Bishop of Ripon seeking clarification, but the Bishop – wisely – simply repeated the relevant clauses in the order without offering any comment.[60] However, burials continued nonetheless, and, at another evidently heated meeting, the Reverend Gray defended his position: 'For what purpose had burials been continued in the Old Churchyards? To get fees? He was not so mercenary. He would be thankful if a hard and fast line could be drawn as to when burials in the churchyards were legal and when not so.'[61] Furthermore, it was argued, the definition of 'human remains' was moot, and without any legal definition the Reverend Gray felt justified in putting 'his own construction on the Order in Council'.[62] A response to the letter sent to the 'Burial Acts department' offered no further enlightenment, and simply noted that it had no authority to interpret the regulation.[63]

Alternative provision not yet available

The continuation of interments also took place in settlements where replacement burial provision was not yet available. As has been seen, some parishes applied for postponements but this was not always the case. At Northallerton, the closure order was issued before the cemetery was available for interment. As a consequence, burials in the churchyard evidently continued, and on the same scale as previously. Following its 'closure' in 1854, there were 82 interments in that year, and 79 in the following year; the first interment in the cemetery did not take place until September 1856.[64] Similarly, in Sutton-on-the-Forest, the Order in Council allowed continued interment in bricked family graves, and officially took effect in 1864 but the first interment in the newly established detached churchyard extension did not take place until December 1867. In the intervening period interments continued in the old churchyard at the same scale.

Non-compliance

Finally, there is some evidence that communities chose not to act in accordance with the spirit of the order regulations, even where some flexibility had been allowed with the exemption of vaults and walled graves. In 1880, the Reverend George Alexander England of Gate Helmsley found himself under investigation by the Burials Office for allowing the interment of Ann Patrick in the part of the churchyard that had been closed. England was informed that he rendered himself 'liable to a penalty under Section 2 of the act 18&19 Vict. Cap 128'. The penalty was a sum 'not exceeding ten pounds', if the perpetrator was convicted before two Justices of the Peace.[65] The case against England was dropped on his explaining the circumstances of the case which were not, unfortunately, represented in the documentation. However, it was clear that England had interred Ann Patrick, aged 84, in the grave next to that of her husband, who had died thirteen years earlier. The desire of families to evade the regulations and secure continued burial in proximity to each other is evident in other documentation. In 1881, J. Hulme Goodier, vicar of Trinity, Ripon, sent a printed leaflet to his parishioners, following Dr Hoffman's visit to the Trinity churchyard. Dr Hoffman had indicated that although closure did not need to be imminent, it would allow for continued interment in existing vaults and family graves. Goodier published a note of clarification, the intent of which was barely hidden:

> I beg my readers to understand (for their comfort) that this order will require that the *rights of all owners of vaults and family graves, which shall exist in June, 1883, shall be carefully and scrupulously allowed.* I have also permission to state that, in view of this Government order, our rule for forbidding any one to secure (before it is wanted) a portion of land for vault or family grave, will be relaxed; and that *(within the next two years,) any parishioner or person interested in Trinity churchyard may obtain a new vault or family grave,* provided only, *that such transaction be completed before the month of June, 1883.*[66]

Non-compliance could also result from the fact that there was not always widespread consensus that a closure had been needed. At Helmsley, the Reverend Charles Norris Gray sought an end to further burials in the old churchyard because, although '99 per cent' of parishioners were using the new extension, 'some few persons ... insist on being buried in the old yard to the great annoyance of the friends of those who are buried there, to the disgust of bystanders and to the serious inconvenience and distress of the officiating minister'.[67] Dr Hoffman's inspection at Ripon was said to be 'owing to certain unnecessary complaints from some anonymous quarter'.[68] At Great Ayton, the vestry records included the following resolution:

> this meeting wishes to record its deep sense of regret that any memorial should have been forwarded to the Home Secretary requiring the closing of its ancient burial ground without first calling a meeting of the parishioners to consider whether some plan could not have been adopted whereby it might have been maintained in such efficient sanitary condition as would have allowed of its continued use.[69]

Thus, the community could be divided on the need to close the churchyard, and it is probably this division that explains continued use of the site long after a closure order had been passed. This is perhaps why, at Kirkby Fleetham and despite the issuing of an order in 1878 prohibiting interments in all but existing vaults, interments continued at the same rate.[70] There was no evident extension to the churchyard and no clarifying note in the burial register. Indeed, there appears to be no reason at all why the initial order was pursued.

Conclusion

The closure of parish churchyards by Order in Council constituted a rather different process in operation than might be first supposed. First, it has to be stressed that the regulations were permissive rather than obligatory. Local communities themselves invited inspectors to visit their churchyards, and there was discussion and negotiation around the timetable for closure and allowed exceptions. The churchyards of the market towns and large villages were more likely to be subject to closure orders, but there was not an exclusive association between scale of use with application for closure. Inspections were also invited for small churchyards that had only limited numbers of burials a year, and where it might be presumed that overcrowding was not immediately evident in the manner so vividly described by Dr Walker. It is possible that the rationale for closure did not necessarily reflect intensive use per se, but changing attitudes towards the disturbance of even long-buried remains. Such disturbance was increasingly deemed to be inappropriate as Victorian society embraced the notion of 'perpetuity' burial. However, there is a duality evident in attitudes towards disturbance of the dead. The closure orders reflected a principled objection to disturbance but, in practice, burials often continued. Most importantly, conditions attached to closure orders generally allowed continued burial within existing family graves. For many families, the desire to secure interment close to a previous family burial could still excuse disturbance of existing remains.

For the most part, closures meant that new interments were relocated to an extension that had been added to the old part of the churchyard. In central North Riding, it was very rare for a churchyard to be closed absolutely by Order in Council, with the community then required to use a newly established cemetery. Indeed, closure orders have to be understood in the broader context of churchyard extension: in this period, a closure order was a strong indicator that a churchyard extension had recently taken place, or was about to happen.

Notes

1 NYRO, PR/RI (HT) 12/2, Terrier and inventory, 20 Jun 1905, Appended printed leaflet, 'To the congregation and parishioners of Trinity Church, Ripon' (nd).

2 The 25 Orders in Council issued between 1853 and 1894 were printed in the *London Gazette*, but copies of these Orders are also held at various record offices.

3 BI, N/MAL/M 10, St Michael's Burials, 1813–1850; BI, N/MAL/L 18 & 19, St Leonard's Burials, 1813–1907; R. Rawlinson, *Report to the General Board of Health on a Preliminary Inquiry into the Sewerage, Drainage and Supply of Water, and the Sanitary Condition of the Inhabitants of the Parliamentary Borough of Malton* (London: HMSO, 1854).

4 G. Milner, *On Cemetery Burial: Or Sepulture Ancient and Modern* (London, Joseph Masters, 1846), p. 39; *York Herald*, 28 Aug 1836.

5 C. Hamlin, *Public Health and Social Justice in the Age of Chadwick, Britain 1800–1854* (Cambridge: Cambridge University Press, 1998), pp. 275ff.

6 Hamlin, *Public Health*, p. 278.
7 W. Ranger, *Report to the General Board of Health on a Preliminary Inquiry into the Sewerage, Drainage, and Supply of Water, and the Sanitary Condition of the Inhabitants of the Township of Ripon* (London: HMSO, 1854).
8 W. Ranger, *Report to the General Board of Health, on a Preliminary Inquiry into the Sewerage, Drainage, and Supply of Water, and the Sanitary Condition of the Inhabitants of the Town of Northallerton, in the County of York* (London: HMSO, 1850).
9 *Ibid*, p. 16.
10 *Ibid.*, p. 17.
11 NYRO, PR/NO 1/16–17, Burials, 1813–1865.
12 *London Gazette*, 21 Feb 1854.
13 Mirroring the provisions for London included in the Burial Act (1852), s. 2.
14 Mr T. Duncombe, *Hansard* HC Debates vol. 122 col. 879, 17 Jun 1852.
15 See, for example, NA, HO 45/9814/B7338, Burials in populous centres, including a report by Dr Hoffman dated 1888.
16 J. Pellew, *The Home Office 1848–1914. From Clerks to Bureaucrats* (London: Heinemann Educational Books, 1982); NA, HO 45/4460, Letter of appointment of Dr Sutherland.
17 NA, HO 45/9814/B7338, Burials: Burials Bill. Reports of deputations, correspondence etc. aiming at promotion of Bill for amendment and consolidation of burial law. Contains a report by Dr Hoffman.
18 NYRO, PC/AYG 2/1, Great Ayton Sanitary Committee, 1876–1898, Minute book with appended copy of letter from the Reverend John Collins, 28 May 1880.
19 NYRO, PC/HEL 7/1, Correspondence and papers relating to the old churchyard and its extensions, 1880–1989, Letter from churchwardens to Home Department, 11 May 1880.
20 Mr Apsley Pellatt, *Hansard* HC Debates, vol. 131 col. 453, 7 Mar 1854.
21 Burial Act (1855), s. 1.
22 NYRO, PR/RI (HT) 12/2, Terrier and inventory, 20 Jun 1905, Appended printed leaflet, 'To the congregation and parishioners of Trinity Church, Ripon' (nd).
23 NA: HO 45/9949/B31354, Burials – Great Smeaton.
24 BI: PR G/HEL 22, Records relating to the closure of the old churchyard.
25 *London Gazette*, 26 Oct 1877.

26 *London Gazette*, 2 Dec 1859.
27 NYRO: PR/WAT 7/5, Correspondence relating to the extension of the churchyard, 1886–90.
28 *London Gazette*, 19 May 1871; 6 Feb 1872; 1 Jul 1873; 10 Jul 1874.
29 V. Harding, *The Dead and the Living in Paris and London, 1500–1670* (Cambridge: Cambridge University Press, 2002), p. 65; R. J. Morris, *Cholera 1832: The Social Response to an Epidemic* (London: Croom Helm, 1976).
30 NYRO, PK/KN 3/1/2, Vestry minutes, 1849–62, 23 Jan 1852.
31 NYRO, PR/RI 1/39–41, Ripon Parish Register burials, 1813–1881.
32 *Ibid.*
33 *London Gazette*, 17 Aug 1855.
34 T. Bulmer, *History, Topography and Directory of North Yorkshire* (Preston: T. Bulmer & Sons, 1890), p. 967.
35 S. Tarlow, 'Wormie clay and blessed sleep: death and disgust in later historic Britain,' in Tarlow, S. and West, S. (eds), *The Familiar Past? Archaeologies of Later Historical Britain* (London: Routledge, 1999) p. 193.
36 G. Walker, *Gatherings from Graveyards* (London: Longman's and Co., 1839), p. 150.
37 *Ibid.*, p. 157.
38 G. Milner, *On Cemetery Burial; or, Sepulture Ancient and Modern* (Hull, 1846), p. 40.
39 Ranger, *Northallerton*, p. 17.
40 NA, HO 45/9949/B31354, Burials – Great Smeaton, letter from the Reverend S. T. Mosse, dated 2 Jul 1877.
41 NYRO, PR/ALB 2/2, Parish Book, note dated 1866.
42 Boroughbridge Town Council, Aldborough Vestry Minute Book, 1849–1957, circular reproduced at 11 Dec 1871.
43 NYRO, BB/PAT, Minute Books, 1871–1963, 5 May 1877.
44 NYRO, PC/HEL 7/1, Correspondence and papers relating to the old churchyard and its extensions, 1880–1989. Letter from churchwardens to 'Home Department' dated 11 May 1880.
45 NA, HO 45/9949 B31354, Appleton Wiske.
46 BI, CD/Add. 1868/4, Gate Helmsley, addition to churchyard, 1868.
47 1877 (438) *Churchyards. Return of all parishes in England and Wales in which any new portion of ground has been consecrated to serve as a churchyard since the last return made to Parliament in 1863; distinguishing those which have been purchased by the parish and those which have been purchased by voluntary subscription, or presented as a free gift.*
48 *London Gazette*, 20 Jan 1891.
49 *London Gazette*, 11 May 1886.

50 NYRO, PR/KN 9/2/8, Correspondence relating to the acquisition of land for a new burial ground, Order in Council, 14 August 1855; *London Gazette*, 2 April 1878.
51 NYRO, PR/ALB 7/2, Closure of churchyard: notice of intention to close by Order in Council, 1880.
52 NYRO, PR/KN 9/2/8, Correspondence relating to the acquisition of land for a new burial ground, Order in Council, 14 Aug 1855.
53 NYRO, PR/TH 1/22, Burials, 1869–1948.
54 NYRO, PR/CRA1/2, Burials, 1840–1918.
55 *London Gazette*, 16 Nov 1858; 15 Aug 1913.
56 NYRO, PR/OSM 6, Papers relating to the discontinuance of burials in the churchyard, 1877–1904.
57 *Ibid.*
58 *Ibid.*
59 NYRO, BB/PAT, Minute Books, 1871–1963, 1 Jan 1876.
60 NYRO: BB/PAT, Minute Books, 1871–1963, 6 Feb 1876.
61 NYRO, BB/PAT, Minute Books, 1871–1963, 5 May 1877.
62 *Ibid.*
63 NYRO, BB/PAT, Minute Books, 1871–1963, 13 Jun 1877.
64 NYRO, PR/NO 1/17, Burials, 1840–1865.
65 BI, PR G/HEL 22, Records relating to the closure of the old churchyard), letter dated 23 Feb 1880 from Mr Liddell to the Reverend G. A. England; Burial Act (1855), s. 1.
66 NYRO, PR/RI (HT) 12/2, Terrier and inventory, 20 June 1905, leaflet appended to terrier. Underlining and italics original.
67 NYRO, PR/HEL, Correspondence and papers relating to the old churchyard and its extensions, 1880–1989.
68 NYRO, PR/RI (HT) 12/2, Terrier and inventory, 20 Jun 1905.
69 NYRO, PC/AYG 5/1 (Parish Meeting Minutes, 1852–1964), 29 Nov 1881.
70 NYRO, PR/KRF 1/9 (Burials 1813–1889).

4

'A very modern act':[1] the Churchyard Consecration Act and churchyard extensions

Chapter 3 indicated that formal closure of the churchyard was a common response to its 'insufficiency' but, in almost all these cases, new land for interment was made available elsewhere. In central North Riding, this space was generally provided through the addition of land to the existing churchyard. Indeed, in most of the settlements in the study, the commonest response to lack of space in the churchyard was not to seek a closure order at all, but simply to extend the churchyard. The history of burial has generally overlooked the incidence and significance of this action, which occurred with frequency and – in the case study area – much more commonly than the opening of a cemetery. Of the 273 churchyards in the study, 154 were extended; indeed, some churchyards were extended two or three times, and in total some 256 individual extensions have been recorded for this area alone. It is probable that, in reality, there were more but evidence for some churchyards is scanty and inconclusive.[2] Wiggins considered that, aside from the frenzied debate relating to Nonconformist rights culminating in the Burial Laws Amendment Act, the churchyard could be characterised in terms of 'ancient calm, devoid of controversy and bereft of drama'.[3] This claim overlooks the financial, technical and legal difficulties that were often a consequence of adding land to the existing churchyard. Two detailed case studies – of extensions at Knaresborough and Bedale – indicate how fraught this course of action could become.

Change to this process came in the late 1860s. Until 1867, addition to the churchyard took place under the aegis of the numerous Church Building Acts which were used to transfer land to Church ownership. The Churchyard Consecration Act of 1867 aimed to simplify the process and reduce the consequent legal fees and, in the long term, succeeded in offering an incentive to landlowners to donate land, and in streamlining what had been a highly bureaucratic process. Nevertheless, it remained the case that extension could be costly to the community. On the larger estates, landowners could be more or less proactive about their tenants' need for burial space, and even cover attendant legal costs in addition to donating land. However, there was usually some cost to the vestry, which was often met with a mortgage raised against the church rate or the poor rate. In 1868, the abolition of the church rate removed one option for funding expansion of the churchyard, but that option had been a controversial one and the cause of tension and disagreement at the local level; after this date it was much more common for payments to be met through voluntary subscription. The amount required could be substantial. Even where land had been donated, raising the required funds to cover the costs of enclosure and drainage and the consecration fee could prove challenging. The vicar often made the majority contribution by donating land from the glebe or personally meeting the shortfall between the cost and the collected donations.

The previous chapter indicated that unwillingness to disturb previous burials led to the closure of churchyards in some cases, and there is evidence that churchyard extension had its basis in similar concerns. However, a much more substantial inducement rested in the increased complexity of the churchyard landscape through the accretion of more or less formal monumentation. From the first half of the nineteenth century, the desire to erect a stone memorial over the grave had expanded considerably and the needs of a growing middle class were met through the increased commercial sophistication of the trade in monumental masonry. Cemetery establishment had created a new type of burial landscape where each family was afforded an individual headstone and had the opportunity to erect more elaborate statuary. This trend began to be reflected in substantial change to the churchyard landscape. However, the erection of headstones, kerbsets and railings and the construction of brick vaults here all provided obstacles to the traditional reuse of graves as generations passed. The need for extension became almost inevitable, and the landscape of the new extension gradually became indistinguishable from an urban cemetery.

Furthermore, guidance that was issued by the government to accompany the Burial Acts created new management protocols, the application of which reached beyond the cemetery and into the churchyard. In the second half of the nineteenth century, adding an extension was in many places the context for the introduction of more consistent practices for managing churchyard space including the creation of grave registers and use of plot numbers. These practices produced a formally arranged landscape that was similar to that of the cemetery, and created expectations on issues such as the ability to reserve particular graves, and their permanency. These expectations, and the proliferation of grave 'furniture', created difficulties for vicars who considered themselves responsible for ensuring that churchyard burial space was available to all parishioners. The trend also introduced questions about what made the churchyard distinctive and sacred. Overall, therefore, local churches increased their provision of burial space in the second half of the nineteenth century, but the nature of that space was beginning to alter.

The incidence of churchyard extension

Churchyard extension was by no means a new development in the second half of the nineteenth century. There were instances of additions in the earlier part of the century, to churchyards in places such as Knaresborough (1828), Burneston (1840) Sutton-on-the-Forest (1841) and Kirkby Overblow (1849). However, the pace at which addition took place increased after 1850: there were at least 61 instances up to 1894. In a handful of cases, the churchyard was extended twice during this period. For example, at Thornton-le-Dale, All Saints' churchyard was extended in 1854 and again in 1890. Extension of the churchyard generally comprised the addition of land in a single block to the existing churchyard, sometimes as a square or rectangle of land simply attached to one side. This type of extension is readily recognisable on contemporary OS Maps. For example, the addition to St Hilda at Skelton-on-Ure in 1850 comprised 22 perches, which elongated the extended churchyard 'rectangle' eastwards.[4] On other occasions, the addition comprised a strip which edged the churchyard further out a few feet on one or more sides. The extension to St Helen's in Amotherby in 1873 included a portion 207 square yards to the east and a further 988 square yards to the north of the existing churchyard.[5] In some cases, it was not possible to extend the existing churchyard at all, and a 'detached' churchyard extension was created in another part of the settlement or out of the village entirely: at Sutton-on-the-Forest and Kirby Misperton the sites were situated away from the church and in more open countryside, in what was probably a better location for all the townships using the site. The amount of land given to extend the churchyard was rarely over an acre in size. Portions of donated land measuring a quarter or half an acre were common. However, additions could be very small indeed: at North Stainley, the churchyard was extended by just 129 square yards in 1893. Size was no doubt determined by the limited resources available to vestries where land had to be purchased, but was also restricted by the requirements of the

Churchyard Consecration Act, which was applicable only to sites not exceeding one acre. In the second half of the nineteenth century, only Stokesley was extended by more than this amount: in 1877, 1.272a was gifted by the vicar and added to a new detached churchyard which itself had only been created in 1850. As will be seen, the nature of the extension in terms of its shape, location and size could in themselves be an encouragement to more formal management.

Figure 4.1 indicates the chronology of churchyard extensions compared with closure by Order in Council. The period from 1850 to 1880 was the most active, and mirrors the growing number of cemeteries nationally at this time, although – as Chapter 10 will demonstrate – the interwar period was also notable in this regard. The task of donating land was made cheaper and easier by the Churchyard Consecration Act, but numbers in central North Riding do not indicate a substantial growth in the incidence of extensions as a consequence. Before 1867, there was an average of just over one extension a year; in 1868–94, the average had increased to just over 1.5.

In terms of location, the churchyards that were extended were spread right across the case study region, as indeed

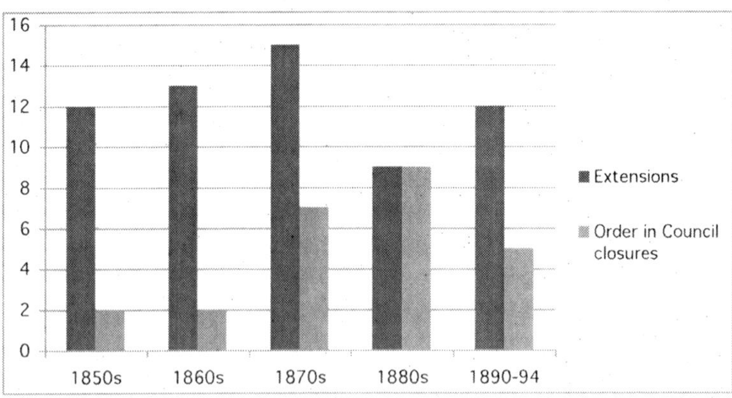

Figure 4.1 Churchyard closures and extensions, 1850–1894

churchyard closures had been. The previous chapter indicated that there was little evidence of a link between change in population and the incidence of churchyard closure. Similarly, the extension of the churchyard was not a consequence of changing use patterns judged purely in terms of number. Figure 4.2 takes a random selection of three churchyards, to demonstrate that – as in the case of closures – interments were remarkably variable year-on-year, and there was no clear linear progression of increased usage. Similarly, although there were places in which the number of interments was remarkably high – St John's, Knaresborough, and Ripon Cathedral being the obvious examples – extension also took place in locations where the number of interments over the previous twenty years was relatively small: for example, at St Hilda's, Skelton-on-Ure, which had 147 burials in that time, or St John the Baptist at Hunsingore which had 230. In a small handful of cases, the number of interments was tiny: North Stainley, Leathley and Arkendale all had fewer than a hundred interments in the twenty years prior to extension, and it was not unknown in those places for over a year to pass with no burial at all in the churchyard.

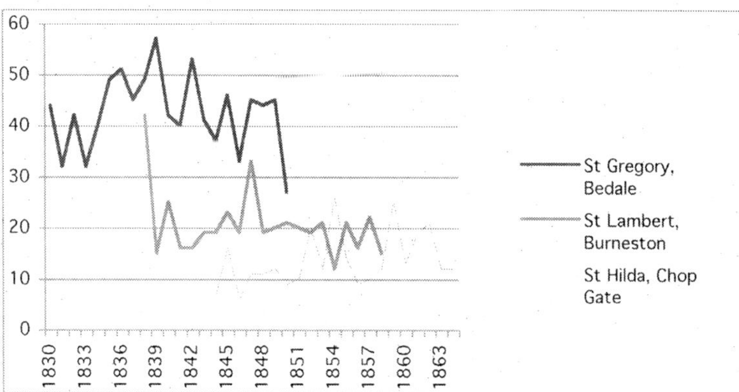

Figure 4.2 Burials in selected churchyards twenty years prior to their extension

Scale of use evidently did have an impact on the timing if not the incidence of extension. As the century progressed, extensions were taking place in churchyards where demand for space was lower: pressure on space was taking longer to accrue. Insufficient information is available on the size of churchyards prior to extension, so it is not possible to draw any conclusions on link between churchyard sizes per se and the likelihood of extension.

The rationale for extension

Vestry minutes tended not to dwell on the reasons why an extension to the churchyard was thought necessary. In very many parishes, only annual vestry minutes are available, and an addition to the churchyard might be afforded little more than an elliptical comment especially since – as will be seen – this task was often overseen by a sub-committee which took this business outside the central concern of the annual vestry, which was the appointment of parish officers.

Church rebuilding

One very obvious factor that might be considered pertinent to churchyard extension is the massive programme of church rebuilding which took place across England and Wales in the second half of the nineteenth century. There were very few churches in the central belt of North Riding that were not demolished and rebuilt or substantially altered in this period. It might be thought that church improvement would carry with it the desire to expand and re-order the churchyard. Certainly at Nunnington, John Rutson took the opportunity to extend the churchyard at the same time as rebuilding the church in 1884: the extension was consecrated by the Archbishop of York straight after the service to re-open the church.[6] The churchyard of St John the Baptist at Hunsingore was extended in 1859 and again in 1868, and this second expansion was entirely a consequence of the rebuilding of the church, financed by the local landowner

Joseph Dent of Ribston Hall. The new church was relocated – by a few feet – to the north of the existing one, and as a consequence a compensatory quarter-acre strip of land was added to the churchyard also to the north. Nevertheless, it was much more common to find no link between new church building and any change to the churchyard. For example, at Easingwold a substantial rebuilding took place of St John the Baptist church in 1858, just two years after the vestry decided on the need to purchase a section of land adjacent to the churchyard. None of the documentation relating to the two developments links them in any way: indeed, newspaper clippings relating to the church restoration make no mention of the churchyard at all.[7] Similarly, in Wath, a parish history – written by successive vicars in the baptism register – noted that a new churchyard extension was consecrated in 1861 by the Bishop of Ripon, and that in 1888 the churchyard was improved by the addition of yews. In the intervening period the church was rebuilt and re-opened: a long newspaper clipping on the ceremony again makes no mention of the churchyard. The parish history similarly makes no connection between churchyard and church improvement.[8] Perhaps the only link that appears to connect the two developments is the desire to minimise any expenditure on the churchyard extension where a vestry might have borne the cost of church rebuilding.

'Insufficiency'

Once church rebuilding is dismissed as a contributory factor, it is necessary to work with the hints and intimations offered in the vestry minutes. Where a vestry did give any kind of rationale for extension, it was for the most part simply stated that the existing churchyard was deemed 'insufficient'. At Thornton-le-Dale, the churchyard of All Saints comprised 0.375a in 1854. This was considered to be 'very small and circumscribed', a view compounded by the fact that it was bounded in part by a cottage and joiner's shop.[9] The last chapter indicated that, in many parishes, the churchyard was deemed to be full in terms of the inability to add further interments without disturbing prior burials. In Bedale, this was certainly a concern. Here, in a notebook relating to the new churchyard extension, it was written that that the existing ground had 'become overcrowded to an extent dangerous to public health, and painful to the feelings of everyone'.[10] In Hunsingore, a scrap book containing 'parochialia' written by the vicar indicated that in 1852 he took the step of increasing the burial fee for non-parishioners to £1 – the usual cost was 1s – 'in consequence of the burial ground being too full'.[11]

The belief that a churchyard was 'full' was not simply restricted to the capacity of the site to take further burials. Pressure on space could be evident both below and above the ground. Churchyard memorials have often been studied as in terms of archaeology and aesthetics, but rarely as a management problem for vestries. According to Houlbrooke, the erection of substantial stone churchyard memorials was not widespread until the seventeenth century: in Ralph Bigland's nineteenth-century survey of Gloucester churchyards, a minority had monuments before 1700.[12] From the mid-eighteenth century, more elaborate memorialisation was becoming commonplace. Industrialisation, not least in the creation of a canal and rail infrastructure, made dressed stone cheaper and more readily available as the nineteenth century progressed.[13] Concern relating to the public health consequences of burial in the church itself relocated interments, and expensive monuments, to the churchyard. The creation of major urban cemeteries encouraged the development of the monumental masonry industry, which was becoming increasingly sophisticated and attuned to a 'mass market.'[14] In her study of commemorative practice in the Orkney islands, Tarlow noted an exponential increase in gravestone erection from the beginning of the nineteenth century, which accelerated rapidly from 1841.[15] Cannon's study of 3,500 gravestones in rural Cambridgeshire also found a substantial increase in the number of monuments erected

Plate 4.1 All Saints, Thornton-le-Dale. The edges of the churchyard have not been subject to clearance, and the congestion of monumentation gives a rare indication of the chaos of the Victorian churchyard landscape.

annually, which climbed rapidly from 1850 to 1860 and continued growing until the 1880s.[16]

There is no similar study of monument erection in the Yorkshire parishes included here, but qualitative data indicates that commemorative practices were changing to the degree that problems were beginning to emerge. Difficulties related to both formal and informal monumentation. In terms of large, structural monuments, it was felt by 1860 that diocesan intervention was required. The Archdeaconry of Cleveland issued a directive as a consequence of the 'inconvenience' arising from the 'multiplying of vaults, walled or bricked graves, and inclosure of burial places with iron-rails in churchyards'. Clerics would 'do well to object to persons, who desire these private enclosures, making them to the injury of the common right'.[17] The directive pointedly included walled and bricked graves. In these cases, the grave was given 'walls' or lined with bricks to protect the coffin and define the grave more formally. This type of grave was often excluded from Order in Council closures, which then constituted an incentive to arrange for their construction. But this kind of grave created particular problems, and was singled out for censure in a pamphlet issued by the Church of England Burial, Funeral and Mourning Reform Association in 1888: 'the space required for a brick grave is more than double that required for an earthen grave, being 36ft instead of 16¼ft ... it is obvious that the use of brick graves tend to fill up a churchyard more rapidly than the use of earthen graves only would do'.[18]

Commemoration of grave space extended from formal built structures that included a large headstone and railings to the common practice of mounding the grave. In the nineteenth century, mounds were integral to the churchyard landscape, and comprised a raised and flattened platform perhaps a foot above the ground level. In 1843, Loudon commented that 'every grave, whether private or common, to which there is to be no monumental stone, should be finished with a green mound' since its absence 'destroys the distinctive feature of a graveyard'.[19] Guidance issued to burial boards mentions the raising of a 'high mound over the grave' as being 'generally practiced at present'.[20] At Helmsley, the Reverend Charles Norris Gray noted that the old churchyard had been full of 'mounds, or hollows, [which] were still means of recognising the spot where some friend or relative was buried in years gone by, we say advisedly mounds or hollows; for hollows caused by fallen in graves were as much marks as the mounds'.[21] The mound was augmented over time with additional soil to accommodate any subsidence, and items such as flowers and *immortelles* placed on its surface. *Immortelles* were commemorative items often placed on the grave, comprising an arrangement of artificial flowers under a large glass dome. Although they were sometimes covered with a protective wire 'basket',

Plate 4.2 St Gregory's, Kirkdale. An ancient church with mounds still visible in the churchyard landscape.

immortelles were extremely fragile and harzardous to staff cutting the grass.

This combination of types of commemoration contributed to an extremely complicated landscape: indeed, at Northallerton the churchyard was reported as containing 314 headstones, 77 more formal tombs and 1,544 mounds.[22] The sexton had expected to be able to reuse the churchyard every twenty years, but this level of complexity markedly undermined the ability to go over the ground again. This issue was at the heart of difficulties with new commemorative practices. Again, the Church of England Burial Funeral and Mourning Reform Association noted the difficulty:

> A corpse buried in a wooden coffin, and in an earthen grave, disappears entirely in a certain number of years, which number varies according to the nature of the soil, and the ground can be used again for burial. This has been the

> practice in the churchyards of England for centuries, and, in rural districts, might continue for centuries to come, if wooden coffins and earthen graves are only allowed.[23]

Thus the Association's objection to built graves rested on the belief that 'burial in a brick grave prevents that spot being used for centuries'.[24] Thus, the proliferation of different types of memorial placed substantial pressure on what were often very small rural churchyards. The expectation that remains would lie undisturbed, 'in perpetuity', was matched by an understanding that formal and informal monumentation would also remain intact. In these circumstances, the only possible option was to extend the space available.

Two churchyard extensions: Knaresborough and Bedale

Enlargement of the churchyard was a hugely complicated business, even after the Consecration of Churchyards Act in 1867 introduced some simplification. Prior to that date, churchyard extension took place within the legal context of a succession of Church Building Acts which had aimed to increase the number of new churches. In this, the Acts had probably been successful, but at the same time they created a mystifying accretion of regulations which – in conjunction with the legalities around the proposed use of the church rate – created a great deal of uncertainty for incumbents and vestries. From 1836, the Ecclesiastical Commissioners played a central role. The Commission's creation had signalled the intent for the Church of England to organise its financial affairs, including estate management, in a much more rational fashion.[25] All purchased or donated land for use as a churchyard had to be conveyed through the Commissioners, to be added to the freehold of the local incumbent. In addition, the regulations and expectations that arose as a consequence of the Burial Acts also created a further legal dimension, for example, on the proximity of the churchyard extension to dwellings and on requirements which might arise as a consequence of any closure order served on the churchyard. Finally, the Bishop also had certain conditions which had to be met before it was agreed that consecration could take place, this in addition to the expensive nature of petitioning for a sentence of consecration and having the relevant documentation lodged at the Diocesan Registry Office.

Knaresborough

An indication of the complexity of the process of securing and financing land to enlarge the churchyard is indicated by the example of Knaresborough, where the churchyard of St John the Baptist was extended in 1857. In September 1854, the vestry had called a special meeting to consider 'what measures should be adopted to supply additional burial ground'. The meeting resolved that the churchwardens be instructed to make enquiries as to the rate at which land adjacent to the existing churchyard might be procured.[26] Ostensibly, the land was regarded as suitable since it was already in the ownership of the Ecclesiastical Commissioners, although it was being leased at that time to Lord Rosslyn. Correspondence with Lord Rosslyn's solicitor, Mr Tottie, revealed that Lord Rosslyn was willing to give up the land, but the tenant in question could not be given notice until 1857.[27]

The churchyard of St John the Baptist was closed by Order in Council in 1855, which carried perhaps unforeseen consequences for the vestry's progress towards securing an extension. Closure by Order in Council carried the requirement that the Secretary of State had to be informed of and approve any new burial ground within two miles of the closed site.[28] The Burials Office required the production of surveyor's plans and reports to demonstrate that the proposed land was suitable for burial, particularly with regard to drainage. A more onerous and problematic requirement was that the Secretary of State also ordered that any new burial space should include provision for Anglicans and Dissenters. It was clear that the Burials Office did not agree that Knareborough's burial needs could be met with a churchyard extension: in May, 1855 an official wrote from Whitehall: 'I feel great difficulty about the case of Knaresborough churchyard. I am strongly of the opinion that the best thing for the parish to do would be to get a new burial ground out of the town.'[29] The vestry's difficulty was resolved to some degree by a change in legislation. In 1855, the Burial Act allowed that any new ground provided under the Burial Acts 'shall be held and used in like manner and subject to the same laws and regulations in all respects as the existing burial ground or churchyard of the said parish', providing that within ten years an *unconsecrated* portion of land be made available.[30] In October 1855, the vestry resolved that 'a separate unconsecrated burial ground be provided for Roman Catholics and other non conformists and that a like sum be paid for them as will be expended on purchasing additional church ground'.[31] In actuality, a new burial board cemetery was not opened in Knaresborough until 1876. Further complication ensued in 1856, as the vestry was served with 'a bill' forbidding them to use land for burial within 100 yards of the dwelling house of the plaintiff, Dr Simpson.[32] A long and expensive legal battle followed, which the vestry eventually won.

In December 1855, the vestry laid a rate of 6d in the pound to cover the expenses of securing the extension. However, not all the townships in the parish agreed that they had responsibility for meeting the cost. Arkendale and Brearton had both had new churches built in the 1830s, and the communities there were no doubt already dissatisfied with the fact that they still had to pay church rate to the older parish church for a period of twenty years in addition to supporting their own church financially. The churchwardens in Arkendale and Brearton simply refused to collect the rate, since they were no longer reliant on St John the Baptist for burial space. Again, the Knaresborough vestry resolved to take Counsel's opinion on the townships' responsibility to pay the rate. The issue again took some time to resolve; in 1860, the vestry decided to raise a voluntary subscription to defray expenses as yet unpaid relating to the new churchyard including a further sum to make its drainage more efficient.[33] A final comment on the complexity of the process is the bill presented to the vestry by Powell and Sons, solicitors. The bill runs to a number of pages and included fees for: 'attending you on having been served with Bill in Chancery at the suit of John Simpson esq to prevent our completing and using the piece of ground recently purchased as for a Burial Ground'; 'attending at the Vestry and on the vicar to obtain copies of minutes made at the several meetings held respecting the obtaining of a churchyard and to ascertain what passed between the Vicar and the Secretary of State'; 'attending adjourned meeting held at the court house this evening when in consequence of the Deputation appointed at the meeting having failed in making any amicable arrangement with Dr Simpson a resolution was passed authorising you to take Counsel's opinion and report to a vestry meeting'; 'attending on Mr Fawcett [the vicar] to procure considerable information as to the facts and to read over same to him engaged 2 hours'; 'attending the meeting of committee appointed when they waited on Mr Simpson and 2 of them afterwards went on to the ground to point out what would be sold to him and he was to give an answer in a few days as to whether he would accede to the proposal made by the committee'; and 'attending at Dr Simpson's House to ascertain if he was prepared with his answer when we found he had gone to Scarbro'. This last task was itemised as costing 3s 4d.[34]

Bedale

Perhaps a key difficulty for all the actors concerned – the vicar, vestry, patron of the benefice and any legal adviser brought in to draw up the necessary documentation – was that every extension carried a different play of administrative, legal and financial contexts. Each parish had to 'learn' the process for itself. Dissimilarity in the play and number of variables stymied the ability of incumbents to pass their knowledge between each other; furthermore, the Ecclesiastical Commissioners were not forthcoming with regard to guidance. In Bedale, two principal problems beset the Reverend Thomas Monson as he sought to enlarge the churchyard in 1849–50. First, it was decided that, rather than purchasing space, Monson would donate a portion from his glebe land. However, to do so he had to deal with the Ecclesiastical Commissioners' Office which outlined the required course of action:

> if the Patron and Incumbent of the living are consenting parties to your voluntarily alienating half an acre of the glebe land belonging to your rectory, for the purpose of enlarging the churchyard of the parish of Bedale, and you will forward an intimation to that effect, with the name or names of that latter party and a plan on a scale and a description of the land in question (in the words to be inserted into the conveyance) and a certificate from some professional gentlemen acquainted therewith, that such land is freehold and forms part of the ancient professions of the rectory and is free from incumbrances and in your possession as rector the same will be laid before the board at their next meeting.[35]

This procedure appeared to be straightforward, but Monson soon became entangled in legal complexities and required the services of Mr Williams, a solicitor. Williams considered that the best option was for Monson to sell the glebe land for a nominal price, and on visiting the offices of the Commissioners for confirmation reported that 'the gentleman who I saw seemed to favour my view'. Williams then reconsidered the situation and, returning to the Commissioners with a further query, found 'if the transaction were done by means of sale that a valuation would be required'. If the land was valued at any sum about £20 then it might be necessary to involve the Bank of England and establish trustees.[36] By the following month, Williams appeared to be floundering, and advised Monson to refer matters to another and more experienced solicitor – William Haggard – who was 'able to advise on the questions arising under the Church Building Acts'.[37]

The second problem facing Monson related to payment for the extension. Although the land itself had been donated, there remained the cost of enclosure and the rapidly accumulating legal cost consequent to dealing with the Ecclesiastical Commissioners. Monson was uncertain whether it might be possible to defray those costs through the church rate. This was a step that had been taken by other settlements. For example, in Norton in 1852, the detached churchyard extension for St Nicholas's church cost £250 for the land and a further £160 for enclosure of the land and legal costs. The sum was met by taking a loan against the church rate, to be repaid over a ten-year period.[38] The vestry at Thornton-le-Dale had taken a similar step in 1854.[39] However, Monson was himself uncertain as to the legality of this action. He wrote in a note to himself prior to a special vestry meeting on the subject: 'It seems to be doubtful. I have not been able to find any authority for doing so. If such expenses are included, the rate must be made for the whole estimated amount *at once* I think, it cannot be extended over a period of years yet to come.'[40] He took advice from the Reverend Scott Surtees, vicar at Crakehall, who confirmed that, although his vestry had voted to put the cost on the church rate, 'there was so much objection made, that we thought it better to drop it'.[41] Instead, the expenses there were, were met through voluntary subscription. Surtees recommended that Monson should purchase a legal textbook: 'I would strongly advise you laying out 25s on "Cripps Law of the Clergy", no clergyman of a town parish ought to be without it. We could not have got through without it.'[42] Monson clearly took this advice, since from this point his letters and notes made reference to various pages in 'Cripps'. From this source it appeared that a clause within one of the many Church Building Acts might provide a solution, and he wrote to the Church Building

Commissioners. His letter met with a carefully worded rebuff: 'without giving any opinion on the construction of the words in such sections quoted by you, [we] have no funds applicable to the purposes mentioned in your letter'.[43] Indeed, it appeared that dealing with the Church Buildings Commissioners might in itself incur costs, since Monson's papers also included a proforma relative to the conveyance of land to the Commission indicating an agreement to 'undertake to pay to the said Commissioners or their solicitors, all the law costs and charges arising from or incidental to such conveyance, which the Board may incur'.[44]

The Churchyard Consecration Act, 1867

Contemporaries acknowledged that the various Church Building Acts had become 'a most complicated mess of confusion'.[45] Administrative records of the Ecclesiastical Commissioners indicate that considerable bad feeling had begun to arise on the matter. From notes and correspondence it was clear that particular ire was directed by diocesan authorities towards the needlessly complicated process of research into the titles of properties conveyed for use as churchyards. In 1858, a letter forwarded from the Registrar of the Welsh Diocese of St Asaph complained that local solicitors should be used since 'We believe that this would facilitate business and be less expensive. A local man who in most cases knows the tenure of the land and has ready access to papers is always within reach of parties employed for parishes'.[46] This measure also ensured better communication with the diocesan offices, so there would be no postponement in making arrangements with the bishop to secure consecration. Complaints were also made to White, Barrett and White, the London solicitors who took on the conveyancing work, that they were 'needlessly stringent' with regard to proof of title.[47] Certainly by the 1860s it was understood that some alteration needed to be effected in the case of churchyards specifically. The preamble to the Churchyard

Consecration Act of 1867 commented on the expediency of diminishing the expense associated with churchyard extension, and introduced simplification to the process of enlarging the churchyard in two respects. First, it would be possible for the sentence of consecration for a churchyard extension to be signed by the bishop at the churchyard without the presence of the diocesan chancellor or registrar: indeed, the signature of two clergymen of the diocese only would be required. Generally, it became common for neighbouring clergy to serve this duty. Furthermore, no officer of the Bishop would be permitted to charge a fee for attendance or travel expenses.[48]

Second, the Act also provided a form of conveyance of land, which reduced the legal cost of drawing up a separate conveyance document, and enacted that a gift of land for the purpose of extending the churchyard would not be subject to stamp duty.[49] Perhaps more importantly, and subsumed under this requirement, it would no longer be necessary to use the Ecclesiastical Commissioners' London solicitors. Indeed, the new system enabled the by-passing of the Commissioners almost entirely, where the Act was invoked. The Commissioners were by no means satisfied with this arrangement, and administrative documentation indicates ongoing rumbles between the Commissioners and local bishops, who had been very much in favour of a measure that simplified their own diocesan business. Indeed, the Commissioners actively sidestepped the Act by recommending in response to enquiries on the matter that vestries should continue to use the more cumbersome provisions of the Church Building Act. A letter of complaint to the Commissioners from R. H. Momsey via the Bishop of Carlisle's office reviewed the situation in the 1870s:

> The Consecration of Churchyards Act is a very modern act, and, as was intended, provides an extremely cheap and easy form of conveyance; and to put in force the recommendations of the Commissioners would simply be throwing away the benefit intended to be given in the act. Take for instance the

> numerous cases of lands parts of glebes that are added to churchyards at present. The conveyance of such lands costs from £1 10s 0 to £2 2 0 or even sometimes less. The costs of the Commissioners solicitors for an ordinary conveyance usually amounts to from £10 to £20, and in addition to this increased cost not only would no advantage from the change accrue but additional delay and trouble would be entailed on all parties concerned.[50]

Nevertheless, the Commissioners – with no small duplicity – continued to recommend use of the Church Building Act to all those who enquired about the legal process of extension.

Churchyard extensions: legalities and technicalities

It is uncertain whether the Churchyard Consecration Act, 1867 so simplified the process of extending the churchyard that vestries were more likely to take this action than to establish burial boards and lay out a cemetery. Certainly after 1867, the vast majority of extensions took place under the aegis of the Act, which remains in place. However, this is not to say that after this date the enlargement of the churchyard was easy to achieve: there was still a series of hurdles to overcome. Furthermore, although a great deal of regulation remained in place, there were areas where there was no statutory duty or responsibility and the interplay between church and civic law created a great deal of uncertainty.

Initial stages

The decision to extend the churchyard often emerged in the vestry minutes as a resolution that a problem existed with the existing site and that a sub-committee be appointed to consider possible options. After the early 1850s, the vestry had a choice between establishing a burial board and extending the churchyard, and in some cases – for example, in Stokesley – both were considered before the decision was made in favour of an extension. In Ripon, following closure of part of the Cathedral churchyard, the town council had gone so far as to seek permission from the Secretary of State to create a burial board. However, this plan was suspended after the Cathedral's Dean and Chapter donated a large section of land to the east of the churchyard.[51] The vestry often appointed an extension sub-committee, and on occasion its report back to the vestry is detailed in the vestry minutes. For example, at Thornton-le-Dale in 1854, the sub-committee reported that it had considered all possible options, decided on a piece of land, negotiated on price, reviewed the land again and then concluded that purchase would be the most satisfactory outcome. In commending their conclusion to the vestry, the sub-committee:

> Beg[ged] to add that they have especially taken the subject into consideration in an economical point of view and that they are also of opinion that while they have just grounds on the one hand for believing that such a purchase will strictly speaking be positively moderate under all circumstances, that on the other the increase to the churchyard thus proposed will – whether ratepayers or not – be according to the wishes and the feelings of their fellow parishioners at large.[52]

A much larger task of project management faced the vestry at Wath. Here, further extension to the churchyard was deemed necessary in 1884, as an Order in Council to close the churchyard began to take effect. The Third Marquis of Ailsbury died in 1886, evidently leaving his estate in some disarray, and a letter from the solicitors of the Fourth Marquis in 1887 indicated that he had 'no interest in the Yorkshire estates, they having been conveyed away to Trustees under a scheme of arrangement'. A donation of £20 was offered.[53] This sum was little compensation for the substantial difficulties which then arose as a consequence of proving land ownership in order to secure consecration. The vestry was also subject to the legal steps that were taken by the vicar to prevent the location of the extension close to the rectory. An extended series of letters is extant between the vestry and various legal representatives of the vicar. The clergyman in question – the polymath and antiquarian William Collings Lukis – objected to the plan in terms of the possible threat to his family's health. Indeed, his opposition was so marked that he threatened the vestry in February 1887 to 'apply to the Supreme Court of Indicature for an injunction restraining you and other persons from proceeding forthwith'. Lukis evidently considered that the sanitary authority was the 'proper and only authority that has power to form a new burial ground'. However, the vestry appeared not to favour this option, because it would carry a heavier burden in terms of rate. The following month Lukis finally allowed the plan to go ahead if

> only the farest [*sic*] portion of the ground from the church yard wall shall be used as a burial ground and that the other half shall not be so used without the written consent of the Rector for the time being such written consent to be attested by two disinterested and respectable witnesses then their client will not object to the scheme as the incumbent of the rectory from a sanitary point of view will be safe.[54]

There was some consternation from the vestry that the proposal extended the rector's control so far into the proposed extension – Mr Richardson, vestry representative, noted 'I had no idea that the 100 yards from the Rectory ran so far into the half acre', taking up as it did close to two-thirds of the area.[55] Thus the task of securing an extension could absorb a great deal of vestry representatives' and churchwardens' time.

Estate management and donation from estates

At Wath, the 1880s extension contrasted markedly with an earlier churchyard enlargement, in 1860. In this year minutes recorded that the vestry had been notified by Samuel West, Registrar of the diocese, that 25 perches of land had been conveyed to the Ecclesiastical Commissioners by the Third Marquis of Ailsbury to enlarge the churchyard. All the consequent expenses were paid as part of the donation, leaving the vestry with little to do.[56] The donation of land from an estate was common throughout the period. Many of the settlements in the study were estate villages with one principal landowner. In these cases, it might be expected that the landowner would be proactive in understanding and responding to the community's need for additional burial space. However, estate management was hugely variable in quality, depending to a large degree on the professionalism of the agents employed.[57] At Wath, the first extension had perhaps been arranged by the 'conscientious agent' who Thompson notes had at one time managed the Yorkshire property.[58] Even where the landowner was less proactive, it was clear in the case of estate villages where responsibility for providing land lay, and the vestry could then request space. At Chop Gate in July 1864, the vestry decided that 'a petition be drawn up for signature, to solicit Lord Feversham to make a grant for enlarging the churchyard'.[59] The petition was successful, and the vestry proposed a vote of thanks to Lord Feversham in November 1864. Lord Feversham also gave land for the extension of All Saints in Kirkbymoorside in 1871.[60] It was not always the case that the principal land owner took action. The possessor of the advowson – the right to present a vicar to the parish – had some responsibility for the upkeep of the church and the churchyard. In 1884, it was the patron of the living, Mr Russell, who donated land to extend St Lambert's at Burneston.[61] At Pickhill, in 1889, a quarter-acre extension was added to All Saints by Trinity College, Cambridge, also patrons of the church; and Henrietta Kendal, who lived in Clapham, donated a strip of land at Sinnington, with the understanding that trees in that strip would not be uprooted.[62]

From the perspective of the donor of land, the Consecration of Churchyards Act did carry a further advantage, beyond the simplification of the conveyance. The Act also allowed that one-sixth of the extension could be reserved by the donors, in which they were granted 'the exclusive right in perpetuity of burial and of placing monuments and gravestones in a part of the land so added'.[63] This option probably carried a great deal of attraction at a time when interments within churches themselves had become restricted. A local landowner's need for burial space following a death in the family explains the timing and incidence of churchyard extension in a couple of cases. At Sawley in 1871, the death of H. Wormald, who was the principal local landowner, led to the temporary blessing of a piece of land attached to the churchyard: 'The Bishop granted a licence to bury in this ground subject to the promise that it should be as soon as possible conveyed to the Ecclesiastical Commissioners for a burial ground and connected.'[64]

Other types of donation

It was equally common for donations of land to be made from the glebe held by the rector himself. The nature of this donation sits within the long tradition of clergy using their own income to support the welfare of a parish.[65] In addition, some clergy may have felt a responsibility for the provision of additional space when it was required. In the nineteenth century, the freehold of the churchyard was owned by the incumbent of the church, who materially benefited from the burial fees charged. However, it remained the case that all parishioners were entitled to Christian burial, and so space had to be available.[66] In addition, there were probably practical considerations: land surrounding the churchyard was often glebe land. In Gate Helmsley, an addition of 14 perches was made to the front southern portion of the churchyard in 1868 with land gifted by the vicar, John Farrow.[67] In 1860, 1 rood 36 perches were conveyed by the Reverend Thomas Headley to the Ecclesiastical Commissioners to extend the churchyard at Masham.[68] The Reverend John Richard Green also gifted glebe land to extend the churchyard at Ellerburn in 1890.[69] In other cases, vestries were less fortunate, in finding that the vicar insisted on financial remuneration.

Donations of land also came from local landowners who were not necessarily the principal estate owner in an area: vestry records might simply indicate that the land had been given without mentioning an individual. In some instances, where land was purchased, the vestry was quoted a below-market price which amounted to a donation. Land for the churchyard extension was purchased at Thornton-le-Dale in 1854 at a cost of £236; the price was considered reasonable, since the land had a cottage and workshops which would have to be demolished, and for which the landowner agreed to make no charge.[70] However, in cases where an outright 'market' purchase had to be made, then the vestry had to decide how much land it was prepared to buy. At Easingwold in 1858, land was available next to the churchyard, owned by a Mr Hobson. The vicar – the Reverend Henry Aislie – wanted the vestry to purchase an entire 3-acre field at £200 an acre and place the entire sum on the church rate. To make the decision, it was proposed that the vestry make a show of hands but, following a protest against that method, a more formal poll decided in favour of buying just a portion, at £35 plus expenses.[71] At Staveley in 1890, the vestry approached the owner of a field – a Mr Morrell – next to the churchyard, but his price was deemed to be too high, at £125 for half an acre. The vestry had been willing to offer £100, taking into account the other costs which would be incurred, which it calculated would probably also amount to £100. The meeting recorded that vestry members offered donations, including – oddly – one from Mr Morrell himself, of £5 providing the vestry agreed his price of £125. The vestry meeting for the following year recorded that 'several interviews had been held with the owner during the year and many letters had been passed between Messrs Hirst and Capes acting for the Rector and Churchwardens and Mr Powell for the vendor but no agreement had been arrived at'. Negotiations must have gone badly for the vestry, since the price finally agreed was £130.[72] Perhaps mindful of this kind of outcome, the vestry at North Stainley decided on an alternative course of action. At the 1891 vestry meeting, it was decided to add the village pinfold to the churchyard, 'if it could be done legally and without great cost'. This commonly held enclosure for the penning of stray farm animals was conveniently located next to the churchyard, and a portion of 129 square feet was consecrated in 1893.[73]

Ecclesiastical Commissioners and diocesan requirements

Irrespective of the manner in which land was secured for an extension, it had to be conveyed to the Ecclesiastical Commissioners before being then given to the incumbent. This step, in itself a complex bureaucractic process, at least ensured that the land was securely in the ownership of the Church before interments began. Ownership of the land had to be clearly settled, and the necessary documents presented to the diocesan office before the bishop would consider consecration. It has been seen that, at Wath, the Bishop of Ripon was uncertain about consecrating the proposed extension since no clear title could be ascertained: the vestry had to argue the legalities of the case with the Registrar, and a deputation from the village was sent to meet with the Bishop himself.[74] At Bedale, the Reverend Thomas Monson's many difficulties included an inability to prove ownership of the glebe land he hoped to donate. The Diocesan Registrar wrote that 'with reference to the additional piece of ground you mention, in strictness I fear there is some difficulty as to consecrating it, as there is apparently no title to it', although a way around the problem was arrived at: if the parish had been in possession of the land for more than twenty years, it was sufficient to present declaration of that fact signed by individuals with appropriate local authority.[75] The Churchyard Consecration Act allowed that where a parcel of land had been conveyed and enclosed along with the existing churchyard, after a period of five years the ground would become vested with the incumbent even if neither consecration nor burial had taken place, and ownership could not be questioned.[76] Putting such difficulties to one side, even where ownership was clear the vestry still had to meet the cost of the conveyance.

Evidence of land ownership was perhaps not the most expensive of the Bishop's requirements in order for consecration to take place. It was also necessary for the churchyard to be enclosed, which usually required the construction of a stone wall. Vestries were required to make a formal petition for consecration – another expense – which generally mentioned the fact that the extension was 'properly enclosed'. Canon law underlined the importance of proper enclosure of the churchyard: in 1229, the Bishop of Worcester directed that the churchyard should be enclosed by a wall, hedge or ditch; in 1603, canon law 85 defined this as a responsibility of churchwardens and questmen, who were required to make sure that 'churchyards be well and sufficiently repaired, fenced and maintained with walls, rails or pales'.[77] Upkeep of the churchyard boundary remained an important duty, and vicars were required to include information on the matter in the terrier.[78] Thus, vestries had to meet the cost of erecting a stone wall. In Chop Gate, much of the expense was met through the voluntary donation of

Plate 4.3 St Lambert's, Burneston. Sentence of consecration for churchyard extension, with map (BI, PR/BUE 1/7).

labour and the vestry was able to reduce the cost to just £9.[79] The land had to be properly drained. At Burneston, land was donated but much of the remaining cost, which totalled £259, related to drainage.[80] The combination of land, legal, consecration and infrastructure costs generally left vestries with bills of between £200 and £300, depending on whether the land had been donated.

Meeting the cost

Up until 1868 it had been possible for the cost of churchyard extension to be met through use of the church rate although – as Monson discovered – it was not always certain whether the rate could be applied for this purpose. Furthermore, in the years preceding its abolition, setting and collecting the church rate had become a hugely contentious religious–political issue, as Nonconformists refused to make payments to support the Church of England. After the passage of the Compulsory Church Rates Abolition Act in 1868, vestries had little option but to seek subscriptions to meet the cost. In some areas, formal assessment was made of a voluntary church rate, which carried the advantage of sharing the cost fairly between two or more townships reliant on the churchyard. In many cases, although there was an intension to meet costs through voluntary subscription, the vicar himself often repaid much of the debt. For example, in Stokesley in 1877, the expansion of the Lady Cross Cemetery – the churchyard extension – cost £317, some £100 of which was 'lent' by the Reverend Francis Digby Legard who was never repaid. The Reverend John Thorneycroft Hartley at St Lambert, Burneston, also donated the difference between the amount raised by voluntary subscription and the amount owed.[81]

New churchyard management

The extension of the churchyard brought to the fore issues relating to its management. After 1850, the acquisition of new land for burial encouraged in many places a review of the ways in which the 'old' churchyard had been used.

Planning and layout

Communities had been heavily reliant on the knowledge of the sexton with respect to ongoing interments in the churchyard. Sexton's notebooks, which exist in some locations as an informal supplement to the burial register, give some indication of the way in which a sexton might map the churchyard mentally. Thus, at Great Ayton, a small notebook lists burials chronologically, noting the name and age of the deceased, with a note on the grave's location: in 1856, George Wetherill, nine weeks old, was buried in the 'sw corner, beside his brother', Sarah Sanderson, 46 and buried in 1851 was 'beside her son James, herself next the church'; and in 1870, Robert Ward, 82, was buried 'behind church among friends'.[82]

With the introduction of new land came the possibility that burials might take place on a more ordered footing, particularly with regard to the layout of graves. In 1850, the Sentence of Consecration of the addition to St Hilda's churchyard in Skelton-on-Ure carried the following memorandum: 'At the time of the consecration of the burial ground, it was arranged that interments should be made first along the eastern boundary wall; and that a second row should not be begun before the first should be filled up, and so on throughout.'[83] It followed that ordering of the ground, with the graves numbered and in rows, might facilitate the keeping of a grave register. In Helmsley, after the churchyard extension of 1875, the vicar informed the parishioners that 'Iron markers have been placed at the head of each grave, each with numbers, these numbers correspond to numbers in a book kept by the sexton so that every grave can henceforth be always known.'[84] This 'grave registrar' still exists and contains variously formatted attempts to log the date of burial, name of the deceased and grave number.[85] A similar grave register was also created for the extension at

Knaresborough, and contained instructions on the numbering system:

> commencing on the first row on the south of Robert Ewebank's headstone and numbers in the row counted from the wall towards the church thus – ½ is number one in the second row the fractional number to be read the denominator as the row, the numerator as the number in the row. So Robert Ewbank number is number one in second row. The D standards for double grave – V is for vault.

After three pages the entries end with the comment: 'further entries useless on account of change in sexton – lines deviated from and the remainder thrown into confusion'.[86] It was common for 'new management' to extend to the parish burial register: in Kirk Deighton, the register began to include some grave numbers after the extension was created in 1885; and in Bedale, 'NG' was written into the margin to indicate an interment in the 'new ground'.[87] The extension also offered an excuse to review commemorative practice. At Helmsley, the Reverend C. N. Gray also hoped that better, and more restrained taste would prevail:

> With regard to the future arrangements of the ground, people will be at liberty to be buried with their friends where they choose. As regards the gravestones: it is indeed very much to be wished that the new churchyard may look as neat and nice as possible, and without doubt very large gravestones do not add to the beauty of the ground: it is earnestly hoped that parishioners will be content with stones of smaller size and of some more elegant form than hitherto.[88]

Regulations

In the case of the larger churchyard extensions, where the scale of interment was substantial, there was a more determined attempt to consider the application of government guidance aimed at burial boards. This guidance was produced alongside the regulations, and – as will be indicated in Chapter 5 – intended to advise on day-to-day management of a site dictated by scientific principles. At Knaresborough, it was agreed by the vestry that regulations 13, 14, and 15 be adopted for the extension to St John the Baptist in 1855. These regulations related to pathways and the planting of appropriate vegetation.[89] The vestry concluded also that 'the vicar be requested to carry the same into effect for the old ground as far as practicable'.[90] At Norton it became clear that in the new churchyard extension, the vicar had been following ministry guidance that specified that only one coffin be placed in each grave.[91] There was little wonder, therefore, that the larger detached churchyard extensions could be mistaken for cemeteries: in 1890, Bulmer referred to Stokesley where 'a small cemetery, half an acre in extent, was laid out and consecrated in 1851'.[92] The site became known as the Lady Cross Cemetery, and was itself further extended in 1877. However, the land was a churchyard extension, wholly consecrated and containing a small Church of England mortuary chapel.

Grave spaces in perpetuity

The formality of the churchyard extension layout and consciousness of new practices introduced in the cemetery were also an encouragement for parishioners to seek grave spaces granted in perpetuity. This last requirement was problematic for many vicars, since it could be considered that these requests absorbed, for private and family use, land in the churchyard that was intended for all parishioners. The Church of England Burial, Funeral and Mourning Reform Association addressed the matter in *The Interment of the Dead*, in which it was asserted that no parishioner should expect to establish rights in perpetuity, since once remains have decayed then the land should be available for further interment. Indeed, the pamphlet further argued that formal monumentation delayed the decomposition of the body, and brick vaults took up more space than a parishioner had any right to expect. Vicars charged parishioners more to erect larger memorials, but this practice in itself became 'a direct inducement to him to permit these abuses, and act against the interests of his parishioners. It is in fact in the nature of a bribe to him to commit a breach of trust.'[93]

The changing nature of the churchyard

Fears were expressed that, as a consequence of the proliferation of monuments, the churchyard was losing its essential character. Matthews has commented on the dichotomised nature of literary tropes surrounding the rural churchyard and city cemetery,[94] but even in the nineteenth century it appears that the sentiments were largely rhetorical, particularly as they related to the 'rustic' churchyard. The image of the old country churchyard appealed as a site of 'true Christian piety', but vicars could not be over-bold in their claims for churchyard burial. Post-Reformation, the consecration of the churchyard could have no influence on the soul's destiny, and, unlike Roman Catholic memorials, passers-by could not be exhorted to 'pray for the soul of . . . '. The Reverend J. J. D. Dent, vicar of Hunsingore, expressed his view of the churchyard, in a pamphlet to his parishioners in 1868:

> It is indeed 'God's acre', a plot of ground full of seed, if it be true as we are taught that all the bones therein must in some way rise again, and the incorruptible body, there sown in hope, become in God's own time, incorruptible. The churchyard is hallowed not only by the Bishop's blessing, but by the mourner's tears and prayers; while I wish it to be ever free to all, I pray all who frequent it, to walk therein with sober gait, and quiet step.[95]

Dent is perhaps a little ambiguous with regard to belief in bodily resurrection ('if it be true ... '), but considered that the churchyard's sacredness rested in its consecration and its location as site of grief and prayer. However, these elements were equally present in the cemetery and the churchyard. Furthermore, as the aesthetic of the churchyard extension shifted towards ordered rows and numbered grave markers, it was clear that 'cemetery' practices were becoming absorbed. In Masham, in 1884, the Reverend G. M. Gorham admonished his congregation, through the vehicle of the parish magazine: 'Next to the Church *fabric* and *Services*, the Church*yard* claims our reverent attention and care.' He continued:

> It is hoped one practice, which has recently been adopted, will not be extended further; that of depositing fragile memorials – artificial wreaths, and printed cards – beneath glass covers; which are objectionable on many accounts, and savour of the mixed Cemeteries of huge towns than of the grass-grown mounds of a peaceful country Churchyard.'[96]

Villagers were evidently not persuaded by an idealised churchyard aesthetic, and indeed through the course of the nineteenth and twentieth century the churchyard landscape was moulded by expectations with regard to commemorative practice that had been fostered in the cemetery context.

Conclusion

In rural North Yorkshire, in the second half of the nineteenth century the passage of the Burial Acts did not signal disinvestment or disinterest in churchyard burial. Indeed, during the period to 1894, many communities extended their churchyard space. As much of this chapter has indicated, even the ostensibly straightforward task of accepting a donation of land or absorbing adjacent glebe land carried legal and financial burden. Indeed, the workings of the Ecclesiastical Commissioners alone were in themselves a substantial obstacle. The continued operation of myriad Church Building Acts clearly did not assist matters, and although the Consecration of Churchyards Act was adopted by the majority of parishes seeking to enlarge their churchyard, the legislation did not provide an unambiguous framework. The desire to extend the churchyard reflected the reluctance to disturb earlier burials, but also demonstrated that use of space above the ground could become equally pressured. Even before the introduction of the Burial Acts, the churchyard had begun to resemble a cemetery, in terms of the erection of more, and more complex, monumentation. The addition of an extension to the churchyard introduced a spatial framework for new management practices. At a very basic level, extensions provided space in which order became possible. Graves could be numbered and laid in rows, and burial could be purchased on the assumption that a certain level of monumentation would be allowed and would remain undisturbed. As the century progressed, extensions began to recreate churchyard space as 'cemetery' space, in being visually indistinguishable from burial board sites, and in carrying identical expectations in terms of perpetuity burial. As will be seen, these expectations fuelled further cycles of extension as the proliferation of monuments undermined the traditional practice of reusing the churchyard.

Notes

1 CERC, 11686/4 1875–1881, Church Commissioners: Churches, burial grounds and parsonages, conveyance of sites, general file, letter from R. H. Momsey, via the Bishop of Carlisle, Apr 1876.

2 In some instances, the only information available is inclusion in the House of Commons report, 1877 (438) *Churchyards. Return of all parishes in England and Wales in which any new portion of ground has been consecrated to serve as a churchyard since the last return made to Parliament in 1863; distinguishing those which have been purchased by the parish and those which have been purchased by voluntary subscription, or presented as a free gift.*

3 D. Wiggins, 'The Burial Act of 1880, The Liberation Society and George Osborne Morgan', *Parliamentary History*, 15:2 (1996), p. 189.

4 Yorkshire (North Riding, West Riding) sheet CXIX.16 (1909).

5 BI, CD. Add.1873/1, Addition to churchyard, 1873.

6 NYRO, PR/NU 6/5, Notes on the history of parish church, compiled 1959.

7 BI, PR/EAS 179, Papers relating to church restoration in 1858, unattributed newspaper clipping dated 11 Jun 1858.
8 NYRO, PR/WAT 1/6, Baptisms and parish diary, 1850–1893.
9 NYRO, PR/TND 5/1, Churchwardens' accounts and minutes, 1852–1921, 1854.
10 NYRO, PR/BED 17 2/1, 1849 Churchyard.
11 NYRO, PR/HSG 5/3, Hunsingore Parochialia, 1855–1966, unpaginated.
12 R. Houlbrooke, *Death, Religion and the Family in England 1480–1750* (Oxford: Clarendon Press, 1998), p. 362.
13 F. Burgess, *English Churchyard Memorials* (London: Lutterworth Press, 1963).
14 S. Buckham, '"The men that worked for England, they have their graves at home": consumerist issues within the production and purchase of gravestones in Victorian York' in Tarlow, S. and West, S. (eds), *The Familiar Past? Archaeologies of Later Historical Britain* (London: Routledge, 1999).
15 S. Tarlow, *Bereavement and Commemoration: An Archaeology of Mortality* (Oxford: Blackwell, 1999), pp. 58ff.
16 A. Cannon, 'The historical dimension in mortuary expressions of status and sentiment', *Current Anthropology*, 30:4 (1989), 437–58, figure 4.
17 NYRO, PR/AYG, Great Ayton Burials, 1850–1875. The circular is pasted into the burial register.
18 A. Sington, *The Interment of the Dead*, Church of England, Burial, Funeral and Mourning Reform Association (Manchester: John Heywood, 1888), p. 9.
19 J. C. Loudon, *On the Laying Out, Planting and Managing of Cemeteries; and on the Improvement of Churchyards* (London: Longman, Brown, Green, 1843), p. 41.
20 'Instructions for Burial Boards in providing cemeteries, and marking arrangements for interments under the Burial Acts 15 & 16 Vict cap 85, and 16 & 17 Vict, cap 134, XXXI' in Cunningham Glen, W. *The Burial Board Acts for England and Wales, with the Regulations of the Secretary of State, and Copious Notes of Decided Cases upon the Construction of the Acts and also the Law Relating to the Burial of the Dead* (London: Shaw and Sons, 1869), p. 154.
21 NYRO, PR/HEL 7/1, Correspondence and papers relating to the old churchyard and its extensions, 1880–1989, handwritten extract from the parish magazine, 1879.
22 Ranger, *Report to the General Board of Health, on a Preliminary Inquiry into the Sewerage, Drainage, and Supply of Water, and the Sanitary*

Condition of the Inhabitants of the Town of Northallerton, in the County of York (London: HMSO, 1850), p. 17.
23 Sington, *Interment of the Dead*, p. 9.
24 *Ibid.*
25 K. A. Thompson, *Bureaucracy and Church Reform: The Organisational Response of the Church of England to Social Change, 1800–1965* (Oxford: Clarendon Press, 1970).
26 NYRO, PR/KN 3/2/2, Vestry minutes, 1849–62, 5 Sep 1854.
27 NYRO, PR/KN 9/2/10, Correspondence relating to the acquisition of land for a new burial ground, letter from Mr Tottie, dated 15 Dec 1855.
28 Burial Act (1852), s. 9.
29 NYRO: PR/KN 9/2/10, Correspondence relating to the acquisition of land for a new burial ground), letter from the Home Office, dated 22 May 1855.
30 Burial Act (1855), s. 10.
31 NYRO, PR/KN 3/2/2, Vestry minutes, 1849–62, 19 Oct 1855.
32 NYRO, PR/KN 3/2/2, Vestry minutes, 1849–62, 14 Aug 1856.
33 NYRO, PR/KN 3/2/2, Vestry minutes, 1849–62, 16 Mar 1860.
34 NYRO, PR/KN 9/5, Receipted bill for expenses relating to a new burial ground between Aug 1856 and Jan 1857.
35 NYRO, PR/BED 17/1/1, Letters and papers relating to the enlargement of the churchyard, 1849–1850, letter from Ecclesiastical Commissioners Office to the Reverend Thomas Monson, 10 Apr 1849.
36 NYRO, PR/BED 17/1/3, Letters and papers relating to the enlargement of the churchyard, 1849–1850, letter from Mr Williams to the Reverend Thomas Monson, 17 Apr 1849.
37 NYRO, PR/BED 17/1/7, Letters and papers relating to the enlargement of the churchyard, 1849–1850, letter from Mr Williams to the Reverend Thomas Monson, 12 May 1849.
38 BI, PR/NORT 40, Conveyance document, 1851.
39 NYRO, PR/TND 5/1, Churchwardens' accounts and minutes, 1852–1921, 1854.
40 NYRO, PR/BED 17/1/1, Letters and papers relating to the enlargement of the churchyard, 1849–1850, Notes for agenda for vestry meeting, 14 Apr 1849.
41 NYRO, PR/BED 17/1/25 (Letters and papers relating to the enlargement of the churchyard, 1849–1850), Letter from the Reverend Scott Surtees to the Reverend Thomas Monson, nd.
42 *Ibid.*
43 NYRO, PR/BED 17/1/6 (Letters and papers relating to the enlarge-

ment of the churchyard, 1849–1850), Letter from Church Commissioners to the Reverend Thomas Monson, 11 May 1849.

44 NYRO, PR/BED 17/1/24 (Letters and papers relating to the enlargement of the churchyard, 1849–1850), Proforma 'Conveyance of sites under the Church Building Acts'.

45 Dr Stephen Lushingon, undated quotation used by M. H. Port, *Six Hundred New Churches: A Study of the Church Building Commission, 1818–1856, and Its Church Building Activities* (London: SPCK, 1961), p. 111.

46 Church of England: Church Commissioners (Churches, burial grounds and parsonages, conveyance of sites, general file, 11686/2, 1845–65), letter dated 23 Jan 1858.

47 Church of England: Church Commissioners (Churches, burial grounds and parsonages, conveyance of sites, general file, 11686/2, 1845–65).

48 Consecration of Churchyards Act (1867), ss.1 and 2.

49 Consecration of Churchyards Act (1867), ss. 5 and 6.

50 CERC, 11686/4 1875–1881, Church Commissioners: Churches, burial grounds and parsonages, conveyance of sites, general file, letter from R. H. Momsey, via the Bishop of Carlisle, Apr 1876.

51 *Ripon Millenary: a record of the festival also a history of the city arranged under its wakemen and mayors from the year 1400* (Ripon: W. Harrison, Printer & Publisher, 1892), p. 176.

52 NYRO, PR/TND 5/1, Churchwardens' accounts and minutes, 1852–1921, 1854.

53 NYRO, PR/WAT 7/5, Correspondence relating to extension of the churchyard, 1886–90, Letter from Walker and Newborn-Walker, solicitors to the vestry, dated 15 Feb 1887.

54 NYRO, PR/WAT 7/5, Correspondence relating to extension of the churchyard, 1886–90, Letter from Edmonson and Gowland, solicitors to the vestry, dated 15 Feb 1887.

55 NYRO, PR/WAT 7/5, Correspondence relating to extension of the churchyard, 1886–90, Letter from John Richardson to the vestry dated 22 Apr 1887.

56 NYRO, PR/WAT 1/6, Baptisms and parish diary, 1850–1893.

57 Barbara English, *The Great Landowners of East Yorkshire, 1530–1910* (Howden: Hull Academic Press, 1990); F. M. L. Thompson, *English Landed Society in the Nineteenth Century* (London: Routledge and Kegan Paul, 1963).

58 Thompson, *English Landed Society*, p. 176.

59 NYRO, PR/BLK 2/2, Vestry and churchwardens' minute book, 1860–1927, July 1864.

60 NYRO, PC/KMO 2/1, Minute book of vestry, ratepayers and annual public meetings, 1810–1975, 1 Feb 1871.
61 NYRO, PR/BUE 4/1, Minute Book, 1858–1925, 26 Mar 1884.
62 NYRO, PR/PIC 2/3, Church land account and vestry minutes, 1854–1900; NYRO, PR/SIT 5/1, Churchyard trees.
63 Consecration of Churchyards Act (1867), s. 9.
64 NYRO, PR/SAW 8/11, Bound volume of copies of the *London Gazette*, containing MS diary of parish events, 1856–1881, 1871.
65 M. G. Hinton, *The Anglican Parochial Clergy* (London: SCM, 1964).
66 See, for example, H. W. Cripps, *A Practical Treatise on the Law Relating to the Church and the Clergy* (London: Sweet and Maxwell, 1937, 8th edn), p. 564.
67 BI, CD/Add.1868/4, Gate Helmsley, addition to churchyard, 1868.
68 NYRO, PR/MAS 10/1, Conveyance from the Reverend Thomas Headley to the Ecclesiastical Commissioners for England.
69 NYRO, PR/ELL 8/1/1, Accounts for the addition of land to Ellerburn churchyard, 1890; NYRO, PR/TND 3/1, Terrier, 1911.
70 NYRO, PR/TND 5/1, Churchwardens' accounts and minutes, 1852–1921, 1854.
71 BI, PR/EAS 185, Report of ratepayers' meeting on a new burial ground.
72 NYRO, PR/SVL 5/3 , Vestry Minute Book, 1850–1930, 1890, 1891, 1892.
73 NYRO, PR/SNN 3/1–6, North Stainley Vestry Minute Book, 1890–1924, 31 March 1891; NYRO, PC/SNN 4/4, North Stainley, statutory record of consecration, 1893.
74 NYRO, PR/WAT 7/5, Correspondence relating to extension of the churchyard, 1886–90.
75 NYRO, PR/BED 17/1, Letters and papers relating to the enlargement of the churchyard, 1849–1850.
76 Consecration of Churchyards Act (1867), s. 7.
77 Burgess, *English Churchyard Memorials*, p. 23; G. Bray (ed.), *The Anglican Canons 1529–1947* (Woodbridge: The Boydell Press, 1998), pp. 379–80.
78 See Appendix Three, Note on Sources.
79 NYRO, PR/BLK 2/2, Vestry and Churchwardens' Minute Book, 1860–1927, 7 Dec 1864.
80 NYRO, PR/BUE 4/1, Minute Book, 1858–1925, 22 Dec 1884.
81 *Ibid.*
82 NYRO, PR/AYG 7/34, List of burials, with fees paid and place of burial. Examples from 1851, 1856 and 1870.
83 NYRO, PR/SKO 12/1, Sentence of consecration, Skelton burial ground, 1850.

84 NYRO, PR/HEL 7/1, Correspondence and papers relating to the old churchyard and its extensions, 1880–1989, parish magazine extract, 1875.

85 NYRO, PR/HEL 7/2, Registrar [*sic*] of deaths in the new burial ground, 1874–1900.

86 NYRO, PR/KN 9/6, Book of reference for plan of additional burial ground, nd post 1860.

87 NYRO, PR/DEK 1/6, Kirk Deighton burials, 1813–1909; NYRO, PR/BED 1/27, Bedale burials, 1849–1870.

88 NYRO, PR/HEL 7/1, Correspondence and papers relating to the old churchyard and its extensions, 1880–1989, parish magazine extract, 1874.

89 Cunningham Glen, *The Burial Board Acts for England and Wales*, appendix one.

90 NYRO, PK/KN 3/1/2, Vestry minutes, 1849–62, 24 Dec 1855.

91 BI, PR/NORT 35, Vestry meetings, 1867–1933, 1882.

92 T. Bulmer, *History, Topography and Directory of North Yorkshire* (Preston: T. Bulmer and Co., 1890), p. 209.

93 A. Sington, *The Interment of the Dead* (Manchester: John Heywood, 1888), p. 22.

94 S. Matthews, *Poetical Remains: Poets' Graves, Bodies, and Books in the Nineteenth Century* (Oxford: Oxford University Press, 2004).

95 NYRO, PR/HSG 12/1, Letter to the inhabitants of the parish of Hunsingore by the Reverend J. J. D. Dent, MA, 1868, p. 8.

96 NYRO, PR/MAS 21/1, Masham and Healey Magazines, 1884–1901, Jul 1884. Italics original.

5

'It was entirely a question for the parishioners':[1] *burial board management*

The extension of existing churchyards was by far the most common response to the need to expand burial space in rural North Yorkshire: before 1894 there were more than sixty individual instances. However, in eighteen villages and towns the vestry decided instead to establish a burial board as permitted by the Burial Acts. As will be seen in the next chapter, Anglican–Dissenting relations in these settlements had a part to play in the decision not to extend the churchyard. This chapter will concentrate on perhaps more prosaic concerns, and aims both to illustrate a narrative point and illuminate a more theoretical concern. First, the chapter takes a cue from the work of Christopher Hamlin, who in 1988 observed that 'a useful direction for research in urban history and the history of public health and public works would be to give substance to the claim that urban improvement was a matter of staggering complexity'.[2] Chapters 3 and 4 have already indicated that both closure of the churchyard and its extension could engender local consternation. The establishment of a burial board cemetery was infinitely more bewildering, and involved vestries in technical, legal, financial and political decision-making where error was almost inevitable.

The chapter will also use the narrative of burial board establishment to address a more theoretical contention: that

Ministry directives on cemetery management constituted a Foucauldian intrusion, in which scientific agendas overtook traditional approaches to burial provision. Ragon characterised cemeteries as 'the high place of the embodiment of administrative rationality'.[3] The compilation by the General Board of Health of detailed 'Instructions' for burial boards on the operation of cemeteries underlined the need to approach the management of burial space in a more scientific manner, and introduced unfamiliar and in some cases unwelcome practices such as the restriction to one body per grave. Hitherto, family members had been buried together in the same grave. However, in the UK much of the new burial legislation and its attached guidance were permissive, not least the fact that communities could themselves decide on the provision of additional burial space. Furthermore, where a burial board was set up, its operation was closely geared to longstanding local ratepayer democracy, in that all the Board's substantive decisions – including the amount borrowed and the fees charged – had to garner a majority vestry vote.

Third, the chapter considers how far the cemetery was a new type of burial space which constituted a dislocation from the tradition of churchyard interment. As the last chapters have intimated, change in the way that communities used churchyards had begun to gather pace from the mid-century onwards. The new burial guidance sought to contain the proliferation of commemorative practices which hampered decomposition, and to institutionalise a system of periodic grave reuse. Indeed, it could be argued that – initially at least – the cemetery aimed to re-engage with some churchyard customs which had begun to fall out of favour. However, it is notable that the regulations were more fluid than might be supposed and within a decade of their introduction were subject to modification. Thus the 'science' of cemetery management was itself moulded by what was practicable and acceptable, in the same way that that churchyard practice had begun to alter. From the mid-nineteenth century, the landscapes of both types of burial site evidenced the importance of the family grave and the opportunity for appropriate commemoration.

Burial boards in central North Riding, 1853–94

Before discussion the nature of burial boards and their cemeteries, it is useful to consider basic details of their incidence and timing in the period up to 1894. Although burial boards are generally associated with large urban developments, the existence of eighteen boards in a largely rural part of the country indicates that this format was thought to carry some advantages even in smaller settlements. The small-scale burial boards will be discussed in more detail in Chapter 8. Table 5.1 lists the larger burial boards in operation in central North Riding in this period. Almost all these settlements were in places where the churchyard had been completely or partly closed by Order in Council, the exception being New Malton where interment in the churchyard of St Michael had ceased 'by consent'.

Although many of the settlements in this list are included amongst the ten largest towns and villages in the study – leaving Harrogate to one side – there is not necessarily a conclusive correlation between the size of town and the decision to form a burial board rather than extend the churchyard. In Ripon, the 1854 burial board was disbanded after land to extend the churchyard was donated by the Cathedral Dean and Chapter; in Knaresborough, the burial board of 1876 was preceded by a churchyard extension in the 1850s, as was the burial board in Norton. There was sole reliance on one or more extensions in four of the ten largest settlements in the second half of the nineteenth century: Bedale, Pickering, Kirkbymoorside and Easingwold. However, it seems that burial board establishment was common amongst the larger settlements, and with initial expenditure on a relatively large scale. Borrowings were usually well in excess of £1,000; buildings including lodges and chapels were commonplace, and the size of the site generally measured in acres rather than roods. At 7 acres, the Knaresborough Burial Board site was by far the largest, but both Harrogate Burial Board's Grove Road Cemetery and the site at New Malton probably constituted the grandest. The Grove Road chapels have now been demolished, but at Malton the long drive upwards remains impressive. The double chapel is connected with a porte-cochère, or a covered area providing shelter for the hearse and mourners.

Burial board procedure

The means by which a vestry could establish a burial board was laid down in the various Burial Acts, and comprised a number of stages even before any decisions were made on land purchase. Two principal themes emerge from an account of the early history of burial boards in central North Riding: the fact that both vestry approval and Burials Office ratification were required for all substantive decisions, but – as will be seen – neither local nor central agreement always came readily; and that – over time – complexity led to the development of expertise, and an understanding of the accretion of increasingly arcane burial laws provided a cornerstone of the development of cemetery management as a profession. At the risk of labouring the point, there were at least half a dozen distinct sets of tasks or stages from the meeting at which the decision was made to establish a board rather than extend the churchyard, to the day when it became possible to open the cemetery for business. The vexed issue of consecration and chapel provision for Anglicans and Nonconformists will be discussed in more detail in the next chapter. Nevertheless, it should be remembered here that vestries and burial boards were at all stages required to negotiate compromise and agreement between denominational factions quite capable of stymieing progress if they felt that their interests were not respected.

Table 5.1 Larger burial boards, 1853–1894

	Date	*Initial acreage*	*Buildings*	*Total initial loan (£)*
Ripon Burial Board	1856	*No cemetery*		
Northallerton and Romanby Burial Board	1856	4a	CoE and N chapels; lodge in 1876	1600
Burial Board for the Ecclesiastical Parishes of St Michael and St Leonard New Malton in the County of York	1859	5a	CoE and N chapels	2500
Harrogate Burial Board (later, Bilton and Starbeck Joint Burial Board) (Grove Road)	1864	4.5a	CoE and N chapels and lodge	c. 5000
St Mary's Burial Board, Harrogate (Harlow Hill)	1871	1a 2r	Attached to mission church	1000
Knaresborough Burial Board	1876	7a 29p	CoE and N chapels and lodge	5500
Burial Board of High and Low Bishopside and Bewerley within the Parish or Ecclesiastical District of Pateley Bridge	1876	3a	Lodge and 'hearse room'	1400
Thirsk Burial Board	1880	3a	CoE and N chapels	2500
Great Ayton and Little Ayton Burial Board	1882	2a	Caretaker's house only	1800
Norton Burial Board	1886	1.948a	Repairs to existing mortuary chapel in churchyard extension	1500
Ripon Burial Board	1894	5a 2r 14p	Single chapel and lodge	5500

The settlements to be served

Perhaps the first substantive decision to be made – once it had been decided that a burial board was wanted – was to consider which settlements the cemetery would serve. The larger parishes might contain a number of townships, and all had to be in agreement that they were willing to contribute rates for the production of a large cemetery that in some cases might be some distance away. The issue was further complicated as smaller villages grew or chapels of ease were built within larger parishes. For example, the two villages of High Harrogate and Low Harrogate were originally in two different parishes: Christ Church, High Harrogate was originally a chapel of ease for St John the Baptist at Knaresborough. High Harrogate was also part of the township of Bilton-with-Harrogate, which itself became a new parish in 1855. Low Harrogate had been in the parish of Pannal. A cemetery for the rapidly developing town of Harrogate therefore required co-operation between a number of townships and parishes. It had evidently been thought that the Harrogate Improvement Commissioners might constitute a burial board, as permitted by the regulations, but its catchment area did not entirely encompass both High and Low Harrogate.[4] At an early stage, the township of Bilton declared that it would not contribute: a new church had been built in the village in 1855 and its churchyard 'was not likely to be full for many years to come, the number of interments being few'.[5] Despite a willingness in principle to act in concert, full vestry meetings of neither High Harrogate nor Low Harrogate agreed the move, and two separate burial boards were created. Similarly, in Great Ayton the decision was made to include the townships of Great Ayton, Little Ayton with Tunstal and Nunthorpe but to exclude Easby although it was within the ecclesiastical parish. A wider catchment area increased the number of contributing ratepayers, but also added to the administrative complexity in terms of rate collection and formal meetings.

Secretary of State approval

At the same time as arriving at a decision as to which townships and parishes should be covered by the burial board, vestries had to bear in mind the fact that both the vestry and the Secretary of State had to agree to the establishment of a board. Where a churchyard had been closed by Order in Council, Secretary of State approval had to be garnered for any new burial ground.[6] The Burial Act of 1860 also specified that permission needed to be sought in cases where parishes had been subject to recent division.[7] Locally, all meetings relating to burial board business had to be announced using very specific notification procedures, and a decision could be negated if these were not scrupulously observed. Under s. 10 of the Burial Act (1852), ten or more ratepayers had to order the churchwardens to call a vestry meeting,

> for the special purpose of determining whether a burial board shall be provided under this Act for the parish; and public notice of such vestry meeting, and the place and hour of holding the same, and the special purpose thereof, shall be given in the usual manner in which notices of the meetings of the vestry are given, at least seven days before holding such vestry meeting.[8]

If the meeting agreed that a burial board should be established, a copy of this resolution 'extracted from the minutes of the vestry, and signed by the chairman' was to be sent to the Secretary of State.[9] Knaresborough Burial Board failed even in this requirement, since its application to the Secretary of State was worded incorrectly. A letter from Whitehall indicated that the submission was 'not quite in the right form' since it 'ought to have declared the expedience of appointing a burial board'. However, the official was 'willing to waive any formal objection, and to take the Resolution as meaning that such appointment is expedient'.[10] The involvement of a number of townships meant that separate meetings had to be arranged for each, with ratepayers' votes secured accordingly: at Great Ayton the burial board minutes record that separate ratepayer meetings took place at Great Ayton, Little Ayton and Nunthorpe.[11] The circuitous nature of the notification procedures led the burial board at Pateley Bridge to ask in 1872 whether they needed vestry approval before seeking the approval of the Secretary of State.[12] The Board had been right to be wary: it was discovered later in the year that the notification procedure had in fact been incorrect, and the legality of the Board was called into question. The Board was obliged to disband and re-constitute itself, and was only able to return to the task of establishing a cemetery six months later. In the meantime, the tricky issue of the catchment area for the Board was again replayed.[13]

Appointing the Board

A burial board comprised a group of – always, in the nineteenth century – men, numbering not fewer than three and no more than nine individuals who were ratepayers. Each year a third of the board was required to step down and elections at full vestry meetings would be held for new members, although individuals could put themselves forward for immediate re-election. A vote for founding members was in general held at the initial meeting to formally establish a burial board: the vicar was invariably included, although, in its submission to the Secretary of State, the burial board at Harrogate pointedly mentioned the fact that it comprised 'churchmen, Independents and Methodists'.[14] In Norton and in Old Malton the board was constituted from members of the respective wards of the Borough of Malton Local Board of Health.[15] This study does not include detailed prosopographical analysis of board members, but the play of local politics was evident. There could be substantial interest in burial board membership, particularly at early stages when major decisions were being made. In Knaresborough in 1877 there was some disagreement during the vestry meeting as to vote counting, and another election was held on a separate date: it is notable that the leading candidate polled 341 and others over 200 each, which indicates a high level of interest in cemetery affairs amongst ratepayers.[16] The election of board members in Pateley Bridge in 1875 was something of a gala event, as substantial controversy had built over the borrowing of an additional sum to deal with drainage problems at the site: 'printed bills, written placards and squibs, both in prose and in poetry, were distributed all over the Burial Board district'. On the day of the election, the local newspaper reported

> groups of eager talkers in the streets, and the animated countenances of those passing to and fro showed that something unusual was occurring. As each batch of voters came into town, they were pounced on by the partisans of one side or the other and accompanied in some cases up to the doors of the Hall itself, by those who were wishful to convince and convert them from the errors of their ways.[17]

Thus ratepayers were active participants in burial board business, and could readily influence the decision of the board through both vestry votes and board member election.

Finding a suitable site

Following from decisions as to a board's catchment area and its members the next two stages were to secure a site and pay for it. However, these ostensibly simple tasks were usually completed in a storm of confusion which could last months. Perhaps only Old Malton and St Mary's, Harrogate, found these tasks straightforward, since their initial sites comprised donated land. The other boards had to decide how much land was required; find the land; persuade the owner to sell or to sell only the amount required; test its suitability for interment; negotiate a cost and any associated conditions such as compensation to existing tenants; and invite tenders for laying out the ground and buildings. It was only once these tasks had been fulfilled that it became possible to arrive at an estimated overall cost, which then had to be submitted for vestry approval before a loan was secured. Where the vestry decided that the cost was too high, then the proposal had to be unpicked and reframed, perhaps with other land since by this time the original landowner might have withdrawn their offer or revised the price upwards as a

PARISH OF KNARESBOROUGH.

The Secretary of State having signified his approval of the appointment of a BURIAL BOARD for such parts of the several Townships of Knaresborough, Scriven-with-Tentergate, and Bilton-with-Harrogate, in the Parish of Knaresborough, as are not already provided with sufficient Burial Ground,

NOTICE IS HEREBY GIVEN,

THAT A

MEETING of the VESTRY of this PARISH,

WILL BE HELD AT THE

VESTRY OF THE PARISH CHURCH, KNARESBRO',

AT TWO O'CLOCK IN THE AFTERNOON,

Of Friday, the Seventh day of March, 1873,

For the purpose of appointing not less than three, nor more than nine persons, being Ratepayers of the Parish, to be the BURIAL BOARD of such Parish or District for which such Burial Board shall be provided, and to carry out the resolution adopted at the Vestry Meeting of the said Parish, held on the 27th day of December, 1872.

Dated this Twenty-fifth day of February, 1873.

JOSEPH BENSON,
STEPHEN ROBINSON,
MEADLEY WOOD, } *Churchwardens of the Parish of Knaresborough.*

HANNAM, PRINTER, KNARESBOROUGH.

Plate 5.1 Knaresborough vestry meeting notice. Election notice for burial board, worded according to regulations (NYRO, PR/KN 18/1).

consequence of the vexation. At Norton, the process lasted over two years, and included a wrangle with local residents who lived within 100 yards of a proposed site. Their claim for compensation was deemed to be 'so unreasonable in amount that this Board cannot further entertain the question'.[18] Harrogate Burial Board was a further case in point: at one stage it had negotiations open on three different tracts of land. The first was 1.5a, owned by a Mrs Bayley and costing £1,000. This cost was thought 'very high' but she had been unwilling to negotiate on price 'as she was not anxious to have a cemetery to adjoin on her land which might be injuriously affected by its contiguity'. However, the Board nevertheless sent a member to discuss the matter with her during her visit to London. Mr Greenwood had slightly less land – 1.25a – but this was being offered at a slightly higher price, of £1,030. The Duchy of Lancaster had 8.837a available for just £883 but the land was tenanted. The tenant absolutely refused to give up the lease until its expiry in 1866 which led the Board to consider the expediency of adding a small tract to the churchyard at Christ Church as a temporary measure. The consequent negotiations, opened with owners of the Stray and with the North Eastern Railway Company, came to nothing. Overall, the issue took around a year to resolve, with the Board agreeing finally the purchase of a completely different tract of land, at Far Jenny Field.[19]

The problems of simply finding and securing land were accompanied by a concern that the land met Burials Office requirements of a site that would be suitable for a cemetery, in terms of size and soil composition. Burial boards were required to complete a detailed proforma on their proposed site in their application for permission from the Burials Office (see Box 5.1). Advice was available since the Home Office had issued 'Instructions for Burial Boards', which was a set of scientific guidelines relating to the purchase, laying out and management of a burial board cemetery. The 'Instructions' were the work of Dr John Sutherland, a General Board of Health medical inspector who was 'well acquainted' with the issue of intramural interment.[20] The 'Instructions' were ordered in numbered paragraphs, which burial boards later referred to as regulations, and by number. The guidelines covered a number of technicalities including assessment of the amount of space required,

Box 5.1 Ministry proforma queries relating to site application

- By what number of persons is the intended burial ground likely to be used?
- What has been the average number of burials annually for a period of ten years? And how many per annum are expected?
- What is the area of the proposed ground?
- What is the distance from the nearest inhabited part of the burial district, – from the mass of the population, – and also from the remotest part of the district?
- What is the distance from the nearest dwelling house to the boundary of the ground? Are there any and how many dwellings within 100 yards of the part to be used for burial? And have the consents, in writing, of the owners, lessees, and occupiers of such dwellings been obtained?
- Do the local authorities of the district consent to the site being used for burial, and are any persons known to object to the site proposed? If so, for what alleged reason?
- Describe the existing means of access to the ground, and state whether it will be necessary to make any new road to it.
- What is the nature of the soil, as ascertained by trial holes at least eight feet deep?
- Is water found, and at what depth?
- Can the ground be thoroughly drained? If so, will the drainage flow into any water now used, or likely to be used, for domestic purposes; and at what distance are the nearest pumps or wells supplying water for drinking from the boundary?
- Has any other ground been proposed? If so, why has this been preferred?
- Send in duplicate tracings of the plan of the ground, drawn to scale, with a sufficient description for its identification; having the position of the trial holes marked upon it; and showing the situation of the ground with respect to the town, adjoining property and points of the compass.
- Send surveyor's certificate, stating whether the ground can be thoroughly drained to the depth of eight feet at least, and as to the outlet for the drainage mentioned in query 11.
- State the name by which the site is now best known.
- What is the number on the tithe or other public map?

helpfully indicating that 'town populations living under defective sanitary conditions require a larger amount of burial space, in proportion to the number of inhabitants, than is necessary in more healthy districts', but in the more insanitary districts a larger proportion of deaths comprised children so that 'more space would be required to bury an annual average of 100 deaths in Hertfordshire than in Whitechapel'.[21] In Pateley Bridge, the Burial Board decided that a larger tract of land was required after it was agreed that a boost in local manufacturing in the area was likely to lead to growth in the population.[22] At Norton, it was initially proposed that no less than 5 acres would be 'fully adequate for a burial ground for such a parish'[23] although they finally settled on just under two acres.

The 'Instructions' also dealt with the nature of the soil and optimal conditions for swift decomposition. Light and aerated soil was ideal, since it was air that effected rapid decomposition. Heavy clay and a high water table were both undesirable, and so the guidance included technical detail on drainage and soil improvement. At St Mary's, Harrogate, the Board had benefited from the assistance of Mr Thomas, resident engineer to the Harrogate Waterworks Company, and so presented to the vestry a relatively detailed report on the proposed site, a plan of which – including the location of the noted bore-holes – was pasted in to the end covers of the vestry minute book. The vestry was told that

> the results of digging and boring, carefully executed in various parts of the ground, tend to show: – 1, that the natural slope, both of the surface of the ground, and of the strata which compose the soil, in a remarkable degree, favourable to natural drainage; 2, that the soil is of a nature very suitable for interments, being free from moisture, and presenting no obstacle to excavation.[24]

Site approval also required the visit of a medical officer of health, to check land suitability. In Aldborough, Dr Holland declared that the proposed site was indeed satisfactory but that the Board had failed to seek the necessary Secretary of State permission under the Burial Act 1860, so leading to a new round of vestry meetings and votes.[25]

Paying for the cemetery

The cost of the cemetery was generally met through a loan, which required the permission of the vestry; indeed, any board expenditure above £100 required vestry approval. It was generally at this point that objections were raised. At Harlow Hill, the Burial Board looked set to achieve its objectives with minimal expenditure, since land for a cemetery had become available as a consequence of the donation by Earl Fitzwilliam of the site and for the building of a chapel of ease for the further reaches of what was becoming a populous parish. The Earl had agreed to provide an extended churchyard, and that it should be managed under the Burial Acts by a board. Even so, the vestry grumbled about the cost since it was thought equitable that an unconsecrated chapel also be built at the cemetery: it was suggested that only £1,000 need be spent. A Mr Corker asserted that 'it seemed to him there was a chance of their spending more money than he should approve ... if there was a talk of spending thousands, he should withdraw his support'. His argument appeared to carry the day, and no such chapel was built.[26] At Great Ayton, three separate vestry meetings – held in May, June and July 1882 – approved costs of £1,500, revised upwards to £2,000 and then downwards to £1,800.[27] The situation was further muddied by the fact that many burial boards simply did not appreciate the range of expenditures that would accrue to opening a cemetery: in almost every case, the estimates were well below the actual cost.

Once the amount of loan had been decided by the vestry, the board had to consider how to secure the finance. Central government loans were available for large-scale public projects, from the Public Works Loan Board (PWLB). The PWLB had evolved from a government scheme established in 1817 to facilitate access to loans for public works as a measure to deal with unemployment.[28] Prest noted in 1990 that no history had been written of the PWLB, and this omission remains, unfortunately, the case.[29] Formal annual reporting by the Board began only in 1876, by which time, it noted, a total of £827,636 had already been loaned to burial boards.[30] PWLB finance to burial boards was generally available at a rate of 5 per cent per annum, repayable over 20 years. Burial boards tended to agree that better deals could be had elsewhere; indeed, the Board itself offered a better rate of interest for larger sanitary projects. At Thirsk, the Burial Board borrowed £2,500 from a local gentleman, paying 4.5 per cent per annum for a period of 21 years. Great Ayton and Pateley Bridge also looked to the marketplace for better options, the latter advertising in the local papers for a loan of £1,000 or perhaps two loans of £500 at an interest rate of 4.5 per cent, but found no business and so had to turn to the PWLB. At Aldborough, it was agreed that the Burial Board need borrow only £350 of the estimated £570 expenditure, since subscriptions had already raised the remainder.[31] Applying to the Secretary of State for permission to establish a cemetery was simplicity itself compared with dealings with the Loan Board. Pateley Bridge explained to the vestry in 1873 that slow progress with the cemetery had been a consequence of the loan application. The PWLB had required copies of all Vestry minutes, copies of the placards advertising the vestries, plans describing the boundaries between Bewerley and Pateley Bridge, and a copy of the *London Gazette* indicating a parish boundary change. They also wanted full particulars of every rate levied in the town over the last three years. 'All these things necessitated not only a vast amount of labour in copying, but, which was of more importance, the loss of much valuable time, which might have been better employed in preparing the cemetery for interments.'[32] Harrogate Burial Board also fell at this hurdle, since its application to the Board contained an error relating to the amount of land it intended to purchase. It was informed in May 1863 that a fresh application would have to be made. Mr Powell, clerk to the Board, was sent to London to call in at the Home Office to secure a second letter confirming the proper quantity of land which was then sent to the solicitors of the Loan Office who 'had since wrote expressing themselves satisfied'.[33] Similarly, at New Malton, the Burial Board found that its loan application had been delayed because board membership had not been submitted to the required vestry vote.[34] It is ironic that Harrogate Burial Board had written to New Malton in 1862 seeking advice on that very matter.[35] Furthermore, both boards looked to secure additional loans since their original costings had proved to be underestimates; New Malton was perhaps fortunate in being able to secure this further loan from Earl Fitzwilliam. However, it also took what in retrospect was perhaps a brave step in re-approaching the PWLB in 1860 for a reduction in the interest rate payable, using the rather circuitous argument:

> being desirous of reducing as much as possible the expenses of providing and upholding the said new burial ground which fall upon the ratepayers of the said parishes and considering that the interest on the said loan which is fixed by the Security at £5 per cent per ann if reduced to £4 per cent per ann would be beneficial to such ratepayers are induced to memorialise your Lordship for a reduction of interest accordingly.[36]

Approval was granted.

Design and layout

Once finances had been secured, the burial board could consider cemetery design and the layout of the site. Where expenditure was laid out on chapel and/or lodges, then the burial boards announced an architectural competition – in the cases of Ripon and of Harrogate Grove Road these were advertised in the *Builder*. At Ripon more than twenty letters were received from architects applying for the plans in order to submit competition entries. Even at this stage there were quibbles related to the expected cost: for example, Frederick Peate complained that 'the amount allowed for forming and making roads, footpaths, shrubs &c is far too little' and there were problems in integrating into the design entrance gates already in the possession of the Corporation. This cost-saving measure was later abandoned.[37] As might be expected, once a design was decided on, further negotiation took place on price between the board, the vestry and the architect. As will be seen in the next chapter, cemetery chapels were of deep interest to bishops and archbishops, but Ministry 'Instructions' had nothing to say on this particular matter, beyond stressing that interment in chapels was forbidden.

Of greater import was the formal preparation of the cemetery for interment. Here, the 'Instructions' were voluble in recommendations on plot sizes. The guidance indicated that churchyard overcrowding had hindered effective decomposition, offering plot sizes 'no more than sufficient to hold the coffin'; as a consequence the ground became 'a mass of corruption' and 'saturated with organic matter' so slowing decomposition. A more sanitary approach would be to reduce the number of bodies in each grave and increase the size of each plot, so that decomposition would be swifter and the option to reuse the space more readily available.[38] Under the guidance, grave plots of 9ft by 4ft would be the new standard, reduced to 7ft by 3ft for a young adult and 5ft 9in by 2ft 9in for a child. Burial boards created cemeteries accordingly, laying out the ground and creating grave plans with numbered plots; in the site itself, each plot had the corresponding number on a metal marker.

Establishing bureaucratic processes

It was evident that this more scientific approach would require the development of expertise in terms of ongoing cemetery management. In 1843, John Claudius Loudon had anticipated in the employment of an office clerk to deal with the paperwork, and what he termed a cemetery 'curator' or gardener who would keep the ground 'in the neatest possible manner' and ensure that 'graves men' completed burials according to sanitary principles.[39] In North Yorkshire, boards were rather more likely to employ a single caretaker – who was essentially a sexton – whose work included the manual labour required to dig and maintain graves, and to keep the cemetery in order, and who was able to live in the lodge rent-free where one was built. Of greater importance in the long run was the employment of a clerk to the burial board. In the early years of the burial board, this individual had responsibility for putting together all the information needed for the board and site applications to the Secretary of State and, where required, to the PWLB; for notifying the vestry to set up a meeting when decisions had to be ratified; and for taking the meeting minutes and keeping accounts. The clerk was generally also asked to draw up a schedule of fees and a list of rules and regulations.

Once the cemetery was opened, the clerk or a newly appointed registrar continued to service the burial board but also to manage the cemetery, in keeping the relevant books in order. Parish burial registers recorded, for each interment, the name of the deceased, age, place of residence, date of burial and the name of the officiating minister. The bureaucracy attached to cemetery management was far more detailed. Indeed, it was very quickly the case that companies – such as Shaw and Sons of Fetter Lane, London – specialised in printing the required ledgers, of which there could be many: separate grave registers, ordered by grave number and listing the interments in each grave; a burial register which included all the usual headings found in a parish burial record plus the grave location and whether the interment was in consecrated or unconsecrated land; and account books. These records had to distinguish the fees that were payable to the burial board and those to which the local incumbent was entitled, in cases where interment had taken place in the consecrated section of the cemetery. Further paperwork was required for each funeral, as boards generally required the funeral director or family of the deceased to complete a notice of interment, which included details about the deceased, the time of the funeral and the officiating minister. Where the family had opted to purchase a burial right, then a burial rights register was generally kept. Issuing a burial right was a conveyance that fell under the Stamp Duty regulations, and so record had to be kept that the duty had been paid accordingly. Also, burial rights were a legal document: without the burial right, no one could prove that they had the right to burial in a particular 'purchased' or 'private' grave. Some boards offered the purchasers the option – on payment of a premium – a burial right printed on vellum. The transference of burial rights from one family member to another comprised another complex bureaucratic responsibility.

In these circumstances, it was perhaps small wonder that burial clerks frequently wrote to each other for advice and guidance. Records are not extant for the early years of Northallerton and Romanby Burial Board, but it was certainly the case that New Malton – also a 1850s board – received a number of enquiries from the boards established subsequently. The burial clerk, George Simpkin Cattle, attended the vestry meeting Norton held to discuss the establishment of a burial board there, and offered advice on finance.[40] Tables of fees were circulated readily, as were rules and regulations. For example, in the early 1860s, the burial clerk at New Malton sent a questionnaire to various burial boards in Yorkshire and Cleveland to ask about policy relating to Sunday burials, and received 24 responses.[41] Professionalised cemetery management was beginning to emerge, and manifested itself in the foundation of the National Association of Cemetery Superintendents, in 1913.

A centralising tendency?

It is at this stage that it becomes necessary to ask how far the procedure to establish burial boards constituted a kind of Foucauldian intervention in the development of 'governing

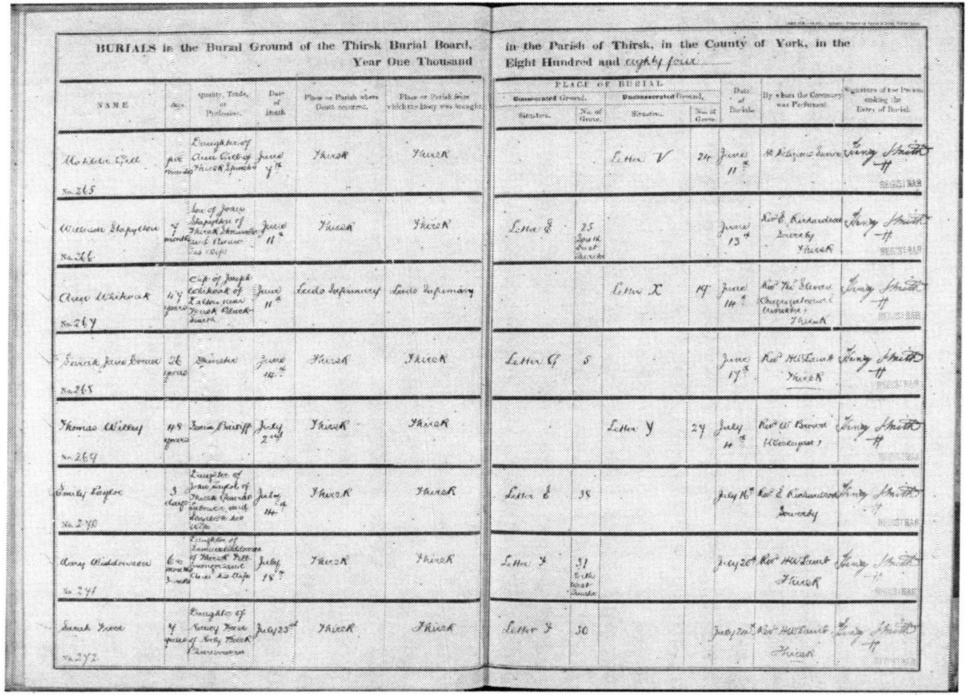

Plate 5.2 Thirsk Burial Board grave register. The bureaucratic regime of new cemetery management encouraged the emergence of the professionalised cemetery manager.

strategies that constituted and disciplined the modern subject through modern networks of power and knowledge',[42] in this case specifically, through scientific guidelines for the laying out of cemeteries and their management, and regulations suggested by Whitehall. Even in the market towns of North Yorkshire, burial board activity was closely monitored by the Burials Office, which required substantial information in order to approve a burial board, and then further and more technical detail on the proposed site before approving a cemetery. There is evidence from almost every site that an inspector from the Burials Office paid a visit. In his history of sanitary institutions, Sir John Simon noted that the centralising tendency was indeed problematic: 'in those early experimental days, neither legislators nor administrators had yet sounded the depths of the difficult problem of finding in local-government politics the happy mean between *too much* and *too little* of central interference'.[43] With regard to burial boards, the kind of interference is also of substantive importance. Central government did require compliance with a raft of bureaucratic and technical requirements, but it is notable that – beyond those contraventions relating to overly complex paperwork – errors tended to fall under the heading of insufficient *vestry* notification. The Burials Office required evidence that all substantive decisions had been subject to vestry vote, and that the vote had been called in the specified manner, to ensure maximum attendance. Essentially, the Burials Office required proof that decision-making had indeed taken place at a local level. In this regard, control of burial matters lay firmly at the parish rather than national level. It was perhaps both despite and because of the Burial Acts that local communities in the second half of the nineteenth century retained direct control of their burial space.

The 'novelty' of burial board cemeteries

Once a cemetery had opened for interment, the burial board had to make decisions with regard to its ongoing management. In analysing elements of this management, some commentators have noted 'the specific novelty of cemetery burial',[44] which provokes the essential question of how far burial board management practices constituted a radical change from churchyard interment. Presumptions of a distinct shift have generally been predicated on a false dichotomy, comparing largely London-based early nineteenth-century cemetery company practice with a rural churchyard 'ideal', where the company cemetery comprised a dynamic agency of modern capitalism and the churchyard presented as 'a world of stasis'.[45] Earlier chapters have indicated that the churchyard interment was not a somehow fixed and unchanging construct, and the incidence of churchyard burial did not come to an end with the introduction of the Burial Acts. As the nineteenth century progressed, churchyard management – particularly in later nineteenth-century extensions – could echo the essential principles of burial board cemetery management. Nevertheless, it is useful to unpick and examine three areas where behaviour might be deemed to have differed, and where new practices or – at the very least – a new tone is deemed to have emerged: the 'science' of grave use and in particular measures to hasten decomposition and effect the periodic reuse of graves; the end of the parish burial ground with its associated parochial burial rights; and behaviour relating to commemoration and the family grave.

Grave reuse and perpetuity burial

'Instructions to Burial Boards' was vociferous in its condemnation of the insanitary practices in the churchyards and small burial grounds in highly populated inner-city areas: grave spaces were only slightly larger than coffins; previous recent interments were cut through to make room; and pauper interments were accommodated in pits. Graves containing a dozen or more coffins were so intensive of land use that the soil was incapable of absorbing the mass of decaying matter and burials at the wrong depth either released 'effluvia' into the atmosphere because they were too shallow or again impeded decomposition because the ingress of air was prevented by excessive depth.[46] As a consequence the 'Instructions' proposed that burials would take place at a shallower depth and that 'no more than one body be buried in any grave at one time'. This was a 'fundamental principle'.[47] Reuse of the grave would happen only after complete decomposition had been effected. This period of time would be variable, depending on the soil type, but fourteen years was a generalised minimum period. An exception to this practice would be family graves, in which more than one burial in each grave might be permitted, although it was recommended that a family 'plot' would be preferable in which two or more graves were used in rotation.

The *Yorkshire Gazette* thought the new regulations were 'absurd', castigating both the single-body grave rule and 'that as the ground becomes filled, the original graves are to be re-opened and the remains of the dead disturbed'.[48] Complaints against the restrictions were also voiced in Norton as the vestry discussed the option of opening a burial board cemetery. The new regulations had been adopted for the earlier detached churchyard extension, and the vicar commented that the poorer parishioners could not reuse the same plot, which added substantially to the expense of burial: new graves were generally more expensive than re-opening an existing family grave. Furthermore, the measure lessened the possibility that families would be buried together: at Norton, one parishioner had five children interred in different parts of the site.[49]

There were two elements to the guidance on grave use offered by the 'Instructions'. First, there was a presiding principle that the grave would be used again following full decomposition of an earlier interment. Objection to the periodic reuse of graves could certainly not rest in this regulation running contrary to any churchyard tradition. In some areas, churchyards had been in use for centuries without any evident extension; and certainly the churchyards of Northallerton, Knaresborough and Ripon could not have accommodated the numbers they did without the land being used again perhaps within a generation. However, as Chapter 3 demonstrated, public opinion of a grave remaining 'inviolable' had certainly intensified from the 1820s. An unwillingness to disturb remains had been heightened not only by overcrowded burial conditions but also by the panic attached to the activity of body snatchers, who removed usually recently interred bodies and offered them for sale to medical schools. Early cemetery companies were particularly pointed in their promise of security. For example, the Liverpool Necropolis promised 'entire security against trespassers of any kind'.[50] In 1845, the City of Canterbury Cemetery Company declared that its ground would be 'faithfully preserved as a place of burial without desecration'; Hull General Cemetery in the same year guaranteed 'decent and undisturbed sepulture'.[51] Company cemeteries were promoted by their directors as places 'where the remains of themselves and their fellow citizens may repose undisturbed until the morning of resurrection'.[52]

It had not been possible to purchase exclusive burial rights in any part of the church or churchyard and be guaranteed that the grave would not at some juncture be used again. This kind of grave – purchased with a right to ensure exclusive use, and offered 'in perpetuity' – was offered by the private cemetery companies. Indeed, the Cemetery Clauses Act, 1847 had followed the lead of earlier private cemetery legislation in allowing the sale of exclusive burial rights 'either in perpetuity or for a limited time, and subject to such conditions as they [i.e. the cemetery owner] think fit'.[53] In this type of grave, no interment could take place without the permission of the owner of the burial rights, no matter how long a period of time had elapsed since the last interment: thus, without family permission, the grave could not be reused. Thus the government's intention to introduce a formalised system of grave reuse ran counter to new practices that themselves overturned a centuries-old custom. As the century progressed, ongoing tension continued between the intent of the guidance to reuse graves, and the exercising of preference to protect remains in perpetuity.

By 1872, the tone of government guidance had begun to shift in favour of public preference. In a revised 'Suggestions' to burial boards, it was noted that there was

> So strong and natural a repugnance to having the bones of the dead dug up, that the plan is frequently adopted of burying at a depth of eight to ten feet (if the ground be free from water), with the intention of opening the grave after a lapse of time, not quite to the original depth, but as nearly as is possible without digging up any bones that may remain; thus the same grave might be buried in many times before it becomes so full of bones as to be unfit for further use.[54]

Thus the 'Suggestions' hinted at a vague compromise, in which the grave was opened to admit further interment, but no bones were actually disturbed although it would remain the case that the grave might be buried in 'many times'.

A second element within the 'Instructions' guidance on grave use was to stress that no more than one body should be buried in each grave, in order to hasten decomposition. In 1872 the 'Suggestions' waspishly noted that 'the economy of burying several bodies in a grave at a time is more apparent than real', and objections to this plan were 'very serious'.[55] The tone reflected the fact that response to this element of the 'Instructions' had been varied. In New Malton, unpurchased graves were used as required, with a single interment in each plot.[56] This burial board was exceptional. At Pateley Bridge, from the inception of the cemetery in 1874, there were four burials in each unpurchased grave.[57] In 1888, the Northallerton and Romanby Burial Board recorded what may have been a shift in policy, in declaring that henceforth all unpurchased graves would be dug at 8ft to allow for further interment.[58] Thus, the science of new cemetery management aimed to trace a return to the tradition of grave reuse, but found itself overtaken. There were stronger new cultural preferences in favour of a system in which, once buried, bodies would remain undisturbed; and the sheer impracticality of permitting just one burial per grave where interments were numerous made this policy impossible to achieve.

The cemetery 'community'

A further way in which cemeteries were deemed to be a departure from the churchyard 'tradition' related to the community that the cemetery intended to serve. For Laqueur, the cemetery 'knew no natural bounds; nor would their inhabitants have known each other'; the churchyard, on the contrary, was 'for the people of the parish'.[59] To a large degree this presumption overlooks two factors. First, the cemetery was often established to accommodate a single parish. As has been seen, burial board establishment rested on vestry initiative, and was strongly integrated into parish government. Even where the parish contained a number of townships, the residents of the townships were often reliant on the 'mother' church for burial space. Under the Burial Acts, consecration of part of the site essentially added that section to the burial space of the ecclesiastical parish. The cemetery *was* parish burial ground.

Furthermore, the vestry took active steps to limit the 'catchment' area of the cemetery so that only local parishioners would be included. Where a ratepayer democracy held sway, as was the case in Victorian England, then the associated services would be restricted to the use of those ratepayers. The distinctions became marked when cases arose to test the definition of 'parishioner' and the right to local burial. This was the case with both churchyard and cemetery. For example, in Easingwold in 1857 the Reverend

Henry Aislie had only lately come to the parish when he had to attend to the burial of an inmate from Easingwold workhouse. Although the woman was the responsibility of Newton-on-Ouse parish, Aislie had charged the parishioner rate, not having had chance to research local practice. However he later revised his policy and, following a complaint by the manager of the workhouse, explained his position: 'I claim double fees, because the double fee is a prohibiting tax, intended to preserve the use of the churchyard to the parishioners alone.' Furthermore, he wrote that pauper inmates were not parishioners, not 'in the ordinary and full meaning of the title'. A double fee had to be paid, 'otherwise the erection of a Union House in any parish, especially in a town, would be very prejudicial to the rights of the parishioners in their churchyard'.[60] Where churchyards were becoming very full, applying an excessive 'prohibiting tax' to deter non-parishioners from using the site was a common strategy. In Hunsingore in 1853, the Reverend H. Bellairs wrote in the parish notebook: 'In consequence of the burial ground being too full, I hereby August 16th 1852 order and direct that no burial of a non-parishioner be allowed from this time unless a fee of £1 instead of 1s be paid.'[61]

Burial boards were directed by a similar imperative, which meant that disincentives applied where a non-parishioner sought interment. Even the owners of purchased graves were generally 'not entitled to have interred therein any parishioner not being husband or wife or indirect ascent or descent of blood relationship or nephew or niece' without the consent of the burial board.[62] Again, there could be confusion with definition. In 1883, Northallerton and Romanby Burial Board sought guidance from the Secretary of State for a judgement on residency where a baby born in Northallerton prison had died, but whose mother was deemed not to be of the parish.[63] All the burial boards either added 50 per cent or doubled the relevant fees where an interment took place that was not local. The burial board cemetery was indeed very firmly and even exclusively for those 'of this parish'.

Social display

A third area in which cemeteries were deemed to be quite different from churchyards rested in the opportunities offered for the display of wealth and social standing, compared with the disrespect routinely meted out to the economically weak and marginal. In 1883, the vicar at Norton was quite adamant that the cemetery at New Malton was for the 'well-to-do' with rates that were too prohibitive for the poor of the parish, who remained the responsibility of the church. He described the common practice of poorer families of 'putting boards up, on which ill-formed letters were written, and little wood kerbings which in time became detached and rotten'. He believed that this informality, contributing to the unkempt appearance of the churchyard, was not likely to be tolerated in a cemetery.[64] It remains to be asked, therefore, what the cemetery offered to the 'well-to-do', and what was available to the poorer members of the community and in which ways these 'offers' differed from the churchyard.

It is undeniable that the cemetery comprised space in which the expression of social difference and more elaborate commemorative practice could be accommodated and even encouraged. In Knaresborough, Pateley Bridge and St Mary's, Harrogate, three classes of graves existed, depending on location within the site. Pateley Bridge even provided an additional 'select' class of interments, for £9 8s. Beyond site location, purchasers could also choose to upgrade from an ordinary earthen grave to a vault or bricked grave. At New Malton, the laying out of the cemetery included the setting aside of a portion where bricked graves and vaults would be ready-built, and at Grove Road, Harrogate, an ongoing contract was arranged with a local mason to ensure that these would always be available. It is understandable that the creation of built infrastructure should carry a cost to the purchaser of a particular type of grave, but it was also the case that fees were charged for permission to erect kerbsets, headstones above a particular size and palisades. Indeed, these fees could look rather bewildering and not a little random: in Knaresborough, for example, fees included a charge of 7s 6d for the erection of headstones not exceeding 4½ft; palisading not exceeding 2ft 6in high around a single grave cost £1 1s; 2s 6d was payable for additional inscription on a memorial after the first; and 'all other memorials of whatever description' carried a fee of £2 2d.[65] In the churchyard, these fees were an understandable style of 'prohibitive tax', and could be equally complex. However, in the cemetery where – ostensibly – space was plentiful, then the rationale for the charges appeared thin.

It is possible, as Sarah Tarlow suggests, to be rather transfixed by the sudden extravagance of monumentation in the nineteenth century and its meanings in terms of the dynamics of power. In the nineteenth century, commercial consumption was not always about class and in the case of funerary expenditure it is easy to lose an appreciation of its emotional underpinning.[66] So much writing on burial practice has simply overlooked the desire for family unity in death. In Leathley, the parish notebook included a request from Reverend Henry Canham, brother of the previous incumbent, who asked his successor, simply 'when I am dead lay my bones beside his bones'.[67] By the second half of the nineteenth century, this desire was becoming more achievable. In churchyard extensions it was often recorded where a new grave had been dug to double depth to ensure further burial – usually of a spouse – in the same grave. However, for those able to pay, cemeteries offered the certainty that families could be buried together, as the purchaser of a right of burial decided who should be interred in a particular grave. Beyond this key principle, above-ground monuments reflected little more than personal taste and income. Indeed, Buckham provided a useful corrective in demonstrating that, for York Cemetery, 'elite' families tended to purchase modest headstones, similar to other families. In some instances, private graves had no memorials at all.[68]

It is usually considered that improved conditions for the 'rich' generally meant deliberate degradation for the poor, and that the cemetery was another instrument of humiliation and punishment for the socially marginal. There is a tendency here to conflate issues. The 'package' of welfare offered to the destitute under the Poor Law was designed on the principle of less eligibility, and a deliberately degrading funeral was often part of that package, although practices could vary.[69] Poor law guardians were encouraged to negotiate a good deal for burial contracts, and cemeteries met demand for intensively used and unmarked burial space. Indeed, studies have shown that some cemetery companies did particularly well in this line of business.[70] It is necessary to stress that, after 1834, paupers would be afforded limited respect in both churchyard and in cemetery. A more cogent question is to consider the treatment of the poorer classes who were seeking decent but affordable burial. It would be a mistake to presume that, for families with restricted income, the cemetery constituted an essentially 'alienating' environment that was markedly different from the churchyard or indeed from any circumstance in which rates of consumption would be variable according to a family's resources. It seems perverse to presume that the cemetery should in some manner be egalitarian, when no other aspect of social life carried that characteristic. Furthermore, as Strange argues, a whole range of mourning rites – from the most elaborate and costly to the simplest – carried emotional meaning.[71] Here, it is perhaps illuminating to review two areas: cost, and restrictions on commemoration and preference that might be directed at the lower-priced burials.

In theory, churchyard interment carried no cost to parishioners: under ancient canon law, such fees were deemed 'simonical' since consecrated ground was *res sacæ*. However, since the Reformation it had been the case that clergy could demonstrate that a charge was due, 'by custom'.[72] Cressy notes that, by the seventeenth century, in some areas a voluntary system of 'tipping' the clergy had become formalised into fee tables, and disputes could arise in which clergy refused burial without payment of a fee.[73] Practice was extremely variable across regions: some dioceses retained the ancient principle that a fee should not be charged, although it was commented in 1897 that 'the spirit that dictated those early canons does not seem now to prevail'.[74] Even within North Yorkshire, terriers indicate variation, but some kind of fee was generally required for one or more aspects of the burial. So, for example, incumbents charged a 'surplice' fee of between 1s and 6s for taking the burial service. An additional fee for the erection of any monument might also be charged. A further fee was payable to the sexton for digging the grave and perhaps also for tolling the bell, and in some instances a small charge was made by the parish clerk. The use of the parish hearse and pall might also increase the cost. The establishment of a burial board cemetery meant that aspects of these fee charges were also applicable in the consecrated section of the new cemetery, since it constituted parish burial ground. Further, the Burial Act 1857 ordered that fees must be identical in consecrated and unconsecrated sections; and all fees were in any case subject to Secretary of State approval.[75] In some places, therefore, the range of burial board fees could reflect the complexity of existing churchyard fee structures.

However, this was not always the case. In Norton, the vicar had been apprehensive about the laying out of a cemetery, which be believed would take the burial fees out of reach of those 'in an humbler sphere of life'.[76] The difficulty lay in the fact that a churchyard and burial board interments were charged in slightly different ways. The minister's fees were the same as in the churchyard, but in the cemetery a fee was always payable for the burial. Even where the grave was 'common' – also termed confusingly 'unpurchased' – and shared with other, unrelated individuals, a fee was still payable and included the administrative costs. The cost of digging might also be defined as a further, additional fee. 'Private' or 'purchased' graves were more expensive, in carrying with them the right to exclusive use.

It has been noted that burial boards generally circulated information on fees charged, and this was the case at Pateley Bridge where in 1874 the burial clerk visited Otley, Wetherby, Harrogate and Bingley. His conclusion from these visits and fee tables from other locations was that 'in all those towns they had a system of public graves in which interments were made at a merely nominal rate, in many cases the charge being only 7s 6d including digging, the ground and minister's fee'. However, at Pateley Bridge, the fourth-class graves – which were the cheapest, aside from the pauper rate – had been initially set at 19s, which included 7s 6d for the ground, 5s for the minister and 6s 6d for the sexton. Board members themselves complained that this fee was considered 'so high that poor people could not possibly pay them', but it was decided only to halve the minister's fee.[77] The Secretary of State wrote reminding the board that vestry approval was needed for the fees, which needed to be 'publically promulgated' so any objection could be launched and, indeed, objections were. The high fee was one of the reasons why the Board's elections proved so fractious in 1876, and explains why the cemetery did little business in its early years, with some parishioners preferring to seek interment in churchyards in the surrounding villages.

Pateley Bridge was certainly expensive, in offering basic interment for the revised fee of 16s 6d. But it is clear that costs could be remarkably variable. St Mary's, Harrogate, charged 12s 6d for a basic 'package' of 10s for a common grave, inclusive of excavation and location chosen by the Board, and a fee to the minister of 2s 6d if the funeral took place within a specified time slot. Knaresborough was cheaper, offering single interments – again with no choice of location – at 5s, with a fee to the minister again set at 2s 6d, with a total cost of 7s 6d; Thirsk Burial Board set the same rate.[78] The high levels of variation and the opaque nature of churchyard fees make comparison less than straightforward. Certainly it appears that burial board fees could be higher than those that might be charged for churchyard interment. However, it is difficult – in the absence of evidence – to assess how this situation was viewed by the poorer members of the community. The churchyard might be cheaper, but in locations such as Northallerton, Knaresborough and Ripon, where there was substantial pressure on space, the quality of the landscape must have offered little consolation. Furthermore, as Strange's work on working-class funerary practice indicates, poorer families had rather more agency within cemetery space than might be supposed: when families were able to purchase grave rights, these became significant financial and cultural currency.[79]

Much has also been made of the restricted commemorative options that were available to the poor in cemeteries. The assumption that the cemetery repressed 'any personal significance or individuality' by 'restricting distinctive identities to those who could afford a headstone'[80] contains the presumption that such class demarcation was absent in the churchyard, or that alternative strategies of commemoration were not available. For example, it remained the case that graves in cemeteries were marked by mounds, as they had been in the churchyard. The 1850s guidance had pointedly indicated that mounds – in heaping additional soil above a grave – essentially created a deep grave which hindered decomposition and so should be avoided. However, mounds remained a feature of cemeteries, which made it possible for a bereaved family to return to a particular spot and lay flowers or other items. Indeed, through the twentieth century, the creation of the 'lawned' grave resulted from the concerted attempt of cemetery managers to remove mounds and flatten the landscape.[81] Furthermore, the fact that a cemetery often charged a fee to 'garden' a grave did not mean that families could not plant flowers themselves. In New Malton in 1860, the Burial Board received a letter from a Mr Wrigglesworth asking for permission to place a stone kerb around the grave of his child. The request was denied because the grave was not purchased, but Mr Wrigglesworth was informed that he was at liberty to plant up the grave.[82] Furthermore, although the cemetery generally forbade the erection of complex stone or brickwork on unpurchased grave, headstones were not forbidden.[83] In Northallerton, it was acknowledged that people buying unpurchased graves 'may yet desire to be buried close to their friends'. As a consequence the Board advertised its intent to leave – as long as was practical – a vacant space by the side of each unpurchased grave for the purpose of interring near relatives.[84]

The willingness of burial boards to offer concessions was also evident in the ability to hold funerals on Sundays. This was a preferred day for families on lower incomes, since it meant that those attending the funeral would not lose wages as a consequence. The burial board at New Malton had canvassed opinion on the matter in 1866, and found that of 22 responses, 21 burial boards allowed Sunday burial, although in a couple of cases it was clear that the preference was against this practice. Indeed, Scarborough imposed an additional fee for Sunday funerals of 10s 6d and double fees to the sexton.[85] However, as the response from Sunderland indicated,

> altho' we would wish to discourage Sunday interments and abolish them entirely it is feared that such a step would lead to much dissatisfaction among our numerous working class, who prefer the Sunday for the purpose, as they do not lose any wages in that case and can gather their friends together afterwards (which in the minds of others is a practice leading to great evil and the chief reason for making a change but still one that among themselves is universally upheld) that it would be found impossible to contend against it.[86]

Generally speaking, however, boards responding to the survey indicated that Sundays were available for interment as was the case with any other day. Overall, therefore, it is clear that there could be flexibility and compassion within an ostensibly rigid framework. Arguably, cemeteries presented opportunities that had been less certain in the churchyard, in granting to lower-income groups a guarantee of close family burial with the option of some form of commemoration.

Reviewing practice in the rural rather than principally urban context does allow reflection on the probability that burial practice in the city was driven by rather harsh exigencies. Ratepayers were vastly outnumbered by non-ratepayers, pauperism was endemic and vestries consequently had limited resources. City cemeteries were slowly crammed to capacity, in the same way that urban housing was massively overcrowded. There needed to be more stringent application of regulations on issues such as memorialisation, as pressure to reuse grave spaces was substantially higher. Common graves were deeper in the big cities, and contained many more burials, as later government reports indicated.[87] However, the urban cemeteries were simply replicating practices in their churchyard predecessors. Indeed, it could be argued that the churchyard 'idyll' had not been a reality for much of central London for quite some time, and in the larger cities – such as Manchester, Birmingham and Liverpool – it was probably a relief to all classes when the old churchyards were closed.

Conclusion

The question remains why a community might choose to establish a burial board, when the process was so onerous in terms of bureaucracy with an outcome little different from the existing churchyard. Some communities were able to meet burial need through periodic extension of the churchyard. This strategy had been successful – in the medium term – in the larger settlements of Ripon and Knaresborough, where pressure on burial space was substantial. Finance was almost always a deciding factor for vestries, and the creation of a burial board did create a structure in which ratepayers could share the cost equitably. Churchyard extension relied heavily on the goodwill of leading landowners, and on voluntary subscriptions which were generally augmented by the incumbent themselves. In terms of scale, churchyard extensions tended to be small, at no more than an acre, and the prospect of increasing space incrementally – with the concomitant expense of rebuilding the wall – was perhaps not welcome. There are indications that Church management of burial space was not always desirable politically, and these will be explored in more detail in the next chapter.

In considering the wider picture, it is clear that the cemetery did not necessarily constitute a radical disruption in burial tradition in the second half of the nineteenth century. Substantive elements of burial board management were grounded in local control of burial space and of the centrality of parish and community. Although the State was entirely present in all aspects of burial board activity, the largely permissive nature of much of the legislation meant that more intrusive guidance on the scientific management of burial space could simply be disregarded. Thus cemetery space was little different from churchyard space in many respects, and indeed burial boards borrowed heavily from churchyard traditions. Where change was evident, it was evident across all kinds of burial space – churchyard and cemetery – and included the desire both to achieve control of family burial space and to establish a grave in perpetuity. All providers of burial space were fully aware of the opportunities to maximise income from burials, particularly with regard to charges to erect memorials. It was perhaps this latter development that was to prove the more explosive issue in the longer term, and helped to undermine public acceptance of the continued hold of the Church of England on local burial space. However, the next chapter will consider the wider play of religious politics, which constituted an essential context for change in burial practice in the second half of the nineteenth century.

Notes

1 BI, PR/NORT, Vestry minutes, 1867–1933, 1882.
2 C. Hamlin, 'Muddling in bumbledom: on the enormity of large sanitary improvements in four British towns, 1855–1885', *Victorian Studies*, 32:1 (1988), p. 83.
3 M. Ragon, *The Space of Death: A Study of Funerary Architecture, Decoration and Urbanism*, trans. Alan Sheridan (Charlottesville, VA: University Press of Virginia, 1983), p. 40.
4 Burial Act (1857), s. 4; NYRO, BB/HRG, Harrogate Burial Board minutes, 1861–91, 6 Aug 1861.
5 NYRO, BB/HRG, Harrogate Burial Board minutes, 1861–91, 4 Oct 1861.
6 Burial Act (1853), s. 7.
7 Burial Act (1860), s. 4.
8 Burial Act (1852), s. 10.
9 Burial Act (1852), s. 10.
10 NYRO, PR/KN 3/1/3, Vestry minutes, 1862–1895, letter dated 20 Feb 1873 and pasted into vestry minute book.
11 NYRO, BB/AYG 1/1, Great Ayton and Little Ayton Burial Board/Committee, Minute Books 1881–1894, 31 Mar 1881.
12 NYRO, BB/PAT, Minute Books, 1871–1963, 27 Jan 1872.
13 NYRO, BB/PAT, Minute Books, 1871–1963, Jun to Dec 1872, passim.
14 NYRO, BB/HRG, Harrogate Burial Board minutes, 1861–91, 16 Aug 1861.
15 NYRO, DC/NRU, Minute book, Norton Burial Board Committee, 1883–1915, 22 Jun 1883.
16 NYRO, PR/KN 3/1/3, Vestry minutes, 1862–1895, Jan 1877.
17 NYRO, BB/PAT, Minute Book, 1871–1963, inserted undated, unsourced newspaper clipping, probably April 1876.
18 NYRO, DC/NRU, Norton Burial Board Committee, Jun 1884.
19 NYRO, BB/HRG, Harrogate Burial Board minutes, 1861–91, Oct 1861–Sep 1862, passim.
20 NA, HO 45/4460, Letter of appointment of Dr Sutherland; *Yorkshire Gazette*, 20 Oct 1855.
21 Regulations of the Secretary of State for the Home Department, 'Instructions for Burial Boards in Providing Cemeteries and making arrangement for interments under the Burial Acts 15 & 16 Vict. cap. 85., and 16 &17 Vict. cap. 134'. Reprinted in William Cunningham Glen, *The Burial Board Acts of England and Wales* (London: Shaw and Sons, 1858). Hereafter referred to as 'Instructions'.
22 NYRO, BB/PAT (Minute Books, 1871–1963), 21 Feb 1872.

23 BI, PR/NORT, Vestry minutes, 1867–1933, 18 Feb 1884.
24 NYRO, PR/HRG, M, 1/5/1, Vestry meeting Minute Book, 1830–1988, 28 Oct 1869.
25 Boroughbridge Town Council, Aldborough Vestry Minute Book, 1849–1957, 25 Jan 1872.
26 NYRO, PR/HRG, M, 1/5/1, Vestry Meeting Minute Book, 1830–1988. At front: proposed plan of burial ground, 28 Oct 1869.
27 NYRO, BB/AYG 1/1, Minute Books 1881–1894, May 1882–July 1882, passim.
28 1876 (269) *Public Works Loan Board. First annual report of the Public Works Loan Board.*
29 J. Prest, *Liberty and Locality: Parliament, Permissive Legislation and Ratepayers' Democracies in the Nineteenth Century* (Oxford: Clarendon Press, 1990).
30 *Public Works Loan Board. First annual report*, p. 20.
31 Boroughbridge Town Council, Aldborough Vestry Minute Book, 1849–1957, 11 Dec 1871.
32 NYRO, BB/PAT, Minute Books, 1871–1963, unsourced undated newspaper report of vestry meeting, 1873.
33 NYRO, BB/HRG, Harrogate Burial Board minutes, 1861–91, 6 May 1863.
34 NYRO, BB/MLN 1/1, Minute Book, 1858–1894, 15 Aug 1859.
35 NYRO, BB/MNL 2/1, Correspondence, general, 1859–1874, Letter from Mr Powell to New Malton Burial Board, dated 29 Sep 1862.
36 NYRO, BB/MLN 3/4, Memorial of burial board to Treasury regarding reduction of mortgage, 20 Aug 1860.
37 NYRO, DC/RIC II 9/26/31–33 and 33–66, Ripon Cemetery, passim.
38 'Instructions', Regulation 17.
39 J. C. Loudon, *On the Laying Out, Planting and Managing of Cemeteries; and on the Improvement of Churchyards* (London: Longman, Brown, Green, 1843), pp. 65–6.
40 BI: PR/NORT 35, Vestry meetings, 1867–1933, unsourced newspaper clipping, 22 Jun 1883.
41 NYRO, BB/MLN 2/2, Interment on Sundays, 1860.
42 A. Herman, 'Death has a touch of class: society and space in Brookwood Cemetery, 1853–1903', *Journal of Historic Geography*, 36:3 (2010), p. 312.
43 J. Simon, *English Sanitary Institutions* (London: Cassell and Co., 1970 [1890]), p. 222, underlining original.
44 T. Laqueur, 'Cemeteries, religion and the culture of capitalism' in Garnett, J. and Matthew, C. (eds), *Revival and Religion since 1700* (London: Hambleton Press, 1993), p. 185.

45 *Ibid.*, p. 186.
46 'Instructions', Regulation 18.
47 'Instructions', Regulation 19.
48 *Yorkshire Gazette*, 20 Oct 1855.
49 BI, PR/NORT 35, Vestry meeting minutes, 1867–1929, undated unsourced newspaper clipping, from 1882.
50 *Liverpool Mercury*, 19 Sep 1823.
51 *Kentish Gazette*, 9 Sep 1845; Hull Record Office, Hull General Cemetery Company, Registered Provisionally, 1845.
52 York City Archives, Annual Report of the York Public Cemetery Company, 1850.
53 Cemetery Clauses Act (1847), s. 40.
54 'Suggestions to burial boards providing and managing burial grounds, and making arrangements for interments by the Inspector under the Burial Acts 1853–55, 1857–59, 1860, and 1871'. Reprinted in Brooke Little, J. *The Law of Burial* (London: Shaw and Sons, 3rd edn, 1902), hereafter referred to as 'Suggestions', p. 704.
55 *Ibid.*, p. 705.
56 Malton Town Council, New Malton Burial Register.
57 Harrogate District Council, Pateley Bridge Burial Register.
58 NYRO, BB/NO 1/1, Minute book, 1872–1893, 11 Jul 1888.
59 Laqueur, 'Cemeteries, religion and the culture of capitalism', p. 186.
60 BI, PR/EAS 212, Fees for the burial of paupers from the union workhouse, letter from the Reverend H. Aislie, 8 Jun 1857.
61 NYRO, PR/HSG 5/3, Hunsingore Parochialia, 1855–1966, unpaginated.
62 NYRO, BB/MLN 4/1/1–4, Draft rules and regulations. This quotation relates to New Malton, but the regulation was commonplace amongst burial boards.
63 NYRO, BB/NO 1/1, Minute Book, 1872–1893, 10 Oct 1883.
64 BI, PR/NORT, Vestry minutes, 1867–1933, 1883.
65 NYRO, DC/RIC II 9/26/1–29, Other cemeteries, handbill for Knaresborough Cemetery, 1889.
66 S. Tarlow, 'Each slow dusk a drawing-down of blinds', *Archaeological Review from Cambridge*, 11:1 (1992), 125–40.
67 NYRO, PR/LTH 7/3, Register of grave spaces, informal notes at the back of the notebook.
68 S. Buckham, 'Delusions of grandeur? The influence of company management, civic pride and private sentiment upon the cemetery landscape at York' in Denk, C. and Ziesemer, J. (eds), *Der*

Bürgerliche Tod: Städtische Bestattungskultur von der Aufklärung bis zum Frühen 20. Jarhundert (München: ICOMOS, 2007).

69 A. Crowther, *The Workhouse System, 1834–1929* (London: Batsford, 1981); E. Hurren and S. King, '"Begging for a burial": form, function and conflict in nineteenth-century pauper burial', *Social History*, 30:3 (2005), 321–41.

70 Herman, 'Death has a touch of class',' p. 310.

71 J.-M. Strange, *Death, Grief and Poverty in Britain, 1870–1914* (Cambridge: Cambridge University Press, 2005), p. 155.

72 See judgement by Lord Stowell in *Gilbert* vs *Buzzard*, 1820, quoted in Brook Little, *Law of Burial*, p. 44.

73 D. Cressy, *Birth, Marrriage and Death: Ritual, Religion and the Life-Cycle in Tudor and Stuart England* (Oxford: Oxford University Press, 1999).

74 Sir W. Harcourt, *Hansard* HC Debate, vol. 31 col. 514, 6 Mar 1895.

75 Burial Act (1857), s. 17; Burial Act (1855), s. 7.

76 BI, PR/NORT, Vestry minutes, 1867–1933, 1883.

77 NYRO, BB/PAT, Minute Books, 1871–1963, 7 Nov 1874.

78 NYRO, BB/TH 10/1, Table of fees dated 1879.

79 Strange, *Death, Grief and Poverty*, chapter six, passim.

80 Herman, 'Death has a touch of class', 306.

81 J. Rugg, 'Lawn cemeteries: the emergence of a new landscape of death', *Urban History*, 33:2 (2006), 213–33.

82 NYRO, BB/MLN 1/1, Minute Book, 1858–1894, 18 Mar 1860.

83 NYRO, BB/MLN 4/1/1–4, Draft rules and regulations.

84 NYRO, BB/MLN 4/2/1–6, Other authorities, undated copy of Northallerton and Romanby Burial Board regulations.

85 NYRO, BB/MLN 2/2, Interment on Sundays, 1860, letter from Scarborough Burial Board, dated 8 Nov 1866.

86 NYRO, BB/MLN 2/2, Interment on Sundays, 1860, letter from Sunderland Burial Board, dated 3 Nov 1866.

87 1890–1 (30) *Cemeteries (provincial towns).*

6

'No differences are so deep as those which arise over the grave':[1] *the religious politics of burial*

It has been commented – not least by this writer – that the introduction of the cemetery undermined the Church of England's near-monopoly of burial provision. Evidence from changing burial provision in North Yorkshire provokes a return to that supposition, and raises the question of how far the Church of England did indeed lose control of burial space in the second half of the nineteenth century. This chapter will consider two of the key mechanisms for this shift of fortunes for the Church: the introduction of cemeteries under the Burial Acts and the passage of the Burial Laws Amendment Act 1880, which allowed Nonconformist ministers to conduct burials in churchyards and in the consecrated sections of cemeteries. Additional legislation that established cemeteries outside the Burial Acts and reduced the power of the local vestry will be discussed in more detail in the following chapter. Central North Riding presents an interesting case study area in which to watch the unfolding of these regulations. In the village of Topcliffe – like so many in this area – the Saxon church of St Columba squares up to the substantial Wesleyan Methodist Chapel, built in 1840. When asked on the Bishop's visitation return in 1868 what obstacles lay in his ministry, the vicar of Topcliffe stated simply, 'the difficulty is to find a churchman'.[2] In an area where

Nonconformity had taken such a strong hold, it might be presumed that any threat to Church of England monopolies would be exploited with vigour.

Again this chapter provides a reminder that scrutinising the local response to legislation is the only way in which its impact can be judged. Although the extension of the churchyard was the most common way to provide new burial space in smaller settlements, burial boards predominated in the market towns which were notable for adherence to both Old and New Dissent. Independents – always the vanguard in matters of burial reform – were active in Helmsley, Pickering, Great Ayton and other locations in which change in burial provision was accompanied by religious political tension. For burial boards, conflict and consternation were likely to arise on the consecration of the site, the building of chapels for both Nonconformist and Anglican burial services and the allotment of land between different denominations. Where records exist for the case study burial boards, there is evidence of difficulty in negotiating the complex religious politics involved. However, it is not necessarily the case that the Church of England lost ground as a consequence. Indeed, much as Nonconformist burial reformers at the time feared, under the Burial Acts a new supply of consecrated burial space was funded through the secular rates. Nevertheless, analysis of burial registers demonstrates that, in a number of market towns, non-Anglicans did indeed make use of unconsecrated ground, although the proportions of interments in these sections were remarkably variable.

This chapter also considers local responses to the Burial Laws Amendment Act of 1880, as indicated in the parish burial register. It might be supposed that in villages throughout North Yorkshire, where the numeric and economic strength of Methodism had led to the building and rebuilding of hundreds of Wesleyan and Primitive Methodist chapels, the opportunities presented by the Act would have been understood and exploited. In a 1981 study of

Methodism, Nigel Scotland indicated that rural Methodists 'had learned to wrestle with the clergyman and his farmer-dominated vestry over the control of education, the churchyard and the distribution of village charities'.[3] For Timothy Larson, Primitive Methodists felt the impact of burial grievances more strongly than any other Nonconformist group, with the exception of Baptists.[4] Both these comments intimate that Methodists were involved in localised burial controversy. However, there was in central North Yorkshire a more muted reaction to the opportunities presented by the Burial Laws Amendment Act. In explanation, it may be possible that limited take-up reflected the nature of Methodist organisation: in dispersed rural areas particularly, there may have been no Methodist minister *in situ* to perform funeral services, and ministers who were available were simply not conversant with local funerary tradition. Furthermore, the fact that Anglican clergy often served for long periods in the same parish added a degree of comfort in continuity that in smaller settlements perhaps carried a greater weight than the desire to express religious political independence.

Non-Anglican worship in North Yorkshire

According to the religious census of 1851, the index of attendance at places of worship in Yorkshire on the census Sunday was highest in North Riding, at 63.6 per cent, with East Riding at 58.8 per cent and West Riding at 52.9 per cent.[5] Attendance in individual towns and villages within North Riding could be very high: the registration district of Bedale, for example, had 79.1 per cent, compared with Northallerton's 57.0 per cent. However, it was attendance at chapel rather than church that was the key characteristic of North Yorkshire observance. The religious census indicated that a total of 41.6 per cent of attendances were in Church of England churches, but 45.4 per cent were in Methodist chapels.[6] In Pateley Bridge registration district, where

Methodist adherence was strongest, 76.9 per cent of worshippers were of that denomination, with just 22.6 per cent designated Church of England (see Table 6.1). However, in many places, attendance at more than one type of service was common: in Helmsley in 1870, Newton Mant noted that 'there was only one "church" family who did not also attend the meeting houses'.[7]

Table 6.1 Religious census 1851: index of attendance at selected locations (%)

Registration district	*Church of England*	*Methodists*			*Roman Catholic*	*Other*	*Total number of worshippers*
		Wesleyan	*Primitive*	*Other*			
Bedale	50.7	35.3	6.6	–	1.0	6.3	3787
Easingwold	52.3	36.4	6.7	1.3	3.2	–	4279
Helmsley	39.7	46.0	8.4	2.4	3.1	0.3	4184
Knaresborough	45.1	34.5	7.7	8.6	3.0	0.9	9179
Malton	38.1	34.9	15.4	5.1	2.8	3.8	7222
Northallerton	51.7	20.4	18.2	–	0.4	9.1	4944
Pateley Bridge	22.6	43.1	33.8	–	–	0.7	2907
Pickering	35.3	32.6	26.4	–	–	0.3	3767
Ripon	45.7	28.5	7.9	7.5	3.8	6.5	6111
Stokesley	43.8	25.6	21.1	4.4	0.8	4.3	2464
Thirsk	45.7	37.7	6.8	6.7	1.5	1.5	5234

Source: W. Shiels and R. Lawton, 'The Religious Census of 1851', in Butlin, R. (ed.), *Historical Atlas of North Yorkshire* (Otley: Westbury, 2003), p. 139.

Everett makes a connection between 'decayed' market towns and Nonconformity, and it was certainly the case that Dissent was pronounced in, for example, Kirkbymoorside, Pickering, Helmsley, Great Ayton and Easingwold.[8] In central North Riding, small and scattered villages constitute the commonest settlement patterns but, nevertheless, Dissent permeated even the most dispersed rural areas. Archbishop's visitation returns for the Diocese of York in 1868 give the impression of livings and churches which had been neglected for some time and where interest had recently revived, but, in the meantime, Dissent had proliferated. The Return asked incumbents the question: 'What Dissenting places of worship are there, and what is the probable number of Dissenters in your Parish or Chapelry?' For 127 of the parishes making returns and that are also included in this study, only 12 wrote that there were no Nonconformist chapels in their parish, and that either there were no Dissenters or the number was negligible. In 23 parishes, Dissenters comprised a minority – for example, in Bossal, Skipton and Coxwold. For around a quarter of the parishes – 34 – Dissenters were thought to comprise at least 'half the parish' or were in the majority. For example, in the Wolds village of Butterwick, the Reverend J. L. S. Hatton noted that no chapel had been built 'but the few cottages there are, are chiefly Dissenters'. In close to half the parishes, vicars noted that there were one or more chapels: in fact, the Returns indicated the existence of over 170 Methodist chapels in the 127 parishes. However, it was not always possible for the vicar to estimate numbers. The Reverend R. Skelton in Rosedale – where Dissent was particularly strong – noted tersely 'Cannot tell what is the number of Dissenters. I never go to a Dissenting place of worship.'[9]

Thus, Nonconformity – and particularly Wesleyan Methodism – was strong in North Yorkshire. However, in a number of cases vicars noted that chapel-goers continued to attend Church services and were in many instances communicants. Indeed, the Dissenters themselves were thought to underplay their Nonconformity. In East Acklam, the Reverend Thomas Briarly Browne commented that 'perhaps three quarters are Dissenters, though many of these attend our Church service'; in Dalby, the Primitive Methodists were 'all well disposed to the church'; and in Seamer-in-Cleveland 'There are a few Wesleyans in the parish who meet at their Minister's house but as soon as the church bells ring they come to church and have good attendance at sacraments'. Thus it appeared common for Dissenting families also to attend at the Church, and for Church-goers to attend chapel: according to Reverend William Abbey at Salton, 'no lines can be drawn'.[10]

Burial grounds in North Yorkshire

Although the Church of England had a strong hold on burial provision in the nineteenth century, its monopoly was not quite complete since a number of denominations also had burial space attached to their churches, chapels and meeting houses. Nationally, the pattern of 'alternative' provision is highly diverse, region by region. In central North Riding, the principal Protestant Nonconformist denominations – Methodism, Congregationalism and Quakerism – had some access to independent burial provision, but this was remarkably limited.

Methodists

Perhaps most surprising is the fact that the number of Methodist burial grounds was tiny, given the strength of the denomination in the area. Hundreds of chapels were built and rebuilt in the area throughout the nineteenth century but only a handful had attached burial space; all these were Wesleyan Methodists. Of the very many eighteenth-century Methodist chapels, only those at West Tanfield and Tockwith had an attached burial ground in operation by 1850. In Tockwith, there was no Anglican church, and so the fact that a burial ground was attached to the Wesleyan chapel appears to require no explanation. By contrast, in West Tanfield, churchyard space in the village had been readily available at St Nicholas's since the thirteenth century but nevertheless the Wesleyan chapel built in 1789 had a burial ground. It is not possible to draw any generalisations from just these two examples, particularly given a lack of local historical documentation. Two further Wesleyan chapels, both built in the 1840s, had burial grounds: at Kirkby Overblow and Pickering. Again, there is no indication in extant records as to why this measure was deemed necessary. Generally, John Wesley had himself cast doubt on the need for burial in consecrated ground, but there was no objection to church burial that was deeply rooted in Methodist doctrine. Robert Newton – by far the most prominent Methodist in central North Riding, and a preacher of national renown – was interred in 1854 in a family grave in the Anglican church of St John the Baptist, Easingwold.[11] His monument remains the most conspicuous, and is amongst the largest memorials in any churchyard in the area.

Independents

From around 1760 to 1820, an evangelical revival amongst Independents in Yorkshire increased their number, and twenty new churches were built, generally in the market towns.[12] Independent chapels were evident in almost all the larger settlements in the study. Many of these chapels had attached burial space, and this was the case at New Malton, Pickering, Northallerton, Thirsk and Pateley Bridge. To the west of Pateley Bridge, rural Nidderdale supported a further large chapel – Providence Chapel – erected at Dacre in 1827 and still in use in 2007. Independents between York and Knaresborough were also sufficiently strong to support the building of chapels in the villages of Great Ouseburn and Green Hammerton; both had burial grounds. The ethos of the Independent Church – that each congregation should comprise a separate, self-governed unit with control of its own affairs – presumed a level of self-sufficiency which included access to separate burial space which was to remain unconsecrated. Views on this particular issue had been published in *Cemetery Interment* by George Collison in 1840. Collison had an undeniable Independent pedigree: his father – also named George – was the President of the Hackney Congregational Theological College.[13] For Collison, there was little harm in consecrating burial space as an indication that this act set the land aside for 'solemn purpose'. However, it was clearly wrong to see the act as being necessary 'to the repose of the dead': this was little more than Popish superstition. Furthermore, the act of consecration was used to justify an 'invidious distinction' between Christians, and separate them in death.[14]

Independents could be relied on as being at the forefront of any local initiative to provide burial space outside the aegis of the Established Church. Early cemetery company development centred on Liverpool and Manchester, and action was led by prominent local Independents. Collison himself was responsible for the establishment of Abney Park Cemetery Company in London, which was the only such company to lay out a completely unconsecrated cemetery in the capital. Independent interest in cemetery reform was further galvanised by the fact that their burial spaces were vulnerable to closure under the Burial Acts. In the market towns, Independent chapels were – like the parish church – generally situated on principal thoroughfares, where burials constituted a danger to public health. Thus, in central North Riding a number of closure orders included specific reference to Independent burial grounds: for example, the Salem Chapel at Bridgehouse Gate, Pateley Bridge, was closed by Order in Council in 1871.[15] Similarly, the Zion burial ground was inspected at Northallerton by William Ranger in 1854. Although just 22 interments had taken place since the opening of the burial ground in 1836, it was located in one of the most densely populated closes just off the High Street and so was included in the closure order of 1854.[16] This was also the case at the Independent Wheelgate Chapel in New Malton, where interments were taking place in an overcrowded neighbourhood. The final interment in this ground took place in 1857, and further entries in the chapel book – which included a burial register – indicated that actual interments took place in the cemeteries at either New Malton or Norton.[17]

Quakers

Also in contrast to the 'absence' of Methodist burial grounds, Quaker burial space was laid out all over central North Riding. The incidence of Quakerism was marked in this part of North Yorkshire, and unlike other Old Dissent denominations extended even into the most remote areas: the road over the Yorkshire Moors from Rosedale to Danby was known as 'the Quaker road'.[18] The denomination was particularly strong in Great Ayton. Here, the religious census of 1851 indicated that perhaps 80 per cent of the village attended some form of worship on census Sunday, and 22 per cent of those attendances were at Quaker meetings.[19] Indeed, the response from the vicar of Great Ayton to the Archbishop's visitation return in 1868 indicated that a key problem in impeding the Church's ministry was 'the persecuting influence of the Quakers – encouraging dispute'.[20] Later in the century, their influence was still notable. Bulmer noted in 1890 that this community was large and respectable: they had founded a library and a school. The Friends' Meeting House had its own burial ground; both were mentioned by Bulmer: the Quaker meeting house is 'a commodious building with a pretty graveyard attached'.[21] Of all denominations, Quakers were the most prolific in their laying out of burial space, either attached to their meeting houses or detached in sometimes remote locations. Indeed, according to Stock, 'early Quakers cared little where their mortal remains were buried so long as it was not a churchyard'.[22] Consecration of burial space was considered to be unnecessary and superstitious, and sentimental attachment to burial space was discouraged. Quaker meetings often sold their burial grounds to augment their finances: there is evidence of early Quaker burial grounds in Northallerton, Crayke and Masham, whose use was discontinued and which were sold in the first half of the nineteenth century.[23]

Roman Catholics

There has been a long tradition of Roman Catholicism in North Yorkshire, supported largely by Roman Catholic gentry.[24] However, there is a very limited incidence of separate burial provision: in this study, just six sites have been located. The church of St Joseph's in Bishop Thornton dates from the fifteenth century, and has attached burial space which is still in use. The remaining sites date from the nineteenth century, and demonstrate both the importance of Ampleforth Abbey and the influence of individual landed families in supporting Roman Catholicism in the area. Ampleforth Abbey dates from 1802 and has a small attached burial ground for the Abbey's Benedictines. The Abbey supported the Mission at Easingwold where St Austin's – later rededicated to St John the Baptist – was built in 1830 and had attached burial space. In Ampleforth itself, Our Lady and St Benedict was opened in around 1900. At Sicklinghall, the Church of the Immaculate Conception was built alongside a monastery in the early 1850s by the Middleton Family of Stockeld Park, again a family with a long tradition of Roman Catholicism. A Roman Catholic burial ground was attached to the churchyard of St Martin's at Allerton Mauleverer at around the same time. The consecration of burial space is central to Roman Catholic funerary rites, reflecting a belief that the body is 'sanctified in baptism, and by other sacraments, and that it is destined to share in the Resurrection'.[25] Generally, Roman Catholics have not been denied interment in Anglican churchyards. Indeed, in North Yorkshire there were 'high' Anglicans whose practices might have been regarded favourably by local Roman Catholic inhabitants: for example, the Reverend Gray at Helmsley was anti-Roman Catholic in principle but notoriously 'Romish' in practice, to the dismay of his largely Dissenting parish.

It is difficult to be conclusive about the reasons for the very small number of non-Anglican burial grounds in central North Riding in the nineteenth century. An association is often made between the spread of Dissent generally and the willingness of a largely Anglican landed gentry to accommodate Nonconformity. Across central North Riding, the experience was probably mixed. For example, Sir Tatton Sykes I was intolerant of Primitive Methodists, and refused permission for the erection of chapels on his land.[26] He was also, incidentally, intolerant of Anglican clergymen, and refused to let one live within four miles of his residence. By contrast, the Fitzwilliams had donated land for the Independent chapel and burial ground in New Malton and there were indications that this ground was at some point extended. However, aside from this single instance, landowner support for independent burial provision was – relative to the assistance given with churchyards and churchyard extension – markedly absent. Indications as to why this might be the case might become evident through comparison of North Yorkshire with regions where Methodist burial grounds were more numerous, and remain outwith the bounds of this study.

Progress to eradicate the burial grievance

The apparent complaisance amongst Methodists in central North Riding on the issue of burials could be regarded as surprising. In the first half of the century, Nonconformists had seen a number of civic disabilities or 'grievances' being gradually removed, such as the repeal of the Test and Corporation Act, and marriage in Dissenting chapels having no standing in law. A third issue – payment of the church rate – had been creating increasingly acrimonious local exchanges from the 1830s; in some areas majority Nonconformist vestries had simply voted to collect no or negligible rates. A compulsory church rate was finally abolished in 1868, leaving just one principal grievance remaining: burial.

The burial grievance

The second half of the nineteenth century saw agitation on the issue of burials being played out nationally, through successive Burial Acts and through a series of failed bills which finally culminated in the passage of the Burial Laws Amendment Act and – beyond that – the Burial Act, 1900.[27] Bishop Blomfield died in 1857 but had spliced the interests of the Established Church so far into the roots of the Burial Acts that, as the century progressed, their operation became overwhelmingly religious-political. The fact that there was a rapid succession of Burial Acts in the 1850s alone is an indication that it was proving to be impossible to settle matters in a fashion considered equitable. For Nonconformists, the burial grievance carried a bundle of theological, ideological, emotional and more practically economic concerns. As has been noted, there was a belief amongst some Dissenters that the consecration of land was intrinsically wrong: at best, it was a relic of superstition, at worst, evidence of Roman Catholic leanings. Anglican ministers might refuse to read the burial service at the funerals of unbaptised children of Baptists, or indeed deny such children interment in the churchyard altogether. Parents could be deprived of Christian consolation, and might perhaps need to find alternative provision. More generally, there was dismay at every funeral being led by an Anglican minister, reading the Church of England funeral service. This factor struck at the rights to free belief and worship; the act also constituted an unpalatable symbol of a final acceptance of Anglican tenets. Lastly, having a burial within a churchyard perforce meant the payment of burial and monument permission fees to the clergy. It was simply inequitable for the Church to have a monopoly of this essential service: parishioners had a right to burial in the churchyard, but they were also under obligation to pay the Church to exercise this right, and consequently Anglican clergy derived substantial financial benefit.

Cemetery companies and the burial grievance

The introduction of cemeteries in the first half of the nineteenth century muddied the waters in a number of ways. It has been seen that the earliest cemetery companies carried the intention of negating the burial grievance. For more radical companies, the cemetery remained wholly unconsecrated, although others – in a spirit of tolerance and inclusion – consecrated part, so that all denominations could be accommodated. This was the case at Nottingham's General Cemetery Company, which was part-consecrated on the insistence of the Quaker Samuel Fox, who had donated land for the cemetery in 1836.[28] Furthermore, although the Dissenting cemetery companies might offer the services of a minister, families would be able to dispense with his services. Thus, Portsea Island Cemetery Company promised: 'Those who bring their own minister with them, will be at liberty to use what form they please; while others, who prefer it, may inter their dead without any service whatever.'[29] It was possible to argue that by the middle of the nineteenth century the burial grievance had been 'met' by this alternative provision. However, by the 1850s cemetery companies had made little inroads into the less populous towns, and certainly none was in operation in the more rural districts. The format was simply uneconomic in locations where there were limited numbers of potential shareholders and where the scale of interments would be unlikely to make even modest returns. In addition even the most benign cemetery company was beginning to be viewed with suspicion, since they were not subject to public control.[30] The company cemetery could not therefore answer the needs of all Nonconformists, although Churchmen could – when it suited – blithely claim that it did.

The Burial Acts: continued agitation

The advent of the burial board offered the opportunity to redress the imbalance since, through payment of a rate to cover the cost, land for both Anglicans and Nonconformists would be supplied on an equitable basis. Anglicans would be satisfied that the consecrated portion of the cemetery constituted an addition to the freehold of the local incumbent and was 'deemed the burial ground of the parish', and Nonconformists had access to unconsecrated space.[31] However, it appeared that neither side could consider itself satisfied, as niggling inconsistencies in the legislation were brought to light. Vestries baulked at the price of achieving equality, in the cost of building two chapels, and Dissenters frequently complained that the separation of consecrated from unconsecrated land within cemeteries introduced a division which somehow signalled the Dissenter as 'other', and not one with the community of Christians. Furthermore, the Burial Acts again did not address the problem of how to deal with burial in rural districts. It still remained necessary to pay for the cemetery through the rates, and in the absence of a substantial community of ratepayers there was little prospect of raising the required funds. Earlier chapters demonstrated that it often proved to be more practicable to extend the churchyard at a cost of a couple of hundreds of pounds rather than establish a cemetery with a possible bill of a thousand or more.

For Dissenters, therefore, their central requirements remained unmet: free access to the parish churchyard, using their own ministers and without the Church of England burial service. Bills on the issue were submitted almost annually from the 1860s, but here is not the place to enter into a detailed history.[32] A typically emotive debate was provided by the Second Reading of a bill brought forward by Sir Morton Peto in 1862. Peto stressed that he had no political intent in bringing forward the Bill – 'he had no object in view to effect the achievement of any Nonconformist triumph' – and in fact was dismayed by the agitations of the Liberation Society, which sought disestablishment.[33] However, in moving to reject the Second Reading, Sir William Harcourt dismissed this claim and argued that the purpose of the Bill was to 'initiate aggression'. According to Harcourt, allowing any service to be permitted in the churchyard would introduce the possibility of funeral services on Sundays, 'at the very time of divine service, with ceremonies perhaps distressing to the Church congregation – perhaps abhorrent to the whole Christian world'. Furthermore, once the churchyard had been breached, the churches themselves would be subject to 'a similar invasion'.[34] More moderate Members felt that the burial boards perhaps met the issue adequately, and wondered if radical national legislation was required for a question which might only occasionally arise in rural districts. On this occasion, it was voted that the Bill be postponed for six months.

The Burial Laws Amendment Act

The act which appeared to settle the matter was passed in 1880, principally through the efforts in Parliament of the Welsh MP George Osborne Morgan. The Burial Laws Amendment Act allowed for interment in the parish churchyard or graveyard without the performance of the Church of England funeral service, provided that 48 hours' notice was given to the incumbent.[35] The nature of the notice was specified in the regulations, and an Annex suggested a proforma for the applicant to use. The burial register at Terrington still includes the copies of two such applications, evidently written by the rector himself but signed by the applicant.[36] It is clear that not all ministers were so obliging, and an early court case related to a refusal by an incumbent to allow a funeral as a consequence of the applicant omitting their address from the burial notice.[37] The burial fee remained payable to the incumbent, even if another minister had taken the service or if no service had been held at all, an option also permitted by the Act. The burials were to be recorded in the parish register, which was to state by whom the service was performed under the Act. Any incumbent failing to register the burial was deemed guilty of a misdemeanour.[38] This element of the legislation does make it possible to count the incidence of burials, since the interment was generally noted – in the column for the person taking the service – as being 'under the BLAA' or 'under the Burial Act'. The Act made clear that Anglican clergy were at liberty to take burial services in unconsecrated ground. As will be seen in the next chapter, the Burial Laws Amendment Act did not bring to a close Nonconformist agitation on the issue: the new regulation had upheld Blomfield's principle of protecting the pecuniary interests of the clergy. Antagonism over burials therefore continued to the end of the nineteenth century: the 1897–8 Select Committee on the subject indicated how little progress there had been. According to Manning, 'Anglicans proved unable to drop their assumption of superiority and privilege or the Dissenters their obstructive tactics'.[39] Neither side emerged from the conflict particularly well: at local and national levels both were quick to see offence and crow ungraciously over the smallest symbolic victory.

Burial politics and burial board management

Thus the ownership and control of burial space was strongly contested in Parliament. At any point in the second half of the nineteenth century, debate on the issue of interments could also be causing ructions locally. It remains to be asked, therefore, whether in central North Riding specifically the overwhelmingly Anglican control of burial space was deemed problematic, and how far the ill-feeling which had been engendered on the issue nationally was reflected in the provision of burial space in the towns and villages in the study. There were perhaps two arenas in which the strength of feeling on the matter was tested: the operation of burial boards, and action in the churchyard consequent to the passage of the Burial Laws Amendment Act. Certainly, the tenor of local religious politics was indicated by the way in which denominational differences were negotiated in the setting up of burial boards, and in the early years of cemetery establishment. Problematic areas included the provision of chapels for burial services; the apportionment of land – what was generally termed 'allotment' – between different denominations; and the act of consecration and the related requirements of the bishop.

The provision of chapels

When the burial board at New Malton was established in 1858 there had already been a couple of changes to the legislation relating to cemetery chapels. Earlier regulation had required that two chapels be built, but the Burial Act, 1857 offered the proviso that where three-quarters of the vestry agreed, a second chapel would not be required on the unconsecrated section. This alteration had left Nonconformists at something of a disadvantage. In 1858, the Burial Board wrote to the Secretary of State for clarification on the matter, asking – perhaps naively – whether it might be possible to permit Nonconformists to conduct burial services in a consecrated cemetery chapel. The Under-Secretary reiterated the regulation that if a majority of three-quarters of the vestry voted that a Dissenting chapel was 'undesirable and unnecessary' then the Burial Board would be regarded as being relieved of this duty.[40] The letter was not entirely helpful to the Board. The vestry had voted overwhelmingly that Nonconformists should have provision, and the Board were of the view that just one chapel might be built, which could be used by both Anglicans and Nonconformists. Indeed, the Board was aware that in York General Cemetery the company directors had built a chapel that sat directly on the dividing line separating the consecrated portion of the cemetery from the unconsecrated: inside the chapel, mourners were guided to the left or to the right depending on their preference. The Burial Board at New Malton considered this to be an ideal solution, and again wrote to the Secretary of State for clarity on the legality of the measure. Typically, the response was noncommittal: 'he must decline to answer the questions which you have submitted as it is not usual for the Secretary of State to give opinions on the construction of Acts of Parliament'.[41] Undeterred, the Burial Board visited York the following month and found that the chapel had been built 'without any apparent division'. A plan was drawn up accordingly and submitted to the Archbishop. He was of a more decided character than the Secretary of State, and wrote that he 'was clearly of the opinion that the law requires two chapels to be erected ... And he should refuse to consecrate a portion of a building.'[42]

Diocesan interference with the plans for chapels was commonplace. At Thirsk in 1878, plans to have joined chapels were rejected, and had to be redesigned as two separate buildings set some distance apart.[43] The Pateley Bridge Burial Board was perhaps in a more favourable position. It had no intention of building any chapels since access remained to the existing mortuary chapel of the old St Mary's Abbey, adjacent to the cemetery; Nonconformists using the cemetery would perforce be reliant on their own chapels in the town. However, this proposal was not regarded as being entirely equitable, and the Board arrived at a compromise. The cemetery lodge would be so constructed to have a board room at one end, and at the other

> a roomy building in which to place the hearse, and by which means of seats placed round the sides would be available for the interment service if the weather was wild. An ornamental gateway to divide the two buildings could be so contrived as to communicate with the hearse room if required and so increase the space available for the service.[44]

Thus a plan – including a marked 'temporary chapel' – was prepared and sent to Dr Holland at the Burials Office, who advised pointedly that 'a room in a lodge in which a burial service might be occasionally read would hardly be considered a chapel, and that it must not be called a chapel'. The Board hastily wrote back that the architect had been mistaken, and that the 'temporary chapel' was in fact a 'hearse room'. In those circumstances, Dr Holland was

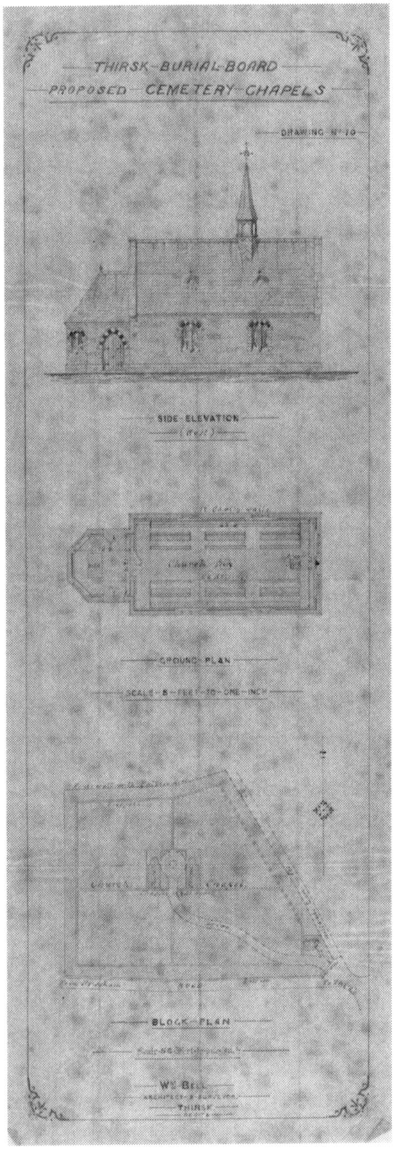

Plate 6.1 Architectural drawing of Thirsk Cemetery chapels. The Bishop required there to be two buildings, some distance apart. They have since been demolished (NYRO, BB/TH 11/8).

satisfied that the approval of the Secretary of State was not required. However, there remained the possibility that the plans would have to be sent for diocesan approval. Holland's advice was again wise: 'it would be better not to send [the plans] to his Lordship lest they should lead him to suppose that the hearse room is to be a chapel'. Indeed, he wrote, the Bishop had no concern with the unconsecrated portion of the cemetery, and should be satisfied with the provision of the mortuary chapel at the Abbey, so 'why trouble him about the rest unless he enquires about it'.[45]

Allotment of space between denominations

The allotment of space within the cemetery was also subject to much debate. Even the symbolic importance of the issue was clear. At Pateley Bridge it was proposed to divide the ground 'as equally as possible' in terms of consecration. It was suggested to the architect that the ground should be divided by a line running north to south: 'giving as it did to each party half of the high ground and half of the low ground, whereas the plan he suggested would give all the high ground to one, and leave all the low to the other'.[46] In New Malton, a more contentious issue remained the specific allotment of ground to the Roman Catholic community. The Reverend William Middlehurst, the Roman Catholic priest, asked for a portion of the site to be consecrated for the use of Roman Catholics in Malton. The Burial Board decided that such consecration be 'deferred for the present'; later, it was agreed that a portion might be set aside, 'providing a price can be agreed'.[47] However, the Roman Catholic community considered that, as ratepayers, they should not have to purchase a portion. At this juncture, Middlehurst wrote a letter that was deemed to be 'offensive and uncourteous ... and not worthy of notice or any further comment or observation on part of the Board', a copy of which is, unfortunately, no longer extant.[48] The vestry was asked to decide on the matter and was presented with a report on matters as they stood. The Board's report was less than gracious, and stated that the population of the Board's combined parishes was deemed to be around five thousand and the Roman Catholic community was thought to be 63. Rather more pertinently, there were 916 ratepayers, just nineteen of whom were estimated to be Roman Catholic. A calculation on the amount of land allowable depending on the rates paid by Roman Catholics indicated that they should be allotted no more than six perches of land. It was thought that claims for a larger amount evidently rested on Middlehurst's intention to use the portion to bury Roman Catholics from beyond the parish, which was clearly untenable to the local ratepayers. Unsurprisingly, the issue was not decided favourably: 'hitherto the Roman Catholics dying in Malton have been interred in the church yard and so far as the Board is aware, without objection on their part'.[49] No allocation was granted. It is perhaps notable that in the twenty years following the opening of the cemetery, Middlehurst conducted 53 interments in the unconsecrated section; many of these interments were of residents from the workhouse.

Concern with the allotment of land to Roman Catholics was also expressed in Harrogate. In 1867, Harrogate Burial Board sent a circular to the burial boards in Barnsley, Wakefield, Pontefract and Otley to enquire whether they had set aside space for Roman Catholics. Questions included: 'Are large crosses permitted to be placed in this space? Is any restriction placed on inscriptions placed on the headstones or monuments placed on the graves generally? Is any control placed over the inscriptions on Roman Catholic monuments? Has any objection been made to such an inscription as "pray for the soul of ..."? Are the graves of Roman Catholics interred with the general graves in the unconsecrated portion or usually in the one locality?' The answers must have proved satisfactory, since it was decided to grant a portion of Section J in the cemetery to the interment of Roman Catholics provided that the community paid for a pathway and that all interments be subject to the Board's general rules and regulations. In Thirsk, a specific area was also set aside for Roman Catholics within the unconsecrated portion of the cemetery, but no comment on the move was made in the minute book.[50]

Consecration and subsequent fees

Once chapels and apportionment were decided, it was necessary to secure the bishop's agreement to consecrate the ground. Even applying for consecration was in itself an onerous undertaking: an application to the bishop for the consecration of a churchyard extension was by comparison a lightweight affair. The Diocese of Ripon and Leeds had by the 1880s produced a proforma application for consecration, which was a useful *aide memoire* for burial boards in terms of the documentation required. One such proforma is extant amongst the records for Kirkby Overblow Cemetery. A burial board was required to send vestry notices and resolutions establishing the burial board, any relevant Secretary of State decisions on the local churchyard, conveyance documents and written consents from any owner of property within 100 yards of the site or a statutory declaration that no such property existed. In addition, the proforma also specified the form of division required by the bishop between the consecrated and unconsecrated portions: 'boundary stones 6 inches square, 18 inches above the surface, and set 18 inches into the ground, marked with the letters B. S. and placed 10 yards apart'. The Board was required to produce a map indicating the division and the placement of the boundary stones.[51]

In October 1882, the Great Ayton Burial Board began the necessary arrangements relating to consecration of its cemetery. The papers were prepared within a month but in the following January the Parish Meeting asked for the Burial Board to delay for as long as possible and this suggestion was adopted. In 1886, perhaps a couple of years after the cemetery opened, the Burial Board received a letter from the Reverend Richard M. Worthington, the local vicar.

The vicar's letter indicated that some local conflict had certainly arisen over the issue: 'I hope that members of the burial board will consent to the consecration of the cemetery taking place next Thursday.'[52] It appears that inhabitants of Great Ayton had 'some time ago expressed their approval of the consecration of that part of the cemetery provided that no portion of the cost of such ceremony be paid out of the rates of the said parish'. Indeed, he was so anxious to ensure the ceremony take place that he was willing himself to cover the cost 'so the rates will not have to be drawn on'.[53] The Board expressed itself appreciative of the 'conciliatory and Christian spirit evinced by the Reverend and Mrs Worthington' in meeting this cost.[54] The consecration of the cemetery took place on 22 July 1886. Puzzlingly, the burial register indicates earlier interments in consecrated space, and it is possible that this may have been dedicated rather than consecrated, as a temporary measure.

Once in operation, there could be further skirmishes between local clergy on the right to fees within the cemetery. In Pateley Bridge, the Reverend Samuel Gray, the Anglican incumbent, complained that the Clerk of the Board had been persuading people to be buried in the unconsecrated section. 'This the clerk indignantly denied affirming that on the contrary, he had acted with the strictest impartiality and declaring that on account of his being a Dissenter, he had been especially careful to show no bias in the matter.'[55] Gray gave the example of Mrs Simpson of Bridge House Gate, who had – reportedly – wanted interment in the consecrated section with himself as officiant. The Clerk insisted that, on the contrary, Mrs Simpson had been a committed Primitive Methodist. The matter was dropped after Gray conceded that he had been 'misinformed'. Gray had in fact been remarkably conciliatory compared with his successor, the Reverend W. Scott. He had come to Pateley Bridge early in the 1880s, and insisted on strict adherence to the requirements of the Burial Laws Amendment Act with regard to interments in the cemetery's consecrated section. The Vicar had put a letter in the *Nidderdale Herald* on 22 November 1884 that 'both he and the curate will always be ready and most willing to take funerals in the unconsecrated portion of the cemetery whenever the friends of the deceased wish it'. In response, a letter was sent to the paper on 13 December 1884, signed by the Congregational Minister, the Wesleyan Minister and the Primitive Methodist Minister: 'Desiring to reciprocate W. Scott's courtesy, we take the opportunity of saying we are prepared to officiate at interments in the consecrated part of the cemetery, in accordance with the provisions of the above act.'[56] In 1887, Scott wrote a reminder to the Burial Board that by right he had to have 48 hours' notice of all interments in consecrated ground, and that all fees for such interment were his even if a Nonconformist minister presided. The Board was unhappy, considering it 'unfair that the Vicar should have all fees from the consecrated section but the reciprocal arrangement not be in place. However, they have to abide by the law as it currently stands.' Over the following months, exchanges between Scott and the Board were reproduced in the local newspaper, and the Board recorded its dissatisfaction:

> It did not seem just that a Cemetery paid for out of the rates should be regarded as a new freehold of the vicar of the parish for the time being, and that he should have the same right to tax them by exacting in the cemetery the same fees which formerly had been claimed in the parish churchyard.[57]

Religious politics in practice

Thus the apportionment of land very clearly carried religious political connotations. However, the extent to which the measure was welcomed can be understood only through analysis of the burial records. For the majority of burial boards in the area, the provision of unconsecrated burial space very clearly met a need, given the rate of interment in those sections. In Pateley Bridge in the first twenty years of the cemetery's operation, around half of all interments took place in the unconsecrated portion of the cemetery, as indicated by Table 6.2. However, there was marked variation in the proportion. Pateley Bridge was – as has been seen – a stronghold of Dissent; in 1851 just 22 per cent of all attendances were at the Anglican church. Half of burials in the cemetery took place in the unconsecrated section, which is a proportion that remains substantially higher than the other cemeteries in the selection. Great Ayton, where it might be presumed that Dissent was similarly strong, had just 18 per cent of burials in the unconsecrated section. The lack of any unconsecrated-portion burials in Kirkby Overblow is remarkable, but may be explained by the fact that the village had had since 1843 a Methodist burial ground, which even Anglicans on occasion preferred. In 1903, the historian Harry Speight wrote about the funeral of David Barrett, churchwarden:

Table 6.2 Interments in unconsecrated ground in selected burial board cemeteries during first 20 years of operation

Cemetery	*Period covered*	*Total burials*	*Number of of burials in unconsecrated section*	*Percentage burials in unconsecrated section*
Knaresborough	1876–1895	2148	653	30
Grove Rd, Harrogate	1864–1883	1807	643	36
New Malton	1859–1878	1660	366	22
Thirsk	1880–1899	1257	279	22
Pateley Bridge	1874–1893	971	484	50
Great Ayton	1882–1901	507	92	18
Harlow Hill, Harrogate	1871–1890	328	5	2
Kirkby Malzeard	1882–1901	257	45	17
Kirkby Overblow	1883–1902	122	0	0

Source: Burial board burial registers.

> He was very conservative of the old ways and customs, and strongly resented the formation of the Burial Board for Kirkby Overblow and the making of the new cemetery. When he died he was at his request interred in the Wesleyan burial-ground, the then rector taking the first part of the service in the church, and concluding it at the grave-side.[58]

Indeed, the scale of burials overall dropped in Kirkby Overblow after the churchyard closed and the cemetery opened, with people using the church at Harewood in preference. Harlow Hill Cemetery, Harrogate, was conceived as a mission church with an expanded 'churchyard' operated by a burial board, which possibly explains the low proportion of unconsecrated interments. The denominational affiliation of those families choosing to inter in the unconsecrated section is available only for some burial boards, since there was no statutory requirement to give this information. However, where this information is available, both Primitive and Wesleyan Methodists evidently made use of the unconsecrated space. It is notable that, in Scarborough, a local newspaper report on interments in 1879 indicated that 54 per cent of interments had taken place in the unconsecrated section, so there clearly were circumstances in which preference was expressed in a numeric fashion.[59]

The Burial Laws Amendment Act in operation

It is evident that, in central North Riding, considerable disagreement could arise between denominations from meeting the provisions of the Burial Acts, and the situation could become more or less inflammatory depending on the willingness of both sides to be conciliatory. On occasion, the burial issue simply ignited other resentments, as was evident in Helmsley. There were sporadic attempts to evade the requirements of the Act but it appears that, despite the politics of the matter, overall demand for non-Anglican ministers to take the funeral service was low.

Helmsley

In Helmsley, attempts to resolve the religious-political issues around burial proved intractable. The town was strongly Nonconformist, and in the early 1870s had probably not welcomed the arrival of the Reverend Charles Norris Gray, whose High Anglicanism was supported by the Earl of Feversham. Indeed, following a scandal attached to the Earl's turning over a Quaker meeting house to Anglican use, the MP, J. W. Pease, wrote that the Earl was 'in the hands of that bigoted priest, the Vicar of Helmsley, and ... we have little or nothing to hope from such a combination'.[60] This judgement also held in the matter of the Burial Laws Amendment Act. Gray had recorded through the medium of the parish magazine – in detail, and at length – his views on the various burial bills which had proposed the possibility of Nonconformist ministers presiding in Anglican churchyards. He reported a meeting of the York Diocesan Conference, commenting that

> It was shown again and again in the debate that if the Church yielded to every cry of a grievance from the Dissenters they must be prepared to yield everything. The cry was now give us the churchyards, the next would be give us the churches. There was no real grievance, they could provide Burial grounds for themselves as they had provided chapels if they disliked the church services in her own churchyards. Rev. R. H. Parr proposed ... 'That this Conference protests against any dealing with the Churchyards which would allow the dissenting minister to claim the right to officiate in the parish churchyard.' This was also unanimously accepted.[61]

For Gray, the matter was very much at hand, since an addition to the churchyard had recently been donated by the Earl of Feversham which was – Gray made clear – 'given specially and solely for the services of the church, by her own appointed minister'.[62]

A further donation of land was made in 1882, following a death in the Earl's family. It was acceded that this site should have both consecrated and unconsecrated sections. This fact with clearly rankled Gray, who was typically testy on the matter in the parish magazine:

> *Of course if there were no desire to have any such bit reserved for burial without the church services* then Lord Feversham would be willing to give the whole for burial with church services, and then the whole would be consecrated. *But he wishes in this matter to act just as people in the parish wish.*[63]

However, the land was given on the understanding that the existing churchyard remained very much under Church control – the implication being that the Dissenting community should be satisfied with provision in the new unconsecrated extension. According to Gray, a general meeting – well attended by the local Nonconformists – agreed this measure. However, the first interment in the unconsecrated section was that of a Methodist. Her family had wanted her to be interred in the churchyard, alongside her husband and with a Methodist minister presiding but the family had been told that the only available space to Dissenters was in the new section. Immediately after the burial, a complaint was made about the interment: the section was deemed to be inferior, and in any case the family had the right to burial in the old churchyard, with their own minister. Gray was clearly enraged by the possibility, and both sides settled into a protracted argument. Gray declared that the Nonconformists were acting dishonourably, in going back on their previous agreement to the conditions imposed by the Earl of Feversham; in response, the Nonconformists ensured that reporters were on hand at the relevant meetings, and the 'mean' entrance way afforded the unconsecrated section was photographed for the newspapers. A letter was written to the Secretary of State requesting permission to exhume the body and inter it in the churchyard. The Home Secretary – Sir William Harcourt – was unlikely to view the request sympathetically. The parish magazine reported that the letter indicated that a licence for disinterment from the Secretary of

State conferred no right of re-interment in any place, and neither did the Burials Act 1880. 'I am to add that the Secretary of State has no reason to think there has been any disregard of that Act in this case.'[64] Reverend Gray's actions were largely futile: in the twenty years following the introduction of the Act, thirty-three funerals with non-Anglican services took place in All Saints' churchyard (see Table 6.3).

Table 6.3 Burial Laws Amendment Act interments in 25 selected churchyards, 1880–1900

Churchyard	*Total interments, 1880–1900*	*Burial Laws Amendment Act interments*
St Peter and St Paul, Pickering	1,200	32
All Saints, Kirkbymoorside	857	101
All Saints, Helmsley	831	33
St Mary the Virgin, Masham	571	19
St Mary the Virgin, Alne	468	6[1]
St Columba, Topcliffe	478	3
All Saints, Spofforth	386[2]	6
St Mary, Leake	342	3
St Thomas à Becket, Hampsthwaite	314	4[3]
St Michael, Well	280	0
All Saints, Terrington	217	2
St John the Baptist, Bishop Monkton	192	3
St Hilda, Ampleforth	188	10
All Saints, Kirk Deighton	156	0
All Saints, Ingleby Arncliffe	141	0
St Michael, Barton-le-Street	134	0
Holy Trinity, Little Ouseburn	119	0
Parish church, Danby Wiske	100	1
St Leonard, Sandhutton	100	2
All Saints, Burythorpe	92	0
St Botolph, Carlton in Cleveland	84	0
St Oswald, Leathley	80	2
All Saints, Yafforth	68	1
St Mary, Birdforth	33	0

Source: Parish burial registers. [1]Includes one interment with no minister at all. [2]To 1897; [3]One is certain; three others are probable.

Evading the Act

The Reverend Gray's machinations in Helmsley indicate that it was possible to try and evade the implementation of the Burial Laws Amendment Act. Such evasion could take place at highest local levels, and in some instances included the principal estate owner. The general opposition of a portion of the Anglican aristocracy to the Burial Laws Amendment Act is evident in correspondence in the Ecclesiastical Commissioners' archive. Prior to the passage of the Act, a petition – dated 1878 – was signed by major 'Donors of Land for Churchyards'. The petition stated that all the signatories had donated land for churchyards in the previous 35 years, and it was their contention

> That such gifts were made in full faith and confidence that the law of England would protect them, untouched and inviolate, to the sacred purpose for which they were given and had we supposed it possible that such perversion of our objects, as that contemplated under the provisions of Mr Osborne Morgan's motion, could ever occur, we would on no consideration have made them to the Church.

Local signatories included Sir Tatton Sykes II and Dowager Viscountess Downe.[65] Local machinations were in evidence. In Pickering, land had been donated to extend the churchyard of St Peter and St Paul's in 1893, on the understanding that only church burials could take place there. Agitation on the issue soured relations between denominations and led to protracted argument over the need for a new cemetery.[66]

In Hovingham, soon after the passage of the Act, Sir William Cayley Worsley employed solicitors to enquire into the legality of his preventing Nonconformist interment in any donated land, and even considered giving two separate portions, each to be administered by a separate trust. The final arrangement, which was highly unusual, entirely evaded the Burial Acts – including the Burial Laws Amendment Act – since the land was essentially leased to a committee which oversaw its management.[67] The site was never consecrated, and so – as in Helmsley – it became theoretically unnecessary for Nonconformist ministers to preside in the churchyard.

It is possible that the flurry of churchyard closures which took place in the 1880s and the dip in the number of churchyard extensions at that time represented further attempts to evade the Act, although there is limited local documentation to support the contention. Some vicars were clearly unhappy, and expressed their dismay in the burial registers. The Reverend G. M. Gorham in Masham scrawled 'No ecclesiastical rites' in the burial register, in the column for the name of the person performing the ceremony; a separate list at the end of the register noted by whom the burial was certified, but he could clearly not bring himself to mention any Nonconformist minister's name: nineteen such interments took place under the act between 1880 and 1900 in St Mary's.[68] At Terrington, the vicar wrote 'cui bono?' (who benefits?) next to the first Act burial in his churchyard.[69] As late as 1908, a *Manual of Parochial Work for the Use of Younger Clergy* advised 'the duty and benefit of meeting on such occasions Dissenting ministers with proper Christian courtesy. Alas that such a caution should still be needed.'[70]

Recourse to the Act

However, despite the passions the matter could evoke, it was clear that recourse to the Act was highly variable, as Table 6.3 indicates. For example, at All Saints, Spofforth, one of the very earliest Act burials in the area took place, on 5 October 1880: 'under new burial act' was written in the margin of the burial register. Nevertheless, only a further six such interments took place in the years up to 1897.[71] In some churchyards, there were no burials under the Act at all. Analysis of a total of 25 burial registers spread across central North Riding demonstrates a correlation between the scale of interments in the churchyard and incidence of Amendment Act interments: they were much more likely to take place in market towns, as indicated by the example of

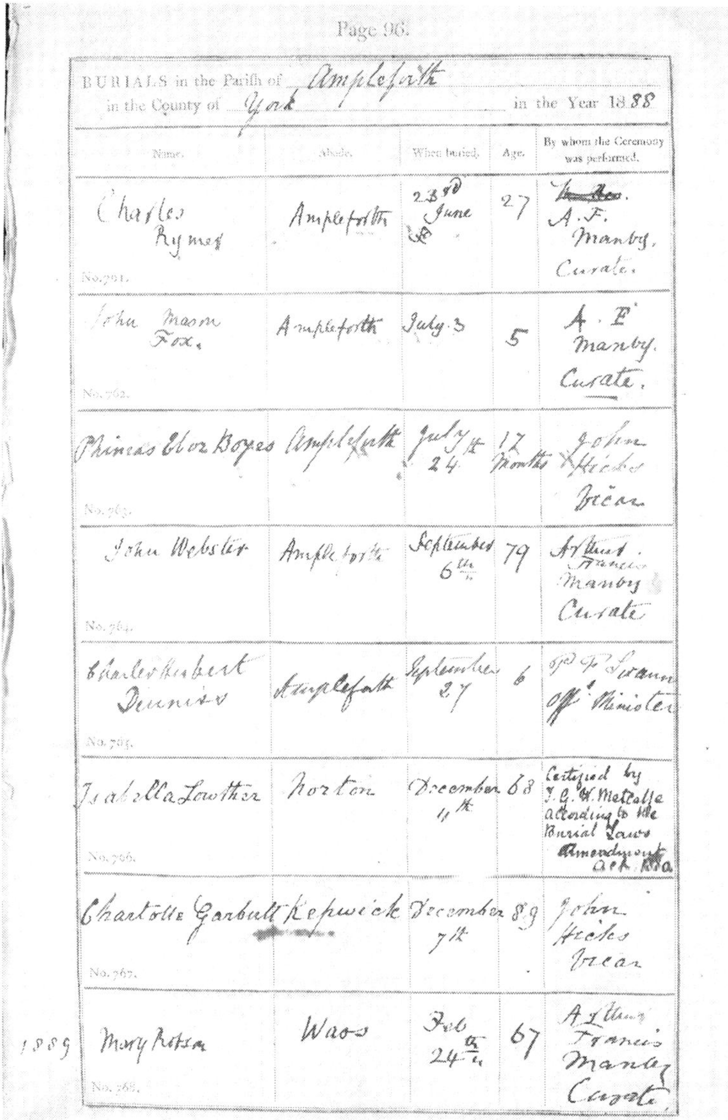

Page 96.

BURIALS in the Parish of Ampleforth in the County of York in the Year 1888

Name.	Abode.	When buried.	Age.	By whom the Ceremony was performed.
Charles Rymer No. 761.	Ampleforth	23rd June	27	A. F. Manby, Curate.
John Mason Fox. No. 762.	Ampleforth	July 3	5	A. F. Manby. Curate.
Phineas Eboz Boyes No. 763.	Ampleforth	July 24th	17 Months	John Hicks Vicar
John Webster No. 764.	Ampleforth	September 6th	79	Arthur Francis Manby Curate
Charles Hubert Dennis No. 765.	Ampleforth	September 27	6	[illegible] Offg Minister
Isabella Lowther No. 766.	Norton	December 4th	68	Certified by J. G. W. Metcalfe according to the Burial Laws Amendment Act 1880
Charlotte Garbutt No. 767.	Kepwick	December 7th	89	John Hicks Vicar
1889 Mary Robson No. 768.	Wass	Feb 24th	67	Arthur Francis Manby Curate

Plate 6.2 Page from burial register of St Hilda's, Ampleforth. Indicates a Burial Laws Amendment Act interment (NYRO, PR/AMP 1/3).

Pickering and – more markedly – of Kirkbymoorside. Here, well over 10 per cent of funerals were presided over by non-Anglican ministers. Of these, around half were given no designation in the burial register but, of the remainder, Wesleyan and Primitive Methodists, and Roman Catholic priests dominated. The Earl of Feversham owned the living at Kirkbymoorside,[72] but this factor was clearly not an inhibiting influence. By contrast, the rate of Amendment Act burials in the smaller settlements did not reflect the extremely strong adherence to Nonconformity in the area. The sample included Topcliffe, where – as has been seen – the vicar in 1868 had declared it impossible to find a Churchman but where just three Amendment Act interments took place, out of a total of 478. Even in places where there was substantial apparently favourable local context, use of the Act was limited. In Burythorpe, the largely Dissenting vestry had through the 1860s been engaged in a well-publicised stand-off with the Reverend H. Walker over church rate support for the Anglican school, and the vicar complained that all the leading landowners but one were Dissenters.[73] Even so, of the 92 interments between 1880 and 1900, none took place under the Act.

The failure to take up the opportunity provided by the Act is remarkable but may perhaps be explained in terms of the extreme rurality of central North Riding and the nature of Methodist organisation. Methodist 'societies' comprised meetings of like-minded individuals who over time would perhaps build a chapel. Societies and/or chapels would join the nearest 'circuit', around which itinerant preachers would travel. Locally, Methodist congregations might be more or less able to afford to pay a full-time minister, or at least pay part-wages to an individual who might also continue to work in a trade.[74] For baptisms and weddings, it might very well be possible to delay the event until a week in which the minister was visiting a particular locality. Funerals were another matter, and it may be that continued use of the Anglican clergy by Dissenters in more dispersed rural areas simply reflected the fact that a Nonconformist clergyman was not on hand to perform the required service. In addition, it remained the case that, even where it was possible to pay a full-time minister, there remained a culture of frequent 'turnover' of clergy: Wesley himself was of the view that ministers should stay no more than a year in a particular locality. Clark, in describing the religious culture of the Yorkshire fishing village of Staithes in the nineteenth and twentieth centuries, underlined the general dislike felt by many Methodist societies for ministers, who were regarded as being 'outsiders, unacquainted with local conditions and attitudes'. One older Primitive Methodist described them as 'ships that pass in the night', to whom little attention needed to be paid.[75]

By contrast, the local Anglican vicar was an individual whose presence was often woven into all the significant events of the community generally, and of families within that community. The Church had recognised its earlier failing of a disconnection between clergy and congregation in the eighteenth and earlier nineteenth century, as the plurality of livings led to many churches being without ministers. St Mary's at Scawton was a case in point. For much of the nineteenth century, the church was subject to neglect, being under the rectorship of Thomas Worsley, who was also Master of Downing College and Vice Chancellor of Cambridge University.[76] The church was deemed to be a disgrace: 'No intelligent passer by would dream of its being intended for a church, unless he should suspect something from the old tombstones which surround it.'[77] However, as the century progressed – and following the apparently poor showing of the Church of England in the religious census of 1851 – massive investment followed in new endowments, and the rebuilding of both churches and vicarages, creating an infrastructure in which the rural clergy as a profession might flourish. Certainly by the end of the nineteenth century, the vicar had become a central figure in rural society and, religious politics notwithstanding, it was expected that he would play a pivotal role in promoting the welfare of the village. Furthermore, both Evangelicalism and Tracterianism tended to increase interest in the pastoral elements of Anglican ministry: handbooks for clergy recommended that effective curacy followed close attention to the lives of parishoners.[78] Indeed, this principle was reflected in recommendations made on parish reorganisation during the Second World War: 'It takes years for country folk to know and trust their parson, and his opportunity of helping them depends on his being on the spot in the hour of need.'[79]

Certainly this was one area where Anglican clergymen of central North Riding showed, on occasion, considerable energy. Burial registers could be one indication of the vicar's local knowledge, and in some instances the record of death is accompanied by notation on the character or family of the deceased. For example, the burial register at Sandhutton indicated, following the death of William and Dinah Hudson, that 'these two were man and wife: they lived together for 64 years, with the greatest affection; and died within seven hours of each other; and are buried in the same grave'.[80] For many settlements in the study, the nineteenth century was remarkable for the number of clergy who served decades in the same parish. The Reverend H. Walker at Burythorpe had been embroiled in argument with his Nonconformist parishioners but continued to serve as vicar from 1855 to 1913. For that whole period, the burial register records that there were no more than a handful of interments taken by other ministers: between 1880 and 1900 there was only one funeral that the Reverend Walker himself did not take. Indeed, he had on one occasion cut short a holiday in Scotland to return to Burythorpe for the funeral of a parishioner.[81] Burythorpe was not exceptional. In Little Ouseburn, of the 85 interments from 1896, all but six are taken by the Reverend William Bannister Tomlinson, who was himself interred in the churchyard at the age of 80 in 1912.[82] In Leake, again between 1880 and 1900, all but 38 of the 342 burials were taken by the Reverend E. A. Houghton;

he had served in the same parish as a curate and was also buried in his own churchyard.[83] Pastoral 'professionalism' underlined the importance of funerals at a time when ministry could be most effective, but it also remained the case that, for many rural communities, the vicar's taking the service himself comprised an important element of the burial tradition. In comparison, the use of a 'fly by night' Methodist minister offered substantially less consolation, despite the politics of the matter.

Conclusion

This chapter has considered the religious politics of burial in central North Riding, with the aim of arriving at an understanding of how far the Church of England lost control of burial space in the area during the second half of the nineteenth century. Methodism was by far the dominant Nonconformist denomination, although pockets of the Old Dissent were evident in the market towns. The operation of the Burial Acts indicated that there were evident tensions in meeting requirements as to consecration and apportionment. In some burial board cemeteries in the study, substantial use was made of unconsecrated sections, which indicated some level of dissatisfaction with the notion of burial with an Anglican minister in consecrated ground. However, in only one instance was it the case that burials in unconsecrated ground approached being a majority option, despite the strength of Dissent generally in this part of Yorkshire. The Burial Acts had meant that the Church of England had indeed extended its provision of consecrated space without recourse to the church rate. Furthermore, it remained the case that the Anglican minister would take payment for all burials in the consecrated sections – irrespective of whether he had indeed taken the service. With the advent of the Burial Laws Amendment Act, it became possible for Nonconformist ministers to hold funeral services in the churchyard. Evidence from 25 churchyards shows that take-up of this option tended to be low in more rural locations, possibly reflecting the practicalities of securing the service of an itinerant Methodist ministry. It may also be the case that a willingness to continue using the vicar reflected a more intrinsic regard for tradition, particularly at a time of extreme emotional vulnerability.

By the end of the nineteenth century, the Burial Acts had not heralded any disconnect in the religious traditions of English burial culture. Although the Church of England no longer had a secure monopoly of burial provision, in actuality its holding of consecrated space increased substantially. From 1850 to 1894, 25 new churches were built in central North Riding, each providing a new churchyard; furthermore – as Chapter 4 demonstrated – numerous churchyards were extended. In addition, in each of the burial board cemeteries, at least half – and often more – of the ground was consecrated. In these spaces, it remained the case that burial fees were payable to the Anglican parish vicar whoever the officiating minister had been. Although Orders in Council were created to close churchyards in the area, these closures generally signalled either the addition of an extension to the site or a new, partly consecrated, cemetery. Nevertheless, the supply of non-Anglican burial space did also increase substantially. In the market towns particularly, there was enthusiastic use of unconsecrated sections of the burial board sites. However, it is perhaps important to reflect that, during the second half of the nineteenth century, any shift away from Anglican burial provision did not reflect a secularising tendency. On the contrary, Nonconformists desire for unconsecrated burial space demonstrated a strength of spiritual resolve and the desire to express religious commitment. Thus, it may be argued that, during the nineteenth century, there had been no substantive alteration to rural burial traditions. It remains to be seen whether, and how far, change became evident in the twentieth century.

Notes

1 *The Times*, 2 Mar 1871.
2 BI, v.1868/Ret 1, Archbishop's Visitation return, 1868.
3 N. Scotland, *Methodism and the Revolt of the Field* (Gloucester: Allan Sutton, 1981), p. 175.
4 T. Larsen, *Friends of Religious Equality: Nonconformist Politics in Mid-Victorian England* (Woodbridge: Boydell Press, 1999).
5 J. Wolffe, *The Religious Census of 1851 in Yorkshire* (York: Borthwick Paper 108, 2005).
6 *Ibid.*
7 N. Mant, *Eighteen Years' Work in a Yorkshire Parish* (Scarborough: E. T. W. Dennis, 1889), p. 25.
8 A. Everett, *The Pattern of Rural Dissent: The Nineteenth Century* (Leicester: Leicester University Press, 1972).
9 BI, v. 1868/Ret 1, Archbishop's Visitation return, 1868. The returns from each parish have been bound into two volumes, ordered alphabetically by parish.
10 *Ibid.*
11 T. Jackson, *The Life of the Rev. Robert Newton, DD* (London: John Mason, 1855).
12 Note that the terms 'Congregationalist' and 'Independents' tend to be used interchangeably but, as the latter was the term most commonly used for this denomination in nineteenth-century rural North Riding, it will be used here; F. Wrigley, *The History of the Yorkshire Congregational Union, 1873–1923* (London: James Clarke and Co., 1923).
13 P. Joyce, *A Guide to Abney Park Cemetery* (London: SAPC, 1984).
14 G. Collison, *Cemetery Interment* (London: Orme, Brown, Green and Longman, 1840), pp. 278–80.
15 *London Gazette*, 19 May 1871.
16 W. Ranger, *Report to the General Board of Health, on a Preliminary Inquiry into the Sewerage, Drainage, and Supply of Water, and the Sanitary Condition of the Inhabitants of the Town of Northallerton, in the County of York* (London, 1850), p. 18.
17 NYRO, R/I/MLT 2, Malton Unitarian chapel book 1829–1876 containing treasurers accounts, minutes and copy letters; church book 1773–1933 containing baptisms, marriages and burial registers, certificates and deeds.
18 J. Rushton, *The History of Ryedale: From the Earliest Times to the Year 2000* (Trowbridge: Blackthorn Press, 2003).
19 D. O'Sullivan, *Great Ayton: A History of the Village* (Great Ayton, private publication, nd).

20 BI, v. 1868/Ret 1, Archbishop's Visitation return, 1868.
21 T. Bulmer, *History, Topography and Directory of North Yorkshire* (Preston: T. Bulmer and Co., 1890), p. 409.
22 G. Stock, 'Quaker burial: doctrine and practice' in Cox, M. (ed.) *Grave Concerns: Death and Burial in England, 1700–1850* (York: Council for British Archaeology, 1998), p. 139.
23 H. E. Roberts, *Researching Yorkshire Quaker History: A Guide to Sources* (Hull: University of Hull Brynmor Jones Library, 2003).
24 W. Shiels, 'Roman Catholic recusancy 1580–1792', in Butlin, R. (ed.) *Historical Atlas of North Yorkshire* (Otley: Westbury, 2003); A. Gramer, 'John the Evangelist, Easingwold: A Century and a Half, 1833–1983', *Ampleforth Journal*, 89 (Spring 1984).
25 'The Roman Catholic view as to consecration', 1897 (312) *Report from the Select Committee on burial grounds; together with the proceedings of the Committee, minutes of evidence, and appendix*, appendix 5.
26 M. R. Watts, *The Dissenters Volume II: The Expansion of Evangelical Nonconformity* (Oxford: Clarendon Press, 1995), p. 116.
27 W. H. Mackintosh, *Disestablishment and Liberation: The Movement for the Separation of the Anglican Church from State Control* (London: Epworth Press, 1972), chapter 21; R. E. Rodes, *Law and Modernisation in the Church of England, Charles II to the Welfare State* (Notre Dame, IN: University of Notre Dame Press, 1991), pp. 140ff.
28 J. Rugg, 'The rise of cemetery companies in Britain, 1820–53' (PhD dissertation, University of Stirling, 1992), p. 182.
29 Portsmouth Central Library: Sanderson Collection, Prospectus of the Portsea Island Cemetery Company, 1830.
30 See, for example, *Yorkshire Gazette*, 8 Aug 1855, 'The York Burial Board'.
31 Burial Act (1852), s. 32.
32 For detailed discussion see B. L. Manning (ed.), O. Greenwood, *The Protestant Dissenting Deputies* (Cambridge: Cambridge University Press, 1952); D. Wiggins, 'The Burial Act of 1880, The Liberation Society and George Osborne Morgan', *Parliamentary History*, 15:2 (1996), 173–89.
33 Sir Morton Peto, *Hansard* HC Debates, vol. 16, col. 1024, 24 Apr 1861.
34 Sir William Heathcote, *Hansard* HC Debates, vol. 16, cols 1029 and 1031, 24 Apr 1861.
35 Burial Laws Amendment Act (1880), s. 1.
36 BI, PR/TER 61, Burials 1893–1979.
37 J. Brook Little, *The Law of Burial* (London: Shaw and Sons, 3rd edn, 1902), pp. 267–8.

38 Burial Laws Amendment Act (1880), s. 10.
39 Manning, *The Protestant Dissenting Deputies*, p. 303.
40 NYRO, BB/MLN 1/1, Minute Book, 1858–1894, 22 Nov 1858.
41 *Ibid.*
42 NYRO, BB/MLN 1/1, Minute Book, 1858–1894, 13 Dec 1858.
43 NYRO, BB/TH 8/1, Minute Book, 1878–1889, 28 Nov 1878.
44 NYRO, BB/PAT, Minute Books, 1871–1963, 20 Sep 1873.
45 NYRO, BB/PAT, Minute Books, 1871–1963, 1 Nov 1873.
46 NYRO, BB/PAT, Minute Books, 1871–1963, 28 Aug 1873.
47 NYRO, BB/MLN 1/5, Extracts re Roman Catholic section of cemetery.
48 NYRO, BB/MLN 1/1, Minute Book, 1858–1894, 7 Nov 1858.
49 NYRO, BB/MLN 1/1, Minute Book, 1858–1894, 7 Nov 1859.
50 NYRO, BB/TH 8/1, Minute Book, 1878–1889, 27 Jan 1880.
51 WYRO, RDP49/65, Papers re churchyard and cemetery, 1881–1883.
52 *Ibid.*, 19 Jul 1886.
53 *Ibid.*
54 *Ibid.*
55 NYRO, BB/PAT, Minute Books, 1871–1963, 19 Dec 1874.
56 NYRO, BB/PAT, Minute Books, 1871–1963, 10 Dec 1887.
57 NYRO, BB/PAT, Minute Books, 1871–1963, Mar 1888.
58 H. Speight, *Kirkby Overblow and District* (London: Eliot Stock, 1903), p. 91.
59 *York Herald*, 9 Jan 1880.
60 NYRO, R/Q/G 10, Guisborough Monthly Meeting, letter from J. W. Pease, 31 Mar 1882.
61 *Helmsley Parish Magazine*, Nov 1876.
62 *Helmsley Parish Magazine*, Mar 1878.
63 NYRO, PR/HEL 7/1, Correspondence and papers relating to the old churchyard and its extensions, 1880–1989, Handwritten parish magazine extracts, 1882.
64 *Helmsley Parish Magazine*, Jun 1883.
65 CERC, 11686/4 1875–1881, Church Commissioners: Churches, burial grounds and parsonages, conveyance of sites, general file. Petition in correspondence dated 23 Mar 1878.
66 NYRO, CRONT/1712, Honouring the Dead – essays in the social and cultural history of death and remembrance in Pickering by Andrew Husband.
67 NYRO, PC/HOV 3/5, Letters and papers relating to the new cemetery, 1880–1882, 1885, 1887.
68 NYRO, PR/MAS 15, Burials, 1843–1957.

69 BI, 627, Burials, 1813–1885, 2 Jul 1881.
70 J. Ellerton (ed.), *A Manual of Parochial Work for the Use of Younger Clergy* (London: SPCK, 1908), p. 81.
71 WYRO, RDP96 12/2, Burials, 1843–1897. Note that no later burial register was available.
72 T. Bulmer, *History, Topography and Directory of North Yorkshire* (Preston: T. Bulmer and Co., 1890), p. 972.
73 F. Francis and J. Smithson, *A History of Burythorpe, A Yorkshire Village* (Private publication, nd, probably post 2000).
74 Watts, *The Dissenters*.
75 D. Clark, *Between Pulpit and Pew: Folk Religion in a North Yorkshire Fishing Village* (Cambridge: Cambridge University Press, 1982), p. 78.
76 www.scawton.org; BI, v. 1868/Ret 1, Archbishop's Visitation return, 1868.
77 H. Brierley, 'The oldest unrestored church in Yorkshire, St Mary's Scawton', *Illustrated Church News*, 29 Oct 1897.
78 B. Heeney, *A Different Kind of Gentleman: Parish Clergy as Professional Men in Early and Mid-Victorian England* (Hamden, CT: Archon Books, 1976).
79 *The Church in Country Parishes* (London: SPCK, 1940).
80 NYRO, PR/SAT 1/9, Burials, 1813–1988.
81 F. Francis and J. Smithson, *History of Burythorpe: A Yorkshire Village* (private publication, nd probably post 2000).
82 NYRO, PR/OUL 1/10, Burials, 1813–1935.
83 NYRO, PR/LEA 1/17, Burials, 1857–1902.

7

'Casting into the great crucible of the present ferment all manner of time-honoured traditions':[1] *new legislative contexts for twentieth-century burial*

This chapter acts as a vantage point and looks back to survey the changes which the Burial Acts and other developments had brought to central North Riding by the end of the nineteenth century, and then forward to consider the new legislative contexts for burial in the twentieth. It is important to stress that any change, where it happened, was taking place in a general context of de-population: industrial activity was continuing to trickle away from central North Riding. However, despite decreasing population numbers, the amount of burial space was increasing. Between 1850 and 1894, 22 cemeteries had been laid out and over 60 churchyards were extended. In addition, 22 new churches were built in the area, so adding further churchyards. In a further handful of cases, church renovation also provided a context for bringing an existing churchyard into use for burial for the first time. By contrast, just 25 Orders in Council to close churchyards were issued. These closures tended to be partial or conditional, and, in almost all cases, burial continued. Perhaps the principal question asked in this chapter is whether and how far the Church of England had lost the near-monopoly position it held in 1850. It is arguably the case that, before 1900, the Church had lost very little. The Burial Acts had brought some concessions to Nonconformist interests in the passage of the Burial Laws Amendment Act and more substantially in the provision of unconsecrated burial space in the new cemeteries. However, as has been seen, burial in consecrated ground, with an Anglican minister, remained by far the majority option. Thus, the Church was probably in an even stronger position at the end of the nineteenth century than it had been at mid-point.

However, four unrelated Acts of Parliament passed between 1879 and 1902 together provided a much less supportive context for the continued dominance of the Anglican Church in funerary matters, and mark the final decades around the turn of the century as a watershed. It is from this point that a serious threat existed to the centrality of the Church of England as a provider of burial space. The first was the Local Government Act, passed in 1894. This Act changed the nature of rural governance and divested the vestry of a number of civic roles. From 1894, new parish councils would take the lead in parish affairs. The second piece of legislation was the Public Health (Interments) Act, 1879, which sat outside the framework of the Burial Acts, and appears in the statute books as little more than an amendment to earlier legislation on mortuaries. However, this Act permitted local authorities to establish cemeteries under the aegis of the Cemetery Clauses Act, 1847, so providing a new legislative framework for cemetery provision in which consecration would not be compulsory. Cemeteries under the Public Health Act were not presumed to have augmented parish churchyard space, as was the case under the Burial Acts. For the first time, it was possible to provide – on the rates – a cemetery completely free of Church of England control. The Public Health (Interment) Act and the Burial Acts were unrelated and operated side-by-side, further confusing an already confused area of law. The distinction between 'local authority' and 'burial board' cemeteries continued until the 1974 Local Government Act abolished burial boards and brought these two types of cemetery under the same regulations.

A third measure which looked set to challenge the dominance of the Church in burial matters was the passage of the penultimate Burial Act: the Burial Act, 1900. The Burial Laws Amendment Act had not brought to a close Nonconformist agitation against burial inequality. There remained the matter of continued payment to the parish clergy of fees charged in churchyards and in the consecrated portions of cemeteries even when ministers from other denominations had taken the services. Campaigning continued through the 1880s and 1890s, and a parliamentary inquiry specifically on the issue of mortuary fees was held in 1882. A second parliamentary inquiry in 1898–9 underlined just how impossible it had become to understand burial legislation. The 1900 Act was the result. From this date, burial fees would be paid 'for services rendered' to whichever minister took the funeral, no matter what denomination, and whether or not the land was consecrated. Furthermore, rather than presuming that consecration would take place, a case would have to be made that consecration was required. One of very last of the Burial Acts finally removed the privileged position held by the Church and the protected status of the clergy: after nearly fifty years, Bishop Blomfield's principle had been abandoned.

The fourth measure followed renewed agitation on the issue of sanitary interment. The final decades of the century were marked with scandal attached to the supposed public health consequences of overcrowding in the new burial board cemeteries located in London and the more populous cities including Manchester and Liverpool. The Reverend F. Lawrence from the small Ryedale village of Westow was the founder and secretary of the Church of England Burial, Funeral and Mourning Reform Association, which was at the forefront of campaigning on the issue and sought re-engagement with the earliest Board of Health principles which had aimed for swifter decomposition. However, the work of the Association was eclipsed by interest in a new technology: the Cremation Act of 1902 expressly permitted local authorities and burial boards to provide crematoria. Cremation in a separate, secular crematorium introduced the possibility of a complete break from all the religious connotations of burial in churchyard or in cemetery, and the Church of England was quickly aware of the implications. In rural areas, parishioners' use of a crematorium located in one of the larger cities meant a substantial spatial dislocation. Indeed, the subsequent scattering of remains at crematoria gardens of remembrance might mean that a final resting place could be twenty or thirty miles distant, and the local churchyard could become an irrelevance.

Burial in North Yorkshire, 1894

By 1894, the central belt of rural North Riding was – with the exception of Nidderdale, perhaps – very firmly agricultural in character.[2] For the rest of the region, much of the earlier industrial activity had, for the most part, fallen away. In 1901–2 the writer and agricultural reformer Rider Haggard undertook a tour to assess the state of English agriculture following a period of severe national depression in the sector. Haggard found farming in North Yorkshire to be in a more prosperous state than 'other counties with equal if not greater advantage'.[3] Neverthless, farmers throughout the region complained of shortages of labour.

Population decline

After mid-century, rural de-population had become evident in much of the county. In the registration districts of Bedale, Ripon, Pateley Bridge, Great Ouseburn, Thirsk, Northallerton, Easingwold, Helmsley and Malton, net outward migration between 1851 and 1901 was greater than the natural increase in population. Only in Stokesley and Knaresborough districts was increase evident: in the latter, the rapid development of Harrogate contributed substantially to a population increase of 109.7 per cent.[4] Table 7.1 indicates that many villages included in the study that were already small in the first half of the nineteenth century diminished further in size in the second half. For example, Allerston near Pickering fell from a population of 450 in 1850 to 369 fifty years later; and the number of inhabitants in Kirby Wiske dropped from 888 to 577 over the same period.

Table 7.1 Population change in a selection of parishes, listing all the warpentakes wholly or partly included in the study

Warpentake	*1851*	*1901*	*+/- percentage change*
East Riding: Buckrose*			
Acklam (*Acklam with Barthorpe, Leavening*)	781	528	–32
Norton	2983	3842	+29
Wintringham (*Knapton Chapelry, Wintringham*)	131	121	–8
North Riding: Allertonshire			
Birkby (*Birkby, Hutton Bonville Chapelry, Little Smeaton*)	243	251	+3
Sessay (*Sessay Hutton, Sessay*)	473	391	–17
Osmotherley (*Ellerbeck, West Harsley, Osmotherley, Thimbleby*)	1354	895	–34
North Riding: Birdforth			
Cold Kirby	179	127	–29
Felixkirk (*Boltby, Felixkirk, Sutton-under-Whitestone Cliffe, Thirlby*)	900	722	–18
South Kilvington (*South Kilvington, Thornborough, Upsall*)	389	383	–2
North Riding: Bulmer			
Alne (*Aldwark, Alne, Flawith, Tholthorpe, Tollerton, Youlton*)	1659	1392	–16
Gate Helmsley	293	171	–42

Table 7.1 *continued*

Warpentake	*1851*	*1901*	*+/- percentage change*
North Riding: Gilling East*			
Kirby Wiske	888	577	–35
East Cowton	461	351	–24
North Riding: Hallikeld			
Kirby Hill (*Humberton with Milby, Kirby Hill, Langthorpe*)	648	592	–9
West Tanfield	628	527	–16
Burneston (*Burneston, Carthorpe, Exelby, Leeming & Newton, Gatenby, Theakston*)	1635	1211	–26
North Riding: Hang East*			
Kirkby Fleetham	605	579	–4
Masham (*Common Lands, Burton-upon-Ure, Ellingstring, Ellingtons, Fearby, Healey & Sutton, Ilton with Pott, Masham, Swainton with Wathermaske*)	2695	1955	–27
Thornton Watlass (*Clifton-upon-Ure, Rookwith, Thirn, Thornton Watlass*)	1,044	713	–32
North Riding: Langbaurgh Liberty West*			
Appleton Wiske	559	291	–48
Kildale	145	247	+70
Seamer-in-Cleveland	247	208	–16
North Riding: Pickering*			
Kirby Misperton (*Barughs Ambo, Great Habton, Little Habton, Kirby Misperton, Ryton*)	993	767	–23
Allerston	450	369	–18
North Riding: Ryedale			
Lastingham (*Common Lands, Appleton-le-Moors, Farndale East Side, Hutton-le-Hole, Lastingham, Rosedale West Side, Spaunton*)	1380	1485	+8
(New) Malton (*St Leonard, St Michael*)	3841	2615	–32
Slingsby	632	457	–28

West Riding: Claro – Lower			
Burton Leonard	475	363	–24
Farnham (*Farnham, Ferrensiby, Scotton*)	580	514	–11
South Stainley with Cayton	247	190	–23
West Riding: Claro – Upper*			
Hunsingore (*Cattal, Hunsingore, Great Ribson with Walshford*)	586	442	–25
Kirkby Overblow (*Kearby with Netherby, Kirkby Overblow with Swindon, Rigton, Sicklinghall, Stainburn*)	1598	1197	–25
Kirk Deighton (*Kirk Deighton, North Deighton*)	480	466	–3
West Riding: Ripon Liberty			
Nidd	114	193	+69

* Indicates that only part of this warpentake is included in the study. Parishes included here do not include any affected by the Divided Parishes Act, and are wholly located in the named warpentake. Townships in the parish are included in parentheses. *Source: Victoria History of the Counties of England: Yorkshire* (1974 [1913]).

Overall, therefore, in this area, demand for burial space decreased through the second half of the nineteenth century. Figure 7.1 includes a small selection of churchyards in towns and villages of various sizes. For St Hilda's at Ampleforth, the average number of burials annually through the 1850s was twelve a year, but in the 1880s this had dropped to nine; All Saints' annual average burials at Kirkbymoorside was 58 in the 1850s, but this decreased to 40 in the 1880s; in Stokesley, interment averages in the churchyard of St Peter and St Paul fell from 46 to 34 in the same period.

With this broader context in view it is useful to ask two questions: how did burial provision change, and whether any change constituted a major challenge to the Church of England's near-monopoly of burial provision in the area, so evident at the mid-century point.

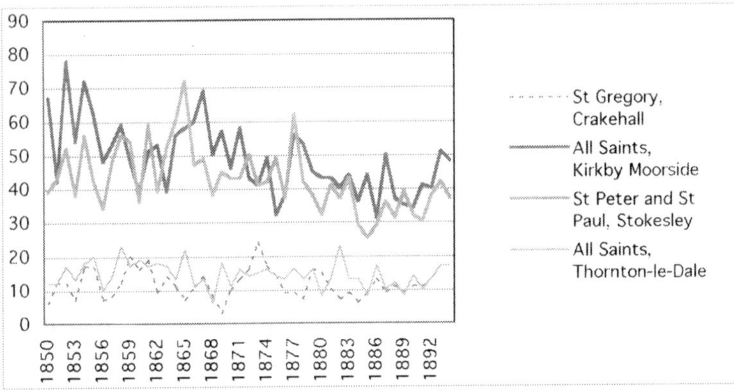

Figure 7.1 Burials in selected churchyards, 1850–1894

Trajectories of change in provision

Analysis of the settlements in the study allows for the mapping of 'trajectories' that compare burial provision in each location in 1850 with provision in 1894. This approach gives the advantage of being able to assess what were the commonest 'narratives' of change. Reviewing the history of burial nationally, it might be supposed that the nineteenth century saw, with the introduction of the Burial Acts, a massive replacement of churchyard provision with new cemeteries. It is clear from this text that this story does not pertain to rural areas, and certainly not in an extremely rural location such as central North Riding. In fact, of the 277 settlements in the study, 153 experienced no substantive change: the churchyard that was open for interments in 1850 remained open for interments half a century later, with no evident alteration to the site's boundary. It would seem that, in these places, the storm of religious burial controversy and tides of successive burial legislation had had no impact at all by the end of the nineteenth century.

Table 7.2 Change in burial provision in case study settlements between 1850 and 1894

No change	153
Extension to churchyard	63
New cemetery	22
New church or churchyard	18
No provision as yet in 1894	13
Other	8
Total	277

However, this rather static picture of 'no change' masks substantial and dynamic development in the remaining settlements. Perhaps the biggest corrective that this study presents to the existing literature on burial is the fact that the Church of England was – throughout the nineteenth century – remarkably active in augmenting its provision, not least through the building of new churches. Eighteen of the settlements in the study had had no burial provision at all in 1850, but by 1894 had been provided with a new church, or with space that became available for interment around an existing chapel of ease. Church building, endemic in the first half of the nineteenth century, expanded even more rapidly in the second half. The findings of the religious census of 1851 were taken as indicating that the Church of England had too few churches and too few sittings particularly in towns and cities. However, new church building was not restricted to just urban areas. In central North Riding, church renovation and new church building had been embraced with energy by the gentry. This was a not insubstantial group. At the end of the nineteenth century, titled estate-owners in rural North Yorkshire continued to dominate rural affairs: the county had the highest concentration of country seats still occupied by the landed gentry.[5] In February 1861, the *York Herald* recorded a meeting held in York to establish the York Diocesan Church Building and Endowment Society. This meeting – one of the most eminent to grace the city, according to the newspaper – was attended by the Archbishop of York and Earl Fitzwilliam and other prominent landowners including Admiral Duncombe, the Honorable Payan Dawnay, J. D. Dent and E. S. Cayley. The meeting had stressed the need for new places of worship in the industrialised areas of South and West Yorkshire, but the North of the county also required attention. According to the Dean of York 'there were in other parts of the Diocese the agricultural and the rural – Wold villages and moorland townships scattered over a vast area, occupied by an industrious and hardworking class, who reside two, three, and more miles from a parish church'.[6] Whether or not the Society was directly responsible, investment in church building in the area was considerable. Sir Tatton Sykes II, who was one of the largest landowners nationally, built fifteen churches on his Wolds estates. Lady Frankland-Russell of Thirkleby Park was also an assiduous church builder, and funded the construction of St Stephen's, Aldwark, and All Saints, Great Thirkleby. In total, 25 new churches were constructed in central North Riding between 1850 and 1894, at least thirteen of which were funded either by local aristocracy or other landed estate owners or through individual acts of philanthropy. The new burial provision brought by this development was not necessarily welcomed. The traditional burial of Aldwark residents at St Mary's, Alne, continued despite the greater proximity of St Stephen's, the use of which has always been limited.

By far the most common change between 1850 and 1894 was extension to an existing churchyard, which took place in 63 settlements. Even in the larger market towns, often the first response to the need for additional burial space was to add land to the space already available. It is notable that both Knaresborough and Ripon – the settlements with heaviest levels of demand at mid-nineteenth century – took the option of extending the churchyard in preference to adopting the Burial Acts. Both St John the Baptist and the Cathedral were augmented substantially by new provision

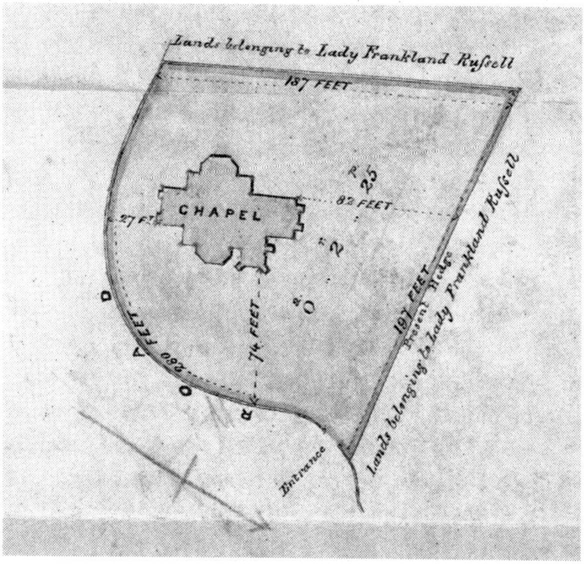

Plate 7.1 Plan of St Stephen's, Aldwark. The church was built in 1853 and provided additional burial space for the parish of Alne (BI, CD251).

which was able to accommodate the continuation of high levels of demand. Indeed, average annual burials in the twenty years following the extensions in both places in 1855 were around 150 in St John the Baptist and 120 at Ripon Cathedral. St Mary's at Thirsk had also been extended in 1844. In all these three places, the need to resort to the Burial Acts was delayed until after the 1880s. Thus, the Burial Acts had in no way negated the validity of continued and even extended reliance on churchyard space.

For 22 settlements in the study, at the period's end the biggest change had been the creation of a cemetery. This change was concentrated mostly in the larger market towns of Norton, Northallerton, New Malton, Pateley Bridge, Thirsk and Great Ayton. In these places, it was often the case that the new cemetery did indeed signal the closure of an ancient churchyard that was more centrally located. There is no question that, for the first time, new cemeteries provided substantial and new provision of more accessible unconsecrated burial space that was available to all Nonconformist denominations. Hitherto, in central North Yorkshire, that provision had been small-scale, with each burial ground's use restricted to a particular denomination.

However, as has been indicated, the consecration of half the cemetery did also materially increase the amount of Anglican burial space. Furthermore, more detailed study of burial boards indicates that there was more than one way in which the Burial Acts could be adopted. Chapters 5 and 6 reviewed the operation of the larger burial boards. In addition to these, there were eight smaller-scale burial boards that were established between 1853 and 1894: at Kirby Misperton, Aldborough, Boroughbridge, Crakehall, Kirkby Overblow, West Rounton, Appleton Wiske and Old Malton (see Table 7.3). The status of these smaller burial boards, and the sites they laid out, is not a little ambiguous. It appears that, in certain circumstances, vestries used the Burial Acts largely as a means to access finance to add an extension to the churchyard. At Appleton Wiske, the

Table 7.3 Smaller burial boards, 1853–1894

	Date	*Initial acreage*	*Buildings*	*Total initial loan (£)*
Kirby Misperton Burial Board	1861	1½ r	None	320
Kirkby Overblow Burial Board	1883	3 r	Single chapel only	na
Old Malton Burial Board	1883	na	None – attached to existing churchyard	c. 165
Appleton Wiske Burial Board	1892	na	None – attached to existing churchyard	na
Crakehall Burial Board	1892	na	None – attached to existing churchyard	na
West Rounton Burial Board	1892	na	None	130
Aldborough Burial Board	1893	1 r 28p	None – attached to existing churchyard	570
Boroughbridge Burial Board	1894	na	None	na

churchyard had been closed by Order in Council in 1892 but the vestry had been declined funding for a new burial site from the Public Works Loan Board. The vestry explained their difficulties in a letter to the Burials Office:

> The Loan Commissioners write us to say that they 'can only lend to burial boards, and they are not aware churchwardens and overseers have any power of borrowing for the purposes mentioned.' A majority of the ratepayers [...] decided that a burial board is quite uncalled for in so small a parish, and decided to carry out the order as stated; but will be quite unable to do so, unless it be in the powers of the churchwardens and overseers or some other authority to obtain a loan for the purpose. If you can advise us how to legally carry out the Order, we shall feel obliged, and shall take the necessary steps at once.[7]

The vestry was advised to proceed under the Public Health (Interments) Act 1879, but decided instead to form a 'temporary' burial board, 'for three years ... who shall raise a loan for fencing, draining and properly laying out the ground for the purpose'. The money borrowed and interest were to be repaid in the course of the three years, at which time the burial board would cease to function.[8] Dr Hoffman, on visiting the site, noted that the 'The Resolution as to the formation of the board appears to be somewhat irregular', but nevertheless the process was agreed by the Home Office.[9]

Similar circumstances seemed to pertain to other burial boards in this group. In Kirby Misperton, a burial board was set up in 1861. Very little information is available about the board, beyond the fact that it borrowed a small sum – just £320 – to lay out less than an acre of land which was managed for the most part as a detached churchyard: by 1910 the entire site had been consecrated and its management was passed to the rector.[10] Similarly, at Old Malton a board was set up and borrowed a sum of £165 to add a portion of land to the existing churchyard attached to St Mary's Abbey; the low cost reflected the fact that the land had been donated, and the principal expenditure was on an extension of the existing wall. The Board purchased further land in 1905, but again the total cost of that venture was relatively minor, at £550. Aldborough Burial Board also borrowed just £570 to add an extension to the churchyard, using land that was being offered at a preferential rate by the local large landowner; the Board opened another equally modest detached site in 1894.[11] The intent to use the Burial Acts to finance a churchyard extension was clearly explicit at West Rounton, where the vestry resolved that, although it had established a burial board, the new cemetery adjacent to the churchyard was to be 'held and used in *like manner subject* to the *same laws* and *regulations* in *all respects* as the existing churchyard of the parish'.[12] It seems, therefore, that the foundation of a burial boards did not always necessarily lead to the laying out of a site that that was unambiguously regarded as a cemetery.

Thus a clear trajectory – churchyard closure and new cemetery establishment – was evident in perhaps only a dozen places in central North Riding. As a consequence, therefore, it is reasonable to contend that by the end of the nineteenth century the Church of England had almost certainly retained its hold on burial space in rural areas. Furthermore, it might be possible to argue that the Church had – nationally – expanded its holdings of consecrated ground within the many hundreds of burial board cemeteries established in towns and cities. Indeed, in the most rapidly expanding locations – Harrogate being a case in point – the Burial Acts created Church-controlled parish burial space where there had been none previously. However, as will be seen, the last decades of the nineteenth century introduced new legislative contexts which reframed the provision of burial space in the twentieth, and so placed the Church of England on a much less firm footing.

New legislative contexts

The law of burial could never be characterised as tidy or straightforward. An internal Home Office memo written in 1888 declared – perhaps with a sigh – that 'the burial laws are a frightful imbroglio',[13] which civil servants were unwilling to unpick for fear of inflaming Nonconformist and Anglican opposition. In 1854, it had been recognised that 'from time immemorial the parochial authorities had been entrusted with the burial of the dead'.[14] By the beginning of the twentieth century, this situation had changed entirely and these old foundations had been demolished. New legislation offered the opportunity to provide interment as an entirely civic function, and promoted technology which would marginalise burial itself.

The Local Government Act, 1894

In positing the Local Government Act, 1894, as a pivotal point, this book takes the view that the disempowerment of the ecclesiastical vestry was a highly significant event in the social history of burial. The vestry had had control of burial and other civic administrative functions for centuries, and by 1835 was spending one-fifth of the budget of the national government.[15] However, as the century progressed, the accretion of new additions to local government – such as Improvement Commissioners and later Boards of Health – began to peel away certain responsibilities. Indeed, it was recognised in a report of the Convocation of Canterbury in 1902 that 'the tendency of modern legislation has been uniformly in the direction of . . . separating ecclesiastical civic offices and duties'.[16] The final agency of this separation was the Local Government Act of 1894, which removed all civic functions from the vestry, and placed them within the authority of a parish council or, in smaller rural areas, a parish meeting. It was recognised at the time that a substantial rupture had taken place. W. C. E. Newbolt, Canon and

Chancellor of St Paul's Cathedral, declared in 1899: 'we are casting into the great crucible of the present ferment all manner of time-honoured institutions'.[17] Certainly, at the local level, the Act underlined a crucial shift in meaning: in 1902 it was acknowledged that '"parishioner" now meant a ratepayer in a given locality, not a member of a Church in a given area'.[18]

At the local level, the churchyard remained the responsibility of the vestry which retained the ancient offices of churchwarden and sexton. However, the Act fractured village governance, and introduced the possibility that in villages a wholly civic authority – the parish council – might assume responsibility for providing burial space without any vestry involvement. Under the Burial Acts, the vestry had held the power to pass a resolution to provide burial space, and to raise funds for that purpose; this power was now passed to the parish council. It could be argued that the change made little difference, in the short term at least, in terms of the play of local democracies. Individuals featuring regularly in vestry minutes were often the same individuals who had put themselves forward to serve as parish councillors. However, at the village level, the greatest difference lay in the changing economics of churchyard management. Vestries no longer had access to traditional ratepayer mechanisms from which to draw voluntary precepts to support the maintenance or extension of the churchyard. Although in most villages the churchyard continued to serve the larger civic parish, its costs were borne by a decreasing Church congregation.

Public Health (Interments) Act, 1879

Much of the first half of this book has dealt with the workings of the many Burial Acts, and left to one side the passage of a completely anomalous piece of legislation: the Public Health (Interments) Act of 1879. This Act was, at the time, commonly referred to as Marten's Act after Alfred Marten, Conservative MP for Cambridge, who had steered its speedy passage through Parliament as a private member's bill. Deborah Wiggins, the only historian to have hitherto noted the import of this act, characterised the legislation as having 'sneaked through' Parliament 'much to the later discomfort of both parties'.[19] Alfred Marten did not have a particularly distinguished parliamentary career, and served as MP for just six years. He had, however, contributed to debate on the many proposed acts which had culminated in the Burial Laws Amendment Act in 1880, and had clearly been frustrated at the degree to which religious politics had hampered the closure of over-filled churchyards and the opening of new cemeteries. He had calculated that around two-thirds of the rural population had not yet been provided with cemeteries, an issue which in his view 'should be treated wholly as a sanitary question'.[20] He believed that the problem lay with the requirement for land to be consecrated. For Marten, there was no ecclesiastical requirement for consecration, and so some form of dedication would be sufficient: the site should simply be 'appropriated by law to purposes of burial, and should not require any other or more formal service of consecration'.[21] The MP had evidently been light on his feet in taking advantage of a series of opportunities: the second reading of his bill had taken place in Osborne Morgan's absence, and so bypassed what would have been substantial opposition; the third took advantage of the 'half past twelve rule' and passed in a tired House of Commons, where none of the Members present understood its ramifications, perhaps Marten least of all.

Marten had characterised his act as 'merely a Bill to enable the sanitary authorities, in certain cases, if they thought fit, to provide cemeteries',[22] and it was in this ostensibly simple guise that the measure had passed through the parliamentary process. On paper, Marten's Act appears to be one of the simpler pieces of nineteenth-century burial legislation: indeed, it contains just three clauses, one of which specifies its short title and construction. The Act makes reference to the earlier Public Health Act, 1875, which had permitted local authorities to build mortuaries for the reception of bodies prior to interment. Marten's Act simply extended that permission to include 'a place for the interment of the dead, in this Act called a cemetery'.[23] The principal difficulty lay in the final clause: 'The Cemeteries Clauses Act, 1847, shall be incorporated with this Act.'[24] Local authorities establishing cemeteries under Marten's Act were not required to operate under the Burial Acts. Rather, they were bound by the regulations included in the Cemetery Clauses Act. Under s. 23 of that Act, consecration of a cemetery *might* take place, but it was also possible that the whole of the site could remain unconsecrated. Chapels were not required by the Act unless part of the site was consecrated, and it was not obligatory to provide two chapels. Even when part of the site was consecrated it was not required for any payment to be made to the local incumbent as compensation for lost interment fees. The Cemetery Clauses Act had presumed that those fees would have been laid out under the specific Act into which the Clauses had been incorporated. The bishop had no authority to appoint a cemetery chaplain. Furthermore, the Marten's Act cemeteries were intended to serve sanitary districts and not parishes: there was no canon law right of burial in these cemeteries as there was in land provided by burial boards for the use of the parish.[25] Essentially, the Act had permitted the creation of rate-funded cemeteries that stood wholly outside the ecclesiastical authorities: 'under Marten's Act', commented MP J. Carvell Williams, 'the parochial incumbent disappeared from the scene as completely as though he were disestablished'.[26]

The impact of Marten's Act became evident almost immediately, as local authorities quickly grasped the freedoms it provided. By 1897, 97 urban districts and 35 rural districts had applied to the Local Government Board for funding for loans to establish cemeteries under the Marten's Act.[27] It should be noted that this list was probably not comprehensive, and did not include the authorities that sought alternative finance – for example, the cemetery at Kirkby

Malzeard that was opened by Ripon Union Rural Sanitary Authority in 1882. Use of the legislation might have been greater had it been available to parish councils, but the Act was not amongst those translated to councils in 1894, and they were obliged to continue making recourse to the Burial Acts. Unsurprisingly, the operation of Marten's Act provoked no little controversy. In 1897–8, a Parliamentary inquiry was held to explore the specific subject of cemeteries established under this legislation.[28] Marten's intention – for the Act to promote speedier and cheaper cemetery provision – had been realised by a number of local authorities. However, they often also took the opportunity to provide new burial space that was entirely unconsecrated, much to the dismay of the local Anglican community. Agitation around the introduction of the Burial Laws Amendment Act in 1880 has perhaps overshadowed the substantial local and national consternation caused by this development.

Respondents to the Select Committee indicated that the opening of cemeteries under the Act could become a very thorny problem indeed at the local level. For example, in Denton, Lancashire, the decision was made to establish a new cemetery in 1890 as accommodation in the parish churchyard was becoming limited. The local authority proceeded under Marten's Act, and the land remained wholly unconsecrated although internally land was set aside for the use of Nonconformists, Anglicans and Roman Catholics. The Bishop declined to dedicate the Anglican section since dedication carried no legal authority. The issue of whether or not the cemetery should be part-consecrated dominated Denton's elections, creating considerable ill-feeling between denominations. The town clerk reported to the Select Committee that the local council elections were fought wholly on the issue, with candidates aligning themselves as pro- or anti-consecration: 'Very strong speeches were made on both sides, and a great deal of election literature issued.'[29] The clerk acknowledged that such agitation would not have arisen had consecration carried no more than ritual intent: the entire problem rested with the legal ramifications which allowed the appropriation of that land by the Church. The issue had become further complicated in Hyde. Here, it was reported that the council had purchased three cemeteries under the Public Health Act with a loan secured from the Local Government Board (LGB). However, the LGB refused a further loan to lay out the cemeteries following the council's resolution not to consecrate any of the three sites: the LGB considered the sites financially unviable if local Anglicans were likely to seek interment elsewhere. This intervention by the LGB in what was considered to be a matter of religious political principle was regarded by the Select Committee as extremely unfortunate. Indeed, its members included the MP for Hyde, J. W. Sidebotham, who had agitated for legislative change on the matter throughout the early 1890s, and whose experience contributed substantially to the framing of the Committee's enquiry and the subsequent bill.

The Burial Act, 1900

The principal recommendations of the Select Committee on Burial Grounds passed almost entirely into law, in the Burial Act of 1900.[30] It would be a mistake to consider that this penultimate Burial Act – coming a long way after the major ructions caused by the 1880 Burial Laws Amendment Act – constituted a return to burial matters after a species of hiatus. In actuality, there had been continued effort to draft legislation that would resolve the very many problems inherent in the operation of two sets of burial legislation, including any number of consolidating bills. However, internally, the Home Office admitted there was a general reluctance to 'bring on a debate between Churchmen and Dissenters on the subject of consecration'.[31] Nevertheless, by 1885, new proposals began to acquire a more radical tone than anything which had gone before, and carried deeper objectives than the desire to rationalise the administration of burial regulations. According to an internal Home Office memorandum dated 1887, another bill had been framed which aimed 'solely to withdraw the local public business of providing for the burial of the dead altogether from the control or influence of any officers of the Church of England', and 'obliterate for the future all distinction between Church of England and Nonconformist in the operation of the Burial Acts or of any Acts under which the expenses of burial come out of the rates'.[32] Essentially, proposals aimed to extend the secular tone of Marten's Act to the Burial Board cemeteries, and remove the diocesan interference that was a consequence of consecration. Unsuccessful bills were presented and failed in 1895 and 1897, but by the century's end it appeared that broad support could be found for the recommendations proposed by the 1897–8 Select Committee. Indeed, bishops attending the Convocation of York had passed a resolution agreeing that the Committee's recommendations were 'a satisfactory basis for legislation'.[33]

This degree of support suggests that the Church of England was fully aware of the untenable nature of its position by the end of the century, with regard to an issue that was tangential to the central concerns regarding consecration. By 1900, there had been considerable agitation on the subject of the fees charged by clergy in both churchyards and the consecrated sections of cemeteries. The subject of mortuary fees was revisited in part by the 1897–8 Select Committee, reiterating findings into an early Select Committee on that specific subject, held in 1882. Sir Alexander Gordon, who had introduced the motion for a Select Committee on mortuary fees in the House of Commons, believed that 'regulation or reduction' was required. The question was not one of denominational politics, since the imposition was universal: 'while these burial fees were a benefit to a few thousand clergymen, they were injurious to 25,000,000 Englishmen'.[34] Earlier chapters have indicated that fee-paying structures for burial in the Church of England could in many cases be as complex as those charges set by burial boards. Canon law and common law pertained to the setting of burial fees, and both had been overridden by the accretion of practices that varied widely: 'there was so much uncertainty that no-one knew what he had to pay'.[35] Inequities had become endemic, and had been further heightened by the operation of the Burial Laws Amendment Act, under which incumbents continued to receive fees for burial services in consecrated sections, even if they themselves did not take the service.[36]

An element of the issue that appeared to be hugely unpopular was the benefit derived by the clergy from the practice of charging permission fees for the construction of brick graves and erection of monuments and railings. Variation in these fees was also substantial, so much so that the Committee found 'it is almost impossible to classify them'.[37] What was certain, however, was that the fees were payable both in the churchyard and in the consecrated sections of burial board cemeteries. This latter charge was extremely difficult to justify. One written submission to the Select Committee was a leaflet issued by the Reverend R. J. Thorpe, vicar of Hovingham, listing monument permission fees and also containing a defence for their imposition. Thorpe stressed that the vicar was also the guardian of public rights in a new cemetery as he had been in the churchyard, and it was incumbent on him to exact substantial fees particularly where larger monuments were involved:

> A large tombstone is, moreover, as a rule, offensive to the public eye, not only for its own ponderous ugliness, but because it has always a tendency to get out of the perpendicular in the course of time. A coping is in nine cases out of ten also an obvious encroachment. It may be said that in all these cases the encroachment is only a matter of a few inches or at the most a foot, but many tombstones mean many inches, and there is little doubt that a piece of ground reserved for plain burials would hold twice as many graves as a piece of equal size in which every grave had a coping and a tombstone.[38]

The Committee was clearly not persuaded by the argument that the fees operated as a deterrent, and instead viewed the income from permissions as 'a direct inducement ... to grant such permission'.[39] The Committee recommended a radical revision of the whole mortuary fees structure.

Nevertheless, legislation was not immediately forthcoming. After a decade, the abuses still pertained and by the 1890s it was generally believed that the clergy were actively profiting from the Burial Acts, to ratepayers' cost. In 1893, Thirsk Burial Board received a circular from the City of Worcester, requiring support for a petition on the matter. The indignation expressed in the petition was stated strongly:

> Your Memorialists would not have been surprised to find that the excessive regard for vested interests which prompted the provision of the Burial Acts dealing with the fees of the clergy, had led to the introduction of a clause securing such fees to every incumbent or minster who had possession of a benefice at the date of the passing of those acts.[40]

The issue was raised with fervour in the House, as it discussed two proposed burial bills in 1895 and 1897. Again the MP J. Carvell Williams – secretary of the Liberation Society, and so very much a partisan activist in the matter – was much to the fore, characterising the fees as 'a particularly odious form of taxation'.[41] The resentment was heightened by the fact that cemeteries required continued subsidy from the rates, and monument erection fees in particular might usefully offset the high costs of maintenance. For example, at Hampstead, the vestry had paid the vicar £9,000 in fees over a ten-year period, while at the same time the cemetery had constituted a net loss of around £15,000 to the ratepayers.[42]

When it finally came, the Burial Act, 1900, brought radical change in a number of areas, almost none to the benefit of the Church of England. The framers of the Act had taken a clear steer from the recommendations of the Select Committee on mortuary fees. It was enacted that within any consecrated portion of any cemetery provided by a local authority after the passage of the Act, ecclesiastical fees –

'other than for services rendered' – were no longer payable. This included the fees charged for permission to erect memorials, and fees for burial services taken by Nonconformist ministers in the consecrated section. For cemeteries established before 1900, the fees would be payable only to the current incumbent or for a period of fifteen years whichever was longer.[43] Furthermore, the Act also removed the obligation of poor law guardians to arrange the interment of paupers in the churchyard or other consecrated ground. This requirement – added to the Poor Law Amendment Act, 1844[44] – had secured for the Church of England perhaps its most lucrative source of burial fees.

A second objective of the Burial Act, 1900, was rationalisation at government department level on the way in which burial matters were administered. There had been agitation on this issue certainly since the early 1880s, on the understanding that a shift of responsibility from the Home Office to the Local Government Board would be more likely to bring sanitary improvement at the local level. For example, the Church of England Burial, Funeral and Mourning Reform Association (CoEBFMRA) – of which more in the next section – had since 1878 strongly advocated this measure, which was included as a principal recommendation in its Memorial to the Home Office Secretary of State in 1888.[45] Under the Burial Act, 1900, the Local Government Board absorbed responsibility for burials inspection which would thereafter be undertaken by sanitary engineers, and oversaw financial aspects of provision including ratifying the fees set by the various burial authorities. The Home Office retained matters relating to the ecclesiastical aspects of burial including responsibility for checking on the apportionment of space to different denominations within new cemeteries and any proposed extension, and checking the burial fees set by local clergy. Ostensibly, the measure appears little more than a matter of 'tidying up' a degree of departmental overlap. In reality, a serious blow had been given to the notion that the provision of burial space was essentially a

Church matter, and should therefore stand somewhere outside the normal legislative framework for sanitary issues.

A third substantive change came with new regulations on consecration. The Church had perhaps been gratified by the very first clause in the Act, which allowed the Secretary of State, on petition from local residents, to order a local authority to arrange consecration of a cemetery. This clause then obviated the possibility of the unseemly and divisive tussles over consecration that had taken place under Marten's Act. However, more radical clauses were to come. The previous Burial Acts had followed the presumption that any cemetery provided under the Acts would be consecrated, with an unconsecrated portion conceded 'by way of special exception'.[46] Under the Burial Act, 1900, the opposite presumption held. It was generally considered that all cemeteries would remain unconsecrated unless a case was made for their consecration. The Home Office produced 'Directives to Burial Authorities' which outlined the information which had to be provided to support any new cemetery or new cemetery extension. Burial Authorities were obliged to demonstrate that 'a reasonable number' of people wanted the cemetery to be consecrated; indeed – as a further indicator of demand – data had to be provided on the level of interments in consecrated space locally. As the following chapter demonstrates, these measures by no means prevented the flaring up of local tensions with regard to apportionment. However, they did place cemeteries more firmly within a secularising context that would have been untenable to those framing the first of the Burial Acts.

The Cremation Act, 1902

A fourth development that looked set to undermine the centrality of the Church of England to funerary matters in the longer term was the legalisation of cremation. The Cremation Act 1902 permitted any agency defined as a burial authority – including burial boards, and local authorities operating cemeteries under Marten's Act – to 'provide for cremation'.[47] The history of cremation has been told by historians more expert than this current author, and detailed reiteration is not necessary here.[48] It is perhaps sufficient to say that the development of cremation technology had taken place largely in Continental Europe and an early, pioneering, advocate was Sir Henry Thompson who was surgeon to Queen Victoria. Thompson was markedly successful in galvanising elite opinion in favour of the new technology: the Cremation Society was formed in 1874, and the building of the first UK crematorium began in Woking in 1878. The fact that the new process could not be deemed illegal was established by a ruling in a case brought in 1884 against a Welsh druid who had cremated the body of his infant son, and the first official cremation took place at Woking in 1885.

Much further work needs to be undertaken to integrate fully the history of cremation with the progress of burial issues in the second half of the nineteenth century. Earlier studies have overlooked the unlikely centrality of a small village in North Yorkshire to widespread agitation on the issue of insanitary burial practices. The Reverend Francis Lawrence was vicar of Westow, a village located ten miles south of Norton. In his 1890 gazetteer of North Yorkshire, Bulmer noted that the vicarage in Westow contained the administrative offices of the CoEBFMRA, which by then had evidently gained some repute.[49] The CoEBFMRA had been established in 1878 and had elicited high-level support within the Church of England and beyond. The Association's presidents were the Archbishops of York and Canterbury, and the Duke of Westminster was its principal patron. By the late 1880s the Association had sufficient authority to secure meetings with the Secretary of State at the Home Office. Initially, the aim of the CoEBFMRA had been to 'promote a fuller appreciation of the idea of Christian burial'. Indeed, in its original resolution to the Lambeth Conference, it had advocated a change to funerary practice that reflected more closely the rubric of the Church of England funeral service.[50] Essentially, the Association sought a greater simplicity in funerals. For example, in its Fourth Annual Meeting, it declared itself dedicated to discouraging the use of

> crepe, plumes, and scarves, as also of metal coffins, brick graves, and other things which unduly retard the return of the body to the earth, it would yet have every effort made to mark the solemnity of the occasion, and suggested the adoption of dark attire, the assembling at the church instead of the house of mourning, the use of a bier on wheels or some such contrivance whereby friends and neighbours rather than strangers might render the last offices, the singing of hymns, and the giving of alms to the poor as one means of showing respect to the dead.[51]

The Association aimed to lead by example. Initially there was no call for legislation; rather, as the Archbishop of York declared in an Association meeting held in 1883, 'Our duty is then simply and solely to lay stress on better ideas'.[52]

During the next five years, the tone of the Association's reform activity shifted substantially. By 1888, a proposed Memorial, addressed to the Home Office Secretary of State, evidenced a shift away from ritual aspects of funerary matters, and instead strongly advocated more sanitary burial practice, and addressed a range of areas which it deemed problematic. For example, the Association objected to any activities which unnecessarily prolonged contact with the dead body. In 1843, Edwin Chadwick had expressed the belief that bodies tended to remain in the houses of the poor for long periods because of the time needed to accrue funds to pay for over-elaborate funerals. The Association echoed this belief – considering that excessive funeral cost created 'perpetual paupers' – and also promoted measures by which the speedy decomposition of the body might be effected following interment. The Association was particularly vehement in its opposition to brick vaults and lead coffins. Although its call for a Royal Commission into burials had been rejected by the government in 1888, it had secured a return on burial practices in London cemeteries in 1889. The report indicated that the vast majority of burial boards and private cemetery companies making returns had not adhered to the principle of one interment per grave. The 'common interment system' was in widespread use, and comprised the burial of up to eight adult bodies or fourteen children in each grave.[53] This and other evidence was reproduced in a further Memorial in the same year, which focused on the subject of common interment both in the old company cemeteries and in the newer burial board sites. The Association must have itself collected further information on burial practices. For example, it was asserted that

> At the Ilford Cemetery, the custom has been to dig a trench about 60ft long by 16ft deep, and to place tiers of 20 or more coffins in it, with about three inches of soil between the coffins, until the trench is filled. About 300 coffins have thus been placed in one such trench, and the trench is filled gradually.[54]

The Duke of Westminster summarised some of the worst practices in a letter printed in *The Times* in 1889:

> They have not been *interred*, that is *laid into the earth*, as the Burial Service orders, but simply hidden out of sight; many in underground cells, in coffins of lead or strong wood: the greater part in pits, as in the Tower Hamlets Cemetery, where almost a quarter-of-a-million lie in less than seventeen acres, some to the number of seventy in the same pit. Such modes of disposal of the dead involve an accumulation far too vast for earth and air to purify and disintegrate, a violation of right feeling, natural law, and Christian tradition, a ghastly dishonouring of the dead, and a flagrant imperilling of the public health.[55]

The CoEBFMRA was successful in securing a meeting with the Home Office to present its Memorial. The Duke of Westminster himself headed the meeting, and the Association was clearly delighted by the degree to which it had garnered support from both the Church of England and the scientific community. The Memorial had been signed by over thirty bishops, and dozens of deans, archdeacons and chancellors. A. E. Pease, MP, who was later instrumental in the passage of the Burial Act, 1900, also signed the Memorial, as did presidents of medical and sanitary institutions and Medical Officers of Health from a number of cities. Indeed, Sir Edwin Chadwick himself was also a signatory. The Memorial made six recommendations: 'the protection of the public against the danger arising from the further general use of already overcrowded cemeteries'; 'the concentration of the authority over cemeteries now divided between the Home Office and the Local Government Board'; 'the certification by competent authority of the suitability of soil for the resolution of human remains before a new cemetery is opened'; 'the enforcement of sanitary precautions when death has been the result of an infectious disease'; 'the effectual inspection and supervision of all burial grounds' and 'rendering overcrowding of the dead an offence liable to punishment upon summary conviction before the magistrates'. The Memorial indicated that the Association had travelled some distance from its original remit, and indeed these more radical objectives were problematic to some of its original supporters, not least the Archbishop of Canterbury, E. W. Benson.

It is notable that the Association made little reference to cremation despite the fact that Sir Henry Thompson attended meetings. It was felt that the simplification of burial practice would result in more sanitary disposal of the dead. In particular, the Association sought an end to the use of brick graves and vaults and indeed any practice which might prolong the decomposition of the body including the use of over-sturdy coffins. Common graves – as indicated in earlier Board of Health directives – were particularly problematic, in delaying decomposition through excessive overcrowding. Here, the Association strayed into repudiation of one of its own principal tenets: that of interfering in funerary preference. The Home Office was clearly aware of the ensuing difficulty, in introducing legislation that would perhaps disenfranchise the owners of existing vaults and enforce burial in 'slender' coffins or even shrouds. At a further meeting held between the Association and Home Office officials, representatives were told by Mr Matthews, the Principal Secretary of State to the Home Department, that

> It is hardly possible to legislate in the drastic sense that has been suggested by this deputation without running counter to a good many traditional feelings which are in themselves respectable even though they result perhaps in public mischief.[56]

It is clear that the government had learned that funerary practice was not necessarily amenable to central control, as the widespread failure of burial boards to follow Home Office directives indicated.

It could be argued that the Burial Acts were passed when it became evident that town and city churchyards were demonstrably incapable of dealing with the pressures of urban mortality. It might also be possible that, similarly, the Cremation Act was passed when it became clear that Burial Board cemeteries were incapable of meeting that continued challenge. However, the Church of England was in no position to benefit from the new technology. Jupp reports that the Church 'adopted an ambiguous position' with regard to cremation, and built concessions into the Act to allow unwilling incumbents to opt out of taking cremation services. Much more significant was the fact that crematoria could not be built on consecrated sections of burial board cemeteries, thus denying diocesan authorities an opportunity to influence the course of cremation practice.[57] As the twentieth century progressed, the increasing popularity of cremation looked set to introduce new funerary rituals in which it appeared that the Church of England and the churchyard had, at best, a marginal role.

Conclusion

At the beginning of the twentieth century, the legislative context for the provision of burial space looked very different from the changes which were being embarked on in the first of the Burial Acts in the 1850s. Those Acts had honoured the principle that the Church of England was central to the provision of new burial space, through the aegis of the local vestry. The Burial Acts ensured that new cemetery space was regarded as an extension to the parochial churchyard and continued protection for clerical incomes was enshrined in the new legislation. Even the passage of the Burial Laws Amendment Act, 1880, offered no threat to this position, since a burial fee remained payable to the Anglican clergy where Nonconformist ministers took services in consecrated cemetery sections or in the churchyard. The Burial Act of 1900 brought that system to a close. Henceforth, the clergy would be paid 'for services rendered'. At the start of the twentieth century, the assumption that the Church of England should hold 'preferred provider' status had vanished. The rise of cremation introduced the possibility that the disposal of the dead might become a wholly secular affair. However, as much of this text has demonstrated, legislated enactment does not always have a strong hold on local practice. The following chapters will discuss just how far these new contexts really did alter burial provision in central North Riding during the course of the twentieth century.

Notes

1 W. C. E. Newbolt, *Priestly Ideals* (London: Longmans, Green and Co., 1899), p. 87.

2 B. Jennings (ed.), *A History of Nidderdale* (Huddersfield: Advertiser Press, 1967).

3 R. Haggard, *Rural England: Being an Account of Agricultural and Social Researches Carried Out in the Years 1901 and 1902* (London: Longmans, Green and Co., 1902), p. 282.

4 Richard Lawton, 'Population change, 1700–1900' in Butlin, R. A. (ed.), *Historical Atlas of North Yorkshire* (Otley: Wesbury: 2003), p. 124.
5 E. Waterson, 'The development of the country house' in Butlin, R. A. (ed.), *Historical Atlas of North Yorkshire* (Otley: Wesbury, 2003), p. 229.
6 *York Herald*, 2 Feb 1861.
7 NA, HO 45/9949 B31354, Appleton Wiske.
8 *Ibid.*
9 *Ibid.*
10 BI, Terr 228, Terrier, 1910.
11 Boroughbridge Town Council, Aldborough Vestry Minute Book, 1849–1957, 20 Nov 1871.
12 NYRO, PR/ROW 20/1, Minute book: West Rounton vestry and the Rountons vestry and PCC, 1892–1936, 6 Jul 1893.
13 NA, HO 45/9814/B7338, Burial Bill. Reports of deputations, correspondence etc. aimed at promotion of Bill for amendment and consolidation of Burial Laws. Internal memo dated 8 Dec 1888.
14 Lord John Manners, *Hansard* HC Debates, vol. 122 col. 874, 17 Jun 1852.
15 S. and B. Webb, *British Local Government from the Revolution to the Municipal Corporations Act* (London: Longmans, Green and Co., 1924), p. 4.
16 N. Sykes (ed.), *The Position of the Laity in the Church, being the Report of the Joint Committee of the Convocation of Canterbury, 1902* (London: Church Information Board, 1952 [1902]), p. 51.
17 Newbolt, *Priestly Ideals*, p. 87.
18 Sykes, *Position of the Laity*, p. 54.
19 D. Wiggins, 'The Burial Acts: cemetery reform in Great Britain, 1815–1914' (PhD dissertation, Texas Tech University, 1991), p. 173.
20 A. G. Marten, *Hansard* HC Debates, vol. 243 col. 1470, 19 Feb 1879.
21 *Ibid.*
22 A. G. Marten, *Hansard* HC Debates, vol. 247 col. 287, 19 Jun 1879.
23 Public Health (Interment) Act (1879), s. 2(1).
24 Public Health (Interment) Act (1879), s. 3.
25 For a clear summary of the legal implications of the Act see 1898 (322) *Report from the Select Committee on Burial Grounds; together with the proceedings of the committee, minutes of evidence and appendix*, pp. vi–vii.
26 J. Carvell Williams, *Hansard*, HC Debates., vol. 31 col. 479, 6 Mar 1895.
27 *Select Committee on Burial Grounds*, p. 69.
28 *Select Committee on Burial Grounds*, p. ii.

29 *Select Committee on Burial Grounds*, p. 16.
30 See *The Times*, 27 Mar 1900.
31 NA, HO 45/9814/B7338, Burial Bill. Reports of deputations, correspondence etc. aimed at promotion of Bill for amendment and consolidation of Burial Laws, internal memo dated 8 Dec 1888.
32 NA, HO 45/9653/A39184, Burials: Transfer of administration of Burial Acts to Local Government Board, internal memo dated 19 Mar 1887.
33 S. W. Sidebotham, *Hansard* HC Debates, vol. 70 col. 516, 25 Apr 1899.
34 Sir Alexander Gordon, *Hansard* HC Debates, vol. 268 col. 213, 28 Mar 1882.
35 Mr Osborne Morgan, *Hansard* HC Debates, vol. 268 col. 220, 28 Mar 1882.
36 1882 (309) *Report from the Select Committee on Ecclesiastical and Mortuary Fees, together with the proceedings of the Committee, and minutes of evidence and appendix.*
37 *Report … on Ecclesiastical and Mortuary Fees*, p. viii.
38 *Report … on Ecclesiastical and Mortuary Fees*, p. 346.
39 *Report … on Ecclesiastical and Mortuary Fees*, p. viii.
40 NYRO, BB/TH 10/1, Table of Fees, 'To the Right Honourable the Secretary of State for the Home Department', dated 21 Nov 1893.
41 J. Carvell Williams, *Hansard* HC Debates, vol. 31 col. 477, 6 Mar 1895.
42 J. Carvell Williams, *Hansard* HC Debates, vol. 31 col 476, 6 Mar 1895.
43 Burial Act (1900), s. 1(2) and s. 3(4).
44 Poor Law Amendment Act (1844), s. 31. This act required the burial of paupers 'in the churchyard or other consecrated burial ground in or belonging to the parish, division of parish, chapelry, or place in which the death may have occurred'.
45 LPL, E. W. Benson Papers, Official Letters, 1890, Home B23–C27, vol. 83, p. 28.
46 NA, HO45/9653/A39184, Burials: Transfer of administration of Burial Acts to Local Government Board, internal memo dated 19 Mar 1887.
47 Cremation Act (1902), s. 4.
48 See for example P. C. Jupp, *From Dust to Ashes: Cremation and the British Way of Death* (Basingstoke: Palgrave Macmillan, 2006).
49 T. Bulmer, *History, Topography and Directory of East Yorkshire* (Preston: T. Bulmer and Co., 1892), p. 287.
50 LPL, Lambeth Conference Papers, 1888, 27.

51 LPL, E. W. Benson Papers, Official Letters, 1883, Home D.52–G. 77, vol 3. This volume of correspondence contains a number of inserted pamphlets and Memorials, including reports from the CoEBFMRA.

52 LPL, E. W. Benson Papers, Official Letters, 1883, Home D.52–G. 77, vol 3. Pages 225–6 comprise a pamphlet of the CoEBFMRA.

53 1889 (288) *Metropolitan cemeteries*.

54 LPL, E. W. Benson Papers, Official Letters, 1888, Home F.1–H.19, vol 58, p. 107. This exchange includes a copy of the Association Memorial.

55 Duke of Westminster, letter to *The Times*, 9 Dec 1889.

56 HO 45/9814/B7338, Burial Bill. Reports of deputations, correspondence etc. aimed at promotion of Bill for amendment and consolidation of Burial Laws. Internal notes from meeting dated 6 Jan 1893.

57 Jupp, *Dust to ashes*, p. 89.

Part Two

The cemetery in the churchyard, 1894–2007

8

'It was a task which he would be greatly pleased to hand over to some other person or persons':[1] *centralisation and cemeteries, 1894–1974*

Much of the first half of this book showed that the tenor of legislation is best understood through its implementation. Thomas Kselman's study of death in France in the nineteenth century indicated that local responses to Prairial 23, or the Edict of St Cloud, shaped and modified its impact particularly in rural locations.[2] In England, the passage of the Burial Act, 1900, signalled a determined step away from Church control in burial matters, and it could be argued that, from this juncture, it is possible to view cemeteries as becoming a more innately 'modern' phenomenon. Certainly the contexts for cemetery management were shifting. The Burial Act, 1900, meant that, for the most part, central control was posited with a government department that saw burial as a purely sanitary issue. In rural areas, successive changes to local governance and a restriction in the powers of the vestry meant that responsibility for burial could be removed from the familiar purview of the churchwarden, and instead be overseen by a rural district council with officers in another town. In 1913, the National Association of Cemetery Superintendents was launched to promote cemetery management as a profession. These centralising tenancies came to a climax with the passage of the Local Government Act, 1972. Local government change was the principal purpose of the Act, but it also contained a series of clauses related to burial provision. Under the Act, in operation from 1974, the powers conferred by the Burial Acts, 1852–1906, ceased to be exercisable and the Public Health (Interment) Act, 1879, ceased to operate. Instead, modern 'burial authorities', including district, town and parish, were empowered to absorb existing burial boards. In Harrogate, the higher-tier District Council took over ownership and administration of a number of cemeteries, including Pateley Bridge, Kirkby Malzeard, Ripon and Knaresborough.

Thus it could be argued that the legislation had finally created a context in which the centralisation of burial functions could take place within unitary and district councils, which might oversee a number of cemeteries that were originally established by burial boards. However, by the end of the twentieth century, central North Yorkshire still had a rather confused patchwork of burial providers: the centralisation of burial functions had simply failed to materialise on the ground. Kselman observed that in France *translation*, which required the closure of churchyards and move to municipal cemetery management, floundered in rural areas, where administrators had to be content with a level of illegality.[3] In England, where law did not assign statutory responsibility for the provision of burial space, any centralising tenancy was similarly undermined. It remained largely the case that each village decided for itself whether and how its burial provision should be altered, and villages tended to sidestep the legislation altogether by extending the churchyard. The new rural district councils were not necessarily in a hurry to exercise their freedom to lay out new Public Health cemeteries: indeed, their interest in burial issues overall could be slight. It was small wonder, since burial laws remained hugely difficult to negotiate. At the heart of the matter lay the same concern that drove the provision of new burial space in the nineteenth century: cost.

Contrary to the notion that modernism brought with it an irresistible centralisation of burial function in the secular state, in reality – in the English countryside at least – no civic agency really wanted the responsibility. Indeed, it was a task which agencies actively sought to delegate elsewhere.

The operation of the Burial Act, 1900

The Burial Act, 1900, had ostensibly created a more streamlined legislative framework, in which the interests of the Church of England were no longer represented. A secularised and centralised burial administration might have resulted, if the apparent simplicity had actually materialised. One of the key reasons why burial provision remained stubbornly local was the difficulty of dealing with the legislation. In 1947, Harry Garrett – cemetery superintendent at Brighton, addressing a conference of his cemetery superintendent peers – characterised burial law as being in 'a serious condition of unnecessary complexity'.[4] Although the Burial Act had brought some degree of rationalisation, it remained the case that two government departments were overseeing two different sets of legislation and the application of two sets of guidance. As the twentieth century progressed, the innate inflexibility of the guidance became increasingly evident, particularly given the rather fluid way in which cemetery practice had evolved.

The Home Office

The Burial Act 1900 had transferred many powers to the Local Government Board but the Home Office retained responsibility for two Church-related matters: the regulation of burial fees charged by the clergy, and control on the amount of ground that could be consecrated. Ostensibly, the intent of the legislation was to ensure that denominations were dealt with on equitable terms, but in practice the Act 'policed' the Church of England to ensure that cemetery matters would no longer prove to be divisive. The Home

Office issued a set of Directives which guided burial authorities through the task of securing approval from the Secretary of State as to the setting of fees and the planned apportionment of ground. The Directives were issued routinely to all Burial Authorities making an application.[5] The process could be complex and cumbersome: some applications extended over months or even years. Many local authorities failed to provide sufficient supporting evidence or the required maps and had to re-apply. The maps in particular tended to be of markedly variable quality. Indeed, on occasion the burial authority submitted little more than a rough hand-drawn sketch: in its internal comment on a scrappy application by Thornton-le-Dale, a Home Department official wrote that 'the maps are small but may perhaps be regarded as sufficient'.[6] Local appeals against particular decisions could also delay matters considerably.

The intention of the Burial Act, 1900, had been to clear away all the confusion and inequity relating to the payment of compensation to incumbents under the existing Burial Acts, and to ensure that the tradition of 'mortuary fees' did not continue. To this end, the Directives regulated 'fees for services rendered' by enacting that all such fees were to be presented to the Secretary of State in a table, which would be subject to approval. In order to maximise confusion on the matter, the Home Office did not propose to issue a model table of fees which burial authorities could adopt. Rather, it required burial authorities to present a suggested table supported with evidence of the 'full concurrence of all the ministers of religion concerned'. These evidences might include written statements from local ministers to signal their agreement.[7] The process occasionally ran into difficulty. For example, the Home Office did not interfere in cases where the burial fee might be considered unfeasibly low. Northallerton RDC had taken the lead in ensuring the establishment of a cemetery at Osmotherley and the site's management was lodged with a local committee. In 1907, the committee clerk sent a confused table of fees to the Home

Office for ratification. The civil servants suggested a number of amendments to the clerk, who had been 'unable to make any effort to reduce his extraordinary table to an intelligible form'.[8] However, the suggested changes did not include amendment to what had been an exceptionally low burial fee. In 1921, a letter of complaint on the matter was received by the Home Office from the local clergyman, who claimed that the parish council had refused even to hold a meeting to consider revising the fee upwards. The incumbent acknowledged that he could not under canon law refuse burial to a parishioner, but stated that he would

> Decline to take further funerals of Nonconformists and they can send 8 miles for a minister from Northallerton or 14 miles to Stokesley for a RC priest whose conveyance costs £3. The fee is 1/- which is an *insult* and I shall put up with it no longer! Would *you* in a similar position on notice of a funeral have to send someone 4½ miles to tell the organist and go all over the place getting a choir to come and sing; and then have ½ mile to walk in my robes, sometimes in heavy rain and wet through to my cassock and the fee is 1/- – one shilling! It is disgraceful the way the clergy are treated nowadays.[9]

In May 1922, the parish council – after much prevarication – increased the fee to 2s.

By contrast, the Home Office did intervene where fees were considered unreasonably high. For example, the Home Office internal case files include an application to extend Stonefall Cemetery, which had been laid out on the edge of Harrogate by Harrogate District Council in 1914. The new cemetery had been justified by District's claim that cheaper-cost graves had run out at Grove Road: none of the grave spaces in the consecrated section was available at a lower cost than £4 4s, 'therefore a cemetery is urgently needed for use of persons who cannot afford to give us as much as £4 4s for a grave'.[10] This regard for affordability appeared short-lived. In its application for an extension to the site in 1947, the Borough proposed that the clerical burial fee should be 12s

6d. This fee was deemed excessive by the Secretary of State, and the Department wrote that the charge would

> tend to press somewhat hardly on the poorer members of the community. Such fees seldom exceed 7s 6d although one of 10s 6d, where it has been adopted as a standard fee for all burials whether in public or private graves, and travelling expenses have to be incurred, has been approved on those grounds.[11]

The burial authority was advised that the Department would consider favourably a table with a burial fee not exceeding 7s 6d for common burials, and 12s 6d for burials in private graves and vaults. The fee was amended accordingly.

The Home Office Directives also related to consecration, where the intent of the Burial Act 1900 was to require evidence of demand for consecrated space and ensure fair apportionment between denominations. The Secretary of State required that each application for approval should be accompanied by a plan of the cemetery showing the whole of the site, with approaching roads, and any buildings adjoining the boundary. The plans had to show the apportionment, but were also required to include a detailed representation of the internal layout, including roads, pathways and flower beds, and any chapels, lodges or other built structures. In addition to a visual representation of the site, the burial authority had to include a number of statements (see Box 8.1). The Directives also applied where there was an intention to extend a cemetery and consecrate part of the extension.

The noble intent of the legislation did not necessarily reflect the widespread desire of denominations to deal fairly with each other at the local level. The law remained inadequate in cases where communities were split against each other, and wilfully incapable of coming to a resolution. Perhaps the most spectacular falling-out occurred in Pickering, which was unusual in central North Riding in having Quaker, Wesleyan Methodist and Independent burial

Box 8.1 Statements on consecration required by the Home Department Directions, 1900

(a) The population of the area for which the ground is to be provided.
(b) The estimated number of burials annually.
(c) The estimated proportion of burials in consecrated ground to others. If a burial ground has been in use for some time the actual figures should be given.
(d) Whether applications have been received for allotments, and, if so, on behalf of what denomination.
(e) The estimated number of persons belonging to such denominations and residing within the district.
(f) Whether the allotments proposed, if any, are approved by the representatives of such denominations.
(g) The nature of any objection which may have been raised to the proposed division of allotments.

space still in operation prior to 1900. The churchyard of St Peter and St Paul's had been extended in the 1840s and 1870s. Local Nonconformists had been enthusiastic in their adoption of the opportunity afforded by the Burial Laws Amendment Act. However, donors of a new section to the churchyard in 1893 gave the land on the condition that no non-Anglican services should take place there. Pressure on available space increased at the turn of the century: the 'old' part of the churchyard was closed in 1899, and the Independent burial ground was deemed to be full at around the same time. In 1900, the town was clearly in need of new burial space but the majority Anglican council refused to take action, and upheld their view that it was the Church's responsibility to provide burial space for the parish. However, Dissenters again petitioned for a site in 1904 and a majority of Dissenters on the Council in that year meant that they were successful. As a consequence, a new cemetery was established by Pickering Urban District Council in 1905, using land that had been bought and donated for the purpose by local Nonconformists. The site remained unconsecrated, and it appeared that the issue had been resolved.

However, the question was replayed with vengeance over 1920–1, when it became evident that the churchyard extension at St Peter and St Paul's had started to run out of space. Local Anglicans wanted part of the new cemetery to be consecrated, and so permission had to be secured from the Home Office. An application was made by the – again now majority – Anglican Council.[12] However, the amount of ground required and its location within the cemetery was disputed locally: the Anglicans sought too large a portion, it was claimed, and wanted a favoured section, close to the road. In response, the Anglicans argued that they wanted no more than a third of the unused space in the cemetery, and to be given a section further back signalled that they were to be 'treated as pariahs to be kept out of sight'.[13] Furthermore, the Council announced that – enabled by a regulation in the Cemetery Clauses Act – it would debar Nonconformist ministers from taking services in the newly consecrated portion. Through the summer of 1920, the Home Department was faced with claim and counter-claim from the Church party, in which the vicar was most voluble, and from the Free Church Council which represented Nonconformist interests in the town. It was, as an internal Home Office comment on the case notes indicated, 'an awkward situation'. The attempt to debar Nonconformists from use of the consecrated section was clearly illegal, and the Home Office internally noted that Council 'have been less than just and they know it', especially given the fact that the Nonconformists had themselves purchased and donated the land. In June 1920, the Anglicans pressurised the Home Office for a decision, claiming that the Bishop of Beverley was ready to consecrate, and a date of 1 September had been booked. The Home Office demurred, and in October suggested a meeting at which two representatives from each party should be present. There was a frank refusal to negotiate – or, indeed, be in the same room – and it was left finally to the Home Office to decide: the issue was resolved by defining two equal portions of consecrated and unconsecrated ground, with a third reserved portion available to whichever denomination first needed the space.

A similarly sour relationship between the denominations was evident in Leavening in 1937–8. Here, the need for new burial space had led to conflict between the incumbent and the parish council, reflected in a tense exchange of letters between the parish council, the incumbent and Norton Rural District Council (RDC), which had been contacted by the parish council for advice on steps it needed to take in order to lay out a cemetery.[14] The village of Leavening had long been reliant on the churchyard of St John the Baptist at Acklam, but it was generally known that the parish was running out of burial space. However, there was evident disagreement locally on what action was then required. The incumbent evidently believed that extension of the churchyard was the logical step, and wrote to Norton RDC to that effect:

> I have not canvassed, but it is reasonable to suppose that most people would desire to have their dead laid in consecrated ground, and with the services they are accustomed to. It is reasonable to believe that they will desire to be buried near relatives and friends, and that a churchyard or cemetery at Leavening will be little used for years. Most will continue to go to Acklam. The statements made about Acklam churchyard being full are exaggerated. I have taken nearly every burial for 8 years, and I cannot say it is full.[15]

His intent was for the rates to cover the addition of new space to the existing churchyard at Acklam: he argued that most people locally were 'Church' people, and one Methodist funeral had been taken at the churchyard in the eight years he had been at the parish. It was conceded that the new addition could be managed as a 'public cemetery' but 'the only condition we would make would be, and it is the usual practice, that part or all the ground should be consecrated. It might also be convenient if the rector or a church member should be ex officio one of the committee.'[16] However, the parish council clearly did not view this proposal favourably: the parish clerk argued that the reason why more Methodist funerals had not taken place in the churchyard was that 'the church clergy are against it'. For the parish council, the importance was the establishment of burial space in which all the parish was 'to be equal both Church and Methodist, no-one having more say than the other'. The Home Department case file on Leavening indicated that a separate application had been made for consecration of the cemetery, which evidently did not carry the support of the parish council. Included in the application, as required, was a minute from a parish council meeting which stated: 'we do not apply for consecration but if the Church wish to do it free of cost to the parish to raise no objection, the ground to be divided equal Church, and Methodist'. The cemetery is still defined as having 'Church' and 'Methodist' ends.[17] Dismay at plans to consecrate was also evident at Terrington, where a new cemetery was laid out in 1905. The application to the Department noted that 'the only objection raised has been some members of the Methodist denomination against the service of consecration of any portion of the ground'.[18] It should perhaps be noted that these difficulties were not always evident. An application to consecrate a new cemetery in Sicklinghall in 1925 included a declaration from the local Wesleyan minister that 'the Wesleyans do not require a separate allotment but will inter in the consecrated part'.[19]

As the century progressed, the issue of consecration began to adopt a different character. By the interwar period, many burial authorities clearly found the legislation irksome and even costly since it constituted a restraint in terms of ongoing land apportionment. The desire not to consecrate had clearly been a religious-political act which defined a degree of denominational independence from the Church. However, use of the cemetery in many locations indicated strong preference for burial in consecrated ground (see Figure 8.1).

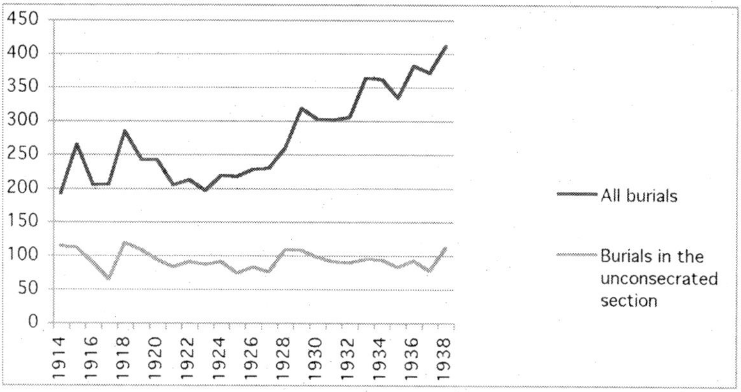

Figure 8.1 Total burials and unconsecrated burials in Grove Road and Stonefall Cemeteries, Harrogate

As the consecrated sections became full, burial authorities concluded that, rather than extend the cemetery, it might be possible to consecrate a portion of the as yet unused unconsecrated section. This was clearly a much cheaper option than purchasing a new section. The Home Office received an application from Kirkby Malzeard in 1949, for permission to consecrate an entire extension: land was in good supply in the unconsecrated section, where – it was claimed, incorrectly – there had been no interment for thirty years.[20] The situation was similar in Great Ayton. Here, the consecrated portion of the cemetery had begun to run out of space in 1914. The Burial Board's review of its options were summarised in a letter sent to the Secretary of State in October 1915.[21] Land had been offered to the Board adjacent to the existing cemetery, but at what was thought to be an expensive rate: in total, the five acres would have amounted to £1,270 10s. A smaller, cheaper plot of land was also available, for £400. It was suggested that instead a section of the as yet unconsecrated portion of the site be consecrated, which was an economical approach favoured by the majority of parishioners. The move would add 320 spaces to the sum of consecrated graves, giving the site another eight years' capacity and costing little beyond the consecration fee. However, the Home Office foresaw problems: the proposed section already contained eleven bodies, and so the Secretary of State 'would not be prepared to approve for consecration any ground in which remains have already been interred unless he were satisfied that the relatives of the deceased persons as buried offered no objection to consecration'.[22] The three townships could not agree which way to move the issue forward. However, it was decided that, as a consequence of the war, it was an 'inopportune time' to buy land and the issue was shelved temporarily.[23]

Similarly, in Northallerton, it was also concluded that problems with land supply could be resolved by an alteration to the existing apportionment. In 1940, an application was received by the Department from the Northallerton and Romanby Burial Board, which sought to apply retrospective consecration to the entire cemetery. There were few spaces left in the consecrated section, but 'ample accommodation' in the unconsecrated side. The Department advised that the Burial Act 1900 required some space to remain unconsecrated, 'having regard to the possibility of appeals being made for the allocation of portions of the burial ground to particular denominations'.[24] The notion of consecrating land in which interment had already taken place was again regarded as problematic. Although the Home Office itself had no objection in principle, it was suggested that relatives of those buried in the unconsecrated section could oppose the move, and so the Board had to be satisfied with part-consecration.

Thus, clerical fees and consecration remained issues for cemetery management through much of the twentieth century. Home Office oversight tended to exacerbate rather than simplify matters: regulations remained inflexible given the changing nature of burial preference and practice.

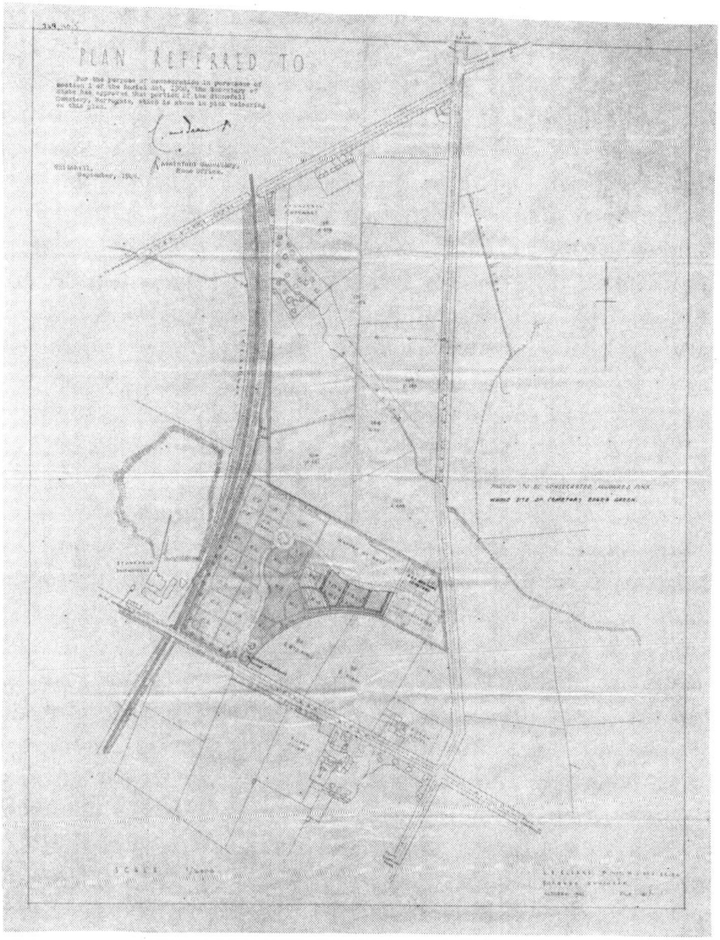

Plate 8.1 Stonefall Cemetery and Crematorium. Map submitted to the Home Office in 1943 to support an application for consecrating the extension (NA, H045/20870).

The Local Government Board

The Home Office had retained some functions, but the Burial Act transferred to the Local Government Board (LGB) the central authority for almost all other aspects of the

Burial Acts.[25] These functions included oversight of sanitary aspects of burial management. The Home Office lost its burial inspectorate, and these duties were devolved to local Medical Officers of Health. Centrally, the LGB retained responsibility for defining sanitary practice and ensuring that new burial ground met specified requirements – for example, in terms of proximity to water courses and residential property. The Board's sanction was also required for a burial board to borrow funds with which to purchase land and lay out a cemetery. As with the Home Office, these various permissions were also required in the case of churchyard or cemetery extensions. The Home Office had oversight of clerical fees, but all other fees – such as the basic burial fee – had to be approved by the LGB, which became the Ministry of Health in 1919.[26] Confusion was inevitable. For example, burial authorities were required to submit details of any sexton fees to the Home Department for approval *if* the sexton was an ecclesiastical officer. Where the sexton was nothing more than the gravedigger appointed by the burial authority, gravedigging fees were to be included within the general burial fee and submitted to the LGB. As with the Home Office, the LGB did not set out a set of model fees and charges, but did actively review the fees presented for its approval and – on occasion – sought to revise them downwards. It remained the case that, where the cemetery had been established under the Burial Acts, the requisite local notifications also had to be given for fee changes, as they had been to the vestry prior to 1894. After 1894, even defining which agency should be approached for permission became a perplexing matter. Guidance printed by the Ministry of Housing and Local Government indicated that 'the present position varies according to the character of the area' and went on to define nine alternative scenarios.[27]

Again, the tenor of these controls and the mode of implementation were regarded as burdensome by local burial boards, particularly since guidance could be less than useful. For example, it emerged during the 1930s that the supply of burial space in Ripon Cemetery had become restricted, and at the heart of the difficulty was an anomaly in the regulations. Earlier chapters have indicated that from the early years of burial board establishment, an attempt had been made to give some consideration to families able only to purchase the lower-cost interments. At Ripon it was generally agreed that no further interment would take place in a common or unpurchased grave for twelve years following the first burial: during this 'grace' period any further family deaths could secure interment in this reserved space. However, in practice this agreement translated to a cut-price purchased grave; after this first grace period, a further twelve years could be purchased for just 7s 6d. Ordinarily, the minimum cost of a new grave with burial right amounted to over £3. The anomaly had caught the attention of other users of the cemetery, as the Corporation indicated in its letter to the Ministry:

> The practice of reserving graves has been used primarily by two classes, firstly, those who would normally have had a public grave and secondly, those who would normally have purchased the exclusive right of burial in perpetuity but saw no reason to do so when they could secure a family grave for 7s 6d each 12 years.[28]

Single interments in 'reserved' graves amounted to a lavish use of space, and the Corporation calculated that it had in excess of seven hundred such graves in the cemetery. Ripon Corporation sought permission from the Ministry of Health to revise its burial fees and amend its regulations to discourage the practice. However, the Ministry's model by-laws made no reference at all to the practice, and it became unclear under what legal framework such an amendment to the by-laws could be made. Correspondence on the matter continued from the late 1930s through to 1944, as the Ministry refused to sanction proposed changes in fees or in working practices. The matter was not resolved until 1944, by which time the legislative basis on which a fee could be charged for scattering remains on a private grave had provoked further confusion.[29]

Overall, therefore, it was clear that the legislative framework for burials for much of the twentieth century remained mired in confusion and largely unresponsive to changing practice, tending to restrict burial boards and local councils on essential issues such as setting fees and establishing workable by-laws. In these circumstances, it was difficult to arrive at efficient and economic management practices. It was perhaps unsurprising, therefore, that, when powers to establish cemeteries were extended to higher tiers of local government, the response from councils was less than enthusiastic.

Rural district councils and 'longstop' cemetery provision

In the final quarter of the nineteenth century a change in rural governance, coupled with the powers granted by the Public Health (Interment) Act, 1879, brought new opportunities for a shift in the basis on which burial space was owned and managed. It had become possible for change in burial provision in a particular settlement to be initiated through the interference of an external agency, acting outside the Burial Acts. Under the Local Government Act, 1888, existing sanitary districts were realigned into urban and rural districts (see Table 8.1). From this period, all the villages of central North Riding sat under the aegis of a rural district council, which had some oversight of burial as it pertained to public health. This was not necessarily a new development. Before this date, some villages had been subject to the sporadic attention of a Rural Sanitary Authority. For example at Osmotherley, concerns about conditions in the churchyard were raised at meetings of the Northallerton Rural Sanitary Authority, which was established in 1873: a report from the Medical Officer of Health was read on St Peter's churchyard in October 1874, although no further details were noted in the Authority minutes at that time.[30] Two years later, in April 1876, the Medical Officer of Health was again requested to visit the churchyard and consider whether additional burial ground was required and later in the same year a report on the matter was forwarded to the Local Government Board.[31] The inspector also visited the churchyard at West Rounton in 1891: disturbance of previous interments and its central location meant that the site was regarded as 'injurious to health'.[32] Similarly, a Medical Officer of Health from the Malton Rural Sanitary Authority was sent to inspect the churchyard at Hovingham in 1880, and concluded that 'a new place of interment is urgently required with as little delay as possible'.[33] The Wetherby Rural Sanitary Authority heard reports on Kirk Deighton and Kirkby Overblow in 1879, and wrote to both parishes about the unsatisfactory nature of their churchyards.[34]

Table 8.1 Local government after 1888, in areas now covered by Ryedale, Hambleton and Harrogate districts

	West Riding	*East Riding*	*North Riding*
Municipal borough councils	Ripon Harrogate		
Urban district councils	Knaresborough	Norton	Malton Pickering Northallerton
Rural district councils	Ripon and Pateley Bridge Nidderdale Wetherby	Norton	Bedale Flaxton Easingwold Malton Northallerton Pickering Kirkbymoorside Helmsley Stokesley Thirsk Wath

Source: E. Royle, 'Administrative changes in Local Government, 1600–1900' in Butlin, R. A. (ed.), Historical Atlas of North Yorkshire (Otley: Westbury, 2003).

At Kirkby Malzeard, matters were taken further. In 1879 the vestry minutes recorded the resolution to discontinue use of part of the churchyard, which was deemed to be 'overfull'.[35] For reasons that are not clear, action was taken in 1882 by the Ripon Union Rural Sanitary Authority. RDCs were not able to adopt the Burial Acts. However, the Public Health (Interment) Act had specifically extended the powers of sanitary authorities 'to include the acquisition, construction, and maintenance of a place for the interment of the dead', and the Ripon Union brought this enactment into fairly immediate use. However, this first early use of the Public Health (Interment) Act was not followed by an immediate rush of similar action taken by either this or other RDCs. Between 1900 and 1974 just six cemeteries were opened by various RDCs using the legislation. Northallerton RDC finally took action in Osmotherey, and laid out a cemetery in 1905; Wath RDC established a cemetery at Dishforth (1912); Pickering RDC opened cemeteries at Thornton-le-Dale (1920) and Newton-on-Rawcliffe (1934); Malton RDC laid out a cemetery at Coneysthorpe (1932) and Nidderdale RDC was responsible for a new cemetery at Goldsborough (1948).

It is difficult to generalise about RDCs from this exceedingly small selection, especially when RDC minute books tend to be thin in representing the nuance of a particular set of circumstances. Indeed, Wath RDC minutes simply note that new ground for a cemetery had been inspected at Dishforth, and no other reference to the site appears. There is slightly more detail in the case of Newton-on-Rawcliffe. In this instance, Pickering RDC was contacted by the vicar in October 1936, who stated 'the churchyard was so full that something would have to be done with respect to the provision of additional burial ground'. The RDC resolved to ask the vicar to 'submit a petition from persons resident in Newton asking for additional burial ground to be provided and the Council would then consider it'. Within the month, the vicar had written again expressing concern that the shortage was pressing, and a resolution to the matter needed to be forthcoming.[36] Over the next couple of years, the RDC minutes record the negotiation of site purchase and laying out of the cemetery. For Nidderdale RDC, action was provoked by the receipt of the copy of a letter from the Ministry of Health in 1943 referring to the need for a new burial site for the parishes of Goldsborough and Flaxby. The issue had evidently involved the parishes in some difficulty, and they had been advised by the Ministry to 'consider the desirability of bringing the matter before the RDC with a view to action being taken by the DC under the Public Health Acts'.[37] The matter was dealt with by the Public Health and General Purposes Committee which reviewed options for site purchase and – over the next five years – steered the project to completion. As with any cemetery development, the task was complicated by a number of factors not least of which was the fact of extreme resource limitations which were a consequence of the Second World War. It is notable that, where the RDC did take action, day-to-day management of the site was generally devolved to a cemetery committee which included representatives from the RDC and the local parish council. This was certainly the case at Kirkby Malzeard, Osmotherley and Goldsborough, for example.

However, for RDCs in North Yorkshire a failure to take initiative is more prevalent than examples of active engagement with burial issues, which remained very much on the periphery of interest. On the whole, RDC minutes contained sporadic reference to reports on conditions in churchyards, but action was rarely taken as a consequence. For example, in 1900 a letter from the LGB about the parish churchyard at Danby Wiske was read to a meeting of the Northallerton Rural District Council. Unfortunately, the letter was not reproduced, but the RDC resolved not to act on information given since 'no nuisance likely to be injurious to public health exists'.[38] The RDC also discussed the need for burial space at Thornton-le-Beans. Here, the Reverend Thomas Parkinson had been in correspondence about the difficulty over extending the churchyard, as a consequence of regulations about the prohibition against new burial ground being opened within 100 yards of any dwelling house without the written consent of owners and occupiers.[39] He noted that 'the church funds (voluntary) could not be charged with the maintenance of a burial ground for the whole township'. He concluded that the only way in which the whole township could be made to bear the cost of additional burial space would be for the parish meeting to adopt the Burial Acts, and then seek to purchase land 'on favourable terms'. The District Council did not necessarily agree. It recommended that the best approach would be to encourage the nearby residents to consent to the extension of the churchyard for burials, and the clerk was requested to write accordingly.[40] The following month, the Council resolved to take no further steps in the matter.[41]

It is clear, therefore, that the fact that it was possible for RDCs to intervene and effect the laying out of new burial space did not necessarily mean that this course of action was frequently taken in central North Riding. Indeed, there are intimations that RDCs generally tended not to be particularly proactive nationally on this matter. In 1970, internal comment in the Home Office on a proposed burial bill indicated that in general RDCs 'usually only act as longstops for parish councils, who have their own powers to provide burial grounds'.[42] It does seem to be the case that RDC intervention in cemetery establishment was linked to some local difficulty in finding a resolution to the need for additional space. In Kirkby Malzeard, for example, the vestry appeared to be in financial trouble and so probably unable to finance a church extension; at Newton-on-Rawcliffe it was noted that 'the views of the vicar and of the parish meeting appear to be in conflict'.[43] At Coneysthorpe, the village had never previously had any burial provision, and had long been reliant on interment in the neighbouring village: the parochial church council was therefore not in a position to seek an extension. It was generally the case that, unless provoked by exceptional circumstances, RDCs resisted taking any action directly but might more or less gently bat the issue aside. Northallerton RDC steered Leake Parochial Church Council towards a churchyard extension in 1929, and assisted the PCC with negotiations for a donation of land.[44] In West Rounton in 1956, the RDC did not appear to take any action at all. There was no satisfactory response from the Council to a petition from the PCC on the need for additional burial space, and it was decided instead to reuse the churchyard.[45] It was perhaps unsurprising that, after its five-year-long effort towards establishing a cemetery at Goldsborough, Nidderdale RDC responded to the need for new burial space at Killingham with a curt resolution: 'that the parish council be informed that if they consider further provision should be made for burials the parish council should proceed to adopt the Burial Acts.'[46]

In addition to an understandable unwillingness to engage with the daunting complexity of the burial legislation, other additional factors offer further explanation for RDC reluctance to be proactive in cemetery establishment. First, RDC intervention could be regarded as interference, and elicit a failure to co-operate at parish council level. This was certainly true at Leavening, where Norton RDC had attempted to resolve the fractious relations between the vicar and the parish council. The parish council had simply requested information from Norton RDC on the best means of laying out new burial space, and was told by the RDC that it would be happy to take 'the initial steps in providing the cemetery', allowing parochial representation at the Public Health Committee whilst negotiations were in hand. The RDC would, on completion of the cemetery, 'be prepared to delegate the powers of management thereof to a parochial committee to consist of the members of the Leavening PC and the representative of the parish on the RDC for the time being'.[47] In the meantime, the PC was asked to hold further meetings to ascertain local views on the need for additional burial space, given the inability of the PC and the vicar to agree on the matter. The parish clerk was evidently unhappy with these suggestions, and disputed the need for further administrative interference or for additional meetings. The RDC had no option but to step away, and wrote – in December 1937 – that it would take no further steps 'in view of the obvious lack of co-operation on the part of your council in the matter'.[48] Consequently, the parish was free to go ahead under the provisions of the Burial Acts.

A second and more pragmatic factor was the understanding that had emerged quite definitely in the interwar period that cemeteries required perpetual support from the rates. Sanction for burial fees had become centralised but this did not result in a uniform fee structure for cemeteries across England. In a paper on the administration of cemeteries, given to the cemetery superintendent conference in 1947, Charles Hilton – superintendent and registrar at Deptford – commented that 'If one examines the various cemetery charges up and down the country, the diversity is astonishing'. Indeed, in neighbouring boroughs there might be a variation of as much as 100 per cent.[49] There was a concern to ensure that the lowest fees were indeed low enough to be affordable to those on the lowest income, as Edwin Austin indicated to the Joint Conference in 1933: 'the policy of my council is to provide a grave which the humblest person can buy. The council is able to make it up on the other fees.'[50] However, it was not easy to arrive at an overall balance of charges – cheaper, loss-making but more numerous lower-cost interments against the smaller number of profitable higher-cost burials – that would not result in a deficit. Furthermore, central government control of the fees set was tending to stymie the development of charges that might more adequately reflect the cost of the service. It was becoming clear that the provision of burial space by local authorities and burial boards was a loss-making enterprise. A national report on the matter was published in 1928, as a propaganda exercise by the Cremation Society. The report had elicited returns from 166 municipalities, which between them managed 305 cemeteries covering 8,416 acres. Burial fees varied substantially, and some cemeteries made a slight gain. However, taken together, the sites produced a substantial deficit, of an average of £162,000 over three years, or 18s 9d loss per interment. The key issue was the fact that cemeteries were – and are – a wasting asset. Piggott, the report's author, stated baldly: 'Land used as a cemetery becomes sterile and after use entails an increasing charge in upkeep.'[51] Further evidence was produced in the 1930s. In their detailed report on burial reform in 1938, Wilson and Levy calculated that the deficit between costs and fees required rate-payer support of £458,902 in England and Wales in the years 1933–4.[52] Ripon's attempt to review the practice of reserving grave spaces had reflected the ongoing losses of cemetery undertakings, which in 1938 had amounted to £410.[53] It was small wonder, therefore, that RDCs were wary about assuming a function that would become a perpetual debt.

The rise of the professional cemetery manager

The establishment of RDCs therefore did not necessarily have a particularly strong impact on localised control of burial space up to 1974. Too much of the existing regulation remained permissive, and local communities retained the option to use the Burial Acts or – indeed – to extend their local churchyard. However, another development requires some consideration, and this is the increased professionalism of cemetery managers themselves. The National Association of Cemetery Superintendents was created in 1913 following a meeting of London cemetery managers, under the initiative of J. D. Robertson, superintendent of the City of London Cemetery.[54] This was not an unexpected development. The nascent professionalism of cemetery management had been fostered amongst burial board clerks, who had been quick to create informal advice networks, passing information between each other on the interpretation of legislation, and on what might now be termed 'best practice'. The initial aims of the Institute were printed on its reports and conference proceedings: 'advancing the administration of cemeteries [and later crematoria] by fostering a fuller knowledge of the work required for their efficient management'. The early development of the Association was delayed by the outbreak of the First World War, but a First Congress was arranged in 1920. This meeting announced that the Association already had 93 members, and a number of branches had been created: the Yorkshire branch was set up in Leeds in December 1919. This branch was one of the more prominent, covering cemetery management in major conurbations including Leeds, Bradford, Huddersfield and Wakefield. Indeed, from the 1920s, Headingly-cum-Burley Burial Board became what might now be termed a 'centre of excellence' in training new managers in cremation technology and practice.

In its first few years, the Association set about securing better pay and conditions for its members and a level of professional standing through alliance with the National Association of Local Government Officers. However, by the mid-1920s, it had started to turn its attention to matters relating more specifically to burial practice. An early consideration had been to bring an end to Saturday afternoon and Sunday funerals. In 1922 the Yorkshire branch secretary reported success in this regard in the Leeds cemeteries and stressed that it was the intention of his branch to 'hammer at this until it becomes universal'.[55] Another similar initiative was the abolition of glass *immortelles*, which were extremely fragile and were hazardous to staff who were cutting grass. However, in the 1930s, the Association's attention was turned to the opportunities afforded by the invitation to join with the British Undertakers' Association and the Federation of Cremation Authorities in a National Council for the Disposition of the Dead. The Council was officially launched in 1933, and called for the recasting and codification of burial and cemetery law. The Council failed, ultimately, in its attempt to hold together the disparate interests of cemetery and crematorium superintendents and funeral directors. However, the matter firmly established the clear intent of the National Association to seek national change and arrive at a framework of universal principles in terms of regulations and fee setting. Certainly by the end of the Second World War, the National Association of Cemetery and Crematorium Superintendents had begun to arrive at professional standards that could to a degree override more local preferences: cemetery managers were quick to spread best practice on the reduction of monument sizes, and 'lawning' the burial landscape.[56]

The ability of a parish or even town council to support the professional development of staff depended strongly on its level of operation. Few cemeteries in central North Riding operated on such a scale that the use of a trained professional cemetery manager was deemed a priority. The move was felt to be justified in three locations. In Harrogate, demand for interment at Grove Road Cemetery had increased rapidly, reaching a high point with 240 interments in 1911. Concern about increasingly limited space at the site led to the opening by Harrogate Urban District Council of Stonefall Cemetery. Mr Wylie, who was superintendent of Grove Road, was asked to manage both sites together, which were jointly taking over 400 interments a year by the start of the Second World War. Mr Wylie became a member of NACS in 1923, as in later years did Mr G. Flack of Knaresborough and Mr Albert Greenett of Ripon. In each of these cases, the superintendent was generally required to keep the burial registers in order and supervise maintenance and gravedigging staff.

By contrast, interments at other sites had started to decline, as population decreases became evident. For example, Pateley Bridge burials dropped from an average of 54 a year between 1900 and 1909 to 37 a year between 1930 and 1939. Smaller cemeteries tended to employ part-time 'sextons' who were directed by a local cemetery committee, in who the vicar was often the chair. At Kirkby Malzeard the duties of the sexton were pasted into the end covers of the committee minute book, and included gravedigging, keeping the site 'in good order', cutting the grass and removing clippings twice in the summer months and – from 1953 – setting out the space within which a monumental mason must erect a memorial on any particular grave.[57] These duties filled only a part-time post. In some cases, the parish clerk retained a responsibility for dealing with the paperwork, and gravedigging and maintenance were dealt with in a more *ad hoc* fashion. For the most part, therefore, cemetery management in rural locations came to be subsumed within the increasingly broad range of services covered by the parish clerk.

The Local Government Act, 1972

The Local Government Act, 1972, implemented from 1974, brought with it another wave of substantial change to local government boundaries, wiping away the old rural district councils and replacing them with larger units of London, metropolitan, district and borough councils. It is perhaps less well understood that the Act also encompassed the most substantial change to burial provision since the Burial Act, 1900. The changes brought in 1972 were by no means unheralded: since 1900 it had been widely appreciated that it was extremely difficult to work with the combined Public Health and Burial Act legislation, empowering as it did various tiers of local government and involving two national government departments. A number of attempts to codify the burial legislation had come to nothing. Often failure reflected the fact that reform of the law had become harnessed to another less achievable objective. For example, the National Council for the Disposition of the Dead became embroiled with agitation to register funeral directors in the 1930s. Similarly, Wilson and Levy's comprehensive 1938 report on the industry concluded that 'what is now required is less amendments to the law, though such also are necessary, than the fundamental change to the organisation of burial and funeral'. The authors sought to secure legislation to reduce funeral costs, which – as they themselves acknowledged – would take 'drastic measures'.[58] No change to burial legislation followed. In 1944, and in tune with national discussions of postwar reform and reconstruction, NACCS issued a memorandum which sought full State control of all funerary industries. It was clearly felt by NACCS that the profession had gained some standing during the period of conflict, as members had served with distinction in leading and staffing teams dealing with civilian war fatalities.[59] The Memorandum commented that there had been 'no legislation of general application since 1906'. Indeed,

> The administration has been left to the uncertain guidance of piecemeal (if not haphazard) legislation which is both voluminous and inadequate. This has left the way open for many activities which can only be described as deplorable.[60]

NACCS again called for a single unifying piece of legislation which would cover matters relative to the disposal of the dead. However – again not surprisingly – the opportunity was not taken. Garry Alligan, addressing the Institute conference in 1947, reported that Bevan – as Minister of Health – had stated adamantly: 'I see no possibility that Parliamentary time could be found in the near future for considering legislation amending the statutes relating to burial grounds and cemeteries which would inevitably be very complicated.[61] Within the conference report, this comment was given the exasperated subheading of 'More Shelving'. One further attempt is worth noting. In 1962, Lord Colville, Vice President for the National Association of Parish Councils, introduced a bill that attempted to consolidate the law as it affected parish councils. However, the proposed change concentrated solely on the Burial Acts, and left intact the duality of cemeteries operating separately under either the Burial Acts or the Public Health legislation. Lord Colville was persuaded to withdraw his bill on the understanding that new and more comprehensive legislation would be forthcoming. However, this proposed bill was itself withdrawn 'since there was no chance of Parliamentary time being found for the bill in the immediate future'.[62]

When change finally came, it was substantial and radical. It is remarkable that the majority of the Burial Acts and the Public Health (Interment) Act had continued to operate for well over a century. The legislation had indeed become hoary and anachronistic. A principal intent of the Burial Acts – that local communities should themselves decide how best to provide burial space – had lost its way, and the procedure for securing various permissions from central ministries was unnecessarily bureaucratic. The Local Government Act, 1972, brought changes on two major fronts. Under the existing legislation, burial authorities had been defined as those agencies that had taken up either the Burial Acts or the Public Health (Interment) Act. From 1974, an alternative approach was adopted. Instead, burial authorities were defined as London, metropolitan, district and parish councils and parish meetings, all of which had the authority to operate cemeteries if they chose to do so.[63] The Burial Acts ceased to be exercisable and the Public Health (Interment) Act was repealed in its entirety. Existing burial boards, established under the Burial Act, 1852, no longer operated. The 1972 Act ordered the creation of a single code for burial authorities, which comprised the Local Authorities' Cemeteries Order of 1977.[64] Amongst other things, this regulation required burial authorities to 'satisfy themselves that a sufficient part of the cemetery remains unconsecrated' and to charge 'such fees as they think proper for or in connection with burials in a cemetery'.[65] Central government interference was no longer deemed necessary.

The abolition of burial boards coupled with local government reorganisation created the opportunity for substantial change to the provision of burial space in central North Riding. It is interesting to note that of the three modern local authorities in the study – Rydale, Hambleton and Harrogate – only the last took the opportunity to absorb a number of cemeteries within its area. Ryedale District Council retained control of just one site – Coneysthorpe – and Hambleton maintained ownership of Osmotherley Cemetery. Other burial boards in these locations were simply taken over by the local parish council, as was the case in Thirsk in 1894. The wholesale adoption of burial sites in Harrogate in all probability reflects the fact that the Borough operated at sufficient scale to have developed a more strategic overview of burial provision: unfortunately, the absence of available council minutes precludes more detailed commentary. There is little material on the immediate aftermath of change in the 1970s. At Pateley Bridge, concern was expressed that 'central administration for dealing with funerals etc would be most unsatisfactory'.[66] However, this remark was exceptional. For the most part, the burial boards concerned tended to offer little adverse comment, and certainly no resistance to the development. Indeed, there is a sense in which the opportunity to pass over control constituted a relief from performance of a duty that was less than welcome. In Kirkby Malzeard, parochial cemetery committee meetings could be years apart, and management supervision had been lax. For example, in the 1950s, gravedigging had been insufficiently accurate, and the grave plan had to be realigned. In Fewston, cemetery minutes appear similarly haphazard. Here, a principal difficulty in maintaining the wall had led to conflict with the farmer of the neighbouring field, and court action had been threatened more than once following damage to monuments from livestock escaping into the cemetery. The site had begun with conflict over its financing, and the Burial Board never really achieved a degree of equilibrium.

Conclusion

The notion that 'modernity' encompassed a state desire to control burial space fits perfectly with the tenor of burial history in France, where through much of the nineteenth and twentieth century the State and Church were locked in conflict, and the churchyard comprised a highly contentious and emotionally charged battle ground. French burial legislation offered a deliberate challenge to the centrality of the Church, and had its roots in the secularist intent of eighteenth-century Revolutionaries. This entire paradigm does not transfer easily to England, and certainly finds no echoing development in rural England. During the twentieth century up to 1974 the context was set for a stronger level of state control, as the Burial Act of 1900 deprived the Church of England of its privileged position under the earlier Burial Acts. Changes to local governance removed from the vestry all responsibility for providing civic services, and instead created a framework of rural district councils whose staff of sanitary officers had a clear remit for dealing with any public health nuisance caused by inadequate burial space. Professionalised cemetery management had made substantial inroads in promoting uniform practice. However, the legislation failed to take what might be regarded as the most radical step of all: no new law imposed a *responsibility* for providing burial space. The permissive nature of the regulation meant that decisions remained, largely, local in rural areas.

Furthermore, the disincentives to establish civic cemeteries were legion. By the twentieth century it had become firmly established that burial provision would require a permanent call on the rates. Wilson and Levy's 1938 report had underlined the fact that cemeteries were largely unsustainable in financial terms. As a consequence, no local authority was eager to accept this burden unless forced to do so. Furthermore, even up to the Second World War, cemetery establishment could still bring tension and even conflict between denominations. Laying out and managing cemeteries required compliance with a regulatory framework which was bewilderingly complex. For smaller local authorities – parish and small town councils – the difficulty was increased by the inability to rely on the development of professional expertise, and since burial operations tended to be on a minor scale it was not easy to build skills and knowledge. As a consequence, the provisions of 1974 were in all probability a relief to many burial boards, who were able to pass over responsibility for sites where the costs of maintenance and expansion were becoming difficult to meet from diminishing burial income. For many civic authorities, therefore, ownership and control of cemetery space was not eagerly sought. Indeed, where the need to establish burial space became evident, there was a hurried nudging between the tiers of local government as each abrogated responsibility.

Thus, in central North Riding, it might be argued that the complexity of burial legislation itself constituted a key reason why a complete centralisation of burial function did not take place. This factor, coupled with the dispersed nature of rural settlement in the area and the low and falling level of demand in individual towns and villages, meant that it was possible for interment to be contained within its traditional framework: the churchyard. However, the church remained largely ambivalent about its role as provider of burial space. The clergy – like all various tiers of local government – were of a view with the Reverend John Collins of Bishop Monkton who considered the provision of burial space a 'thankless task', and one 'which he would be greatly pleased to hand over to some other person or persons'.[67] However, as will be seen, the expansion of churchyards constituted the principal source of new burial space during the twentieth century.

Notes

1 NYRO, PR/BPM 5/4, Vestry meeting Minute Book, 1897–1920, vicar of Bishop Monkton, 1 Nov 1923.
2 T. A. Kselman, *Death and the Afterlife in Modern France* (Princeton: Princeton University Press, 1993).
3 *Ibid.*, p. 180.
4 CRGA, H. Garrett, *Official Report of the Scarborough Conference of Members and Officers of Burial and Cremation Authorities* (1947), p. 33.
5 J. Brooke Little, *The Law of Burial* (London: Shaw and Sons, 3rd edn, 1902), appendix A, n. 1. Note that classification HO 45 at the NA includes individual files of applications to the Secretary of State for consecration plan approvals. These files generally include letters and a map in a folder on which Secretary of State decisions are recorded, along with comments on the case by unnamed civil servants.
6 NA, HO 45/22882, Thonton Dale cemetery consecration, 1922–49.
7 Brooke Little, *Law of Burial*, pp. 692ff.
8 NA, HO 45/18679, Burials: Osmotherley Cemetery, Northallerton.
9 NA, HO 45/18679, Burials: Osmotherley Cemetery, Northallerton. Underlining in the original.
10 NA, HO 45/20870, Burials: Harrogate Cemetery: Consecration, 1914–1947.
11 NA, HO 45/20870, Burials: Harrogate Cemetery: Consecration, 1914–1947.
12 NA, HO 45/17295, Pickering Cemetery, 1920–38.
13 *Ibid.*
14 NYRO, PC/LVN 7/2, Correspondence relating to the provision of a cemetery, 1936–7.
15 NYRO, PC/LVN 7/2, Correspondence relating to the provision of a cemetery, 1936–7, letter from incumbent to Norton RDC, 6 Nov 1936.
16 *Ibid.*
17 NA, HO 45/18270, Burials: Leavening burial ground.
18 NA, HO 45/22665, Terrington burial authority, 1905–49.
19 NA, HO 45/11954, Sicklinghall Memorial Cemetery.
20 NA, HO 45/22894, Kirkby Malzeard Cemetery: consecration, 1923–49. Burial records for the cemetery indicate ongoing use of the unconsecrated section.
21 NYRO, BB/AYG 1/1–3, Great Ayton and Little Ayton Burial Board Committee: Minute Books, 1881–1974, 3 Oct 1915.
22 *Ibid.*

23 NYRO, BB/AYG 1/1–3, Great Ayton and Little Ayton Burial Board Committee: Minute Books, 1881–1974, 29 Dec 1915.
24 NA, HO 45/18820, Burials: Northallerton and Romanby Cemetery, 1940–41.
25 Changes in authority were usefully summarised in M. R. R. Davies, *The Law of Burial, Cremation and Legislation* (London: Shaw and Sons, 1956). Functions acquired by the Local Government Board were transferred to the Ministry of Health in 1919, and from there in 1951 to the Ministry of Local Government and Planning, which was renamed in the same year Ministry of Housing and Local Government.
26 Although note that from 1947, *all* fee approvals – including clerical fees – were transferred to this department from the Home Office.
27 NYRO, BB/TH 10/1 (Table of fees), 'Burial Acts 1852–1906 Fees Etc', TS Guidance issued by the Ministry of Housing and Local Government nd, probably 1964.
28 NYRO, DC/RIC II 9/2/13, Town Clerk correspondence files: Cemetery, 1939–1952, letter from the Corporation dated 31 Oct 1944.
29 NYRO, DC/RIC 9/2/13–15, Town Clerk correspondence files: Cemetery, 1939–1952.
30 NYRO, DC/NOR I 1/1, Northallerton Rural District Council: Minutes, 14 Oct 1874.
31 NYRO, DC/NOR I 1/1, Northallerton Rural District Council: Minutes, 26 Apr 1876.
32 NA, HO 45/9949 B31354, Appleton Wiske.
33 NYRO, PC/HOV 3/5, Letters and papers relating to the new cemetery, 1880–1882, 1885, 1887.
34 WYRO III/93/3 (Wetherby Rural Sanitary Authority Minutes, 1873–1889), 20 Nov 1879, 18 Dec 1879.
35 NYRO, PR/KMZ 2/4, Vestry minutes, 1823–1895, 15 Apr 1879.
36 NYRO, DC/PIR, Pickering Rural District Council minutes, 1931–1937, 6 Oct 1936 and 3 Nov 1936.
37 DC/NID 1, Nidderdale Minutes, 1942–44, 24 Feb 1943.
38 NYRO, DC/NOR I 1/1, Northallerton Rural District Council: Minutes, 8 Aug 1900.
39 *Darlington and Stockton Times*, 25 Aug 1900.
40 DC/NOR I 1/1, Northallerton Rural District Council: Minutes, 8 Aug 1900.
41 DC/NOR I 1/1, Northallerton Rural District Council: Minutes, 19 Sep 1900.
42 HLG 29/2250, Burial and cremation bill, 1968–1972, paper

entitled 'Burial Bill: Background Notes, December 1970'.

43 NYRO, DC/PIR, Pickering Rural District Council minutes, 1931–1937, 1 Dec 1936.

44 DC/NOR I 1/6, Northallerton RDC Minutes, 1928–1933, 31 Dec 1939.

45 NYRO, PR/ROW 20/2, Minute book: the Rountons vestry and PCC, 1940–1970, 1 Mar 1956; 4 Jul 1963.

46 DC/NID 1, Nidderdale RDC minutes, 1948–50, 17 May 1950.

47 NYRO, PC/LVN 7/2, Correspondence relating to the provision of a cemetery, 1936–7, letter from Norton RDC to the parish clerk, dated 26 May 1926.

48 NYRO, PC/LVN 7/2, Correspondence relating to the provision of a cemetery, 1936–7, letter from Norton RDC to the parish clerk, dated 7 Dec 1936.

49 CRGA, C. Hilton, 'The administration of cemeteries', *Official Report of the Scarborough Conference of Members and Officers of Burial and Cremation Authorities* (1947), p. 14.

50 CRGA, E. Austin, 'Cemetery administration', paper given to the Second Joint Conference (1933), p. 17.

51 A. E. Piggott, *Municipal Cemetery Undertakings* (London: The Cremation Society, 1928), p. iii.

52 A. Wilson and H. Levy, *Burial Reform and Funeral Costs* (Oxford: Oxford University Press, 1938), p. 110.

53 NYRO, DC/RIC 9/2/13–15, Town Clerk Correspondence files: Cemetery, 1939–44. Inserted clipping from Corporation minutes.

54 'Interview with Mr J. D. Robertson', *The Undertakers' Journal*, June 1915, 165. I am grateful to Dr B. Parsons for this reference. Note that the National Association of Cemetery Superintendents was renamed the National Association of Cemetery and Crematorium Superintendents in 1932, and again renamed in 1947 the Institute of Burial and Cremation Administration. Consequently, the organisation will be referred to as either 'the Association' or 'the Institute' depending on chronology.

55 CRGA, NACS *Year Book, 1922*.

56 J. Rugg, 'Lawn cemeteries: the emergence of a new landscape of death', *Urban History*, 33:2 (2006), pp. 213–33.

57 NYRO, PC/KMZ 1/6, Cemetery parochial committee, 1901–1959.

58 Wilson and Levy, *Burial Reform*, p. 192.

59 CRGA, NACCS, *Memorandum on Planning for Post-War Reform in the Disposition of the Dead* (1944).

60 *Ibid.*, p. 3.

61 CRGA, G. Allighan, 'Burial and the state', paper given to the

Official Report of the Scarborough Conference (1947), p. 33.

62 NA, HLG 29/2250, Burial and cremation bill, 1968–1972. Comment by unnamed civil servants from the Ministry of Housing and Local Government, on internal memorandum.

63 Local Authorities' Cemeteries Order, 1977, SI 1977, no. 204. Note that this replaced the earlier order SI 1974, no. 628.

64 This Statutory Instrument was replaced by a second Local Authorities' Cemetery Order in 1977, and reference will be made to this second SI here.

65 Local Authorities' Cemeteries Order 1974, Article 5 (2) and Article 12 (3).

66 NYRO, BB PAT 1/4, Pateley Bridge Burial Board Minutes, 1963–74, 21 Feb 1974.

67 NYRO, PR/BPM 5/4 (Vestry meeting minute book, 1897–1920), vicar of Bishop Monkton, 1 Nov 1923.

9

'Being desirous of avoiding a burial board'[1]*: the churchyard as cemetery*

The previous chapter has indicated how far statutory civil agencies prevaricated over the need to meet demand for additional burial space in rural areas. In central North Riding, all tiers of local government tended to look to the parochial church council to address any shortage of burial provision. Accordingly, churchyard extension was remarkably common in this area during the twentieth century. Indeed, there were at least 177 separate churchyard extensions, compared with the laying out of just 21 cemeteries over the period 1895–2009. This chapter explores the incidence of churchyard extension by framing questions around the changing nature of the churchyard itself during this period. First, it is necessary to underline the fact that, in pragmatic rural Yorkshire, the desire to extend the churchyard rather than establish a new cemetery did not necessarily reveal a strong spiritual or emotional attachment to the Church of England as burial provider. If this sentiment was felt, it was rarely expressed in the written vestry minutes of the period. Furthermore, the Church of England was not often at the forefront of protecting its interests in this area. Indeed, vicars themselves tended to be the first to suggest the option of a cemetery laid out on the rates. Rather, the extension of the churchyard was favoured as the cheapest option and – as associated legal processes were simplified – usually the easiest. The Burial Acts had again contributed to the Church of England retaining its hold on burial provision, although not necessarily in the way originally intended.

The character of the churchyard shifted in another not wholly unexpected way. The more widespread erection of formal monumentation and a continued aversion to the disturbance of remains meant that churchyard space became finite. The centuries-old tradition of cyclical reuse was for the most part abandoned, and some churchyards were extended two or even three times. Restrictions were placed on the erection of more elaborate monuments, but new designs were simpler, cheaper, and more readily available and affordable. The introduction of a formal grave plan meant that families could make certain that their members were buried close together. Indeed, a family grave in the churchyard with a memorial became a common expectation, often achieved with burials 'side by side' rather than in double-depth plots. Vicars came under pressure to reserve burial spaces, and disagreement around the legality of this practice increased the incidence of more formal reservation of grave space by faculty. All these developments increased the speed at which available land was consumed and, as a consequence, parochial church councils strengthened their policies on non-parishioner burials, which were not always easy to implement.

Churchyard extension or new cemetery?

Despite its otherwise radical intent, the Burial Act, 1900, had still not created a clear responsibility for the provision of burial space. It remained the case that each community had to make its own decision as to how to secure new space for interment. In most villages, it was generally the vicar who was of the view that something needed to be done. In the small village of North Otterington, the church dedicated to St Barnabas was also the burial place of other larger settlements in the benefice, including Thornton-le-Beans and Thornton-le-Moor. By the turn of the century, this provision was proving to be inadequate. In 1904, a report had been lodged with Northallerton Rural District Council that coffins were being interred at insufficient depth: one coffin had been no more than eighteen inches from the surface.[2] Amongst the vestry records is a long note written by the Reverend Thomas Parkinson to himself, which summarised his options. First, he considered consecration of glebe lands, but then this extension would have to be maintained from the church funds. This he regarded as being 'not very desirable' since local Nonconformists would have the right to be buried there without having to make any financial contribution towards maintenance. Second, it might be possible to transfer the land to Church trustees who might restrict use to Anglicans only, but this 'might lead to sectarian jealousy'. Parkinson did not like a third idea, which was to establish a new churchyard immediately outside the chapel of ease at Thornton-le-Beans 'since Dissenters or secular services in the ground might be held at the same time that services were going on in the church, without the vicar or church authorities having any control'. He concluded that 'by far the best plan would be for a public burial ground or cemetery (consecrated, or part not) to be provided from public funds (rates etc) to serve for both townships in some place convenient for both'.[3]

The vicar at Bishop Monkton drew a similar conclusion. Here, the churchyard had been extended in 1899 but in the following couple of decades ongoing problems with maintenance had clearly taxed the vicar's patience. In 1912, vestry minutes recorded that 'a desire was expressed by the vicar that every part of the churchyard should be kept neat and tidy', and perhaps a fund should be established 'towards which it was thought all parishioners, whether church people or not, could gladly contribute'.[4] In 1917, the call for funds was reiterated, again in the hope that 'chapel people as well as church folk' would make donations.[5] In 1920, an application for faculty to reserve grave spaces was made; the applicant promised a contribution of £30 towards the cost of a churchyard extension should the application be successful. However, the vicar expressed opposition. In his view, 'the needs of the district would be best met by the provision of a cemetery', preferably one in which the neighbouring village of Littlethorpe would have equal rights.[6] The matter was deferred somewhat by the technicalities attendant on the establishment of the new parochial church council, which itself addressed the issue again in 1922. It appeared that the PCC was in favour of the purchase of a neighbouring field to extend the churchyard, and the vicar – perhaps wearily – commented that the parishioners knew his view on the issue, but 'he would not stand in the way of such as scheme if church people were in a mind for it'. Again he stressed that 'the legal obligation to provide ground for burial rested upon the civil authorities', but nevertheless the resolution in favour of extension was passed unanimously.[7]

Both these cases indicate that a number of factors played into decisions about how rural settlements chose to provide new burial space. Of all the individuals involved, the vicar was often most conscious of the costs attached to churchyard maintenance, and – above anything else – tended to look for opportunities to rid himself of the burden. However, there was general agreement that extension was preferable, and for a number of reasons. Vestry minutes commonly record – as with Sawley, for example – that 'this public meeting ... approves the extension of the churchyard as the most suitable means of increasing the burial ground accommodation'.[8] Most often, the argument was carried by an understanding of the heavier expense of cemetery establishment. In Kirk Hammerton in 1897, the parish magazine contained an account of a large meeting of parishioners, where the vicar reported his findings from research into costs on the option:

> The land bought, three quarters of an acre, cost £60; building chapel, iron railings and wall round it, £390 10s; legal expenses £37; cost of loan £5 5s; advertising 15s; architects plans, £3 10s. Total £497 1s 1d. Mr Wise (consecration fee)

£10 19s 6d. A cemetery of two acres at Boroughbridge, cost £600.[9]

Initial cemetery establishment was not the only expense. Ongoing management brought a much heavier administrative burden including – as has been seen – the securing of various consents from various ministries. In 1933, the Reverend Henry Archibold Douglas at Salton had evidently undertaken detailed research on the legal aspects of the matter, to support his contention that a churchyard extension using land transferred from the glebe would be preferable. A handwritten copy exists of his report, which was presented to the PCC. The report contains an extended section on the 'civic' option and its disadvantages. These included the fact that any cemetery would have to be located 100 yards from the nearest residential property, and so perhaps consequently be out of Salton or even in Brawby, the adjacent village. This last claim he crossed out, as being possibly insensitive to the parishioners at Brawby who had had to use provision at Salton for generations past. The cost of the site would be four times as much as the churchyard extension, and be added to the rates. 'And the cost would not stop at the beginning', he claimed. 'There might be further charges for management, and the cemetery would be a perpetual burden on the parish.' The imposition carried beyond the expense: 'After a cemetery had been formed, there would be probably be bylaws and regulations and all kinds of rules to comply with quite different from the present easy system.' The situation would be even worse if the Burial Acts were adapted since, according to Douglas, 'this course would mean, literally, a dozen or more meetings, a committee and delay and trouble and expense'.[10]

This heavier burden of secular administration was also an argument put forward by diocesan officers. At Pockley in 1915, decisions around the need for new burial space were coloured by ongoing denominational tension, but the Diocesan Registrar remained of the view that churchyard extension was a better alternative to 'civil control and management with its more or less heavy expenses'.[11] Certainly by the 1930s, the Diocese of York was generally recommending extension as the preferable option, purely in terms of ease and economics:

> When a churchyard is full, the church authorities can either make provision for an extension of the churchyard themselves or they can put upon the local authority the onus of providing a public cemetery or burial ground out of the rates. It should be pointed out, however, that it is much more expeditious and less costly if the former course be adopted.[12]

Churchyard extensions: incidence and chronology

The strength of local opinion in favour of churchyard extension is indicated most forcefully through its growing incidence. As Chapter 4 indicated, there is evidence for 253 extensions for the churchyards in the study for which a definite date can be pinpointed. Although the average annual incidence of extension was very slightly higher in the second half of the nineteenth century, frequency in the twentieth was not far behind. Indeed, with the exception of a dip in activity during the Second World War, churchyard extensions continued with remarkable regularity until the end of the 1950s. It was often the case that, when a site had been extended in the nineteenth century, further extension followed in the twentieth. Indeed, All Saints at Kirkbymoorside was extended in 1875 with four further additions in 1909, 1935, 1949 and 1967. Other churchyards were extended four times in the 157-year period studied. For example, at All Saints in Kirk Deighton, extensions were aded in 1942 and 1959; the site had already been enlarged twice before, in 1885 and 1900.

It is notable that the number of extensions dropped substantially in the 1950s, at a time when investment in new cemeteries nationally also declined.[13] The Cremation Society of Great Britain had been hugely successful in its promotion

Figure 9.1 Incidence of churchyard extension, by decade

of this alternative to burial; indeed, the Society's rhetoric tended to lead debate on the subject, targeting political, medical and religious elite opinion.[14] It was therefore not surprising that in 1955 the Church of England declared itself of the opinion that further extension of churchyards was not necessarily a policy that it could wholeheartedly support. In 1955, the Report of the Maintenance of Churchyards Commission commented that 'In our view the taking of land away from the living for the use of the dead is something that can easily be carried to excess', and so all proposals to extend churchyard space 'should be scrutinised with care'.[15]

Chapter 4 called into question any link between churchyard extension and increase in the number of interments. Similarly, during the twentieth century, a static or declining population was evident in the majority of the smaller settlements in the study, but the churchyard grew nevertheless. North Stainley is a case in point. St Mary the Virgin had been built in 1840, and the first burial took place in the churchyard in 1842. In the following eight years just eighteen interments took place. Despite the fact that there tended to be no more than half a dozen interments a year, the churchyard was extended by 129 square yards in 1893.[16] The need for a further extension was becoming evident in 1924, although there was no evident increase in demand. An extension of 31 square yards was added in the same year, which was clearly a stop-gap measure since, in November 1925, the PCC again discussed the need for more space, 'there being only space for six more graves'.[17] Action was delayed for some time, probably because the scale of usage dropped a little, to around five or fewer a year. Nevertheless, in June 1969 the PCC minutes noted that Captain Staveley drew attention to the urgent need for more space, and within a decade another extension was added.[18]

Figure 9.2 gives a selection of different sizes of settlement where there was more than one churchyard extension during the period of the study. Of the group in this selection, only Sowerby had marked population growth, increasing from a population of around 750 in the second half of the nineteenth century to 3,700 at the 2001 census. However, even in this case the number of burials in the churchyard increased only slightly but nevertheless the churchyard was extended four times: in 1859, 1886, 1912 and 1974. Kirkbymoorside saw a more modest increase in population, from 1,878 in the 1820s to 2,280 in 2001, but its churchyard was also extended four times, as has been seen. Here, the decline in the number of interments annually was more marked. Indeed, for the majority of settlements in the study, a contracting population combined with an overall national decrease in mortality – and in particular, infant mortality – led to a decrease in the number of churchyard interments. Nevertheless, churchyard extension continued. For example, the small village of Aldfield, just to the west of Fountains Abbey, had a population of 80 at the 2001 census; a century earlier the number had been closer to 130. Here, the churchyard was extended in 1905 and 1958. Gate Helmsley had, according to Bulmer, 205 residents in 1881, which had increased only slightly to 290 in 2001; again, the churchyard was augmented four times, in 1868, 1892, 1927 and 1953. In 2007, a further extension was due to come into use.

Figure 9.2 Interment in each decadal year between 1840 and 1960 in selected churchyards with two or more extensions

Attachment to above-ground monumentation also played a role in absorbing space in the churchyard and militating against any system of grave reuse. Through the course of the twentieth century, changing tastes, and 'modernist' aesthetics had encompassed a shift in memorial style, which meant that above-ground monumentation had become simpler in construct. However, as it became simpler, it also became more affordable. Headstones – with or without kerbsets – replaced the use of mounds, which in some churchyards were prohibited, again making the use of some kind of monument more likely. In 1962, *The Churchyard Handbook* complained that churchyards were becoming 'a jumble of individual monuments which bear little or no relation to each other or to the whole of which they are parts'.[19] Aesthetics aside, it was widely acknowledged that grave 'furniture' was taking up a substantial portion of space in the churchyard. However, the Church did not consider prohibition. Indeed, implicit encouragement on the matter was given through the Ecclesiastical Commissioners' issuing of a standardised table of monument permission fees, which PCCs were invited to adopt. Thus graves in the churchyard became – by practice if not strictly legally – perpetuity burials usually with a memorial. The continued extension of the churchyard was an inevitable consequence.

The legal and economic context

By the twentieth century, the legal and economic contexts for churchyard extension had changed. However, it remained the case that – on occasion – extension provoked a protracted and expensive legal wrangle that delayed completion of a scheme. At Carlton Miniott, for example, the vestry had had to deal with the trustees of the estate of William Carlton, which had in 1896 agreed to donate the land provided the vestry paid the conveyance costs. These were unexpectedly high, involving the Chancery Court in London, and the matter took four years to settle.[20] In Hampsthwaite in 1902, the vestry 'resolved unanimously that the committee formed five years ago to enlarge the churchyard be requested to push forward the matter at once'. Here, problems had rested on the need to demolish a tenanted property to effect better access.[21] At Thornton-le-Moor, land had been donated adjacent to the existing churchyard of St Barnabas in 1953. The churchyard had until that time never been used for burial, but the incumbent and the PCC ran into considerable difficulties in ascertaining whether permission was needed before interment could begin. The vicar wrote to the Ministry of Housing and Local Government in 1956: 'I would be glad to know of any rules and regulations that have to be observed (if any) as no one seem capable of telling me, nor even of whom I should enquire!'[22] Sorting out the legal ramifications involved the Church Commissioners and the Diocesan Registrar, who wrote in 1957 that the question 'has entailed a very considerable amount of work and I propose to submit the Registry charges in the matter, which no doubt your Parochial Church Council will meet in due course'.[23] In 1965, the parochial church council of St Oswald's at Sowerby also ran into protracted difficulty on its negotiation to buy land for an extension from the trustees of the estate of Mr Bamlett. The land was thought to be substantially over-valued at £800, and the estate required the building of a boundary wall which would have added an estimated £500 to the overall cost. Contested valuations, negotiations and renegotiations meant that the extension took nearly a decade to secure, with the site finally consecrated by the Bishop of Whitby in 1973.[24]

However, these were exceptional cases. During the course of the twentieth century, extending the churchyard was becoming a simpler option in legal terms, certainly in comparison with the process in the nineteenth century. There had been no radical new legislation that had changed the essential legal frameworks. The Churchyard Consecration Act of 1867 remained in place and is indeed still in force. The Ecclesiastical Commissioners had continued to advise that conveyance *should* take place via the Church Building Acts, and 1900 around half the conveyances it dealt with related to churchyard extensions.[25] However, the Commissioners had halved the legal cost charged to parishes in 1883; thus at Hampsthwaite in 1897 the vicar was told by the Commissioners that 'the costs of the Commissioners' solicitors in cases like the above are systematically kept as low as possible'.[26] Continued complaint about the charges again led the Commissioners to revise their policy, and from January 1902 it no longer used the London solicitor's firm it had employed for decades. Conveyances were dealt with entirely by a solicitor's clerk employed directly by the Commissioners, at no cost to the parishes applying.[27] Locally, diocesan registrars had also introduced standard procedures. Certainly by the First World War the Diocese of York had started to issue a typescript form, covering the essential information and with gaps left for the relevant information to be inserted. An example exists amongst the parish records at Amotherby:

> We the undersigned being the INCUMBENT and CHURCHWARDENS of APPLETON LE STREET with AMOTHERBY do hereby present this our Petition that the

> piece or parcel of ground containing 1049 square yards or thereabouts recently by deed dated 24th February 1899 conveyed as an addition to the churchyard of AMOTHERBY in the North Riding of the County of York within your Grace's diocese and Jurisdiction may be consecrated.[28]

At Marton-le-Moor in 1910 a letter to the Reverend Smithson from the Registrar of the Diocese of York acknowledged receipt of the required conveyance document, enclosed a copy of the above proforma for signature, and indicated that the cost of fees relating to consecration would be £3 3s.[29] This procedure was a substantial improvement on previous practice: the nineteenth-century petition for consecration had been a formal document that was expensive to prepare and required the employment of a legal professional. Thus, by the 1930s – though certainly not so in the previous century – it could reasonably be claimed that 'the legislature has provided expeditious and inexpensive means of adding pieces of land to a churchyard'.[30] Bureaucratic processes had finally started to match the simplicity aimed for in the Churchyard Consecration Act of 1867.

Through the twentieth century, it remained common for land to be donated for extensions. There were some instances still where the incumbent was able to gift land from the glebe, as was the case at Alne: the vestry thanked the vicar formally in 1902 for 'thus saving the parish a large expenditure'.[31] The larger landowners also continued to donate land from their estates. The Fitzwilliams at Malton and the Fevershams at Helmsley granted land where it was required, but it was also the case that the smaller estates made concessions: for example, Charles Thelusson of Brodworth Hall in Amotherby and Colonel Stanyforth in Kirk Hammerton. During the nineteenth century, the ability for the donor to reserve a sixth of the extension space had been an effective incentive, given the prohibition on further burial in the church. In the twentieth century, donation perhaps reflected an inability otherwise to secure a reasonable-sized plot in the churchyard. This was evidently an issue that had been in the mind of John Hutton of Solberge Hall, who in 1904 had proposed extending the churchyard of North Otterington, but only if it could be certain that space could be secured for himself and his family.[32]

Donors of land sometimes covered some or all the cost of conveyance, consecration and preparation of the extension for burial. For the most part, however, these costs were met through voluntary subscription. In the nineteenth century, there had been a clear link between the ratepayer and the service used, which in the case of the churchyard had collapsed completely with the abolition of the church rate and the vestry. Nevertheless, in Salton the vicar strongly argued that the churchyard extension should be paid for out of a formal rate calculated for the two villages of Salton and Brawby, equal to a fifth of the annual civic rate for each ratepaying household. A rate collector was appointed, and the money duly collected.[33] However, a reliance on voluntary subscription was thought to be fair, since – as was concluded in Bedale – 'the cost is borne proportionately by all, and in no case is the burden a heavy one'.[34] In some places, the expectation that the churchyard would need to be extended meant that the parish saved towards the event. Thus, in Great Fencote, money was collected over 1909–12; the higher burial charges for non-parishioners were also paid into the fund.[35] A churchyard extension committee was formed in Alne, with a secretary and treasurer, and 'collectors' for donations for the separate townships in the parish.[36] Even if there was no formal committee, in many cases a special churchyard extension fund was established, into which the funds from designated offertories might be placed. Sales of work, bazaars and fetes were typical, including special teas held on the day of the consecration. In more than one case a door-to-door collection took place: in Masham, this job was undertaken by the churchwardens.[37] The ability to meet the debt incurred was highly variable. In some locations, sums were collected readily, and within a matter of months even generated a surplus which could be used further to improve the churchyard landscape. In Alne, the total cost of the extension had been £77, but collectors had managed to raise closer to £100.[38] It was also the case that the fund-raising task could be protracted, with some debt remaining even years later. Bedale was a case in point: land for the extension was donated in 1900 by Sir Henry Monson on the understanding that the parish would meet the additional costs. However, even by 1904 the funds raised had not yet met the entire cost of drainage, levelling and enclosing the ground. Furthermore, internal road and pathways had not been constructed although interment in the extension had started.[39] It is notable that clergy were no longer able personally to meet any shortfall in subscriptions, as had commonly been the case in the nineteenth century. Certainly by the start of the First World War, parochial clergy were less likely to be the well-cushioned sons of the local elite; clerical incomes became standardised but remained relatively modest with some stipends as low as £240 in 1939.[40]

Churchyard as finite space

Chapter 4 indicated that, during the second half of the nineteenth century, churchyard extensions generally reflected changed attitudes towards disturbance of earlier remains, and changes in commemorative practice. These causative links continued during the twentieth century, and were reflected in and strengthened by changing management practices in the churchyard. These practices indicated a definite shift in the essential nature of the churchyard: it had become finite space.

Managing grave spaces: the increased use of faculty

Users of the churchyard often believed graves to be 'in perpetuity' although assurance that this was the case was never given by the Church of England, except when reservation was granted by faculty. However, there were increased

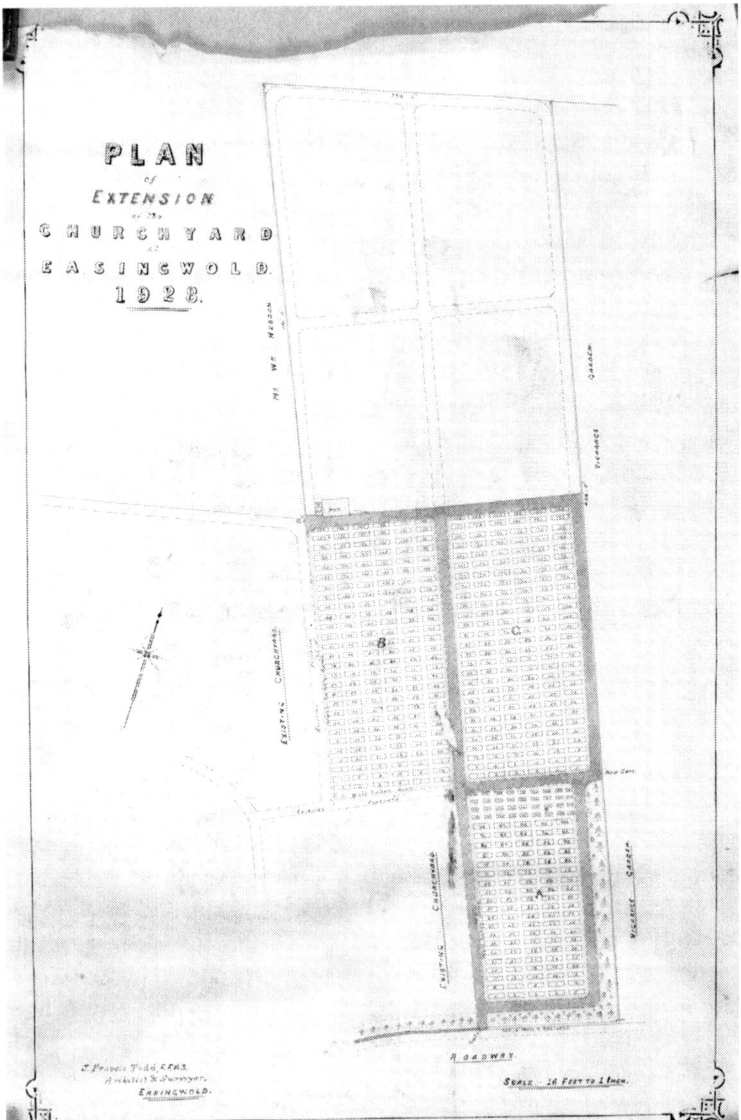

Plate 9.1 Plan of the churchyard extension of St John the Baptist, Easingwold. Map, dated 1928, showing a new attention to order and grave numbering (BI, PR/EAS 48/2).

expectations that it would be possible to reserve space. This development further impeded any ability to use the land economically. New management practices in the churchyard extension encompassed many of the virtues of cemetery administration, including grave numbering systems, but tended to overlook some of the measures that could be employed to maximise land usage. Despite the repeated exhortations of central government, cemetery management had generally continued on the presumption that a single plot would accommodate a number of coffins, one on top of the other, with a foot of earth separating each burial and ensuring that 4 feet of earth remained between the top of the last burial and the surface (see Appendix Two). Common or 'unpurchased' graves, where no burial rights had been bought, provided burial space only and so the burial authority could therefore choose to inter a number of 'unrelated' bodies in a single grave, maximising the use of the space as soil conditions allowed. Where burial rights had been purchased, the owner of the right would decide how many burials would take place in a particular grave, and the first interment would take place at the required depth. So, for example, where a grave was dug to accommodate three interments, the first interment would take place at 9 feet. When a further interment was required, a 're-open' would mean the gravedigger digging to 7 feet, so allowing a foot of earth to above the existing interment, and ensuring that the new burial did not disturb the previous remains. A second interment would again allow a foot of earth between the second and third coffin, with a final 4 feet of earth above the last grave. Thus a large proportion of interments in cemeteries tend to be 're-opens', that is, burial in the as yet unused space in graves dug initially to accommodate more than one burial. Burial authorities were obliged to keep grave registers in addition to burial registers; grave registers contained a sequence of grave numbers, against which were listed the burials that had taken place in that grave.

During the second half of the nineteenth century, and as

the twentieth century progressed, churchyard management adopted elements of this system. For example, at Carlton Miniott the vestry had acquired a formal register of grave spaces, which had been purchased from a stationery office and was similar to the books produced by companies such as Shaw and Sons for the use of burial boards. The register is printed on the cover, 'Register of Grave Spaces. Burial Ground at ____ in the County of ____', and contained the following columns for completion: number of grave space; description (whether grave, vault or catacomb) and situation of grave space; if purchased number of entry in registry of purchased graves; name of person interred, age, sex, date of interment; amount of fees paid at each interment; and number and folio in the register of burials. The final two pages of the register have been used for a hand-drawn grave map, indicating the pathway through the centre of the site and with names written in each grave 'square'.[41] An attempt to replicate this formality was evident in Sharow, where a 'grave register' exists for the period 1889–1985. The register – a notebook – contains entries that list burials chronologically, indicate whether the grave was dug to double or single depth, and whether there was a headstone. Against each entry an 'address' was noted, for example '6th headstone south of F. Clark's headstone', or 'North of Richardson's monument'.[42] Other systems were even less formal. As was the case in the nineteenth century, it was sometimes written in the parish burial register when the first interment had taken place in a new extension, and on occasion thereafter the register would include for each interment a number or an even a row and a number. It was also the case that vicars would attempt to record in the register where a new interment might have taken place to double depth originally, and so leaving the grave with the ability to accommodate a further burial. However, management of the churchyard relied for the most part on vicars, sextons or churchwardens remembering if an initial interment had been deep, and that space was available.

There is evidence in a number of places that a formal system of recording simply broke down, or got into a deep muddle following some basic failures of communication. For example, St Oswald's churchyard in Farnham had been extended in 1899, with a square of land to the south-west. By 1929, it was clear that attempts to manage the extension had either gone awry or simply never been put in place; neither the churchwarden nor the sexton had kept any documentation. A handwritten plan of the site is extant for that year, produced with an accompanying note written by an earlier incumbent to the vicar in 1929, and aiming to represent his memory of where burials had taken place: 'It grieves me to think I have to send you such a mess but I cannot make a good job of it at this distance.' He goes on to advise the present incumbent to make a list of interments out of the burial register, and try to use the location of the existing tombs to try and recreate a grave map.[43]

Even where that information had been somehow retained, it became impossible for use to be made of any remaining space in a double grave if the second interment did not take place as intended – for example, if the family moved away from the area. Individuals who expressed no preference were also interred singly. Some parochial church councils understood that this use of the land was profligate, and attempted to institute appropriate directives. For example, in Winksley, in 1938 it was suggested to the vicar at a church council meeting that 'in the future no single graves be made unless it is definitely a case where the grave will not be required by another member of the family'.[44] In Allerston, it was noted in the burial register 1958 that a particular grave was 'double depth: first of its kind in Allerston churchyard, though probably not last in view of decreasing space for future interments'.[45]

As Allerston indicates, in churchyard extensions it was often the case that 'family' graves were single graves that were grouped together spatially, one next to another. Husband and wife were buried side-by-side rather than together in a double grave as was largely the case in the cemetery. This system rested on a family's being able to 'reserve' a grave space adjacent to the one which had been used. 'Reservation' was not strictly speaking permitted under Church of England regulations but accommodations were made. In Carlton Miniott in 1902, the vestry minutes noted that 'it is illegal to reserve grave spaces for payment, but a space alongside will be left when possible for the wife, husband and child of the deceased'.[46] Here, the use of the register indicated that particular graves were indeed being reserved: indeed, the first three graves in the extension were reserved under a single name. It is clear that some graves were dug to double or triple depth, and a specific list at the back of the register gives a symbol indicating depth for each grave. However, there were a number of grave spaces reserved for which no interment is recorded.

Through the course of the twentieth century, the Church of England made various pronouncements which emphasised the fact that it was not technically permitted for space to be reserved in the churchyard, and that, although the parishioner had a right to burial in the parish burial ground, that right did not confer the ability to be specific about location within the ground. This possibility was little more than a courtesy afforded by the vicar. Furthermore, it had to be stressed that a grave in a churchyard was not the same as a purchased cemetery plot. In 1918, the printed Ecclesiastical Commissioners' table of fees included the warning that 'no exclusive right of burial to a vault or grave is conferred by payment of any of the above fees'.[47] However, the matter was becoming confused. In 1936, the *Care of Churchyards* emphasised, in definitive statement, that:

> Neither the incumbent nor the parochial church council has the power to give or promise to any person a right to be buried in any particular part of the churchyard, and it is hoped that the improper and illegal practice of 'selling' grave-spaces in churchyards (which was formerly prevalent in certain parts of England) has now almost, if not wholly,

> ceased. The law upon the subject has never been in doubt. Upon such a 'sale', the incumbent took money for what he could neither sell nor give, while the 'purchaser' got nothing at all for the money which he paid.'[48]

This issue had become markedly problematic in Leathley in 1950. Here, the vicar gave a lecture on the specific subject of the rights of parishioners in the churchyard. It is clear that promises had been made by a previous incumbent. In an informal burial log, the new vicar noted the revised policy:

> Unless a grave space is acquired by Faculty it is in no sense the property of anyone who may have paid a sum privately to any Rector. There are cases where monies have been paid and accepted & receipts given, in consequence of which various people are under the impression that some rights are transferred to them thereby & they are designed 'owners' in this book. Personally I shall try to grant the facilities which they thought were theirs by right of purchase, but legal ownership of any grave space should by no means be taken for granted until the Faculty is produced or the Registry consulted.[49]

Under one grave space in the book, the vicar wrote that the spot was promised to a named family, and notes 'I advise my successor (if such a question arises) to press the [family] to take out a *faculty* and establish their rights'.[50] It appears that some families heeded this advice: one gentleman asked that space at the foot of his son's grave be reserved, and it is noted in the book that 'A faculty has been granted for this space, and is among the church records'.[51]

Consequently, the reservation of space under faculty became more widespread practice. This option had been available in the nineteenth century, but in the twentieth century the number of applications increased substantially. Records for the Diocese of York include a listing of granted faculties. From 1850 up until the 1920s there were no more than a handful of faculties granted to reserve grave space. In the 1920s alone there were seven successful applications, but this increased to 24 in the 1930s and 51 in the 1940s. The faculty permission made it possible to pinpoint exactly the space required, and ensure that no other burial could take place in that spot. For example, in 1902 the Arton family sought faculty to reserve their plot in St Nicholas churchyard, West Tanfield. This particular petition for faculty was made after interment, indicating that the spot was situate 'on the North side of the said church', 'containing about 11½ square yards' and 'delineated on the plan accompanying the said petition and thereon coloured pink'.[52] It was more commonly the case for faculty to be sought prior to burial, and to ensure interment close to the grave of a family member. By the beginning of the twentieth century, reservation by faculty was clearly regarded as a proxy for the purchase of burial rights. It was generally required that the appropriated space be marked by the laying of kerbs or placing of marker stakes, to ensure that the space would not inadvertently be used for another interment.

The application for faculty to reserve a burial plot would be made to the diocese, which would be guided in its decision on whether to grant the faculty by supporting documentation presented by the vicar and the parochial church council. Parish records do in some instances carry correspondence on the granting of faculty, and diocesan guidance clearly shifts as the century progresses. So, for example, in 1916 a letter from a parishioner requesting the purchase of a grave space at Baldersby St James is rather unsure about what might be offered to the vicar to secure a faculty. A 'bribe' was clearly not out of the question:

> My husband has asked me to write to you about the ground in the churchyard which we are so anxious to have as our own. We should be very grateful to you if you would find out from the authorities if we could have a piece measuring 36 square yards ... As you know we are *very* anxious to have that part of the churchyard kept very nice, and what we hope to be able to do will perhaps be the beginning of a general improvement in the care of the graves, which I know is a matter about which you have several times expressed a wish. Of course what we

> shall be able to do all depends on whether we can have the grounds and what price is fixed.[53]

The Diocesan Registrar wrote to Sir Philip Wilbraham Baker Wilbraham for an informal judgement on the request.[54] Sir Philip was not certain that he agreed with current restrictive diocesan policy: 'I am not sure that this is right for there is a good deal to be said on both sides of the question.' However, he considered it to be unwise to change diocesan policy at that stage. The application had sought to reserve a plot which on the ground would measure perhaps three grave spaces, an amount which Sir Philip viewed as 'larger perhaps than can be easily justified'. The offer of additional funds for churchyard maintenance 'seems a good one in itself – providing that it is understood that this transaction is not merely a matter of purchase'.[55] However, this application was finally refused. Nevertheless, another similar application was approved at Carlton-in-Cleveland in 1921, and allowed the creation of a family burial plot through the reservation of a space measuring 14 ft 4 in by 16 ft, granted on the understanding that the family would donate half an acre to extend the churchyard.[56] At Newton-on-Rawcliffe, another petitioner for burial space was again successful. In this case, the vicar wrote a letter of support, stressing that, although the applicant was a non-parishioner, her husband had lived in the parish and she had herself donated the church clock.[57] The level of local influence over the Diocesan decision to grant faculty was further indicated in Lastingham. In 1935, the Registrar had received a request to extend an existing vault in the churchyard, agreement for which had been granted during the 1920s at a time when there had been no incumbent to offer any objection. The Registrar wrote to the parochial church council that the family had said that the churchyard had been extended, burials seldom took place in the old churchyard and the area which had been applied for was 'in fact, occupied by no graves'. The parochial church council responded vehemently:

> the Council absolutely refuse to consent to it. The last extension to the churchyard was very expensive and not a great deal of land could be acquired. With a view to the future it was decided severely to restrict burials therein, and such a faculty would give to ... a non-parishioner, rights which the people of the parish cannot have.[58]

The PCC at Lastingham was not alone in its concern about faculty reservations. At Sessay, an application was made in 1953 by the daughter of a widow who wished to be buried next to her husband. The PCC expressed 'considerable anxiety about such reservations in view of the rapid filling of the churchyard' but the agreement was made on the understanding that the space could only be used by the widow.[59]

These examples indicate that faculty applications appeared to have been assessed on a case-by-case basis. In 1936 the Diocese of York offered guidance on the issue, indicating a number of factors that would be brought to bear in the decision as to whether reservation would be permitted:

> The right to be buried in a particular consecrated plot at his or her death ought not to be conferred upon a person who in his or her lifetime appears to be taking no interest in the parish church, gives no help towards the upkeep of God's acre, and perhaps does not even practise Christianity at all or try to 'bear witness' to the faith. Considerations of 'sentiment' and especially the natural human wish to be buried near the grave of those whom we love, should have their due weight; but standing alone they are not, it is thought, sufficient.[60]

However, by the end of the Second World War, the Diocese of York had reviewed its position again. A letter from the Registrar's office to the Reverend Bayley at Kirby Hill in 1945 indicated that 'The Chancellor usually makes it a rule that the persons obtaining a faculty should make a contribution in accordance with his financial position towards the cost of maintaining the churchyard'.[61] Thus, there was a shifting emphasis away from evidence of service to the church and towards the possibility that monetary remuneration would be sufficient.

However, it is worth underlining the fact that much of the difficulty in arriving at consistent policy on the matter rested in its substantial emotional impact on the families concerned. As has been seen, the Diocese of York had in 1936 viewed 'sentiment' as being insufficient as a single reason for the granting of faculty for reservation. In actuality – as much of this history demonstrates – 'sentiment' was probably the principal reason why applications were made. In the vast majority of cases, applications were from family members seeking close interment to previously buried relatives. Thus, for much of the first half of the twentieth century, incumbents and PCCs were obliged to seek ways to resolve the conflict between the 'emotional' desire to seek a specific burial space and the shifting rationales in which faculties to reserve grave space would be granted. Thus, active 'evasion' of the faculty regulations could be practised. In Coxwold in 1951 the parish magazine indicated that a plan of the churchyard would be drafted, showing where recent burials had taken place, and indicating remaining spaces:

> The Meeting fully appreciate the natural desire of relatives to be buried near to one another wherever possible, and felt that the drafting of such a plan might be of assistance without in any way infringing the law forbidding the reservation of grave spaces in churchyards without a faculty.[62]

By the 1960s, the situation had become resolved to a degree. It was clear that faculty to reserve burial space would simply be available to anyone with the ability to pay the substantial fee charged. In January 1975, an inquiry about the faculty process sent by the vicar at Kirkbymoorside to the Diocesan Registrar was answered simply by indicating the cost. 'When you are ready to proceed further, no doubt you will communicate with me again, when I would forward you the necessary application form.'[63] No conditions were attached: securing faculty to reserve grave spaces had become little more than a monetary transaction.

There appears to be some correlation between the

incidence of applications to reserve grave spaces and the laying out of a new extension, signalling a desire to secure or protect available space in the 'old' churchyard. Of the 82 applications recorded for the Diocese of York from 1920 to 1949, 35 were from Foston, Whitwell, North Otterington and Middleton. At North Otterington, John Hutton's plans to extend the churchyard had taken some years to materialise, and had included the condition that further interments in the old churchyard should cease unless in reserved grave spaces. The vicar, the Reverend Thomas Parkinson, had intimated that some of the spaces had been reserved by word of mouth agreement, and he had felt morally bound to honour his promises in that regard. Nevertheless, it is possible that local views on Hutton's rather heavy-handed approach to 'tidying up' the churchyard led to fears that only reservations by faculty would be respected.[64] At Foston, the faculty reservations were grouped largely in the 1920s and 1930s: new land for an extension was conveyed in 1935. Similarly, in Middleton, the faculties were applied for in 1938 – the year in which the churchyard was extended – and in the following decade.

Excluding non-parishioners

In these circumstances, it was not surprising that the parochial church councils began to consider that use of the remaining space had to be rationed, concluding that a principal 'saving' could be made by excluding non-parishioners. Policies became restrictive. For example, in Carlton Miniott, the vicar reminded the Easter vestry of 1910 that 'it required the sanction of the two churchwardens as well as his own before a non-parishioner – that is, one who did not reside in the parish – could be buried in the churchyard'.[65] In Alne, there was contemplation of an outright ban. Here, the vicar declared in 1955 that 'he was bound by law to find a grave for any people who died within the boundaries of the ecclesiastical parish. He was not bound to find graves for any, no matter how exalted their rank who died outside the parish.' The PCC remained of the opinion that such burials be allowed, but that £10 should be charged in addition to all the other usual burial fees. The vicar was uneasy, but 'was challenged on this point and reminded that the churchyard is parson's freehold and that he was entitled to all fees, and was responsible for their collection.[66] This imposition of non-parishioner burial rates had already been in use as a 'prohibiting tax'. The Ecclesiastical Commissioners did not set a boundary on the amount that non-parishioners might be charged for interment, giving churchwardens and clergy the right to 'settle the amount of the fee in any case where they may be induced to allow a non-parishioner to be buried in the churchyard'.[67] In parishes all over the region, fees were increased substantially as pressure on space became acute. At West Tanfield in 1911, it was decided to charge non-parishioners a fee four times the normal level; and in Coxwold, in 1951, the additional cost was set at £30 above the normal parishioner fee, with this fee paid into a churchyard extension fund.[68] In these circumstances, definition of 'non-parishioner' began to assume increasing importance, particularly where older family members had moved away to larger settlements to access residential care. In Flaxton, it was proposed in 1953 by the parochial church council that 'a charge of £15 be made to non-parishioners except in the case where a husband or wife has been buried and the remaining party (husband or wife) has subsequently left the parish, and except for those on the *electoral roll* of the *Parish of Flaxton*.'[69]

The fact that particular churches had begun to look again at the use of their burial space brought into question the tradition of a number of townships 'sharing' a single parish burial space. It is notable that during the course of the twentieth century, a number of new churchyards came into existence. Burial space was added to chapels of ease, or completely new detached churchyard extensions were created for settlements that did not have a tradition of their own provision. For example, the small village of Pockley near

Helmsley had had a simple chapel of ease built in 1822 and rebuilt in 1860 by Lord Feversham; a burial space was created to the east of the village in 1915, and extended in 1932. This new provision reflected a desire to husband resources in the existing burial sites. The churchyard of St Columba at Topcliffe had closed and was replaced by a cemetery, in which Topcliffe Parish Council had introduced a non-parishioner rate that failed to respect the traditional reliance of Marton-le-Moor on St Columba churchyard. Double fees were required, which the vicar noted 'in addition to the usual funeral expenses, comes very heavy upon the poorer parishioners'.[70] The addition of burial space to the chapel of ease at Marton-le-Moor was a consequence. Similarly, the churchyard of Appleton-le-Moors came into use for burial only in 1922. The vestry minutes for its mother church of St Mary's at Lastingham indicates that the provision of this burial ground would bring to an end the 'preferential scale' for Appleton-le-Moors residents, underlining the desire to retain St Mary's for Lastingham residents only.[71] Tension on the matter was indicated in an exchange of letters in 1924, relating to the churchyard extension fund for St Mary's. On donating £5 to the fund, a resident at Appleton-le-Moors expressed that hope that 'when the time of my departure comes I may be laid to rest in that beautiful spot (Lastingham), where my own dear ones sleep and many I love'. The response from the vicar was perhaps less than generous of spirit, and provoked another letter from the donor: 'I am sorry if I inferred in any way that my donation was conditional. I only expressed a wish, if it cannot be granted it is quite alright.'[72]

Conclusion

The Church of England had been essentially disenfranchised from its rights in burial terms by a bundle of acts passed towards the end of the nineteenth century. Nevertheless, the continued obscurity of the Burial Acts in themselves underlined the fact that in rural areas there were substantial advantages to the Church remaining the principal agency by which burial space would be provided. As some elements of Church bureaucracy were pared away, the simplification that the Churchyard Consecration Act had aimed for finally became evident. It was not always easy for parochial church councils – no longer able to access the rates – to meet the subsequent expense. Nevertheless, it was generally agreed that this measure was much preferable to the alternative, which was recourse to the overly convoluted and regulation-heavy civic burial legislation, which would result in a continued and compulsory call on the rates.

Putting these pragmatic concerns to one side, it could be argued that the desire to continue using the churchyard expressed an adherence to tradition. However, this chapter indicates that more complex processes were in play. Churchyards were valued because they began to resemble cemeteries. The play of new expectations was most clearly expressed in the management of extensions. Here, Church authorities, the clergy and parishioners had to revise and adjust policies to meet the consequences of a substantial shift in expectations which changed one fundamental aspect of churchyard space: its innate sustainability. The extreme rurality of the central North Riding, with its decreasing population, meant that the region constituted one area in which it might be possible for the churchyard to continue accommodating interments without substantial changes. Indeed, as Chapter 11 will indicate, this was so for very many of the villages in the study. However, it was very often the case that the churchyard ceased to be an infinite resource, reused and reusable for generation after generation. Although no church law supported the presumption, churchyard interment was thought to comprise 'perpetuity' burial, and the memorial was 'expected to last hundreds of years'.[73] Families were more able to secure proximate burial, but often only by using land in a profligate way and burying side-by-side rather than using double-depth graves. The extension of the churchyard was an inevitable consequence, and in many places looks set to continue.

Notes

1 NYRO, PR/SNS 8/1, Correspondence and papers relating to extension of the churchyard, 1913–1920. Notice of meeting, 28 Feb 1913.
2 NYRO, DC/NOR I 1/3, Northallerton RDC, Minutes 1904–1910, 2 Mar 1904.
3 PR/OTN 4/3/5, Newspaper cuttings relating to possible burial ground, 1900, MS notes by the Reverend T. Parkinson.
4 NYRO, PR/BPM 5/4, Vestry meeting Minute Book, 1897–1920, 15 Apr 1912.
5 *Ibid.*, 6 May 1917.
6 *Ibid.*, 8 Apr 1920.
7 *Ibid.*, 22 Apr 1922 and 4 May 1922.
8 PR/SAW 7/1, Minutes of meetings of churchyard extension committee, 1924–25, 8 May 1924.
9 NYRO, PR/HMK 20/1, Parish magazines, 1890–1942, Mar 1897.
10 NYRO, PR/SAL PR/SAL 7/1, Notes and papers relating to the churchyard and its extension; with copy conveyance of additional land, 'Churchyard extension, Salton parish, 14 May 1933'.
11 NYRO, PR/HEL 7/2/1, Correspondence relating to Pockley burial ground, 1913–1947, letter from Diocesan Registrar dated 21 Aug 1915.
12 Diocese of York, *The Care of Churchyards* (London, SPCK, 1936), p. 8.
13 Based on own analysis of data derived from Confederation of Burial Authorities, *The CBA Directory of Cemeteries and Crematoria in the UK* (London: CBA, 2001).
14 P. C. Jupp, *From Dust to Ashes, Cremation and the British Way of Death* (Basingstoke: Palgrave Macmillan, 2006).
15 *Churchyards, Report of the Maintenance of Churchyards Commission*, C. A. 1131, 1955, p. 9.
16 NYRO: PR/SNN 4/1–14 (Records relating to church and churchyard, 1890–1973).
17 *Ibid.*, 15 Nov 1925.
18 NYRO: PR/SNN (North Stainley with Slenningford Parish Council Minutes, 1846–1980), 5 June 1969.
19 Church Information Office, *The Churchyards Handbook* (London: Church Information Office, 1962), p. 6.

20 NYRO, PR/SAT 22/1, Papers relating to the extension of the churchyard, 1900–1.
21 NYRO, PR/HMP 6/8, Church restoration minute book, 1899, 14 Jan 1902; NYRO, PR/HMP 6/18, Churchyard and churchyard extension.
22 PR/OTN 4/4/2 (9) Letter from the Reverend Bateman to Ministry of Housing and Local Government, 22 Mar 1956.
23 PR/OTN/4/4/2 (9) TS letter from Diocesan Registry to the Reverend J. Bateman, 28 Nov 1957.
24 PR/SOW 7/7, Correspondence relating to the extension of the churchyard, 1965–73.
25 Church of England, Church Commissioners, Churches, burial grounds and parsonages, conveyance of sites, general file, 11686/10 1898–1902.
26 NYRO, PR/HMP 6/18, Churchyard and churchyard extension, letter from Ecclesiastical Commissioners dated 29 Jan 1897.
27 Church of England, Church Commissioners, Churches, burial grounds and parsonages, conveyance of sites, general file, 11686/10 1898–1902.
28 BI, PR/AM 11, Petition for consecration of churchyard extension, 1899.
29 PR/DIS 8/13, Correspondence and conveyance relating to the addition of land to the churchyard, 1909–1910.
30 Diocese of York, *Care of Churchyards*, p. 8.
31 PR/ALN, Churchwarden's account book, 1861–1904, 27 May 1902.
32 NYRO, PR/OTN 4/1/4, Correspondence relating to extension of churchyard, 1904–7.
33 NYRO, PR/SAL 7/1, Notes and papers relating to the churchyard and its extension; with copy conveyance of additional land.
34 NYRO, PR/BED 17/4, Parish Magazine, Nov 1904.
35 NYRO, PR/KRF 12/7, Fund for the extension of the churchyard, nd.
36 BI, PR/ALN, Alne Parochial Church Council Minutes, 1928–1958, 1 Jun 1937.
37 PR/MAS 3/1/6, Churchwardens' Minute and account books, 1885–1951, 26 Apr 1905.
38 *Easingwold Advertiser and Weekly News*, 7 Jun 1902.
39 NYRO, PR/BED 17/4, Bedale Parish Magazine, Nov 1904.
40 Charles Loch Mowat, *Britain between the Wars, 1918–1940* (London: Methuen and Co., 1955), p. 224.
41 NYRO, PR/SAT 22/2, Register of grave spaces, 1901–1939, and NYRO, PR/SAT 22/3, List of grave spaces, nd.

42 NYRO, PR/SHA 11, Grave register, 1899–1983.
43 NYRO, PR/FNH 5, Plans of the churchyard with covering letters, three documents, twentieth century.
44 NYRO, PR/WIN 5/1, PCC meeting minutes, 1921–62, 17 Feb 1938.
45 NYRO, PR/ALL 1/8, Burials 1813–1980.
46 NYRO, PR/SAT 13/2, Vestry meeting minutes, 1889–1942, Easter 1902.
47 NYRO, PR/LAS 2/1, Churchwardens' accounts, 1740–1921, reproduced at 21 Nov 1918.
48 Diocese of York, *Care of Churchyards*, p. 10.
49 NYRO: PR.LTH 7/3 (Register of grave spaces), note in the inside cover.
50 NYRO: PR.LTH 7/3 (Register of grave spaces), note under grave 26.
51 NYRO: PR/LTH 7/3 (Register of grave spaces), note under grave 92.
52 NYRO, PR/TAW 7/2, Faculty for the enclosure of a family vault, 1902.
53 BI, DRF 1 D. 11, Baldersby, reservation of grave space, 1917.
54 Sir Philip Wilbraham Baker Wilbraham would serve as Secretary to the National Association of the Church of England, 1920–39 and the First Church Estate Commissioner, 1939–54.
55 BI, DRF 1 D. 11, Baldersby, reservation of grave space, 1917.
56 BI, Fac. 1921B/32, Reserve plot in churchyard for family burial ground; demolish wall to permit churchyard extension, and rebuild at new boundary, 1921.
57 BI, Fac. 1939/1/5, Petition to lead faculty securing right of burial in the old churchyard.
58 NYRO, PR/LAS 5/4–6, Citation to ground faculty ... for right of burial in vault in Lastingham Churchyard.
59 NYRO, PR/SES 10/2, Citation for a faculty and correspondence relating to the reservation of a grave space, 1953.
60 Diocese of York, *Care of Churchyards*, p. 11.
61 NYRO, PR/KM 8/6, Correspondence relating to grave spaces, 1944–48, letter from Registrar to the Reverend Bayley, 25 May 1945.
62 BI, BI, PR/COX 79, Coxwold Parish Magazine, 1951–1971, May 1951.
63 BI, DRF.2/743, Correspondence re reservation of grave spaces, 1975.
64 NYRO, PR/OTN 4/1/4, Correspondence relating to extension of churchyard, 1904–7.

65 NYRO, PR/SAT 13/2, Vestry meeting minutes, 1889–1942, Easter 1910.

66 BI, PR/ALN, Alne Parochial Church Council Minutes, 1928–58, 14 Apr 1955.

67 Church of England, Church Commissioners, Ecclesiastical Fees, general file 14953/4 1900–1910, letter no. 10450.

68 NYRO, PR/TAW 3/2, West Tanfield Church accounts, 1911; BI, PR/COX 79, Coxwold parish magazines, 1951–71, May 1951.

69 BI, PR/FLAX 72, Parochial church council minutes, 1937–54, 17 Feb 1953. Underlining in the original.

70 NYRO, PR/DIS 8/13, Correspondence and conveyance relating to the addition of land to the churchyard, 1909–1910, Letter to the Ecclesiastical Commissioners from the Reverend Smithson, dated 20 Dec 1909.

71 NYRO, PR/LAS 2/1, Churchwardens' accounts, 1740–1921, 21 Nov 1918.

72 NYRO, PR/LAS 5/2, Vouchers, correspondence and statements of accounts relating to Lastingham Churchyard Extension Fund.

73 BI: FAC.1975/20 (Bentley memorial), letter from mason to Diocesan Registrar, 7 Jun 1974.

10

'Unobservable or inconspicuous to the casual visitor'?:[1] *the changing churchyard landscape*

This chapter considers the way in which the landscape of the churchyard changed over the course of the twentieth century and addresses some contentions that have been central to the notion of a new and 'modern' attitude towards disposal of the dead. The introduction and growing popularity of cremation has been taken as evidence of societal disengagement with mortality. A strong contrast can be drawn between the heavy emotional and economic investment in a grave delineated by a kerbset with railings and surmounted by statuary, and the scattering of remains in a communal garden of rest following cremation. In rural locations it is possible to define a progression from the clearance of the mounds that clearly indicated the presence of the dead body to the removal of kerbsets and the eventual 'tidying away' of unvisited memorials until the churchyard bears scant evidence that interment had ever taken place. As congregations dwindled after the Second World War, and following the Pastoral Measure of 1968, the joining together of parishes could leave an orphan church vulnerable to demolition. Any remaining churchyard has in some cases been left literally hidden in the landscape. At the same time, cremation has created an alternative locale and framework for commemorating the dead, eschewing the Church entirely. Overall, this gradual shift in practice is taken as denoting revulsion against mortal remains: the crematorium is a modern 'machine' which takes the matter of disposal out of sight and consciousness; the dead consequently disappear from the rural landscape. This is a persuasive narrative, and one that offers a great deal of comfort to sociologists and historians who like dichotomous representations of 'traditional' and 'modern' death. However, the narrative contains a number of assumptions. A close analysis of the rural landscape of death through the twentieth century indicates that there was without any doubt a substantial change in the appearance of the churchyard. But change did not necessarily denote 'disengagement' with mortality.

This chapter considers three broad developments evident through the course of the twentieth century. First, there is discussion of the 'tidying up' of the churchyard, in the removal of above-ground monumentation including body mounds, and the clearance of monuments and kerbsets to create an 'emptier' landscape. This process was extremely protracted, both in the region generally and in individual churchyards, predating the First World War and extending right through to the 1960s and 1970s. Complaints about the complexity of the churchyard landscape were in evidence by the 1860s, alongside concerns about excessive expenditure on funerary items.[9] The twentieth century saw the emergence of a new aesthetic for funeral landscapes, which eschewed grander statements in favour of a more domestic lawned garden approach: modernism brought simplicity and uniformity in design. These trends were augmented by the desire to contain expenditure on churchyard maintenance but at the same time improve its overall standard.

Second, the chapter considers the incidence of churchyard closure. Unlike the nineteenth century, when churchyard closures generally reflected public health concerns, closures in the twentieth century generally denoted a PCC's desire to save money. Legislation permitted vestries and later parochial church councils to turn over responsibility for paying for grounds maintenance of closed churchyards to the local secular authority – the parish council, and later the rural or district council. Initially, closure had to take place using the formal mechanism of Order in Council but during the twentieth century the regulations were amended so that churchyards could also be deemed closed 'by consent' or simple written confirmation from the vicar that no further interment was to take place. This process of disconnecting the churchyard from the Church was augmented overall by the gradual creation of larger rural benefices as congregations decreased in size, particularly after the Second World War. However, the closure of the church itself was not necessarily accompanied by a discontinuation of burial, and throughout the whole area under consideration there were no more than a small handful of instances where the use of a particular churchyard ceased and the site disappeared. 'Church-less' churchyards could become hidden in the landscape, but they were evidently valued by the communities that still used them.

Finally, the chapter considers the introduction of cremation and its impact on rural burial practice. There was no crematorium in the three districts included in this study until a facility was built at Stonefall Cemetery in Harrogate in 1936. Before that time, North Yorkshire residents had evidently been making use of the crematoria at Darlington and Hull, which both opened in 1902. Nationally, cremation became the majority preference in the 1960s, and for many early commentators threatened the centrality of the Church to funerary practice. Indeed, the physical relocation was complete: it was possible to have a funeral service at the crematorium chapel, followed by the strewing of remains in the adjacent garden of rest. In central North Yorkshire, however, there is more evidence of continuity than dislocation. Although the Church of England was initially uncertain as to the required ritual that should attend a cremation funeral, it quickly understood that the strewing or interment of cremated remains in the churchyard was advantageous pastorally and financially. Indeed, the creation of formal gardens of remembrance within churchyards encouraged the trend, and in some cases brought into use parts of the churchyard that were not suitable for full-body interment. The 'traditional' was readily able to encompass the 'modern'.

Norton: the case of the disappearing churchyard

The study of change in burial culture contains many threads, and this particular book has drawn out one thread relating specifically to rurality. However, central North Riding did have some larger urban settlements, in which a different pattern of change was evident. The closely neighbouring towns of New Malton and Norton were two examples in which the history of the churchyard in the twentieth century was a closer reflection of urban experience than rural. In both towns, churchyard burial was superseded by burial board activity. As use of the churchyard was discontinued, these sites were extremely vulnerable, given pressures to improve and build around their central location. The fate of the churchyard at Norton is particularly well documented. Norton originally had a medieval church on its Church Street which was wholly replaced by St Nicholas's, built in around 1815.[3] The new church was Georgian in style, designed by James Pigott Pritchett, and was – according to comments in contemporary sources – a rather mean and 'unsavoury' structure. The 1815 rebuilding retained a great deal of original Tudor monumentation: indeed, the floor was 'covered with tomb stones of burials from the days of Queen Elizabeth'.[4] No Order in Council was issued for the churchyard; rather, it was closed 'by consent' in 1852, and a new detached churchyard extension was laid out at Langton Road. Pressure to renovate St Nicholas's escalated, and by 1886 a Building Committee for a new church had come into being, with increasing effort paid to fundraising. Initial local meetings had become heated, with disagreement as to whether funds should renovate St Nicholas or build a new church entirely. Pritchett's Georgian design was not regarded with any favour locally, and Hodgeson Fowler, whose architectural services had been secured, indicated that there were a number of practical difficulties precluding the possibility of extensive renovation. The present church was insufficient for the needs of a growing parish, but its location meant that expansion was problematic. The church was too close to the railway 'which causes the present structure to vibrate and shake whenever the trains rush past'.[5] Furthermore, the church and churchyard were full of interments, which would have to be disturbed with the drilling of new foundations.

It was this latter issue which held sway with those people who objected to plans to relocate the church. The problem was brought forward at a Church Building meeting on 15 April 1886 by a Mr Bower, who said that 'under no considerations would he consent to the bodies of his relatives being exhumed and removed from their present resting place'.[6] The issue appeared to divide the community. By December 1888, a site for a new church had been donated, but reservations were still expressed. At a local meeting, Mr I'Anson commented:

> Why was it they had such an enthusiastic meeting? Simply because the parishioners held dear to them the old church and the ground (Hear, hear) Why was it so? First, because it had been a place of worship for generations (Hear, hear). Secondly, because many who were present had friends and relatives who were buried there.[7]

Feelings on the matter continued to run very high indeed, even up to the point at which the new church site was consecrated by the Archbishop of York in 1889. The Archbishop's speech was conciliatory, and pointedly referred to the issue of the disturbance of remains. He noted that a new church building at the St Nicholas site would have meant the disturbance of remains of the dead 'at every turn'. However,

> When he told them that they meant to keep the church undisturbed as a chapel of ease rather than disturb and carry away hundreds of loads of earth, which was the remains of the dead, he thought they could not but approve of the decision. When a church-yard was consecrated, it was a guarantee that the dust should be allowed to rest until the spirits should stand before God and receive their final reward ... The burial ground was closed and would not be touched. It should be planted and beautiful so that those who had friends there would see that it was well taken care of.[8]

The vicar noted that this speech had had the required effect, and opposition to the new church scheme was dropped.[9]

The new church – dedicated to St Peter – was located on Langton Road, adjacent to the detached churchyard extension and new cemetery. A week of special services marking the opening of the church took place in 1894, and the church was finally completed in 1913. However, at the turn of the nineteenth century, the fate of the old church of St Nicholas was yet to be decided. The final service at the old church took place in June 1894, and – according to the vicar's wife, Mrs Chapman – for the following seven years the building remained empty, 'presenting a ruinous appearance'.[10] In 1898 the vestry advertised for tenders to pull the church down, and it was suggested that 'the Council take over the Norton Churchyard and make it a decent and bright spot in the centre of town'.[11] There was some discussion on the legal responsibilities of the council in this matter, noting that the Local Government Act of 1894 did indeed confer on the council the liability to maintain and repair closed churchyards. The churchyard was finally taken over by the Urban District Council but within a few months a planning application was made to build a swimming pool that would encroach on the site of the churchyard. There is little evidence now that a churchyard ever existed.

The disappearance of St Nicholas's churchyard is matched to some degree by successive infringements on other churchyards in the case study area, including the gradual removal of St Michael's churchyard in the marketplace at the centre of New Malton. A similar fate for Christ Church churchyard in Harrogate was probably only prevented by the fact that the church is sited on the large green expanse of the Stray, where no development has ever been permitted. However, the trajectory of churchyards from redundancy to removal generally comprises a story of *urban* change, and is evident only in the larger market towns of the case study area. In the more rural settlements, a different pattern of use emerged, which encompassed aesthetic change but innate continuity.

Tidying up the churchyard

The churchyard is commonly construed as an ancient landscape, and has – in all ages, it seems – been the subject of sometimes romantic musings about the nature of life in bygone times.[12] Many churchyards still contain monuments of undoubted antiquity, but it is doubtful whether many churchyards now would be recognisable to villagers of the nineteenth century or indeed much of the twentieth century. From around the turn of the century to the 1980s, the landscape was simplified in successive waves.

Mounds and lawn

The first wave of change was an assault on the most typical feature of any Victorian churchyard: its 'rude hillocks' or body mounds. It will be recalled from earlier chapters that the body mound constituted a platform of earth above the grave, which was levelled to provide an area on which to place monuments or more ephemeral items. The mound was the simplest of markers, and the one most readily achievable by families unwilling or unable to purchase more elaborate stone monumentation. However, by the beginning of the twentieth century, the body mound was regarded as a problematic element in the landscape. The principal difficulty lay in the challenges it presented to any attempt to keep the churchyard tidy: the mounds made grass cutting impossible by any method other than hand scything. However, removing the mounds and levelling the landscape was understood to be a controversial move which – prior to the First World War certainly – might require persuasion and incentive. Thus, in 1895, the vicar of Carlton Miniott suggested to the parishioners that a reduction in monument erection fees would be available if the mounds in the churchyard were levelled.[13]

At North Otterington in 1904, the Reverend Thomas Parkinson found himself in a dilemma when land was offered as an addition to the churchyard of St Michael and All Angels. As was commonly the case, the principal local landowner offered land for the extension. In this instance, the local landowner was John Hutton, who served as MP for Richmondshire and chairman of North Yorkshire County Council, and was a man of remarkable reforming energy. He was responsible for the erection of the first cottage hospital at Northallerton in 1877, and was a founding chairman of the Northallerton horticultural and floricultural society.[14] Hutton indicated to Parkinson that he was willing to grant a piece of land providing that the old part of the churchyard was closed and all the body mounds were levelled. No doubt these requirements reflected Hutton's public health concerns: the churchyard had recently been visited and criticised by Ministry of Health inspectors.[15] Parkinson wondered at the legality of closure when there might be space remaining, but it was the requirement with regard to levelling that was the greater cause of consternation. Parkinson wrote to Hutton that 'If the closure should take place I can see no objection to the older graves ie those in practically now closed parts of the ground being levelled but there would, I think, be considerable opposition to the levelling of the most recent graves'. Parkinson noted that there was 'sentiment connected with the grave mounds'. Indeed, the mounds were for some families 'the only mark by which they can identify the resting place of their dead ones' and feelings might be hurt by the measure.[16]

Nevertheless, Hutton was very clearly determined to carry through his proposed measure, and to tidy up the churchyard more generally. Removal of the body mounds required a faculty, which was finally secured in 1919 and which specified an even more ambitious programme of 'improvement':

> consisting of the levelling of rough burial mounds to which no claim should be preferred, the removal of all broken headstones on which no legible inscription can be traced and the placing of such stones against the Churchyard boundary walls, the setting upright of such headstones as have fallen over as have any legible inscriptions thereon, the making of a new pathway to connect the disused churchyard with the new part of the churchyard and the planting of trees and shrubs to beautify the ground.[17]

Concern about local responses to the scheme provoked Hutton to ask the Reverend Parkinson to produce a printed circular explaining what would be happening. The circular summarised the improvements listed on the faculty, and asked villagers for contributions to the final bill, estimated at £80.[18] In the course of completing the work, some damage was done to headstones which required Hutton to meet in the churchyard with a member of the family concerned. Hutton reported to Colonel Peckett – who was overseeing the improvements – that the individual was 'of course very grieved … but … most kind and friendly, and I hope and trust he won't press the matter further'.[19] Once the work had been done, Hutton set about establishing a fund to contribute to long-term maintenance of the churchyard. It is notable that, initially, the response was not enthusiastic. In July 1920 Hutton wrote to Peckett that 'It is very disappointing and heart breaking that after all the trouble we took in levelling the churchyard no one has responded to the invitation to form a Guild for its care'.[20]

Throughout the region, and nationally, the desire to remove mounds gathered pace from the 1910s. In Bishop Monkton in 1911 the churchyard committee introduced a restriction in the height of mounds; in 1917 it was decided that 'after due notice', the uncared-for mounds in the old part of the churchyard should be levelled entirely.[21] By the 1930s, the levelling of mounds to create a more even 'lawnscape' in the churchyard had started to become more generally acceptable and implemented less tentatively. In a large part, this was due to the development of a new aesthetic for burial which had been adopted by the then Imperial War Graves Commission. The Commission had created hundreds of cemeteries where each grave contained the remains of just one combatant, whether or not their identity was known. Each headstone was to be uniform, and with no distinction as to rank.[22] An absence has been entirely overlooked in later histories of the military cemeteries: they contained no body mounds. It is clear that the cost of the enterprise and the scale of ongoing maintenance would simply not admit of such a feature. In 1932, Major-General Sir Fabian Ware, founder of the Commission, attended the cemetery managers' conference and showed a series of lantern slides: the principles and design were evidently viewed favourably. In 1934, Alderman Wordsworth in addressing the conference commented that the 'simple effective memorials' of the Commission were 'ideal to aim at ... As you know, the private, the general and the Unknown Warrior receive the same space, the same record, and the same words ... I think that is the thing to aim at.'[23]

It is tempting to view the removal of body mounds as a signal of a revulsion against visible reminders of the rotting body beneath. In actuality, it is more feasible to place this development within a bundle of trends including an 'Anti-Victorianism' which had become more pronounced as the twentieth century progressed. The war cemetery constituted an aesthetic that was clearly modern in design, and antithetical to the Victorian landscape which had become increasingly cluttered and complex. Indeed, Ware himself drew the distinction, and criticised 'communal cemeteries' with their 'jumbled mass of individual monuments of all sorts and sizes and of all variety and quality . . . the result is neither dignified nor inspiring'.[24] A turning away from excessive elaboration of Victorian design complemented continuing calls for greater simplicity in funerary expression. The Church of England Burial, Funeral and Mourning Reform Association had since the 1880s been questioning the costs associated with funerals and their heavy burden on the poorer sections of the community. The Association saw no biblical precedent for excessive grief and high levels of expenditure on monumentation, which were deemed to run counter to a more purely Christian confidence in a heavenly afterlife.[25] Indeed, any excess in terms of funerary monuments could only be regarded as being more expressive of status obsession than any sincere reflection of loss. Percy Dearmer, writer of perhaps the most influential clergyman's handbook of the early twentieth century, wrote in 1899 that standards had deteriorated substantially: 'It may be questioned, however, whether even in the worst period of Georgian paganism, the appearance of our churchyards was half as bad as the ostentation of the last thirty years has made it.'[26] By the interwar period, it became even more common to cast doubt on the sincerity of Victorians' material expressions of grief; indeed, commentary on churchyards or cemeteries invariably included some dismissive barb. For example, in 1933 *The Times* reported favourably on the restrictions placed on memorials by the vicar of Little Gaddesden in Hertfordshire, who was quoted: 'I naturally want to be consistent and treat all parishioners, rich and poor, alike. Anything ornate or ostentatious, or conspicuously costly, is quite out of place in a country churchyard.'[27] Indeed, through much of the 1930s, the newspaper contained letters and even leaders on the subject of excessive monumentation. An associated campaign – to reduce or stop altogether the import of Italian marble statuary – likewise called for simpler monuments on a smaller scale, constructed from local materials by British masons.

The demand for a change in the churchyard landscape

reflected and was augmented by the publication of new guidance issued in a handbook in 1930 by the Central Council for the Care of Churches. *The Care of Churchyards* borrowed a great deal of its condemnatory tone and some of its recommendations from Dearmer, whose handbook was, by the 1920s, reaching its tenth edition. *The Care of Churchyards* was clear that 'the association and atmosphere' of the churchyard was such that its aesthetic should differ from that of any other burial space. Indeed, 'As far as possible it [the churchyard] should suggest something of the nature of a garden. Therefore, the fewer and the smaller the monuments it contains the better. And these monuments should be quiet in themselves and not garish or distracting.'[28] Furthermore, the handbook writer objected to ephemeral items left on the grave, including 'small statuettes or little basins or vases or jam pots'; kerbs containing granite chips were also 'objectionable, and lead to difficulties'.[29] In fact, the ideal churchyard would have no monuments at all aside from a single stone cross. The clearance of monuments was therefore to be a consideration: 'It is far better to have well-kept grass, rosebushes or other flowers than rows of crumbling and meaningless headstones.'[30] The author finally made reference to the body mound, 'cherished so strongly in many parts of the country'. It was adamantly concluded that 'there is no greater obstacle than the mound to the proper care of the churchyard'.[31] It was impossible to mow the grass, and the undulation in the landscape meant that puddles were apt to form. The writer again iterated that 'the feeling against interfering with them is intensely strong in many parts of the country', but nevertheless there were churchyards where a programme of levelling and selective monument clearance had lead to 'extraordinarily good' results: 'The grass is of the right kind and well kept; it has been possible to plant rose trees and arrange flowers, while the old stones are clean, well looked after and well seen.'[32] It is notable that the tenor of this report and its recommendations on changes to the churchyard echoed similar calls for changes to the cemetery landscape, which had begun to be evident in the cemetery managers' journal and conference.[33] The grander statements of the Victorian cemetery had begun to give way to the desire for an intimate landscape, with graves in a more domestic setting. In 1922, the vicar of Kirby Hill expressed his approval of the new churchyard extension: 'It now begins to have a garden-like aspect.'[34] The new 'lawn cemetery' ideal was also a new 'lawn churchyard' ideal, with a similar obsessive attention to the best grass seed for achieving a really fine lawn.

The *Care of Churchyards* report galvanised vicars who had long despaired of the inability to keep the churchyard tidy. For example, in Well in 1935, the vicar had evidently absorbed the report entirely, and in 1936 – with the PCC's support – introduced new protocols for the churchyard:

> Any grave mounds should be kept low and should be carefully sodded in wet weather so that the turf may take root and live. The grass should be kept short at all time. And this is much easier to do if the graves are quite level and no unnecessary stonework is used … Finally may I ask all those who still keep artificial flowers and glass globes on graves to remove them altogether. I can think of nothing more unsightly in a place where real flowers will grow, unless it be the tin and jam jar families which can easily be exchanged for pottery vases at a very small cost.[35]

The addition of land to the churchyard also gave the opportunity to PCCs to aim for this new and simpler aesthetic. For example, in 1944, Acklam PCC asked the rector to place in the parish magazine an order to keep graves level in the new churchyard extension.[36] Certainly by the 1950s some PCCs felt confident in banning body mounds altogether. Thus, in Thornton-le-Beans in 1959, it was declared that 'the surface of the churchyard will be of grass, kept level without mounds and trimly mown'.[37] Similarly, in Coxwold, it was written that in the extension, 'the principle of no mounds be adopted'.[38] Informal work to remove the mounds evidently took place in some locations. For example, at Ainderby Steeple, the PCC minutes indicated the hope that workers from a job creation scheme might be called in to help with churchyard levelling; at Sutton-on-the-Forest, the work continued through much of the 1960s, laboriously and by hand.[39] However, strictly speaking the measure did require permission, and through the 1970s and 1980s a number of faculties were issued that specified the 'levelling' of the churchyard and mound removal: for example, St Andrew's at Ingleby Greenhow in 1973 and St Oswald's, Sowerby, in 1976. It is evident, however, that the practice of mounding lingered through to the 1980s. In 1983, the York Diocesan Advisory Committee noted that in churchyards subject to recent inspection, 'the earth had been "mounded" after recent interments. Obviously gravediggers need to be told only to allow a sufficient surcharge of earth to compensate for settlement'.[40] For this aspect of the churchyard landscape, the process of change was remarkably protracted.

'Re-ordering' the monuments

A contemporaneous trend, again suggested by the *Care of Churchyards* handbook, was the selected clearance of monumentation and general 're-ordering' of the churchyard. As with the removal of mounds, this measure required faculty, and tended to be a gradual feature which first encompassed older and more dilapidated memorials, then kerbsets and finally in some instances almost complete clearance of all remaining monumentation in unused sections of the churchyard. The Diocese of York was very much in favour of this development. In response to questions on the process from the vicar of Carlton Miniott, the Diocesan Registrar indicated in April 1914 that 'The Diocesan Advisory Committee generally supports proposals of this sort'.[41] Indeed, the issuing of faculties for this kind of clearance programme became commonplace from the 1960s, so much so that the Diocese had simplified the process of application by producing a proforma. A typical application was made in 1961 by the vicar of St Helen's in Bilton in Ainsty, who sought permission

> to remove the gravestones in the churchyard on the West, East and South sides of the churchyard of St Helen, Bilton, to re-seed with grass and level the portions wherefrom the gravestones have been removed and to form a paved area on the West side and footpath and the East and South sides of the church using for this purpose the ancient and illegible tombstones.[42]

Hartwith is another typical example. Here, a faculty was issued for works in the churchyard of St Jude, and allowed the removal or burial below the surface of kerbsets where there was no evidence of interment within the last fifty years, and 'the realignment of headstones upon such graves where necessary to cause them to stand in rows' and 'the levelling of mounds upon the graves referred to above'.[43] Any programme of removal required local consultation which allowed for objections to be raised, and the Diocesan authorities generally required the surveying or recording of the landscape prior to clearance. For example, at All Saints, Yafforth, in 1966, the PCC was requested to secure permission 'to remove some very old gravestones in part of the churchyard and the ground cleared and levelled and so tidying it up'.[44] It was thought that it might be difficult to secure permission, and the matter was left in abeyance until finally in 1970 the PCC wrote to the Diocesan Registrar, who specified that a record had to be made of all the stones and their inscriptions, and that stones dating prior to 1810 had to be retained. The Registrar was of the view that the task of surveying need not necessarily be onerous: indeed, he advised that 'it is not necessary to employ a surveyor. Very often an intelligent layman, such as the school-master, can produce a suitable plan and schedule'.[45] Also, an advertisement had to be placed in the newspaper that clearance action was being planned; the Diocese proforma for faculty application generally included a suggested wording. In the event, the Yafforth PCC called in volunteers from the Albertinshire Boys School to complete a survey and diagram, and a faculty for removal was secured in 1971.[46] A similar process was carried through in Sowerby, where the PCC of St Oswald's took the rather more expensive step of using a firm of surveyors to record the churchyard.[47] Despite all the difficulty, it was still evidently felt that application for a faculty to clear was the best option. At Alne in 1971, the chairman asked 'whether it would be more trouble to take up 100 gravestones or put sheep in the churchyard. A faculty would be needed for the removal of the kerbstone[s]. It was proposed and agreed that a faculty be applied for. The sheep would need wiring round'.[48] Perhaps the most substantial work of clearance was completed in 1972–3 around the churchyard of St John the Baptist at Knaresborough. This work took place in the context of ongoing repairs to the church building and facilities around the church. The PCC secured the services of Sylvia Crowe, then President of the Institute of Landscape Architects. A year later, a sum of £1,500 was still outstanding for the work.[49]

Pragmatism and the changing aesthetics of commemoration

The simplification of the churchyard landscape can be explained by the desire to achieve a new aesthetic, deemed attractive in itself but also guaranteed to ensure ease of maintenance and a consequent reduction in cost. The imperative to save money – or, at least, reduce the required expenditure – is a consistent theme through much of the local decision-making around burial provision. Complaints were made immediately after the First World War that labour was impossible to secure, and where it was available then charges were much higher. For example, at Kirk Deighton a letter was sent from the vicar to the Registrar for advice following the resignation of the sexton in 1920:

> Would you kindly tell me the proper procedure to be followed in the matter of the revision of sexton's fees, as the old rate of pay for grave-digging, tolling bell and attending funerals are now out of all proportion to the general rate of wages in these times in the district. Our present sexton is resigning, and I do not suppose for a moment that we should

> get another to take on the job at the old rate of pay, in fact it would not be fair to ask him to, it is enough that the Church should sweat her clergy.[50]

Where workers were employed formally, the need to meet national insurance payments added further to the cost. One strategic response was to introduce mechanisation. Miscellanous documentation relating to Hunsingore churchyard indicates that, in 1917, £2 was paid for a lawn mower with grass box from H. Bushell and Sons, engineers; the PCC was generally unlucky with its choice of machines, and successive receipts chart a history of expensive repair.[51] Twentieth-century PCC minutes invariably include reference to state of the churchyard mower; indeed, the market for second-hand models in central North Riding appears to have been remarkably brisk. However, use of a mower required a change to the landscape. At Appleton Wiske, a new mower had been offered for use in the churchyard, 'but the condition was that the graves would have to be flattened out and all on the same level'.[52] As noted by the York Diocesan Advisory Committee (DAC) in 1983, 'Grass cutting is being carried out with larger heavy duty mowers and by this means working between gravestones and kerbs in confined areas is not possible'.[53]

Pragmatic decisions with regard to economy were just one factor influencing the change. During the twentieth century, it perhaps should be remembered that the task of keeping either cemetery or churchyard tidy was also construed as a service to the bereaved. Indeed, 'a well-cared-for churchyard ... enhances the beauty and dignity of the church itself'.[54] The Victorian burial landscape had been impossibly chaotic. Mourners had to negotiate a highly uneven surface, with broken glass and upturned jam pots hidden by long grass between the body mounds, and a slew of tightly packed, mostly illegible memorials, some teetering on decaying mounds and all in varying states of disrepair. It was thought that this landscape could hardly offer any degree of consolation, and certainly did not honour the church for which it provided an immediate setting. It is notable that work around St John the Baptist at Knaresborough received a local civic achievement award, being considered of great benefit to the town.[55] Better standards of maintenance were increasingly regarded as a priority through the twentieth century, and 'tidying up' was one consequence. However, it has to be remembered that programmes to re-order the churchyard generally took place at sites where new interments were taking place in adjacent extensions. At the same time as they were levelling body mounds in the old sections, parishioners were erecting headstones – often with kerbsets delineating the grave space – in the new sections. Formal memorialisation had become more affordable, as a consequence of the importation of cheap Italian marble. Elements of the aesthetic of commemoration had changed, but there is no evidence of a diminution in the desire to 'place' the dead and invest in funerary materials.

Closing the churchyard, demolishing the church

During the nineteenth century, closure of the churchyard by Order in Council generally reflected concern that the site posed a danger to public health. However, as the twentieth century progressed, churchyard closures tended to reflect other exigencies. Again, it would be tempting to indulge in the symbolism of churchyard closure, which could be interpreted as the Church of England stepping away from its responsibility to provide burial space. The reality was rather more prosaic, and – like churchyard re-ordering – indicated the need to make economies. Section 18 of the Burial Act 1855 ordered that, where a churchyard was closed by Order in Council, then responsibility for its maintenance was vested either in the churchwardens or in the burial board. This regulation rested on an understanding that, for the most part, burial board cemeteries comprised an extension to parish land and so it was consistent to make burial boards responsible for continued churchyard maintenance.

However, because burial boards became detached from vestries following the Local Government Act 1894 and were often absorbed by town and district councils, care of closed churchyards was more frequently lodged with civic authorities. The matter was inevitably subject to a great deal of uncertainty. The Reverend Thomas Parkinson of North Otterington, in compiling his long list of woes in 1904, considered that 'The Burial Acts of the last half century seem to have brought the burial law and ecclesiastical law if not in conflict, into such confusion about closed churchyards that no-one knows who is responsible with respect to them'.[56]

The situation had not necessarily become clearer by the 1920s, when the vicar of St Thomas's at Brompton was considering the steps necessary to close the churchyard. He wrote to the Diocesan Registrar in 1927, who advised that it was not necessary to go through the formal process of closure by Order in Council: 'this course is very seldom taken, and it is usually considered sufficient if notice is given to the Parish Council that the churchyard is full or will be full at a certain specified time'.[57] Consequently, the Reverend Yates wrote formally to the PC announcing that the churchyard was full, and no further interments would take place: 'I hereby give the Council notice that I propose to close the Churchyard early in the New Year say February 1st or March 1st except to such curbed [*sic*] graves where there may be room for a burial of a member of the family.'[58]

Thus, it is possible that by the interwar period, closure by Order in Council may have been superseded by a less formal process which did not require proofs that the churchyard constituted a sanitary nuisance. However, the scale of use of this procedure is extremely difficult to gauge. What is certainly the case is the fact that nationally the number of closures by Order in Council dropped substantially during the interwar period (see Table 10.1). In 1900, there were 35 Orders in Council to close churchyards reported in the *London Gazette*. This figure dropped close to zero in 1930 and 1940 but then had climbed rapidly to 68 by the 1980s.[59]

Similarly, in central North Riding, there appear to be no Orders in Council issued to close churchyards at all between 1910 and 1950. Section 215 of the Local Government Act 1972, implemented in 1974, gave some incentive to PCCs to return to the process of closure by Order in Council. Under this legislation, it became possible for PCCs to turn over responsibility for closed churchyards to local authorities, with just three months' notice. Nationally and locally, numbers of closure orders started to revive from this point in the 1970s; in total, in central North Yorkshire, eight closure Orders were issued in that decade.

Table 10.1 Closures by Order in Council as reported in the *London Gazette*

Year	*Number*
1900	35
1910	15
1920	10
1930	2
1940	1
1950	5
1960	9
1970	16
1980	68

Twentieth-century churchyard closures in rural North Yorkshire are not necessarily easy to research; indeed, it is easier to research closures taking place a century earlier. More recent data are far less readily available, since parish minute books are often still in use, and have generally not yet been deposited at archive offices. Furthermore, there are fewer closures to research: six closures took place between 1900 and the passage of the Local Government Act, and ten between 1974 and 1990. The lack of contextual data and the limited numbers preclude the ability to assess any trends they might represent.

Although it is uncertain why individual PCCs decided to pursue a closure order, it is clear that these orders did not mean the cessation of interment in a particular settlement. In fact, in only one village did this take place. Yearsley's Holy Trinity was a chapel of ease for St Michael's at Coxwold. The chapel had been built in 1839 and its tiny churchyard was closed in 1906 after which time, in all probability, the villagers continued using St Michael's as they had done for centuries. The case of Yearsley was exceptional. It was much more common for closures to be applied for in places where burials had already relocated to another part of the settlement. Thus, for all the remaining instances, alternative burial provision was already available in a village at the point of churchyard closure, either in a detached churchyard extension or in a cemetery. In all cases, this alternative provision had been available for some years. For example, at Gilling East, the churchyard of the Church of the Holy Cross was closed formally in 1979, but a detached churchyard extension had been laid out in 1925. Similarly, at Goldsborough, the churchyard of St Mary was closed in 1979, but a cemetery had been available on the outskirts of the village since the 1950s. Thus, the issuing of a closure order did not necessarily in itself bring discontinuity.

Perhaps a more substantive threat to the continued use of the churchyard was Church of England parochial reorganisation which took place following the passage of the Pastoral Measure in 1968. The Measure was described by one archdeacon to a parochial church council meeting as a means by which the Church could effect the 'best use of money and manpower in the Church', and was 'a large-scale job'.[60] The parish ceased to be the basic organisational unit; in rural areas, larger benefices – uniting neighbouring parishes – were often created. The various churches within a benefice would then 'share' a team of vicars. The reorganisation had followed an understanding that demographic change had left the Church weak in some highly populated urban areas but over-resourced in rural areas, where vicars were by comparison dealing with smaller congregations. Rationalisation of the system inevitably led to a large number of rural church closures. Between 1969 and 1984, nationally some 1,002 churches were declared redundant.[61] In central North Riding, nineteen churches – all with churchyards – were closed between 1970 and 2004. Of these, four buildings were completely demolished, and the remaining fifteen were transferred to the responsibility of the Redundant Churches Fund, which later became the Churches Conservation Trust. In urban areas, the tendency has been for the churchyard to be appropriated by the local authority under the Open Spaces Act, 1906, and landscaped for amenity use: visual reference to a past history of burials has been entirely eradicated. However, there has been little consideration of the fate of rural churchyards in these circumstances.

Plate 10.1 St Cuthbert's, Overton. The church has been demolished but the churchyard is still visited.

In central North Yorkshire, pastoral reorganisation was anticipated with dismay. For congregations of redundant churches, the amalgamation of benefices was something to be heartily regretted: the loss of the church threw the fate of the churchyard into question, and congregations could be uncertain as to likely outcomes. In Allerton Mauleverer, where the church was subject to redundancy in the early 1970s, a note from the Diocese indicated that 'A declaration of redundancy in respect of a church does not bring about any change in the position with regard to the churchyard or other land annexed or belonging to the church: the responsibilities in connection with such land remain as before'.[62] This letter was perhaps too vague to cover the practicalities of the matter, and a letter was sent back to the Diocese from a member of the PCC asking how churchyard maintenance should be financed through the transition: 'I have been wondering whether anything could be done about the churchyard during this "waiting period", and whether any money would be available for cutting the grass. The churchyard seems to get very overgrown, and as my father is buried there, I have a personal interest!'[63]

Uncertainty was perhaps more particularly marked in the case where the redundancy of the church then led directly to its demolition. It might be presumed that, in these circumstances, the churchyard would be extremely vulnerable. However, it appears that diocesan authorities generally assumed that the opportunity would be taken to use for burial the land on which the church had been standing. For example, at Acklam, the church of St John the Baptist was declared redundant and demolished in the early 1970s. The Order in Council for closure made under to the Pastoral Measure 1968 allowed the site of the church to be appropriated for use 'as part of the churchyard or burial ground annexed or belonging thereto'.[64] The fate of the churchyard at Overton was perhaps less clearly stated. St Cuthbert's was demolished in 1967, and within months a spat arose between village residents and the vicar of nearby Shipton-by-

Beningborough. He had appropriated the lych gate at St Cuthbert's – without notice, and without faculty – and the residents wanted it back. In a letter of complaint sent by the PCC to the Diocese, it was stressed that 'these are memorial gates specifically given to this church'.[65] The vicar of Shipton claimed that the lych gates were damaged, and 'In order to prevent the gates from being used as fire-wood' he had simply taken them. It was 'an emergency' and so there was no time to apply for faculty. The vicar considered that at the heart of the problem was the PCC's unhappiness at the fate of St Cuthbert's: 'The Overton people are, in my opinion, still suffering from pique because Overton church was demolished, and they are now, again in my opinion, being plain awkward.'[66]

Congregations were clearly unhappy about their loss of church and vicar, but there is a sense in which the rural churchyard – far from being a threatened element in this new chapter of Church history – provided a point of continuity. At Old Byland in 1975, the erection of a family memorial in the churchyard of All Saints had led to a protracted round of correspondence between the masons, the family involved and the Diocese, since the memorial did not conform to Diocesan guidelines. In making its case, the family argued that 'The clergyman always told me it was the people's church and churchyard and not the clergy's and the clergy come and go'.[67] The designation of 'people's churchyard' seems appropriate in all cases in rural North Yorkshire where the church has been made redundant or demolished, since burials have continued until the time of the current study in 2007. Indeed, at Cowthorpe, Roecliffe and Wintringham the churchyard was extended after the church became redundant; and, in places where the church building remains intact, it is often used for funeral services. Thus, it is evident that the economic exigencies of churchyard closure and pastoral reorganisation could bring short-term confusion and uncertainty, but over the medium and long term did not necessarily cause substantial disruption.

Cremation and the churchyard

The impact of cremation is one final element under consideration in this review of the changing churchyard landscape of the twentieth century. The Cremation Act, 1902 had given cremation legal standing and provided a necessary regulatory framework. Take-up of the option was limited in the first decades, and remained low until the 1940s. However, after the Second World War, the percentage of cremations rose substantially: the 1960s constituted a 'tipping point' where burials were for the first time exceeded by cremations (see Table 10.2).

Table 10.2 Number and percentage of cremations in England and Wales, 1930–1990

	Number of cremations	*Cremations as a percentage of total deaths*
1930	4,287	0.9
1940	22,336	3.8
1950	81,633	15.9
1960	188,294	35.7
1970	327,127	56.8
1980	387,296	66.6
1990	403,290	70.9

Source: www.srgw.demon.co.uk/CremSoc4/Stats/National/ProgressF.html, accessed 27 Jul 2011.

The Church of England was initially ambivalent about cremation, and for decades debated its congruence with the Christian tradition.[68] It remains uncertain how far the Church formed or followed opinion in finally settling the question: in 1944 an Act of Convocation declared that 'the Church's doctrine of the resurrection of the body does not preclude the practice of cremation'; and 'cremation of the dead body is lawful in connection with Christian burial or disposal in sacred ground'.[69] However, some degree of uncertainty remained, and rested in part on the threat posed by cremation to the centrality of the parish church and clergy to funerary culture. As the Bishop of Lancaster commented in 1958, 'A crematorium is as it were in competition with the parish church'.[70] This view was very much understood to be the case at a local level. A report by the Mass Observation Unit, published in 1961, included an Anglican minister's observation, following the opening of a local crematorium, 'If we don't get the ashes or the funeral, not only is the link with the Church broken, but we are losing a lot of revenue ... Since Worktown Crematorium opened we have lost much.'[71] In 1965, the Central Council for the Care of Churches was also concerned about the degree of separation:

> It seems sad that, with the great growth of the practice of cremation in recent years, so many good church people are content that the burial service should take place at the crematorium, away from the atmosphere of Christian fellowship in which their relatives worshipped regularly at the parish church during their earthly life.[72]

It remains to be asked how far the practice of cremation penetrated into the more rural areas of central North Riding. It is notable that, in 1948, Canon T. W. Taylor, Rural Dean of Eccles, Lancashire, declared that people in rural areas were unlikely to view cremation with any degree of favour:

> there is nothing to hold it in the minds of the people. The crematoria are far away, as a rule, in the towns. At the most, cremation is often something people have only heard of and spoken of with uneasy suspicion. The odd one or two who have been cremated or who have expressed a wish to be cremated, are suspected as queer folk who always wanted to be different from others, or who were mildly 'cracked.'[73]

Cremation facilities were early to arrive at the more heavily populated areas on the periphery of North Riding: crematoria were established both in Hull and in Darlington in 1902 and at Lawnswood, Leeds, in 1905. There is evidence from burial registers that these crematoria were used by residents of central North Riding in the absence of closer facilities. Indeed, a separate cremation register kept for St Mary's, Appleton Wiske, indicates that Darlington was the preferred option, and was regularly used by the villagers from the 1940s.[74]

Within the three boroughs covered by this study, Harrogate was the first to build cremation facilities, located at Stonefall Cemetery in 1937. The resources of this current study do not allow for analysis of the proportion of deaths that led to cremation in the settlements of central North Riding, and how that proportion changed over time. Although individual burial registers do indicate that a cremation has taken place, not all funerals in a village resulted in an entry in the burial register. Individual crematoria do not have a set catchment boundary, and indeed the Stonefall records indicate cremation of individuals – presumably holidaying in Harrogate – whose home address was outside the UK. The general declining population of central North Riding would also need to be taken into account. However, it is possible to use the Stonefall records to gauge the degree of penetration of cremation into other parts of the case study area.

As Figure 10.1 demonstrates, use of the crematorium at Stonefall grew slowly in the first decade, and then increased rather more rapidly from around 1949. The majority of cremations came from Harrogate itself, but a considerable number had addresses in Knaresborough and Ripon. However, it is notable that a number of cremations also took place of individuals whose addresses were in the smaller villages in the case study area. By the second half of the 1960s, the number of cremations exceeded the number of deaths in Harrogate. Indeed, by the end of the 1960s, Stonefall Crematorium was accommodating funerals from much of the western portion of central North Riding. The penetration into the more rural areas extended to Pateley

Bridge and smaller settlements such as Winksley, Galphay, Blubberhouses and Burnt Yates. Village burial registers themselves also indicate that cremation was taken up with increasing frequency particularly from the 1970s. For example, in Ainderby Steeple, there were 169 entries in the burial register between 1970 and 1990, 69 of which referred to a cremation having taken place. Even in the tiny village of Birdforth, to the south of Thirsk, the first record of cremation appears in 1946, with an interment of ashes; from 1970 to 1990, there are 22 entries in the burial register, five of which indicate a cremation. It is evident, therefore, that the practice of cremation had indeed penetrated into the more rural areas of central North Riding certainly by the 1940s, and had become commonplace by the 1970s.

Cremation is not in itself a complete process, and decisions have to be made as to the disposal of cremated remains. In the first five years of operation at Stonefall, in just over a third of the funerals, cremated remains were taken away by a family representative for private disposal. These early cremation records actually include a note of the action that

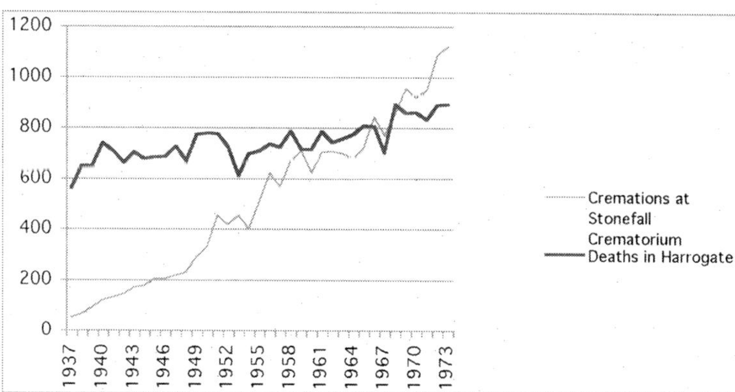

Figure 10.1 Cremations at Stonefall Crematorium and deaths in Harrogate

was intended to be taken in the majority of these cases. It was clear that highly personal preferences were sometimes followed: even in the 1940s, there are instances of scattering on the moors and at sports venues, for example. In many cases, the remains were taken away for burial in a family grave outside the area: where cremation had taken place of an individual from central North Riding, it was common for the remains to be taken away for interment in the local churchyard. This action did tend to be in the minority, but was a large minority. In the first five years of operation, the practice of scattering remains in the garden of remembrance accounted for just over half the disposals, but from the 1950s onwards this proportion increased, and by the 1960s had reached nearly three-quarters. Stonefall appeared to be a little behind the national trend: it appears that scattering was accounting for up to 90 per cent of cremated remains disposals by the 1950s.[75]

Table 10.3 Percentage of disposal options for cremated remains from Stonefall Crematorium, selected years

	1937–41	*1948*	*1958*
Scattering in garden of remembrance at Stonefall	54	65	74
Private disposal	34	26	22
Columbarium	9	2	4
Burial in or scattering on a specified grave in a Harrogate cemetery	3	7	
N=	595	226	669

Source: cremation registers, Stonefall Cemetery and Crematorium, Harrogate.

At Stonefall, variation in practice was rather more marked in the early years of the operation of the crematorium, and it could be argued that there is a linkage between ritual and scale of operation. Indeed, it could be argued that it was only as the numbers of cremations increased that the expression of more individualised funerary ritual appeared to narrow. By the end of the 1960s, the number of cremations had reached close to a thousand a year. Cremations were continuing to come from a wide spread of villages in West Riding, but nevertheless, in the vast majority of cases, scattering took place in the garden of remembrance at the crematorium. Thus the practice of cremation itself does not automatically bring with it a 'disengagement' from more personal and elaborate funerary ritual, as the variation in earlier practices indicates. Rather, it could be argued that the rituals around cremation have been mutable, with a recent return to the earlier 'personalised' post-cremation disposal choices after a period through the 1950s and 1960s when scattering at the crematorium garden of remembrance was by far the majority option.

In the context of this rather complicated narrative, the task of addressing the impact of cremation on the changing landscape of the churchyard becomes difficult. There was a concern that cremation looked set to undermine the hold of the Church of England on funerary ritual, but the new process did present a countervailing opportunity: that closed and/or full churchyards could be landscaped to accommodate gardens of rest. For a number of years from the end of the Second World War almost every official Cremation Society Conference was addressed by a leading clergyman, the majority of whom considered the question of the scattering or burial of cremated remains in churchyards. In urban areas particularly, this measure brought the possibility of a restoration of 'the old sentiment' connecting a community to its church.[76] The formal interment of remains was certainly a preference, in order to replicate the burial service, and to avoid 'those dank little pyramids of grey'.[77] However, favouring interment introduced the problem of commemoration, and this issue could be divisive. The Church wanted to see a revived interest in the churchyard, but not if that interest resulted in a material alteration to the churchyard landscape. In 1954, the Bishop of Plymouth commented that 'there is no suggestion that we are in favour of erecting big memorials over little caskets'.[78] Indeed, it was suggested that the best approach might be to allow only flat memorials: 'small stones laid flat are preferable and produce a more restful appearance', and an even better effect would be achieved if there was no evident disturbance to the turf at all, but inscriptions allowable on plaques on the surrounding wall.[79] A Book of Remembrance in the church would also serve as an appropriate means of commemoration.[80]

In central North Riding, many PCCs considered that the laying out of a more formal garden of rest was a preferred option. Where substantial changes were to be made to the churchyard, then faculty was required, and in these cases the DAC gave guidance on what it considered to be appropriate. Again, the principal consideration appeared to be to restrict the allowable monumentation. For example, the DAC rejected plans proposed for St Wilfred's, South Kilvington, in 1988 to demarcate the cremated remains area with a low post-and-chain fence.[81] At Cropton, there was a proposal to set aside an area for the interment of cremated remains and mark individual graves with horizontally set brass plates. The DAC supported the petition with the proviso that no brass plates be used and with the suggestion that a memorial book be placed inside the church instead.[82] At Ingleby Arncliffe, the PCC were decidedly of the view that it did not favour flat, inset stones, since 'they would readily become overgrown, they would be difficult to avoid with the large lawnmower we use, and water would settle in the lettering promoting the growth of moss'. Rather, it favoured the erection of smaller-scale memorials and asked the DAC if it might be possible to institute regulations, restricting their size. The DAC considered that upright stones were innately problematic: 'In the general part of the churchyard set aside for the interment of cremated remains one would not wish to create something which appears like a mini-cemetery.' However, the PCC was determined, and the vicar argued that 'if upright stones were to be placed a short distance from the wall this would not be a problem. I have not measured the length of wall available, but the population of the village is about 450 so it is not as if there would be serried ranks of memorial stones in a few years' time.'[83] It was clear that in some instances the local desire for a more substantial structure for the commemoration of cremated remains prevailed. At Bedale the highly organised PCC reviewed the practicalities of the matter in 1971:

> Many points were considered – whether the ashes should be buried or scattered, whether a book of remembrance or plaques should be used, the type of hedge, path and so forth. It was unanimously agreed that a garden of rest with a book of remembrance would be of great benefit to the parish.[84]

The result was one of the largest and more recognisably 'designed' gardens of rest in the case study area.

Few churchyards in central North Riding are now without a designated area for cremated remains. Indeed, the interment of cremated remains has re-introduced new

Plate 10.2 St Gregory's, Bedale. The cremated remains area constitutes a substantial development within the churchyard.

funerary practice to churchyards that had previously been closed, such as All Saints at Slingsby, and St Cuthbert's at Pateley Bridge. Furthermore, the interment of cremated remains has introduced a degree of funerary ritual to some churchyards where there has been no previous history of the interment of full-body burials, such as Bewerley Chapel, near Pateley Bridge and St Michael and All Angels at Beckwithshaw, where the area for cremated remains has been delineated by four stones inscribed with crosses.

Conclusion

The churchyard landscape is often used as an idealised representation of unchanging timelessness. In actuality, the churchyard changed considerably during the course of the twentieth century: sites now would be barely recognisable to villagers from before the First World War, and perhaps even the Second. Changes were driven by a number of factors, not least of which was a desire to embrace a new type of aesthetic, which eschewed the fussy ornamentation of the Victorian period. Excessive monumentation was increasingly regarded as showy and insincere, being more readily associated with the wish to impress than a genuine attempt to convey a sense of loss and a desire to commemorate accordingly. The importation of mass-produced stone occurred on such a scale that a campaign to protect the 'native' stone and British craftsmen rose up during the interwar period; increasingly restrictive diocesan regulations on stone materials and design were one consequence. However, at the same time as there were attempts to protect what was innately 'English' about the churchyard, substantial programmes of clearance were being put in place. There are now few churchyards in central North Riding that offer any impression of the earlier chaos and congestion.

The alteration of the landscape is often taken as evidence of a societal disengagement with mortality. However, as the previous chapter indicated, the period was one in which new churchyard extension was commonplace, largely as a consequence of investment in monumentation and to meet the desire of families to be buried together. Cremation did indeed introduce a radical change: use of Harrogate Crematorium indicated that the facility's catchment included many residents from the highly rural hinterland surrounding the city. By the 1960s, cremated remains were more commonly scattered at the crematorium than taken away for personal disposal, perhaps in the village churchyard. But there are indications that more recently the landscape of the churchyard has again altered to accommodate a cultural shift, and it is arguably the case that the creation of cremated remains plots in churchyards has 'recaptured' this final element of funerary ritual.

Through the twentieth century, it was also the case that the churchyard was threatened by changes in Church organisation. In many rural areas – and particularly in widely scattered central North Riding – pastoral reorganisation realigned parishes, and created new benefices that ostensibly gave scant regard to sometimes centuries-old traditions of churchyard use. However, the closure of churches did not necessarily mean closure of the churchyard, and in many instances that use has continued. Indeed, some churchyards have been expanded. There is resonance in the notion that, when vicars come and go and benefices suffer extended interregnums, the churchyard remains 'the people's churchyard'.

Notes

1 NYRO, PR/YAF 7/1, Letters relating to tidying the churchyard, 1969–70, letter from Rectory to the Diocesan Authority, 8 Jun 1980.

2 F. Burgess, *English Churchyard Memorials* (London: Lutterworth Press, 1963), p. 36.

3 BI, PR/NORT 55, Mrs Chapman's notes on the church history for a church handbook preface, nd c.1910s.

4 BI, PR/NORT 40, Proforma reply to the Burial Acts Department, undated but probably 1880s.

5 BI, PR/NORT 55, Mrs Chapman's notes on the church history for a church handbook preface, nd c.1910s, p. 18.
6 BI, PR/NORT 38, Minute Book of the Building Committee of the New Church, Norton, 15 Apr 1886.
7 BI, PR/NORT 38, Unsourced newspaper clipping dated 11 Dec 1888 pasted in Minute Book of the Building Committee.
8 *Malton Gazette*, 19 Oct 1889.
9 BI, PR/NORT 38, Copy of letter by C. J. Chapman dated 21 Oct 1889 reproduced in Minute Book of the Building Committee.
10 BI, PR/NORT 55, Mrs Chapman's notes on the church history for a church handbook preface, nd c. 1910s.
11 BI, PR/NORT 35, Vestry meeting minutes, unsourced newspaper clipping, dated 14 Jul 1898.
12 S. Matthews, 'Representations of the grave in nineteenth-century English poetry: a selected commentary' (PhD dissertation, University College, London, 1997).
13 NYRO, PR/SAT 13/2, Vestry meeting minutes 1889–1942, 1896.
14 'Past lives: legacy of a North Riding colossus', *Northern Echo*, 29 Sep 2000.
15 NYRO, DC/NOR I 1/3, Northallerton Rural District Council minutes, 2 Mar 1904.
16 NYRO, PR/OTN 4/1/4, Correspondence relating to extension of churchyard, 1904–7, letter from the Reverend Parkinson to John Hutton, 9 Oct 1904.
17 NYRO, PR/OTN/1/4/1, Faculty to carry out improvements in the old churchyard, 11 Feb 1919.
18 NYRO. PR/OTN 4/1/9, North Otterington Churchyard, faculty dated 23 Jan 1920.
19 NYRO, PR/OTN 4/1/9, North Otterington Churchyard.
20 *Ibid.*
21 NYRO, PR/BPM 5/4, Vestry meeting minute book, 1897–1920, 17 Apr 1911; 6 May 1917.
22 F. Ware, *The Immortal Heritage* (Cambridge: Cambridge University Press, 1937), p. 30.
23 CRGA, F. Ware, 'British War Cemeteries', *First Joint Conference of Cemetery and Crematoria Authorities, Brighton* (1932), p. 38; CRGA, Alderman Wordsworth, *Third Joint Conference* (1934), p. 36.
24 F. Ware, 'Introduction' in F. Kenyon, *War Graves: How Cemeteries Abroad Will Be Designed* (London: HM Stationery Office, 1918), p. 6.
25 See, for example, the Church of England Burial, Funeral and Mourning Reform Association leaflet, 1883, in LP, E. W. Benson

Papers, Official Letters, 1883, Home D.52–G. 77, vol 3, inserted at pages 335–6.

26 P. Dearmer, *The Parson's Handbook* (London: Grant Richards, 1899), p. 191.

27 *The Times*, 23 Jan 1933.

28 Report of the Central Council for the Care of Churches, *The Care of Churchyards* (London: Church Assembly, 1930), p. 8.

29 *Ibid.*, p. 9.

30 *Ibid.*, p. 22.

31 *Ibid.*, p. 32.

32 *Ibid.*, p. 33.

33 J. Rugg, 'Lawn cemeteries: the emergence of a new landscape of death', *Urban History*, 33:2 (2006), 213–33.

34 NYRO, PR/OUG 16/5, Boroughbridge Deanery Magazine, 1904–1931, Jan 1922.

35 NYRO: PR/WEL 9, *Well and Snape Parish Magazine*, Oct 1935.

36 BI, PR ACK/29, PCC Minute Book, 1920–47, 13 Apr 1944.

37 NYRO, BB/TH 10/2–4, Rules and fees etc., various dates, c. 1940s–1950s. Includes 'Rules for the care of Thornton churchyard'.

38 BI, PR/COX 79, Coxwold parish magazines, 1951–71, October 1959.

39 BI, PR/AIS 5/1–4, Vestry and PCC minutes 1891–1979, 16 Nov 1977; BI, PR SUT/F 51, Parochial Church Council Minutes, 1960–73.

40 BI, PR/TER 67, Papers relating to the upkeep of the churchyard, 5 items, c.1970–1983, copy of DAC, 83 4th Meeting, Agenda Item 9, 1983.

41 PR/SAT 22/11, Correspondence relating to the removal of headstones and kerbs, 1967–68. Letter from Diocesan Registrar dated 25 Apr 1961.

42 BI, PR BIL 17, Faculty: removal of gravestones, 1961.

43 NYRO, PR/HRW 11/8, Faculty for the re-ordering of the churchyard, 1968.

44 NYRO, PR/YAF 9/2, PCC Annual Minutes, 1943–1974, 15 Jun 1966.

45 NYRO, PR/SAT 22/11, Correspondence relating to the removal of headstones and kerbs, 1967–68, letter from Diocesan Registrar to vicar of Carlton Minott, dated 11 Aug 1967.

46 *Ibid.*, 1 Apr 1970.

47 PR/SOW 7/7, Correspondence relating to the extension of the churchyard, 1965–73.

48 NYRO, PR ALN 65, PCC minutes, 1968–80, 18 Jan 1971.
49 NYRO, PR/KN 3/2/7, PCC Annual minutes, 1934–1979, 1 Apr 1973.
50 NYRO: PR/DEK 3/8, File of papers relating to the resignation of the sexton, increase of sexton's fees, etc., 1920–21, letter sent from the vicar to the Diocesan Registrar, dated 8 Sep 1920.
51 NYRO: PR/HSG 8/3, Vouchers relating to the upkeep and rent of the burial ground, 1916–1919.
52 *Ibid.*, 18 Sep 1953.
53 BI: PR/TER 67, Papers relating to the upkeep of the churchyard, 5 items, c. 1970–1983, copy of DAC, 83) 4th Meeting, Agenda Item 9, 1983.
54 Diocese of York, *The Care of Churchyards* (London: SPCK, 1936), p. 13.
55 NYRO, PR/KN 3/2/7, PCC Annual minutes, 1934–1979, 1 Apr 1973.
56 NYRO, PR/OTN 4/1/4, Correspondence relating to extension of churchyard, 1904–7, letter from the Reverend Parkinson to John Hutton, dated 9 Oct 1904.
57 NYRO, PR/BRN 6/4, Churchyard correspondence, 16 Nov 1927.
58 NYRO, PR/BRN 6/4, Churchyard correspondence, 27 Dec 1927.
59 These figures are based on a search of the *London Gazette* in the stated years, using the search terms 'burial' and 'order', and excluding notices of postponement, variations on earlier orders and the standard reprint of each Order.
60 BI, PR SUT/F 51, Parochial Church Council Minutes, 1960–73, 16 Jun 1969.
61 A. Russell, *The Country Parish* (London: SPCK, 1986), p. 241.
62 NYRO: PR/ALM 5, Correspondence file of the secretary of the PCC relating to the redundancy of the church, 1970–72.
63 NYRO: PR/ALM 5, Correspondence file of the secretary of the PCC relating to the redundancy of the church, 1970–72, letter dated 10 Jan 1972.
64 BI, Orders in Council 843, Redundancy of the parish church of East Acklam and demolition of the church, 28 Jul 1971.
65 BI, PR OVE 21, Letters relating to the closure of the churchyard.
66 *Ibid.*
67 BI, FAC.1975/20, Memorial. Letter written by family member to Diocesan Registrar, 8 Feb 1975.
68 P. C. Jupp, *From Dust to Ashes: Cremation and the British Way of Death* (Basingstoke: Palgrave Macmillan, 2006).
69 *Ibid.*, see p. 135ff.

70 CRGA, Bishop of Lancaster, 'The Church and cremation', *Official Conference of the Cremation Society* (1958), p. 19.
71 T. Harrisson, *Britain Revisited* (London: Victor Gollancz, 1961), p. 53. 'Worktown' was an anonymised case study.
72 Central Council for the Care of Churches, *Churchyards Handbook*, p. 70.
73 CRGA, Reverend Canon T. W. Taylor, 'The conversion of the churchyard into a garden of rest', *Official Conference of the Cremation Society* (1948), p. 26.
74 NYRO, PR/APW 1/15, Appleton Wiske: Record of Cremations, 1940–1991.
75 CRGA, Bishop of Lancaster, 'The Church and cremation', p. 20.
76 CRGA, Reverend Canon Taylor, 'The conversion of the churchyard into a garden of rest', p. 23.
77 CRGA, Bishop of Rochester, 'The Church and cremation', p. 29.
78 CRGA, Bishop of Plymouth, 'The Church and cremation', *Official Conference of the Cremation Society* (1954), p. 33.
79 CRGA, Central Council for the Care of Churches, 'Cremation ashes and the construction of crematoria: notes prepared by the Central Council for the Care of Churches', undated pamphlet, probably 1950s.
80 Church Information Office, *The Churchyards Handbook*.
81 BI, FAC 1988. /151, South Kilvington: area for cremated remains, 1988.
82 BI, DAC (88) 11th Meeting, 1 Dec 1988.
83 BI, FAC. 1986/161, Faculty: area for cremated remains, 1986.
84 NYRO, PR/BED 21/1, Vestry, Church AGM and PCC minutes, 1952–85, 5 Jul 1971.

11

'Thoroughly untidy': changing burial culture, 1850–2007

In drawing this study to a conclusion, this text takes the opportunity to survey current burial provision in central North Riding, and consider elements of change and of stasis. Again it needs to be stressed that this area is not presented as being typically English, typically rural or even typically Yorkshire: there is no single English burial history. The permissive nature of English burial law means that patterns of burial provision were and are still played out at a local level, and remain largely chaotic with a multiplicity of providers operating under two sets of legislation: church and civic law. Nevertheless, all parts of England have been subject to the same play of changing burial legislation and – as has been seen on innumerable occasions – the arm of Whitehall still reached into the most remote settlement. In central North Riding even a basic summary of contemporary provision offers rich material for interpretation: in 2007, there were 273 churchyards still in operation, and 43 cemeteries that were owned and managed by parish, town and district councils. It would be as valid to stress elements of change as it would be to stress the larger continuities. Here no dogmatic claim is made either way. Rather, it is sufficient to say that the notion that cemeteries brought 'modern' burial practice collapses under scrutiny. It is clearly necessary to arrive at new discourses to address and analyse burial practice over time.

The second half of the chapter will draw together some of the larger themes addressed by the study, and look outwards towards some of the wider questions that relate to changing attitudes towards death more generally. Gordon and Marshall, in reviewing death and burial in a much earlier period, offer timely advice to 'attempt to avoid juxtaposing sets of neatly contrasting paradigms, to present static "before" and "after" snapshots of a series of processes that were in reality dynamic, evolutionary and thoroughly untidy'.[1] This counsel is also true for the period 1850–2007, where there is in particular a temptation to use the World Wars as crisis points. The decision not to take this approach here appears alarming, particularly given both the number of war memorials that were erected in churchyards throughout the region in the 1920s and 1930s, and the substantial scholarship attached to this subject alone. However, this text has erred on the side of describing rather than ascribing trends, and in doing so finds the chronology of change problematic. In particular, the notion that at some juncture between the nineteenth and twentieth century there is an advent of 'modernity' in terms of burial practice is difficult to support. Walter has stressed that mortality is a multi-tiered phenomenon,[2] and burial is similarly layered. Reviewing actual burial practice is not just useful in gathering material on the changing aesthetics of commemoration but is also helpful in pinpointing alterations in the conceptualisation of the corpse. This research has demonstrated that it is helpful to distinguish two different types of corpse: the massed, undifferentiated dead, and the individuated dead body of a family member. Each of these types of corpse has fared differently over the course of the period in question, and understanding those differences helps to consider what might be 'modern' about burial practice in this period, and what might not have changed at all.

Positing the study in a rural area also helps to pinpoint some new questions about the progress of burial reform, particularly in an industrialising society. The burial board, as a format, applied across all types of parish – rural or urban – and where pressure on space ranged from perhaps twenty burials a year to more than a thousand. It is clear that, where demand for space challenged the ability to provide, then there was a concomitant deterioration in the quality of ritual and even a decrease in the degree of dignity afforded to the dead body. However, the cemetery was not, per se, an agency for the delivery of indignity – particularly to pauper bodies – as some commentators have claimed. Rather, new urban scales of operation on occasion overcame all attempts to contain the massed mortal remains that were a consequence. Cremation rhetoric in the nineteenth century – which is often taken as a signal for disregard or loathing for the corpse – rather, reflects fears that containment of the urban dead may not be possible.

This case study also provokes reflection around issues of burial and secularity. This author has – with others – been guilty of connecting a rise in cemetery use with secularisation and a loss of authority for the Church of England. In actuality, as much as this book has demonstrated, the Church retained substantial control over burial provision until 1900, and even thereafter there was no reduction in demand for burial in consecrated space. A disconnect has been evident between the Church and rites of passage in urban areas. In many of the rural parts of North Yorkshire, continuity – in terms of funerary rites – has remained strong, for the most part. Cremation has entailed some adjustment to ritual but not necessarily undermined the role of the churchyard in village communities.

Finally, the study has provoked some revision in definitions of burial space that distinguish between cemetery and churchyard. In rural areas, cemeteries and churchyards are often impossible to differentiate visually, and in some instances even local communities might mistake ownership of a churchyard located away from a church, or a cemetery laid out next to the churchyard. This raises the question of why it is necessary to bother making any distinction if, culturally, these two types of burial space carry identical meaning and significance for their users. Within archaeology, anthropology and sociology, the differences are perhaps too fine to merit attention. However, within the realms of history and policy, the differences are key. In England the history of cemeteries does not support the notion of a modern, Foucauldian appropriation of the dead body by the State, and the Church has a more central role. In policy terms particularly, the fact that churchyards and consecrated ground lie under Church authority, whilst unconsecrated burial space is subject to civic legislation creates substantial tensions, not least with regard to contemporary issues around the supply of burial space in rural areas. If this research has clearly demonstrated anything, it is that in England no agency – including the Church – actively seeks the responsibility to provide burial space.

Burial provision, 2007

This concluding chapter reviews the provision of burial space at the very end of the research period, in 2007, as a means of commenting on the longer trajectories of change.

Cemeteries

It might be supposed that, over the course of a century and a half, there would have been a substantial shift away from churchyards, and towards the more widespread use of cemeteries. In actuality, this trajectory was much more complex. In 1850, the Church of England dominated supply, but a number of 'mixed economy' settlements existed in which alternatives were available. By the end of the nineteenth century, the larger burial boards had made inroads into Harrogate, which had grown rapidly, and the smaller market towns. After 1894, the number of cemeteries nearly doubled, but there was a change in the legislative processes used to support their establishment. Although use of the Burial Acts continued to be possible right up until 1974, the majority of cemeteries that were laid out after 1894 were purchased and managed using the Public Health (Interment) Act, 1879. Throughout England it remains the case that cemeteries can be operated at district, town and parish levels. In the three local authority areas under consideration, there is a contrast between the proactive absorption of burial space by Harrogate Borough Council, which by 2007 had acquired ten cemeteries, and Ryedale and Hambleton Districts which managed just one each. It is arguably the case that, in rural areas, the provision of burial space has remained strongly wedded to very localised governance. Twenty-eight of the cemeteries in the study are now owned and managed by town and parish councils.

Churchyards

However, the introduction of new cemetery provision did not constitute the strongest trend in changes to burial provision in rural areas since 1850. In 2007 the Church of England continued to dominate the supply of burial space, judged purely in terms of site numbers if not in scale of interment. Indeed, the number of churchyards has increased, easily absorbing any reduction in churchyard numbers that were a consequence of expansion in the more urban areas of the study. Despite – and perhaps because of – the small number of annual interments, a Church of England churchyard remains the only burial provision available locally in the majority of the villages and scattered settlements beyond the market towns. The need for additional space has been more readily met through the extension of the churchyard rather than recourse to a civic cemetery. It would be tempting to see here evidence of substantial continuity and that in some way the remoteness of these Yorkshire churchyards in their very rural settings provided insulation from the wider changes to burial culture reviewed in this study. Indeed, within the study there are more than twenty Norman or even Saxon churchyards whose 'footprint' in the landscape remained unchanged during the period 1850–2007: it appears that a thousand-year tradition remained largely untroubled. However, it would be a mistake to view these churches as having been somehow overlooked. For example, the undedicated church at Danby Wiske – located in farmland in the Vale of York between Northallerton and Darlington – dates from the Norman period. Although the churchyard has been neither closed nor extended during the last two centuries, it has not been immune from wider legislative and cultural change: a Burial Law Amendment Act interment took place here in 1893, conducted by a Roman Catholic priest; the churchyard was the subject of a sanitary report by the Local Government board to Northallerton Rural District Council in 1900; and between 1969 and 1990, 25 of the 45 entries in the burial register indicated that a cremation had taken place.[3]

It is clear that the churchyard has constituted a more dynamic space than has commonly been supposed, in terms of its framing and responding to changes in burial culture. The continued reliance on the Church of England in central North Riding has rested mainly on the fact that its churchyards expanded to accommodate increased demand. There is a sense in which this trend reveals more about local pragmatism than about a strong adherence to the conception of the Anglican Church as a 'favoured provider'. It remains the case that churchyard maintenance rests almost entirely on unpaid voluntary effort: churchwardens continue to scrape together funds from smaller and smaller Church congregations to pay for lawn mower petrol, or let local farmers graze their sheep in older sections. Parish councils would fall under more stringent regulation and – in the way of all local government – would be obliged to put the work out to tender, and pay attention to the expensive niceties of health and safety.

Table 11.1 Change in burial provision, 1850–2007

	In 1850	*By 1894*	*By 2007*
Churchyards			
Subject to Order in Council closure	0	25	38
Extended[1]	na	63	133
TOTAL churchyards in operation[2]	**243**	**268**	**273**
Cemeteries			
Burial Board under the Burial Acts	0	19	22
Parish or RDC under Public Health (Amendment) Act	0	1	12
Post-1974 cemeteries	–	–	5
Trusts/committees/other	0	2	1
TOTAL cemeteries in operation	0	22	43[3]
Burial grounds			
Quaker[4]	11	10	4
Wesleyan Methodist[4]	4	4	2
Independent	7	8	2
Roman Catholic	4	4	5
TOTAL burial grounds in operation	**26**	**26**	**13**
Crematoria	–	–	1

Notes: [1]It was commonly the case that churchyards closed by Order in Council were extended. [2]'In operation' means continuing to accommodate either full-body interment or cremated remains only. [3]There were three cemeteries where details of legislative background were not available. [4]At Scotton, the Quaker burial ground was turned over to use by the Wesleyan Methodists in the 1880s.

Burial grounds

A further element of change which has become clearly evident by 2007 is the reduction in the number of denominational burial grounds. In 1850, central North Riding was not remarkable for its supply of either Roman Catholic or

Protestant Nonconformist burial spaces, and in this regard is probably very different from other rural areas where the Old Dissent had a deeper footprint. Independent and Congregationalist burial grounds in the market towns were always vulnerable to urban development and closure as a consequence of public health concerns. At the same time, new cemeteries increased the supply of unconsecrated burial space substantially. Indeed, it could be argued that although the number of burial grounds specific to non-Anglican communities halved over the period, in actuality over forty new sites became available within the part-unconsecrated cemeteries. However, the political significance of that space has dwindled considerably. The notion of consecration – or more particularly non-consecration – as a religious political statement has disappeared from popular understandings of burial space. Indeed, interviews with local funeral directors, churchwardens and even vicars indicate the presumption that burial in unconsecrated space denotes some level of punishment rather than an active choice.

Cremation

Just one crematorium was established in the case study area, in 1937. There was discussion on the need for a crematorium in Northallerton in the 1960s, but geography told against the ability to arrive at any joint funding arrangement with neighbouring authorities: Ripon and Knaresborough were already well served by Harrogate.[4] As the twentieth century progressed, the number of crematoria on the periphery of central North Riding increased: for example at Skipton (1952), Scarborough (1961), York (1962) and Driffield (1997). British funerary culture has been transformed by the growing incidence of cremation, which has naturally tended to dominate any discussion of disposal of the dead, particularly in the postwar period. However, this research indicates that, although a great deal is known of the 'institutional history' of cremation, its popular and social history merits further and more detailed exploration. For example, methods for the disposal of ashes have been subject to a number of shifts in trends. Studies by Parsons have demonstrated that, in the first couple of decades after the opening of Woking Crematoriun, ashes tended to be interred rather than strewn, creating a 'mini-cemetery' with scaled-down memorials.[5] The strewing of cremated remains at gardens of rest was a subsequent development, further encouraged by the popularity of the Memorial Gardens at Stoke Poges.[6] The intimate family rituals created around the private disposal of cremated remains is not so easy to research. Recent studies have indicated the richness of variation in contemporary practice: cremated remains are not always interred or strewn at traditional places of disposal – the churchyard, crematorium or cemetery – but are taken to places with more personal resonance.[7] A review of the destination of cremated remains taken for private disposal in the early years of Harrogate Crematorium also indicate that very personal choices were made, for example, with instances recorded of strewing in the open countryside. In the last couple of decades, the creation of specific areas within churchyards for the interment of cremated remains has become almost universal. Indeed, it could be argued that funerary culture has begun to return – via the crematorium – to burial.

'Green' burial

One final and hitherto unremarked trend which is evident by 2007 is the growing popularity of 'green' burial. It is now the case that over 250 such sites are now in operation all over the UK. Although definition of 'green' varies substantially, there is a general presumption that such burials will offer some concessions to ecological principles – for example, burial in shrouds rather than coffins – and that stone memorials will be discouraged in favour of natural alternatives.[8] This development began from the initiative of Ken West, who was then manager of the cemetery service at Carlisle, and who opened a natural woodland section in the cemetery at Carlisle in 1993.[9] One of the earliest green burial sites – the Mowthorpe Gardens of Rest – was established at Terrington by a private sector company in 1995. Now many large-scale burial authorities offer at least a section of a cemetery where the presumption is that no stone memorial will be erected, in preference to the development of a more natural wooded area. Green burial has been subject to recent detailed study, and it is clear that the meanings attached to green burial are as varied as the management styles. It could be argued that green burial is perhaps more closely aligned to cremation in its development as a 'niche' initiative catering to a market with very particular ethical concerns. As with early crematoria, green burial sites are not necessarily closely tied to 'place', and their catchment area can be nationwide. Their appeal to the families that use them lies not in their proximity but in the fact that they offer an alternative to churchyard and cemetery provision that is considered somehow dissatisfactory. Initial concerns about regulation were satisfied in the case of crematoria, with the Cremation Act 1902. It is still the case that green burial remains outside any specific regulatory framework, although 'best practice' principles have been endorsed by the Ministry of Justice.[10]

Themes

The disposal of the dead has tended to regarded as a rather minor aspect of wider histories of mortality. Where mention is made of burial, there is generally a concentration on the material culture of commemoration rather than more prosaic concerns such as how burial space was supplied and the regulations by which it was managed. This final section reviews some of the major conclusions that can be drawn from this history of burial, provoking a series of larger questions that are integral to the study of mortality.

From churchyard to cemetery

Perhaps the first notable trend is to consider the trajectory that is commonly held to be the central story of nineteenth-century burial: the closure of an ancient churchyard and its replacement with a new cemetery. The principal corrective brought to this picture is an understanding that cemetery establishment cannot be viewed in isolation, since the laying out of churchyard space continued to take place throughout the nineteenth century. The continued use of churchyards was not restricted to central North Riding. Fiona Stirling has completed a detailed study of burial change in an urban location, using Sheffield as a case study area. Here, in the eighteenth century, burial provision was met by use of the Cathedral churchyard and two small chapels of ease. All three sites were located centrally. However, between 1825 and 1840 four new 'Million Act' churches were established on the periphery of the growing city. All these churches had churchyards, and the drop in interments at the Cathedral was marked. In addition, in 1836, the General Cemetery was established by a joint-stock company. Although this new site absorbed a substantial proportion of the city's interments, its location meant that it tended only to serve the south-east; burials in the 'Million Act' churchyards continued. The city expanded into previously rural parishes, where existing churchyards were often extended to accommodate the increased demand; this was the case at All Saints, Ecclesall, for example. The various townships of Sheffield themselves sought to provide additional burial space, and almost all provided new burial board cemeteries through the 1850s.[11] This rather confused but dynamic picture underlines the fact that, in most of the rapidly growing urban centres of England, changing burial provision through the nineteenth century constituted less a clear progression from churchyard to cemetery than a scramble to meet often rapidly changing demand using whatever process or agency was deemed to be politically acceptable locally. In many urban areas, new burial board cemeteries were being mapped on to a pattern of churchyard provision that had already been shifting for a generation or more.

In addition, there needs to be a clearer regard for the

agency of change, which was for the vast majority of cemeteries in the nineteenth century the local vestry. It was the vestry – essentially, local ratepayers – who decided the way in which local burial needs would be met. Under the Burial Acts, and notwithstanding the local religious politics of the issue, any new cemetery was essentially an organic development from existing churchyard provision and was, to all intents and purposes, a scaled-up churchyard extension that included an unconsecrated section. A focus on the agency of change underlines the continuity inherent in the process of moving from churchyard to cemetery in the vast number of places. This is not to say that, in some areas, new burial provision did not bring a level of dislocating innovation – for example, in York where the new company cemetery achieved a near-monopoly position after all the churchyards of the city were closed. But this study demonstrates that the abrupt shift from churchyard to cemetery is just one possible trajectory – probably not even the most common – of a number of types of trajectory that together constitute recent English burial history. Furthermore, the burial legislation indicates that it is probable that the greatest changes occurred not in the nineteenth century but in the twentieth. Both the Burial Act, 1900, and the bypassing of the Burial Acts by the Public Health (Interment Act), 1879 created a new legislative context for burial provision at the start of the twentieth century, in which the interests of the Church of England were firmly sidelined.

Modernity and the aesthetics of commemoration

A second theme which runs through this text is to question notions of modernity as they attach to changing burial practice. For writers who view the cemetery as an inherently modern construct, the shift in use from the churchyard to the cemetery is generally posited as evidence of a societal disengagement with mortality. The simplification of the landscape and a rejection of Victorian funerary excess are generally regarded in the same light, as is the rapid growth in cremation in the second half of the twentieth century. This research calls into question the need always to consider funerary culture as a dichotomised engagement/acceptance or disengagement/avoidance of mortality. At the heart of the problem is the fact that, as more primary material emerges, this analytical framework becomes less tenable. Indeed, Jalland was recently compelled to conclude that 'acceptance and avoidance can exist side by side in the same society, as well as in the same individual'.[12] Now is perhaps the time to put this framework to one side, and to consider afresh the evidence that is available from which it might be possible to draw some conclusions.

A concentration on burial is particularly useful as a means of addressing attitudes towards mortality, since material is provided on two major aspects of death: commemorative practice, and attitudes towards the corpse. The desire to invest in commemorative practices in and around the grave is carried beyond the style of memorial erected, and includes the emotional attachment to the place of burial: an investment of time as well as pecuniary resource. It is very tempting to use the First World War and Second World War as watershed points, and compare 'before' and 'after' activities. For example, studies published in the 1960s indicate that there may have been a substantial change in the rituals around the funeral itself as a consequence of the Second World War. For example, in 1961, Tom Harrisson, of the Mass Observation Unit, wrote a report considering aspects of 'Worktown' – his anonymised town – in the 1960s and thirty years earlier. A chapter on death included an interview with the local funeral director, who reported that the whole funeral had become 'lighter': 'The day of leaving the body at *home* before burial is completely over. More than 60 per cent take place from a chapel [i.e. funeral director premises] now, and it's increasing every month ... People want *simpler* coffins now, it's natural wood instead of varnished. *The whole occasion is lightened*.'[13] There had also been a change in aesthetics at the cemetery: there was 'a striking truncation and simplification of tombstones. The tall, cured sandstone … is gone.'[14]

However, the comparison of fashions in funerary taste obscures evidence of continuities: aesthetics can change without there being appreciable differences in attitudes towards mortality. Indeed, every age indulges in critical commentary on its own contemporary funeral practice and tends to look backwards to a time in which, somehow, things were done in a much more satisfactory manner. These criticisms are always selective. Commentary in the 1960s tended to focus on the funeral itself, and overlooked commemorative practice in the following weeks, months and years: indeed, Harrisson's study barely mentions this at all. Geoffrey Gorer's 1965 study of death, grief and mourning does include some material on commemoration although again this was not a focus of the study. Indeed, Gorer did not specifically draw out from respondents their commemorative activities where there had been a cremation although he did include direct quotations from respondents that inadvertently indicated that private rituals were in evidence. For example, one widower – whose wife had been cremated – bought flowers for her every Christmas, to 'feel she's still in the house,' and a woman who had lost both husband and son always put flowers by their photographs on their birthdays.[15] Where the funeral included burial, Gorer's evidence indicates that formal commemoration was central. In 23 of the 27 burials included in Gorer's study, families were intending to erect a headstone at the cemetery, and almost all regularly visited the grave: indeed, for some a visit to the cemetery was 'an important part of their weekly routine'.[16]

However, the twentieth-century cemetery has rarely been interpreted as providing evidence of engagement with mortality. Indeed, the opposite is generally posited as being the case. The aesthetics of the lawn cemetery have generally been dismissed as lacking the intense emotionalism of the Victorian necropolis. However, it is as valid to interpret the ranks of seemingly identical imported headstones as a 'democratisation' of commemoration. Wilson and Levy's 1938 report had called for 'a dignified and uniform standard of burial',[17] and, to a large degree, this principle was met through lawn cemetery design. Purchased graves became more affordable, as did the formalised visible expression of loss. Even in the 1960s, national newspapers included advertisements for kerbed memorials – 'simplicity and dignity at low cost' – that could be bought on monthly payment plans.[18] However, the expression of loss was strictly contained by regulations, as cemetery and diocesan authorities introduced more and more stringent guidelines that restricted the size, material and design of memorials: kerbsets were regarded as being particularly contentious. This was not a period in which there was no desire for a material expression of grief at the grave. Perhaps the most telling evidence on commemorative practice in the 1960s is a box of Diocesan Advisory Committee correspondence detailing case after case of rejected monument applications, where the design had failed to meet Diocesan guidelines.[19]

Familial burial: a constant imperative

Studying the management of burial is also a useful framework for understanding changing attitudes towards the dead body itself. Attitudes toward the corpse are regarded as being central to theories about mortality, and in particular there is an understanding that in the medieval world, death was 'tame'. The place of burial constituted a social centre for the town, in being a place for trade and for amusement.[20] Ariès notes that it was even common for people to live in the cemetery, 'utterly oblivious to the sight of burials or to the proximity of large common graves, which were left uncovered until they were full'.[21] Familiarity with the corpse is generally deemed to be an essential facet of 'traditional' attitudes towards death; by contrast, disgust with physical remains of the dead – 'unbearably repulsive in its decay' has been taken as evidence of modernity.[22] However, for this research, it has been useful to distinguish between two types of corpse which evoked different rhetorical and policy responses: the individual dead body of a family member, and the massed, urban dead.

This research suggests that the desire to secure burial in a grave with or immediately adjacent to a previously interred family member was the principal overriding consideration for the majority of users of all kinds of burial space from 1850. This concern was expressed so strongly that it overrode State-sponsored advice based on sanitary principles. The desire to achieve proximate familial burial was not new in the nineteenth century. However, the changing configurations of the burial landscape both reflected and encouraged this aspiration and created new opportunities. Tarlow has underlined the importance of understanding the emotional significance of burial location, particularly in contradistinction to assumptions that choice is more readily explained by status display.[23] The sale of burial rights in perpetuity for the first time afforded the opportunity for families to be guaranteed that their grave would not be appropriated for use by another family; and cemeteries made vaults and double graves more readily available, which increased the amount of space a family could reserve for its exclusive use. Within churchyard extensions, it became possible for families to appropriate contiguous grave spaces by informal oral agreements with clergy, although – as has been seen – these arrangements were technically illegal. Strange has illustrated ways in which people on lower-incomes also negotiated a pathway through cemetery regulations in order to secure burial in proximity to family, and evidence here from burial board records indicates that managers introduced a degree of flexibility in the use of unpurchased graves in order to maximise the opportunity for family members to be buried together.[24] Again – as with elements of commemoration – this desire for close family burial is very clearly a constant aspect of mortality, in evidence from the medieval period onwards.

Massed, urban burial and the degradation of funerary ritual

It is notable that the period which saw the flourishing of Romantic conceptualisations of loss and family reunion in death also saw the introduction of functional process-driven burial management according to scientific principles. However, as Tarlow very appositely commented, 'one is forced to abandon any expectation that people's beliefs about the dead and the bodies of the dead will be consistent and coherent'.[25] From the eighteenth century onwards, a second 'type' of corpse had begun to dominate policy concerns: the accumulating dead of the city, devoid of individuality. The incidence of over-rapid, uncontrolled urbanisation delivered massed corpses on an unprecedented scale. The care and solicitude that was afforded the individuated body of a family member, and which defined the ordering of cemeteries and churchyard extensions, was absent in instances where deaths routinely overwhelmed the ability to deliver decent interment. Some burial boards were compelled to deal with upwards of a thousand corpses annually, year on year and with unceasing regularity. Furthermore, the political exigencies attached to the treatment of pauper corpses directed burial boards to deal with these bodies in a perfunctory way. One consequence was the common grave, in which up to a dozen mixed adult and child coffins would be interred.

The struggle to deliver appropriate levels of decency and ritual in these circumstances can be likened to the emergency procedures adapted during times of crisis. Epidemic and war were both circumstances in which the authorities might be obliged to suspend funerary niceties and arrange the interment of large numbers of bodies. During the Black Death in 1348, two new cemeteries were established on the edge of London and one – at East Smithfield – received over 2,400 bodies. Archaeological research has found that, in parts of the site, bodies were laid in trenches rather than in individual graves.[26] Similarly, in Hull during the Blitz, trench burial became necessary following a few days of successive air raids in 1941. In the six months prior to the intensification of the attacks, the city's cemeteries took an average of 249 interments a month; in the six months of intensive bombardment – between February and July – the monthly average had increased to 510.[27] It is notable that in both instances, and despite the emergency, the use of individual graves continued for as long as was practicable and a breakdown reflected both chronically high levels of demand sustained over a period of time and a shortage of labour to dig graves. The dead were, simply, overwhelming.

Here, it is suggested that the cemetery itself should not be regarded as the 'agency' or reason why many burials became undifferentiated and apparently without ritual during the nineteenth century. Rather, many of the very large urban cemeteries were operating in a chronic state of crisis, as churchyards had been before them. Edwin Chadwick's 1843 *Interment Report* indicated that land in churchyards and burial grounds in the capital amounted to 218 acres, and in 1834 alone took 44,355 interments, excluding those bodies interred in vaults.[28] According to parliamentary return from 1889, average annual interments in Camberwell Cemetery amounted to 2,448, at Brompton Cemetery 3,163 and in Tower Hamlets, 5,145, with burials under the 'common interment system' routine.[29] Where cemeteries were located in more rural or even just less pressured locations, the tone of burial could be quite different. In its first ten years of operation the cemetery at New Malton took, on average, no more than two burials a week, and common or unpurchased graves usually contained a single body.[30]

In the final decades of the nineteenth century, and for much of the twentieth, it was all too easy for the cremation movement to formulate emotive and sometimes hysterical rhetoric to exploit and further foster a sense of unease with the notion of an uncontained urban dead. In fact, it is very difficult to locate any primary material relating to the corpse in the twentieth century that is not imbued with cremationist rhetoric, which – through a remarkably successful propaganda campaign – was translated through elite media such as *The Times* newspaper. It becomes almost impossible to conceive that during the twentieth century families might choose cremation for any other reason than the fact that they were disgusted by the contemplation of the dead body. In actuality, although studies have underlined a number of contexts which aim to explain the increased incidence of cremation, there is a critical absence of substantial data explaining why individuals and families took that decision. As a consequence, evidence around a twentieth-century abhorrence of the dead body is perhaps rather more problematic than might be supposed.

The Church of England in burial history

A further theme that emerges from this study relates to mortality and secularity. The concept of secularisation has engaged the understanding of scholars for some decades, and here is not the place to rehearse what has become a rich and edifying debate.[31] However, there is a general presumption that, since 1850, death has become more 'secular'. Again, the study of burial brings new material forward, in considering both the fate of the Church of England under the new burial legislation and the importance of the consecration of burial space. This history indicates that, even when putting to one side the continued use of churchyards through the period, the Church of England was closely connected to the evolution of burial culture. It was not the case that the Church was superseded by new and secular frameworks for the provision of burial space. Rather, the Church was integral to nineteenth-century cemetery provision, and remained in a dominant position at least until the passage of the Burial Act, 1900. Cemeteries were not in themselves a secularising agency. Indeed, the cemetery was a means by which the Church could extend its holdings of consecrated burial space, and do so with funding made available from ratepayers. The fact that this was the case rests entirely with the early intervention of Bishop Blomfield, who had recognised that the Church looked set to lose substantial burial incomes if cemetery space remained unconsecrated. Indeed, this research indicates that the history of nineteenth-century burial needs to be recast, with the Church of England placed squarely at the centre. A fresh set of questions arises from this new interpretation. For example, the economic history of the church – not least as manager and provider of burial space – would merit detailed consideration; the direct involvement of bishops in interpreting burial legislation and intervening in local burial board management requires study; and variation in and development of diocesan policies on faculties for actions such as grave reservation, monument erection fees and indeed monument erection would reward scrutiny. Overall, the Church of England has played a more forceful and proactive role in burial reform than might generally be supposed.

Viewing secularity in terms of a diminution in the significance of the sacred, then, this study has demonstrated that the importance of consecration has dwindled considerably with regard to burial space. In terms of theology, consecration has had little more than a symbolic importance since the Reformation. Criminals were excluded from consecrated space, but it could be argued that the greater punishment rested with the separation from family and community at death rather than burial in unblessed soil. The Church itself has evidently found the notion of consecration problematic in theological terms, since no spiritual benefit can derive from the practice. After the storms of passionate, and generally political, debate on the merits of consecration in the nineteenth century, the act was regarded as something of an anomaly for much of the twentieth century. For example, included amongst documentation on the proposal to consecrate the whole of Northallerton Cemetery in 1940 is a letter from the local vicar: 'Personally I do not regard the act of consecration as having any spiritual value whatsoever and I look upon it as an ecclesiastical tradition and usage which ought to be relegated to the forgotten things.'[32]

A general disregard for the need to ensure that burial takes place in consecrated space appears to be undermined by the continued use of the churchyard in rural areas. However, interviews in the case study area indicated that, on the whole, the act of consecration had become re-linked to the notion that burial in unconsecrated soil could denote punishment or exclusion. There was a general and vague understanding that consecration should take place or – in the case of a cemetery – certainly had taken place, and that the use of unconsecrated space was a long-distant Victorian practice restricted to cases of suicide, and the unbaptised. On the whole, it could be argued that consecration now falls within what S. J. D. Green referred to as 'popular devotion to sacred things',[33] and constitutes a quasi-superstitious regard for what might be deemed appropriate.

Definitions: what makes a cemetery a cemetery?

A final theme sits around the definition of burial space. This author has assessed the ways in which it is possible to define burial space broadly, and has concluded that four elements are central. First, there are evident landscape differences, particularly with regard to scale of operation and the intent and complexity of internal design; and the ownership of the site – by secular or religious authorities – also has to be taken into account. The site's sacredness has to be considered, and can be defined in terms of the site's permanence and in the level of 'pilgrimage' to the site to visit graves. Finally, the site has to be judged in the way in which it promotes or protects the individuality of the deceased.[34] To some degree, this research challenges that differentiation as it applies to distinctions between cemeteries and churchyards specifically. There are a number of sites in central North Riding which are impossible to categorise as either churchyard or cemetery simply by appearance alone. Detached churchyard extensions, with formal internal layout, are identical to smaller parish council cemeteries. Indeed, in some areas the churchyard space sits next to cemetery space with no visible distinction between the two. It is clear that, in the countryside, cemeteries can be extremely modest in scale, and lack any design intent. There is also confusion on the issue of ownership and management. Many of the smaller burial boards in the study carried the intention of using the Burial Acts as a means of extending the local churchyard. In this case, the legalities of the matter define the space as a cemetery. However, in at least three instances, the ownership and management of the 'cemetery' was transferred to the vestry after the initial loan had been paid, for management as a churchyard. The confusion becomes complete, when it is noted that, in a couple of other instances, part of the churchyard extension was left deliberately unconsecrated. This was the case at Sandhutton, where the churchyard was extended in 1878 with land that was originally part of the vicarage drive. A sketch plan of the site indicated that a small strip of the extension was not consecrated.[35] Is it necessary, therefore, to revise the definitions of different types of burials space, or indeed to dispense with the task of definition altogether as being little more than an academic nicety?

The difficulties notwithstanding, the task of completing this research has underlined the fact that, at the level of local governance, these two types of space are indeed regarded as being distinct and different. Churchyard space – and indeed all consecrated space – remains under the control of the Church, and it is still necessary to secure faculty to institute major works; church legislation applies. For municipal burial authorities, the Local Authorities Cemeteries Order, 1977, is the principal legislation with which they have to work, although some aspects of cemetery management still call on elements of the Burial Acts. This research study has repeatedly demonstrated that legislative context defines activity within burial space. As a consequence, whilst these distinctions appear to be little more than legal technicalities, in actuality these frameworks define the very personal and family decisions on the choice of monument – that, in churchyards, will be subject to faculty – and larger strategic decisions on the future provision of burial space in rural areas. For example, under secular legislation, a strong presumption remains against the possible reuse of grave spaces, since s. 25 of the Burial Act, 1857 remains in operation, preventing the disturbance of remains in unconsecrated space without a licence from the Ministry of Justice. This provision does not apply in the case of churchyards, which are entirely consecrated and where reuse is permitted under faculty provided that any remains are removed from one consecrated place of burial to another. Indeed, in the 25 churchyards in which no change has been noted for the period 1850–2007, a policy of grave reuse been in place since the medieval period. Thus, at this very basic level of management, churchyard space is distinguishable in the ability to adhere to the traditional practice reuse even though – through the nineteenth and twentieth centuries – that tradition was questioned.

Conclusion

This wide-ranging and detailed history of burial in central North Riding has provided a context for the exploration of a number of key questions about mortality, not least of which is the question of where it might be possible to locate 'modern' attitudes to death. It is certain that the period saw substantial change to some aspects of funerary ritual, but in central North Riding the continuities in burial provision are perhaps more marked than the discontinuities. A very different conclusion might have been drawn if this research had been completed some twenty years ago. During the 1980s, the clearance of churchyard landscapes would be in progress, and the proportion of cremations leading to anonymised strewing at the crematorium garden of rest would perhaps be at its height. However, another shift in funerary culture has been in evidence since the early 1990s: a new accommodation with death has emerged. There is space in the churchyard for cremated remains, and the church building itself is used for funerals and for services of commemoration that take place both with and without the body. There is pluralism, certainly – green burials and humanist services are increasing – but in rural North Yorkshire the Church of England has managed to retain a foothold that has been lost in more urban locations. There is also a re-engagement with the 'sacred', as current funerary practice adopts ritual behaviours imbued with a sense of religiosity even where there is no theological belief. It might be argued that funerary culture can now be defined as being 'postmodern', as choices become fractured. Future historians will certainly blanch at the sheer diversity and degree of emotional and financial investment that our current culture affords all aspects of mortality.

This history of burial culture is by no means intended to be a final statement on the vast subject of disposal of the dead in the nineteenth and twentieth centuries. There are a tremendous number of gaps. It is particularly hoped that further progress will be made on the tasks of simply understanding difference between regions and cities, between urban and rural areas, and between Scotland, Wales, England and Northern Ireland. In addition, there needs to be further study of the commemorative preferences and actions that have been overlooked because they leave no trace on the landscape or in formal record. The issue of chronology remains problematic. This history indicates a substantial amount of continuity through the nineteenth century with substantive change really becoming evident only after the Second World War, and in doing so sits at odds with research on other aspects of death, which pinpoint change at an earlier period. It is clear that mortality does indeed have a 'thoroughly untidy' history, full of perplexing contradictions.

Notes

1 B. Gordon and P. Marshall (2000) 'Introduction' in Gordon, B. and Marshall, P. (eds) *The Place of the Dead: Death and Remembrance in Late*

Medieval and Early Modern Europe (Cambridge: Cambridge University Press: , 2000), p. 10.
2 T. Walter, *The Revival of Death* (London: Routledge, 1994).
3 NYRO, DC/NOR I 1/1, Northallerton Rural District Council: Minutes, 8 Aug 1900; NYRO, PR/DAW, Burials 1621–1996.
4 NYRO, BB/NO 1/4, Northallerton Burial Board Minutes, 1957–74, 8 Mar 1968.
5 B. Parsons, *Committed to the Cleansing Flame: The Development of Cremation in Nineteenth-century England* (Reading: Spire Books, 2005), pp. 178ff.
6 B. Parsons, 'Where did the ashes go? Part 2', *Journal of the Institute of Cemetery and Crematorium Management*, 73:2 (2005), p. 28.
7 L. Kellaher, D. Prendergast and J. Hockey, 'In the shadow of the traditional grave', *Morality*, 10:4 (2005), 237–50.
8 A. Clayden, T. Green, J. Hockey and M. Powell, 'From cabbages to cadavers: natural burial down on the farm' in Maddrell, A. and Sideway, J. (eds), *Deathscapes* (Aldershot: Ashgate, 2010).
9 K. West, *A Guide to Woodland Burial* (London: Shaw and Sons, 2010).
10 www.justice.gov.uk/downloads/burials-and-coroners/natural-burial-grounds-guidance.pdf, accessed June 2012.
11 F. Stirling, 'Grave re-use: a feasibility study' (PhD dissertation, University of Sheffield, 2009), pp. 24–63.
12 P. Jalland, *Death in War and Peace: A History of Loss and Grief in England, 1914–1970* (Oxford: Oxford University Press, 2010), p. 179.
13 Tom Harrisson, *Britain Revisited* (London: Victor Gollancz, 1961), p. 43. Italics in the original.
14 *Ibid.*, p. 45.
15 Geoffrey Gorer, *Death, Grief and Mourning in Contemporary Britain* (London: The Cresset Press, 1965), p. 77.
16 *Ibid.*, p. 49.
17 A. Wilson and H. Levy, *Burial Reform and Funeral Costs* (Oxford: Oxford University Press, 1938), p. 115.
18 BI, DAC Correspondence and papers, 1930s–1970s, flier from monumental mason amongst notes on a memorial at Allerston churchyard.
19 BI, DAC Correspondence and papers, 1930s–1970s.
20 D. Dymond, 'God's disputed acre', *Journal of Ecclesiastical History*, 50 (1999), 464–97.
21 P. Ariès, *The Hour of Our Death*, trans. H. Weaver (Harmondsworth: Penguin, 1983), p. 64.

22 A. Herman, 'Death has a touch of class: society and space in Brookwood Cemetery, 1853–1903', *Journal of Historic Geography*, 36:3 (2010), p. 306.
23 S. Tarlow, 'Each slow dusk a drawing-down of blinds', *Archaeological Review from Cambridge*, 11:1 (1992), 125–40.
24 J.-M. Strange, *Death, Grief and Poverty in Britain, 1870–1914* (Cambridge: Cambridge University Press, 2005).
25 S. Tarlow, *Ritual, Belief and the Dead in Early Modern Britain and Ireland* (Cambridge: Cambridge University Press, 2011), p. 173.
26 D. Hawkins, 'The Black Death and the new London cemeteries of 1348', *Antiquity*, 64 (1990), 637–42.
27 HCA, TCR 1/10/7, Committee Reports 1940–41, vol. 6. See J. Rugg, 'Managing "Civilian Deaths due to War Operations": Yorkshire experiences during World War II', *Twentieth Century British History*, 15:2 (2004), 152–73.
28 Edwin Chadwick, *Supplementary Report on the Results of a Special Inquiry into the Practice of Interment in Towns* (London: HMSO, 1843), p. 133.
29 1889 (288) *Metropolitan Cemeteries*.
30 Malton Town Council, Burial Register.
31 See e.g. C. Brown, *The Death of Christian Britain: Understanding Secularisation, 1800–2000* (London: Routledge: 2001). A useful summary is given in S. J. D. Green, *Religion in the Age of Decline: Organisation and Experience in Industrial Yorkshire, 1870–1920* (Cambridge: Cambridge University Press, 1996).
32 NA, HO 45/18820 (Burials: Northallerton and Romanby Cemetery, 1940–41).
33 Green, *Religion in the Age of Decline*, p. 17.
34 J. Rugg, 'Defining the place of burial: what makes a cemetery a cemetery?', *Mortality*, 5:3 (2000), 238–59.
35 NYRO, PR/SAT 21/1, Sketch plans and measurements of land to be annexed to the churchyard.

Appendix One

Glossary

Burial Acts	A series of acts passed between 1852 and 1906, defining the terms under which *burial boards* would operate. The Burial Acts were in force until 1974.
Burial board	Agency appointed under the *Burial Acts* and comprising between three and nine members elected by the local ratepayers. Burial Boards were empowered to take out loans repayable from the rates to lay out cemeteries.
Burial ground	This text uses *burial ground* as a term for burial space intended to serve non-Anglicans, for example Roman Catholics or Quakers.
Burial right	The right to burial in a *purchased* or *private grave*, purchased from the owner of the cemetery. No interment can take place within a *purchased* or *private grave* without the permission of the owner of the burial right. The 'burial right' is defined in a legal document noting the location of the grave within the cemetery, and can be bought, sold and gifted like any other property although the land itself remains in the control of the cemetery owner. It is not possible to purchase a burial right in the churchyard: in this instance, *faculty* is required.

Burials Office — Administrative office within the *Home Office*, dealing with burial issues – including churchyard closures and inspections – until 1900.

Cemetery — Burial space generally including consecrated and unconsecrated sections, subject to civic legislation, and intended to serve the entire parish or community.

Chapel of ease — A building for worship located away from the principal parish church, for the convenience of worshippers.

Church Commissioners — Manage the buildings and property of the Church of England. The Church Commissioners were created in 1948 and inherited the functions of the Governors of Queen Anne's Bounty, which funded church building, and the *Ecclesiastical Commissioners*.

Churchyard — Consecrated parish burial space sometimes but not always surrounding a church, owned by the Church of England and subject to canon law. In this book churchyards are distinguished from cemeteries.

Columbarium — Above-ground construction comprising a series of niches for cremated remains. Families purchase the use of a niche for a given period. The niche is generally covered with a commemorative plaque.

Consecration — A ritual and legal act, dedicating for holy use an object, building or place. Where ground is consecrated for burial, the land falls under the authority of the Anglican bishop.

Diocesan Advisory Committee — Statutory committee that provides advice at a diocesan level on matters relating to church buildings and contents, and on the churchyard, particularly in issues relating to *faculty*. DACs often include members with experience in conservation.

Diocese — The geographical area over which a Church of England bishop exercises authority. The bishop is subject to canon law, but until 1969 could exercise a great deal of personal influence over the tenor of Church activity in his diocese. As a consequence, there has been variation between dioceses on some aspects of Church of England churchyard management. After 1969, bishops were obliged to consult with representatives of laity and clergy.

Ecclesiastical Commissioners — The administrators of Church of England property from 1836 to 1948, when it was superseded by the *Church Commissioners*. The Ecclesiastical Commissioners dealt with matters relating to churchyard management, including fee setting.

Faculty — Formal permission required from the diocese for substantive changes to church property at the local level. Faculty was required to make substantive changes to the churchyard, including the clearance of monumentation; the reservation of grave spaces could take place only by faculty.

General Board of Health — Created by the Public Health Act in 1848 in order to administer the Act, and in operation during the passage of the Burial Acts in 1852 and 1853. The General Board of Health ceased to function in 1854, and burial functions devolved to the *Home Office*.

Grave — Essentially, a hole in the ground with space for a number of coffins – one on top of another, with soil between each coffin. The number of coffins in each grave depends on the depth to which the grave was dug originally. In cemeteries, the grave is located within a defined *plot*.

Grave, bricked	Grave where the walls have been lined with brick.
Grave, common	Grave in which the burial right is retained by the owner of the cemetery, and in which one or more unrelated individuals may be buried. Also termed unpurchased or 'public' grave.
Grave, private	A grave in which the burial right has been purchased for a defined length of time. Also termed a 'purchased' grave.
Grave, public	See *grave, common*.
Grave, purchased	See *grave, private*.
Grave, unpurchased	See *grave, common*.
Home Office	Government office with primary responsibility for burials until the Burial Act 1900, transferred the majority of these functions to the *Local Government Board*. However, the Home Office retained responsibility for aspects of burial legislation until the transfer of those functions to the Department of Constitutional Affairs in 2005. This department was renamed the Ministry of Justice in 2007.
Kerbset	Raised stone edge marking the boundary of a grave.
Local Government Board	Government agency that took over control of the sanitary, planning and environmental aspects of burial in 1900. This agency became the Ministry of Health in 1919. These functions were transferred to the Minister of Local Government and Planning in 1951, renamed in the same year as Minister of Housing and Local Government.

Mausoleum	Large free-standing building covering a below-ground vault or itself containing above-ground receptacles for coffins.
Mound	Level platform of earth standing about one foot above the grave, on which commemorative objects were placed, including headstones.
Non-parishioner	A person not regarded as being a parishioner, and who for that reason can be denied burial in the churchyard or cemetery, or charged a higher fee.
Order in Council	A simple legislative enactment using a framework defined by statute. Churchyards were closed by individual orders in council.
Ordinary	A bishop or archbishop.
Parish	The basic unit of Church of England administration, which may contain one or more settlements, under the care of a priest. For much of the nineteenth century the parish was the principal administrative unit of both Church and local government, and had officers with specific civic and Church responsibilities elected from the body of local ratepayers. Successive enactments have severed the links between the Church of England and local government.
Parish council	Brought into being by the Local Government Act, 1894 and in rural areas replacing the vestry as the principal agency of local government.
Parishioner	Through the nineteenth century, a parishioner was defined as someone who had been born in a particular *parish*, and/or who paid rates there. Parishioners had rights and responsibilities within their own *parish*, for example, the right to welfare and to burial, which did not translate to other parishes.

Parochial church council	The 'management' arm of a local Anglican church, established in 1921 to replace the ancient *vestry* system and with responsibilities for *churchyard* management.
Plot	A portion of land containing a *grave*. Each *cemetery* will be organised into a series of plots. In the nineteenth century, 9ft by 4ft was the plot size recommended for sanitary burial, to ensure sufficient space between interments. As the nineteenth century progressed, churchyard extensions were also sometimes divided into plots.
Registrar	Essentially the legal officer of the diocese, with responsibility for matters such as conveyancing and dealing with applications for *faculty*.
Re-open	A 're-open' – often used as a noun in this context – is burial in a grave in which there has been a previous interment. This process does not disturb any previous burials.
Sentence of consecration	A legal document recording that a *consecration* has taken place and defining, in an enclosed map, the area that has been consecrated.
Vault	Built structure, located under the ground – including under the floor of a church – capable of receiving a number of coffins. Vaults can be extremely elaborate and contain internal 'furniture' such as shelving or be simple functional repositories.
Vestry	Principal agency of local government until 1894, comprising a body of elected ratepayers. Although the vestry had close connections with the Church of England, it could include ratepayers of other denominations.

Appendix Two

Grave types: diagrams

Specifications of the grave itself were subject to a great deal of discussion and controversy, from the publication of guidance to burial boards in 1852 onwards. These diagrams illustrate some of the grave types discussed in the text.

Figure 1

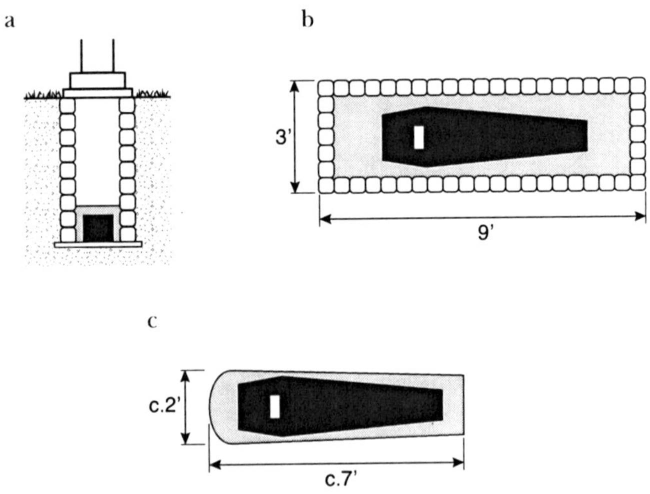

Figure 2

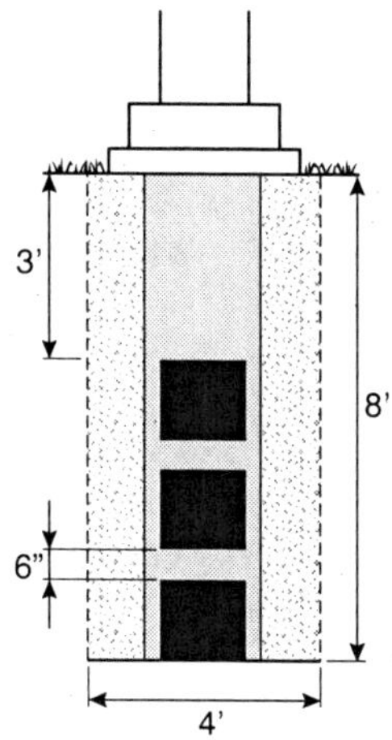

Figure 3

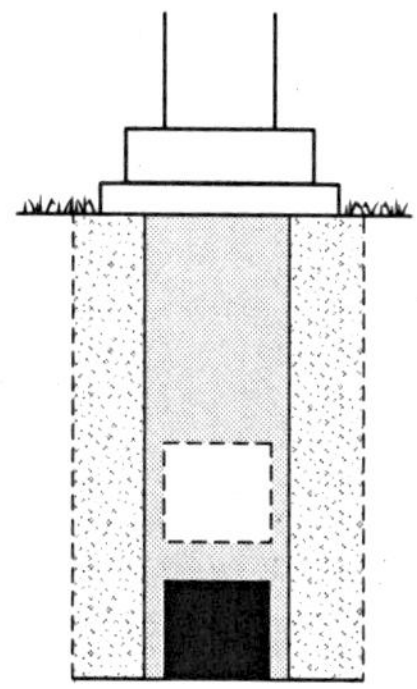

Figure 4

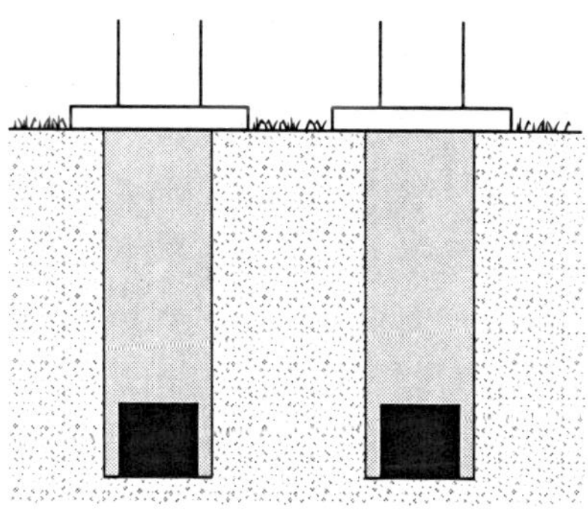

Note on depth: For churchyard burial there is no legislative requirement on the depth of the grave. For cemeteries, 1852 guidance indicated that for adults 4ft of soil above the coffin comprised was a suitable depth, with a foot of soil between each coffin where multiple interments took place. This was later reduced to 6in. The depth of graves generally depends on the intended number of interments.

1a and b. Bricked graves

According to the Burial, Funeral and Mourning Reform Association, the bricked grave prevented the reuse of ground in the churchyard, as it would be unlikely that authorities dismantling any building under the ground would be viewed favourably. The Association also argued that brick graves took up more space than a normal earth grave (1c) but 1852 guidance later specified that 9ft by 4ft should be the standard plot size.

1c. Earth grave

A grave just a few inches larger than the coffin was commonplace in churchyards, but was superseded by graves located centrally within much specified plots (as at 5) in burial board cemeteries and in later churchyard extensions.

2. Triple earth grave, full

This grave has been dug to a depth sufficient to accommodate three interments. Each successive burial does not disturb the last, as gravediggers will be able to calculate achievable depth on the number of previous interments.

3. Double earth grave, with space for a 're-open'

This grave has remaining space for one further burial.

4. Double grave, churchyard

Double graves in churchyard often comprise two single burials side by side, rather than having both interments in one deeper grave, as at 2.

Appendix Three

Sources for researching local burial history

This research required reference to a wide range of sources, the majority of which were parish records available at the North Yorkshire Record Office, Northallerton, the Borthwick Institute, York, and the West Yorkshire Archive Service, Leeds. Commonly used internet resources are also listed here. The study also reviewed additional sources available only at the National Archive at Kew, the Church of England Record Centre at Bermondsey and the Lambeth Palace Library.

Local Sources

Burial registers

From 1813, parishes were obliged to keep burial registers in which interments in the churchyard were recorded. For this study, details of deceased individuals were less important than indications given of overall pressure on burial space over time. Local mortality statistics are available for parishes (see Vision of Britain, below) but these do not specify where interment has taken place. Burial registers also record the abode of the deceased, which gives a good indication of the general 'catchment' area of a churchyard, which could include a number of townships in the parish.

Burial registers name the minister taking the funeral service. The Burial Laws Amendment Act of 1880 specified that interments taken under that Act should be specifically recorded. In some instances, the register simply notes 'Burial under the 1880 Act', but in other instances the name and denomination of a Nonconformist minister are noted. On occasion, a separate register of Burial Laws

Amendment Act interments might be kept with the general burial register.

Burial registers do not comprise 'grave registers', with a location noted for interment. However, when a churchyard was extended, the incumbent sometimes noted a number which indicated that a grave register had been devised. In some instances there is a simple indication of whether burial has taken place in the 'new' or 'old' ground. It is often the case that the first interment in a new extension is noted as being so in the burial register, which is sometimes the only extant documentary evidence that the churchyard has been extended.

Many parish burial registers contain extraneous material, such as a reproduction of the churchyard extension plan. In some instances, relevant Acts of Parliament, diocesan policy notices or other local notices relating to churchyard management are pasted into end boards.

Vestry and parochial church council minutes

Vestry minutes varied substantially in quality and in terms of the amount of information conveyed. Some vestry minutes conveyed little beyond annual elections to parochial officer posts. Others were more detailed, and contained reference to major 'burial' events such as the decisions to close or extend the churchyard. In some cases, specific sub-committees were appointed to deal with the issue, and reported separately within the same minute book.

Terriers

Terriers comprise a regular audit of local church assests, which must be kept up to date. From the second half of the nineteenth century, the information was collected using a proforma which included two specific questions relating to the churchyard and responsibility for its boundary. The form also collected details of the fees charged for particular types of service. Some incumbents gave a detailed breakdown and included all the fees relating to a funeral, such as monument erection fees. Not all terriers carried substantive detail, but in some instances the terrier included extra information on the churchyard and its extension.

Appendix Three

Documents relating to extension

At the Borthwick Institute, the CD.Add archives relate to individual churchyard extensions. Each bundle of documents variously contained conveyancing documentation, a sentence of consecration – the official document declaring a parcel of land to be consecrated, and which included a plan – and some limited associated correspondence.

Churchyard closure

Churchyard closures by Order in Council were announced in the *London Gazette*. Past editions of the *London Gazette* are available on the internet, and are readily searchable. Local documentation held at record offices might also include individual copies of Orders in Council for closure. The documents cite the relevant legislation, and state the conditions on which the churchyard was closed.

Faculties

Faculties constitute 'planning permission' for changes to the fabric of the church and churchyard. The study reviewed in particular faculties relating to the reservation of grave space, and those permitting the 're-ordering' of the churchyard. Faculties for the Diocese of York were listed in the catalogue at the Borthwick Institute.

Miscellaneous documents

Miscellaneous collections relating to the churchyard are sometimes available at record offices and contain – for example – items relating local disputes relating to the churchyard; management material such as receipts or lists of voluntary donations for the churchyard extension, or correspondence on legal matters. Parish magazines are also a useful source, particularly where the vicar adds substantial editorial material that may include comment on use of the churchyard.

Burial boards

Burial boards were often absorbed by town or district councils, and their early documentation did not always survive the transfer. However, there are some instances in which there is a particularly rich collection of material, including minute books, correspondence, and maps and plans. Burial board clerks often wrote to other clerks for information, including fees and by-laws and so some collections can also contain this type of 'survey' material. The records for the Burial Boards at New Malton, Ripon and Knaresborough are particularly diverse and illuminating.

Parish council and other local government minutes

Parish councils were elected for the majority of the settlements in the study, and in some instances were involved in local burial issues. Burial matters within Town and Rural or Urban District Councils were not always dealt with by a separate committee, and tended to be lost in general administrative matters. In some instances, a minute index could be used, but this was not always available or reliable. Issues relating to burial tend to fall between committees, rather than being a central local government concern, and so the amount of information available tended to be limited.

National Sources

General Board of Health, Burials Office and Home Office records

Records are also available for the government departments responsible for dealing with burials, beginning with the General Board of Health, the Burials Office – within the Home Office – and the Local Government Board. Much of this documentation is lodged under the classification HO45 at the National Archive. This heading includes bundles of documents relating to the passage of particular pieces of legislation, to meetings relating to burial issues, and bundles of documents that relate to visits to individual sites for the purposes of inspection or applications following the Burial Act 1900. This research has included review of all the document bundles relating to settlements in the study.

Ecclesiastical Commissioners

At the Church of England Record Centre at Bermondsey, material relating to churchyard management can be found within the Ecclesiastical Commissioners archives, in series of boxed documents entitled 'Churches, burial grounds and parsonages, conveyance of sites, general file'. Boxes are ordered chronologically, and contain day-to-day correspondence, internal records and minutes relating to churchyard issues.

London Gazette

This national resource is available on the internet, and can be searched for particular churches, to check whether an Order in Council for closure has been issued. The Orders were generally published twice, and in some instances there were further notices of amendment or postponement. Unions of benefices are also recorded in the *London Gazette*.

Internet Sources

Completing an audit of local burial spaces has relied heavily on triangulating material from a small number of sources including:

Genuki
Contains local information including local Victoria County Histories, and nineteenth-century gazetteers. Also contains some images of churches.

Geograph
The website aims to contain an image for each OS map square, and so constitutes a valuable visual resource.

A Church Near You
A searchable resource to find churches in a given location, giving local contact details.

Wikimapia/Google Earth
Useful for assessing changes to churchyard boundaries, visible from above but not necessarily discernable on the ground.

Vision of Britain
Gives access to population and mortality data.

Appendix Four

Sites included in the study

Hambleton

Churchyards

Ainderby Steeple, St Helen
Aldwark, St Stephen
Alne, St Mary the Virgin
Appleton Wiske, St Mary
Bagby, St Mary
Bedale, St Gregory
Bilsdale Midcable, St John
Birdforth, St Mary
Birkby, St Peter
Boltby, Holy Trinity
Brafferton, St Peter
Brandsby, All Saints
Brompton (by Northallerton), St Peter
Burneston, St Lambert
Carlton-in-Cleveland, St Botolph
Carlton Miniott, St Lawrence
Chop Gate, St Hilda
Cowesby, St Michael and All Angels
Coxwold, St Michael
Crakehall, St Gregory
Crathorne, All Saints
Crayke, St Cuthbert
Dalton, St John the Evangelist
Danby Wiske Church
Deighton, All Saints
Easingwold, St John the Baptist
East Cowton, St Mary
East Harlsey, St Oswald
East Rounton, St Lawrence
Faceby, St Mary Magdalene
Farlington, St Leonard
Felixkirk, St Felix
Girsby, All Saints
Great Ayton, All Saints
Great Fencote, St Andrew
Great Langton, St Wilfred
Great Smeaton, St Eloy
Husthwaite, St Nicholas
Hutton Bonville, St Lawrence
Hutton Rudby, All Saints
Ingleby Arncliffe, All Saints
Ingleby Greenhow, St Lawrence

Kilburn, St Mary
Kildale, St Cuthbert
Kirby Sigston, St Lawrence
Kirby Wiske, St John the Baptist
Kirkby, St Augustine
Kirkby Fleetham, St Mary
Kirkby Knowle, St Wilfred
Kirklington, St Michael
Leake, St Mary
Leeming, St John the Baptist
Little Sessay, St Cuthbert
Low Worsall, All Saints
Marton-in-the-Forest, St Mary
Maunby, St Michael
Myton-on-Swale, St Mary
Nether Silton, All Saints
Newton-on-Ouse, All Saints
Northallerton, All Saints
North Otterington, St Michael and All Angels
Osmotherley, St Peter
Over Silton, St Mary
Overton, St Cuthbert
Pickhill, All Saints
Raskelf, St Mary
Sandhutton, St Leonard
Scruton, St Radegund
Seamer-in-Cleveland, St Martin
Shipton by Beningbrough, Holy Evangelists
Skipton-on-Swale, St John the Evangelist
South Cowton, St Mary
South Kilvington, St Wilfred
South Otterington, St Andrew
Sowerby, St Oswald
Stillington, St Nicholas
Stokesley, St Peter and St Paul
Sutton-on-the-Forest, All Hallows
Swainby, (Old) Holy Cross
Thirkleby, All Saints
Thirsk, St Mary
Thormanby, St Mary Magdaelen
Thornton-le-Beans, chapel of ease
Thornton-le-Moor, St Barnabas
Thornton-le-Street, St Leonard's
Thornton Watlass, St Mary the Virgin
Topcliffe, St Columba
Well, St Michael
West Rounton, St Oswald
West Tanfield, St Nicholas
Whenby, St Martin
Yafforth, All Saints
Yearsley, Holy Trinity

Cemeteries

Appleton Wiske Cemetery
Bedale Cemetery
Brompton (by Northallerton) Cemetery
Crakehall and Langthorne Cemetery
Great Ayton Cemetery
Husthwaite Cemetery
Hutton Rudby Cemetery
Northallerton and Romanby Cemetery
Osmotherley Cemetery
Thirsk Cemetery
West Rounton (St Oswald) Cemetery

Burial Grounds

Easingwold, St John the Baptist (RC)
Great Ayton, Quaker
Osmotherley Quaker
Thirsk, Barbeck Quaker
Thirsk, Kirkgate Quaker
Thirsk, Salem Independent
West Tanfield, Wesleyan Methodist

Other

Easby Chapel Mausoleum

Harrogate

Churchyards

Aldborough, St Andrew
Aldfield, St Laurence the Martyr
Allerton Mauleverer, St Martin
Arkendale, St Bartholomew
Baldersby St James, St James
Beckwithshaw, St Michael and All Angels
Bewerley, Grange Chapel
Bilton, St John the Evangelist
Bilton in Ainsty, St Helen
Birstwith, St James
Bishop Monkton, St John the Baptist
Bishop Thornton, St John
Bishop Thornton, St John the Evangelist
Boroughbridge, St James
Brearton, St John the Baptist
Burnt Yates, St Andrew
Burton Leonard, St Leonard
Copgrove, St Michael
Copt Hewick, Holy Innocents
Cowthorpe, St Michael

Dacre Banks, Holy Trinity
Dallowgill, Chapel of the Resurrection
Dallowgill, St Peter
Darley, Christ Church
Denton, St Helen
Farnham, St Oswald
Farnley, All Saints
Fewston, St Michael and St Lawrence
Follifoot, St Joseph and St James
Goldsborough, St Mary the Virgin
Great Ouseburn, St Mary the Virgin
Green Hammerton, St Thomas
Greenhow, St Mary
Grewelthorpe, St James
Hampsthwaite, St Thomas à Becket
Harrogate, Christ Church
Harrogate, St John the Evangelist
Hartwith, St Jude
Healey, St Paul
Hunsingore, St John the Baptist
Kettlesing Bottom, Chapel of Ease
Killinghall, St Thomas the Apostle
Kirby Hill / Kirby on the Moor, All Saints
Kirk Deighton, All Saints
Kirk Hammerton, St John the Baptist
Kirkby Malzeard, St Andrew
Kirkby Overblow, All Saints
Knaresborough, St John the Baptist
Leathley, St Oswald
Little Ouseburn, Holy Trinity
Littlethorpe, St Michael and All Angels
Long Marston, All Saints
Lower Dunsforth, St Mary
Markington, St Michael the Archangel
Marton-cum-Grafton churchyard
Marton-le-Moor, St Mary
Masham, St Mary the Virgin
Mickley, St John the Evangelist
Middlesmoor, St Chad
Nidd, St Paul and St Margaret
North Rigton, St John the Evangelist
North Stainley, St Mary the Virgin
Nun Monkton, St Mary
Pannal, St Robert
Pateley Bridge, St Mary the Virgin
Pateley Bridge, St Cuthbert
Ramsgill, St Mary
Ripley, All Saints
Ripon, Holy Trinity
Ripon, Ripon Cathedral
Roecliffe, St Mary
Sawley, St Michael and All Angels
Scotton, St Thomas the Apostle
Sharow, St John the Evangelist
Sicklinghall, St Peter
Skelton-on-Ure, Christ the Consoler
Skelton-on-Ure, St Helen
South Stainley, St Wilfred
Spofforth, All Saints

Stainburn, St Mary
Staveley, All Saints
Thornthwaite, St Saviour
Thruscross, Holy Trinity
Tockwith, The Epiphany
Wath, St Mary
Weeton, St Barnabas
West End, Holy Trinity
Weston, All Saints
Whixley, Church of the Ascension
Wighill, All Saints
Wilsill, St Michael and All Angels
Winksley, St Cuthbert and St Oswald

Cemeteries

Aldborough (St Andrew) Cemetery
Aldborough Cemetery
Boroughbridge, Wetherby Road Cemetery
Dishforth Cemetery
Fewston Cemetery
Goldsborough Cemetery
Harrogate, Grove Road Cemetery
Harrogate, Harlow Hill Cemetery
Harrogate, Stonefall Cemetery and Crematorium
Kirby Malzeard Cemetery
Kirkby Overblow Cemetery
Knaresborough Cemetery
Pateley Bridge Cemetery
Ripon Cemetery
Sicklinghall Cemetery

Burial grounds

Bishop Thornton, St Joseph RC
Dacre, Providence Chapel
Great Ouseburn, Independent
Green Hammerton, Independent
Kirkby Overblow, Wesleyan Methodist
Pateley Bridge, Independent
Scotton, Quaker / Wesleyan Methodist
Sicklinghall, Immaculate Conception RC
Tockwith, Wesleyan Methodist

Other

Little Ouseburn, Thompson Mausoleum

Appendix Four

Ryedale

Churchyards

Acklam, St John the Baptist
Allerston, St John
Amotherby, St Helen's
Ampleforth, St Hilda
Appleton-le-Moors, Christ Church
Appleton-le-Street, All Saints
Barton-le-Street, St Michael
Birdsall, St Mary
Bossall, St Botolph
Bransdale, St Nicholas
Bulmer, St Martin
Burythorpe, All Saints
Buttercrambe, St John the Evangelist
Butterwick, Foxholes, St Nicholas
Church Houses, St Mary
Cold Kirby, St Michael
Crambe, St Michael
Cropton, St Gregory
Dalby, St Peter
East Heslerton, St Andrew
Ebberston, St Mary the Virgin
Ellerburn, St Hilda
Flaxton, St Lawrence
Foston, All Saints
Foxholes, St Mary
Ganton, St Nicholas
Gate Helmsley, St Mary
Gillamoor, St Aiden
Gilling East, Holy Cross
Great Edstone, St Michael and All Angels
Harome, St Saviour
Hawnby, All Saints
Helmsley, All Saints
Helperthorpe, St Peter
Hovingham, All Saints
Howsham. St John
Huttons Ambo, St Margaret of Scotland
Kirby Grindalythe, St Andrew
Kirby Misperton, St Lawrence
Kirkbymoorside, All Saints
Kirkdale, St Gregory
Langton, St Andrew
Lastingham, St Mary
Levisham, St Mary
Lockton, St Giles
Low Marishes, St Francis
Middleton, St Andrew
New Malton, St Leonard
New Malton, St Michael
Newton-on-Rawcliffe, St John
Normanby, St Andrew
North Grimston, St Nicholas
Norton (-on-Derwent), St Nicholas
Nunnington, All Saints and St James
Old Byland, All Saints
Old Malton, St Mary
Oswaldkirk, St Oswald King and Martyr
Pickering, St Peter and St Paul
Pockley, St Chad
Rillington, St Andrew
Rosedale East and West, St Mary and St Laurence
Salton, St John of Beverley
Sand Hutton, St Leonard

Sand Hutton, St Mary
Scackleton, St George the Martyr
Scampston, St Martin
Scawton, St Mary
Scrayingham, St Peter and St Paul
Settrington, All Saints
Sherburn, St Hilda
Sheriff Hutton, St Helen and the Holy Cross
Sinnington, All Saints
Slingsby, All Saints
Stonegrave, Holy Trinity
Terrington, All Saints
Thornton-le-Dale, All Saints
Thorpe Bassett, All Saints
Upper Helmsley, St Peter
Warthill, St Mary
Weaverthorpe, St Andrew
Welburn, St John the Evangelist
West Heslerton, All Saints
West Lutton, St Mary
Westow, St Mary
Wharram-le-Street, St Mary
Whitwell-on-the-Hill, St John the Evangelist
Willerby, St Peter
Wilton, St George
Wintringham, St Peter
Yedingham, St John the Baptist

Cemeteries

Amotherby Cemetery
Ampleforth Cemetery
Coneysthorpe Cemetery
Helmsley Cemetery
Hovingham Cemetery
Kirby Misperton Cemetery
Kirkbymoorside Cemetery
Leavening Cemetery
Lockton Cemetery
New Malton Cemetery
Newton-on-Rawcliffe Cemetery
Norton Cemetery
Old Malton, (St Mary) Cemetery
Old Malton Cemetery
Pickering Cemetery
Slingsby Cemetery
Terrington Cemetery
Thornton-le-Dale Cemetery

Appendix Four

Burial grounds

Ampleforth, Our Lady and St Benedict RC
Ampleforth, Benedictine
Helmsley, Quaker
Hutton-le-Hole, Quaker
Kirkbymoorside, Quaker
Lowna, Quaker
New Malton, Unitarian
Northallerton, Zion Independent
Pickering, Congregational
Pickering, Quaker
Pickering, Wesleyan Methodist
Thornton-le-Clay, Quaker

Other

Castle Howard Mausoleum
Terrington, Mowthorpe Garden of Rest

Select Bibliography

Note that this bibliography does not reference the substantial archival sources used in the study: for these, full references are given as endnotes. However, note that some more recent references have been amended slightly to exclude the mention of individual families, for example where faculties have been granted.

Parliamentary Sources

Hansard HC Debates
Hansard HL Debates

Legislation

Private Acts

An Act for providing an additional cemetery in the parish of Liverpool in the County Palatine of Lancaster, 1826, 7 Geo. IV c. 52, 5 May.

An Act for establishing a general cemetery for the interment of the dead in the neighbourhood of the metropolis, 1832, 2 & 3 Wil. IV c. 110, 11 Jul.

Public Acts

Church Building Act, 1818
An Act for building and promoting the building of additional Churches in Populous Parishes, 58 Geo. III c. 45, 30 May 1818.

Poor Law Amendment Act, 1844
An Act for the further Amendment of the Laws relating to the Poor in England, 7 & 8 Vict. c. 101, 9 Aug 1844.

Cemeteries Clauses Act, 1847
An Act for consolidating in one Act certain provisions usually contained in Acts authorising the making of Cemeteries, 10 & 11 Vict. c. 65, 9 Jul 1847.

Public Health Act, 1848
An Act for Promoting the Public Health, 11 & 12 Vict. c. 63, 31 Aug 1848.

Burial Act, 1852
An Act to amend the Laws concerning the Burial of the Dead in the Metropolis, 15 & 16 Vict. c. 85, 1 Jul 1852.

Burial Act, 1853
An Act to amend the Laws concerning the Burial of the Dead in England beyond the limits of the Metropolis, and to amend the Act concerning the Burial of the Dead in the Metropolis, 16 & 17 Vict. c. 134, 20 Aug 1853.

Burial Act, 1854
An Act to make further Provision for the Burial of the Dead in England beyond the Limits of the Metropolis, 17 & 18 Vict. c. 87, 10 Aug 1854.

Burial Act, 1855
An Act further to amend the Laws concerning the Burial of the Dead in England, 18 & 19 Vict. c. 128, 14 Aug 1855.

Burial Act, 1857
An Act to amend the Burial Acts, 20 & 21 Vict. c. 81, 25 Aug 1857.

Burial Act, 1860
An Act to make further provision for the expenses of Local Boards of Health and Improvement Commissioners acting as burial boards, 23 & 24 Vict. c. 64, 6 Aug 1860.

Consecration of Churchyards Act, 1867
An Act relating to the Consecration of Churchyards, 30 & 31 Vict. c. 133, 20 Aug 1867.

Public Health (Interments) Act, 1879
An Act to amend the Public Health Act, 1875, as to Interments, 42 & 43 Vict. c. 31, 21 Jul 1867.

Burial Laws Amendment Act, 1880
An Act to amend the Burial Laws, 43 & 44 Vict. c. 41, 7 Sep 1880.

Local Government Act 1894
An Act to make Further Provision for Local Government in England and Wales, 56 & 57 Vict. c. 73, 5 Mar 1894.

Burial Act, 1900
An Act to amend the Law relating to Burial Grounds, 63 & 64 Vict. c. 15, 10 Jul 1900.

Cremation Act, 1902
An Act for the Regulation of the Burning of Human Remains, and to enable Burial Authorities to establish Crematoria, 2 Edw. 7, c. 8, 22 Jul 1902.

Local Government Act, 1972
An Act to make provision with respect to local government and the functions of local authorities in England and Wales; to amend Part II of the Transport Act 1968; to confer rights of appeal in respect of decisions relating to licences under the Home Counties (Music and Dancing) Licensing Act 1926; to make further provision with respect to magistrates' courts committees; to abolish certain inferior courts of record; and for connected purposes, 1972, chapter 70, 26 Oct 1972.

Local Authorities Cemeteries' Order, 1977, SI 1977, no. 204.

Parliamentary reports

1842 (327) *Report from the Select Committee on Improvement of the Health of Towns, together with the minutes of evidence, appendix and index. Effect of Interment of Bodies in Towns.*

1843 (509) *Report on the sanitary condition of the labouring population of Great Britain A supplementary report on the results of a special inquiry into the practice of interment in towns. Made at the request of Her Majesty's Principal Secretary of State for the Home Department. By Edwin Chadwick. Esq barrister at law.*

1876 (269) *Public Works Loan Board. First annual report of the Public Works Loan Board.*

1877 (438) *Churchyards. Return of all parishes in England and Wales in which any new portion of ground has been consecrated to serve as a churchyard since the last return made to Parliament in 1863; distinguishing those which have been purchased by the parish and those which have been purchased by voluntary subscription, or presented as a free gift.*

1882 (309) *Report from the Select Committee on Ecclesiastical and Mortuary Fees, together with the proceedings of the Committee, and minutes of evidence and appendix.*

1889 (288) *Metropolitan Cemeteries.*

1890–91 (30) *Cemeteries (provincial towns).*

1897 (312) *Report from the Select Committee on burial grounds; together with the proceedings of the committee, minutes of evidence and appendix.*

1898 (322) *Report from the Select Committee on burial grounds; together with the proceedings of the committee, minutes of evidence and appendix.*

Printed Primary and Secondary Sources

Andersson, T., 'Appearances and beyond: time and change in Swedish landscape architecture', *Journal of Garden History*, 17 (1997), 278–94.

Ariès, P., *The Hour of Our Death*, trans. H. Weaver (Harmondsworth: Penguin, 1983).

Barnard, S. M., *To Prove I'm Not Forgot: Living and Dying in a Victorian City* (Manchester: Manchester University Press, 1990).

Bateman, J., *The Great Landowners of Great Britain and Ireland* (Leicester: Leicester University Press, 1971 [1876])

Bray, G. (ed.), *The Anglican Canons 1529–1947* (Woodbridge: The Boydell Press, 1998).

Briden, T. and Hanson, B., *Moore's Introduction to English Canon Law* (London: Mowbray, 1992).

Brierley, H., 'The oldest unrestored church in Yorkshire, St Mary's Scawton', *Illustrated Church News*, 29 Oct 1897.

Brooke Little, J. *The Law of Burial* (London: Shaw and Sons, 3rd edn, 1902).

Brooks, C. (ed.), *Mortal Remains: The History and Present State of the Victorian and Edwardian Cemetery* (Exeter: Wheaton Publishers Ltd, 1989).

Brown, C., *The Death of Christian Britain: Understanding Secularisation, 1800–2000* (London: Routledge, 2001).
Buckham, S., 'Delusions of grandeur? The influence of company management, civic pride and private sentiment upon the cemetery landscape at York' in Denk, C. and Ziesemer, J. (eds), *Der Bürgerliche Tod: Städtische Bestattungskultur von der Aufklärung bis zum Frühen 20. Jarhundert* (München: ICOMOS, 2007).
—— 'The men that worked for England, they have their graves at home': consumerist issues within the production and purchase of gravestones in Victorian York', in Tarlow S. and West S. (eds), *The Familiar Past? Archaeologies of Later Historical Britain* (London: Routledge, 1999).
Bulmer, T., *History, Topography and Directory of East Yorkshire* (Preston: T. Bulmer and Co., 1892).
—— *History, Topography and Directory of North Yorkshire* (Preston: T. Bulmer and Co., 1890).
Burgess, F., *English Churchyard Memorials* (London: Lutterworth Press, 1963).
Butlin, R. A., 'Agriculture' in Butlin, R. A. (ed.), *Historical Atlas of North Yorkshire* (Otley: Westbury, 2003).
—— (ed.), *Historical Atlas of North Yorkshire* (Otley: Westbury, 2003).
Cannon, A. (1989) 'The historical dimension in mortuary expressions of status and sentiment', *Current Anthropology*, 30:4 (1989), 437–58.
Central Council for the Care of Churches, *The Care of Churchyards* (London: Church Assembly, 1930).
Church in Country Parishes, The (London: SPCK, 1940).
Church Information Board, *Churchyards. Report of the Maintenance of Churchyards Commission* (London: Church Information Board, 1955).
Church Information Office, *The Churchyards Handbook* (London: Church Information Office, 1962).
Clark, D., *Between Pulpit and Pew: Folk Religion in a North Yorkshire Fishing Village* (Cambridge: Cambridge University Press, 1982).
Clayden, A., Green, T., Hockey, J. and Powell, M., 'From cabbages to cadavers: natural burial down on the farm ' in Maddrell, A. and Sideway, J. (eds), *Deathscapes* (Aldershot: Ashgate, 2010).
Collison, G., *Cemetery Interment* (London: Orme, Brown, Green and Longman, 1840).
Confederation of Burial Authorities, *The CBA Directory of Cemeteries*

and Crematoria in the UK (London: CBA, 2001).

Cressy, D., *Birth, Marriage and Death: Ritual, Religion and the Life-Cycle in Tudor and Stuart England* (Oxford: Oxford University Press, 1999).

Cripps, H. W., *A Practical Treatise on the Law Relating to the Church and the Clergy* (London: Sweet and Maxwell, 1937, 8th edn).

Crowther, A., *The Workhouse System, 1834–1929* (London: Batsford, 1981).

Cunningham Glen, W., *The Burial Board Acts for England and Wales, with the Regulations of the Secretary of State, and Copious Notes of Decided Cases upon the Construction of the Acts and also the Law Relating to the Burial of the Dead* (London: Shaw and Sons, 1869).

Curl, J. S. (ed.), *Kensal Green Cemetery* (Chichester: Phillimore & Co., 2001).

—— 'The General Cemetery from 1833 to 1842' in Curl, J. S. (ed.), *Kensal Green Cemetery* (Chichester: Phillimore & Co., 2001).

—— *The Victorian Celebration of Death* (Newton Abbot: David & Charles, 1972).

Daniell, C., *Death and Burial in Medieval England* (London: Routledge, 1997).

Darnton, R., *The Great Cat Massacre and Other Episodes in French Cultural History* (London: Allen Lane, 1984).

Davies, M. R. R., *The Law of Burial, Cremation and Exhumation* (London: Shaw and Sons, 1956).

Dearmer, P., *The Parson's Handbook* (London: Grant Richards, 1899).

Denk, C. and Ziesemer, J. (eds), *Der Bürgerliche Tod: Städtische Bestattungskultur von der Aufklärung bis zum Frühen 20. Jarhundert* (München: ICOMOS, 2007).

Doe, N., *The Legal Framework of the Church of England: A Critical Study in a Comparative Context* (Oxford: Clarendon Press, 1996).

Dymond, D., 'God's disputed acre', *Journal of Ecclesiastical History*, 50 (1999), 464–97.

Ellerton, J. (ed.), *A Manual of Parochial Work for the Use of Younger Clergy* (London: SPCK, 1908).

English, B., *The Great Landowners of East Yorkshire, 1530–1910* (Howden: Hull Academic Press, 1990).

Etlin, R., *The Architecture of Death: The Transformation of the Cemetery in Eighteenth-Century Paris* (Cambridge, MA: MIT Press, 1984).

Everett, A., *The Pattern of Rural Dissent: The Nineteenth Century*

(Leicester: Leicester University Press, 1972).
Finch, J., '"According to the qualitie and degree of the person deceased": funeral monuments and the construction of social identities', *Scottish Archaeological Review*, 8:15 (1991), 105–14.
Finer, S. E., *The Life and Times of Edwin Chadwick* (London: Methuen, 1952).
Flinn, M. (ed.), *Report on the Sanitary Condition of the Labouring Classes* (Edinburgh: Edinburgh University Press, 1965).
Foucault, M. 'Different spaces', trans. R. Hurley in Faubion, J. D. (ed.), *The Essential Works of Foucault, 1954–1984* (Harmondsworth: Penguin, 2000).
Francis, D., Kellaher, L. and Neophytou, G., *The Secret Cemetery* (Oxford: Berg, 2005).
Francis, F. and Smithson J., *A History of Burythorpe, A Yorkshire Village* (Private publication, nd, probably post 2000).
Gittings, C. (1984) *Death, Burial and the Individual* (London: Croom Helm, 1984).
Gittos, H., 'Creating the sacred: Anglo-Saxon rituals for consecrating cemeteries', in Lucy, S. and Reynolds, A. (eds), *Burial in Early Medieval England and Wales* (London: Society for Medieval Archaeology, 2002).
Gordon, B. and Marshall, P., 'Introduction' in Gordon, B. and Marshall, P. (eds), *The Place of the Dead: Death and Remembrance in Late Medieval and Early Modern Europe* (Cambridge: Cambridge University Press, 2000).
Gorer, G., *Death, Grief and Mourning in Contemporary Britain* (London: The Cresset Press, 1965).
Grady, K., *The Georgian Public Buildings of Leeds and the West Riding* (Leeds: Publications of the Thoresby Society, 1989).
Grainge, W., *The History and Topography of Harrogate, and the Forest of Knaresborough* (London: Simkins, Marshall and Co., 1882).
Gramer, A., 'John the Evangelist, Easingwold: A Century and a Half, 1833–1983', *Ampleforth Journal*, 89 (Spring 1984).
Green, S. J. D., *Religion in the Age of Decline: Organisation and Experience in Industrial Yorkshire, 1870–1920* (Cambridge: Cambridge University Press, 1996).
Haggard, R., *Rural England: Being an Account of Agricultural and Social Researches Carried Out in the Years 1901 and 1902* (London: Longmans, Green and Co., 1906).
Hamlin, C., 'Muddling in bumbledom: on the enormity of large

sanitary improvements in four British towns, 1855–1885', *Victorian Studies*, 32:1 (1988), 55–83.

—— *Public Health and Social Justice in the Age of Chadwick, Britain 1800–1854* (Cambridge: Cambridge University Press, 1998).

Harding, V., *The Dead and the Living in Paris and London, 1500–1670* (Cambridge: Cambridge University Press, 2002).

Hargrove, A. E., *The Baneful Custom of Interment in Towns and the Present State of York Graveyards* (York, 1847).

Harrisson, T., *Britain Revisited* (London: Victor Gollancz, 1961).

Hawkins, D., 'The Black Death and the new London cemeteries of 1348', *Antiquity*, 64 (1990), 637–42.

Heeney, B., *A Different Kind of Gentleman: Parish Clergy as Professional Men in Early and Mid-Victorian England* (Hamden, CT: Archon Books, 1976).

Herman, A., 'Death has a touch of class: society and space in Brookwood Cemetery, 1853–1903', *Journal of Historical Geography*, 36:3 (2010), 305–14.

Hinton, M. G., *The Anglican Parochial Clergy* (London: SCM, 1964).

Hotz, M. E., *Literary Remains: Representations of Death and Burial in Victorian England* (Albany, NY: State University of New York Press, 2008).

Houlbrooke, R. 'The age of decency', in Jupp, P. C. and Gittings, C. (eds), *Death in England: An Illustrated History* (Manchester: Manchester University Press, 1999).

—— *Death, Religion and the Family in England 1480–1750* (Oxford: Clarendon Press, 1998).

Hunt, B. C., *The Development of the Business Corporation in England, 1800–1867* (Cambridge, MA: Harvard University Press, 1936).

Hurren, E. and King, S., '"Begging for a burial": form, function and conflict in nineteenth-century pauper burial', *Social History*, 30:3 (2005), 321–41.

Iggers, G. G. (1997) *Historiography in the Twentieth Century: From Scientific Objectivity to the Postmodern Challenge* (Hanover, NH: University Press of New England, 1997).

Jackson, T., *The Life of the Rev. Robert Newton, DD* (London: John Mason, 1855).

Jalland, P., *Death in War and Peace: A History of Loss and Grief in England, 1914–1970* (Oxford: Oxford University Press, 2010).

Jenner, M., 'Death, decomposition and dechristianisation? Public health and Christian burial in eighteenth-century England',

English Historical Studies, 487:CXX (2005), 615–32.
Jennings, B. (ed.), *A History of Nidderdale* (Huddersfield: Advertiser Press, 1967).
Johnson, P., 'The modern cemetery: a design for life', *Social and Cultural Geography*, 9:7 (2008), 777–90.
Jones, A., *A Thousand Years of the English Parish* (Moreton-in-Marsh: Windrush Press, 2000).
Joyce, P., *A Guide to Abney Park Cemetery* (London: SAPC, 1984).
Jupp, P. C., *From Dust to Ashes: Cremation and the British Way of Death* (Basingstoke: Palgrave Macmillan, 2006).
Kellaher, L., Prendergast, D. and Hockey, J., 'In the shadow of the traditional grave', *Mortality*, 10:4 (2005), 237–50.
Kenyon, F., *War Graves: How Cemeteries Abroad Will Be Designed* (London: HM Stationery Office, 1918).
Knighton, L., *Bakewell Church* (Derby: Derbyshire Countryside Ltd, 1985).
Kong, L. 'Cemeteries and columbaria, memorials and mausoleums: narrative and interpretation in the study of deathscapes in geography', *Australian Geographical Studies*, 37:1 (2002), 1–10.
Kselman, T. A., *Death and the Afterlife in Modern France* (Princeton: Princeton University Press, 1993).
Laqueur, T., 'Cemeteries, religion and the culture of capitalism' in Garnett, J. and Matthew, C. (eds), *Revival and Religion since 1700* (London: Hambleton Press, 1993).
—— 'The places of the dead in modernity' in Jones, C. and Wahrman, D. (eds), *The Age of Cultural Revolutions. Britain and France, 1750–1820* (London: University of California Press, 2002).
Larsen, T., *Friends of Religious Equality: Nonconformist Politics in Mid-Victorian England* (Woodbridge: Boydell Press, 1999).
Lawton, R., 'Population change, 1700–1900' in Butler, R. A. (ed.), *Historical Atlas of North Yorkshire* (Otley: Westbury, 2003).
Lewis, R. A., *Edwin Chadwick and the Public Health Movement* (London: Longmans, Green and Co., 1952).
Loudon, J. C., *On the Laying Out, Planting and Managing of Cemeteries; and on the Improvement of Churchyard* (London: Longman, Brown, Green, 1843).
Mackintosh, W. H., *Disestablishment and Liberation: The Movement for the Separation of the Anglican Church from State Control* (London: Epworth Press, 1972).
Manning, B. (ed.), O. Greenwood, *The Protestant Dissenting Deputies*

(Cambridge: Cambridge University Press, 1952).
Mant, N., *Eighteen Years' Work in a Yorkshire Parish* (Scarborough: E. T. W. Dennis, 1889).
Martin, S. K., 'Monuments in the garden: the garden cemetery in Australia', *Postcolonial Studies*, 3:7 (1994), 333–52.
Matthews, S., *Poetical Remains: Poets' Graves, Bodies, and Books in the Nineteenth Century* (Oxford: Oxford University Press, 2004).
McFarland, E. 'Researching death, mourning and commemoration in modern Scotland', *Journal of Scottish Historical Studies*, 24: 1 (2005), 20–44.
Meller, P. A., 'Death in high modernity: the contemporary presence and absence of death' in Clark, D. (ed.), *The Sociology of Death: Theory, Culture and Practice* (Oxford: Blackwell Publishers, 1993).
Milner, G., *On Cemetery Burial; or Sepulture Ancient and Modern* (London: Joseph Masters, 1846).
Mitchie, R. C., *Money, Mania and Markets: Investment Company Formation and the Stock Exchange in Nineteenth-Century Scotland* (Edinburgh: John Donald, 1981).
Morley, J., *Death, Heaven and the Victorians* (Pittsburgh, PA: University of Pittsburgh Press, 1971).
Morris, R. J., *Cholera 1832: The Social Response to an Epidemic* (London: Croom Helm, 1976).
Mowat, C. L., *Britain between the Wars, 1918–1940* (London: Methuen and Co., 1955).
Muncey, R. W., *A History of the Consecration of Churches and Churchyards* (Cambridge: W. Heffer & Sons Ltd, 1930).
Munslow, A. *The Routledge Companion to Historical Studies* (London: Routledge, 2000).
Murray, H., *This Garden of Death: The History of York Cemetery, 1837–2007* (York: Friends of York Cemetery, 2008).
Nash, G., 'Pomp and circumstances: archaeology, modernity and the corporatisation of death: early social and political Victorian attitudes towards burial practice' in Graves-Brown, P. M. (ed.), *Matter, Materiality and Culture* (London: Routledge, 2000).
Newbolt, W. C. E., *Priestly Ideals* (London: Longmans, Green and Co., 1899).
O'Sullivan, D., *Great Ayton: A History of the Village* (Great Ayton: private publication, nd).
Page, W., *A History of the County of York, North Riding: Volume 2* (London: Victoria County History, 1923).

Parsons, B., *Committed to the Cleansing Flame: The Development of Cremation in Nineteenth-century England* (Reading: Spire Books, 2005).

—— 'Where did the ashes go? Part 2', *Journal of the Institute of Cemetery and Crematorium Management*, 73:2 (2005), 28.

Pearson, M. Parker, 'Mortuary practices, society and ideology: an ethnoarchaeological study' in Hodder, I. (ed.), *Symbolic and Structural Archaeology* (Cambridge: Cambridge University Press, 1982).

Pellew, J., *The Home Office 1848–1914. From Clerks to Bureaucrats* (London: Heinemann Educational Books, 1982).

Pevsner, N., *Yorkshire The North Riding* (London: Yale University Press, 2002 [1966]).

—— *Yorkshire The West Riding* (London: Yale University Press, 2003 [1959]).

Pevsner, N., and Neave, D., *Yorkshire: York and the East Riding* (London: Yale University Press, 2005 [1972]).

Piggott, A. E., *Municipal Cemetery Undertakings* (London: The Cremation Society, 1928).

Polson, C. J., *The Disposal of the Dead* (London: English Universities Press, 1953).

Port, M. H., *Six Hundred New Churches: A Study of the Church Building Commission, 1818–1856, and Its Church Building Activities* (London: SPCK, 1961).

Prest, J., *Liberty and Locality: Parliament, Permissive Legislation and Ratepayers' Democracies in the Nineteenth Century* (Oxford: Clarendon Press, 1990).

Ragon, M., *The Space of Death: A Study of Funerary Architecture, Decoration and Urbanism* trans A. Sheridan (Charlottesville, VA: University Press of Virginia, 1983).

Ranger, W., *Report to the General Board of Health, on a Preliminary Inquiry into the Sewerage, Drainage, and Supply of Water, and the Sanitary Condition of the Inhabitants of the Town of Northallerton, in the County of York* (London: HMSO, 1850).

—— *Report to the General Board of Health on a Preliminary Inquiry into the Sewerage, Drainage, and Supply of Water, and the Sanitary Condition of the Inhabitants of the Township of Ripon* (London: HMSO, 1854).

Raven, N., 'De-industrialisation and the urban response: the small towns of the North Riding of Yorkshire c1790–1850' in Weedon,

R. and Milne, A. (eds), *Aspects of Small English Towns in the Eighteenth and Nineteenth Centuries* (Leicester: Centre for Urban History, 1993).

Rawlinson, R., *Report to the General Board of Health on a Preliminary Inquiry into the Sewerage, Drainage and Supply of Water, and the Sanitary Condition of the Inhabitants of the Parliamentary Borough of Malton* (London: HMSO, 1854).

Rawnsley, S. and Reynolds, J. 'Undercliffe Cemetery, Bradford', *History Workshop*, 4 (Autumn, 1977), 215–21.

Richardson, R. and Curl, J. S., 'George Frederick Carden and the genesis of the General Cemetery Company' in Curl, J. S. (ed.), *Kensal Green Cemetery* (Chichester: Phillimore & Co., 2001).

Roach, J., *Cities of the Dead: Circum-Atlantic Performance* (New York: Columbia University Press, 1996).

Roberts, H. E., *Researching Yorkshire Quaker History: A Guide to Sources* (Hull: University of Hull Brynmor Jones Library, 2003).

Rodes, R. E., *Law and Modernisation in the Church of England, Charles II to the Welfare State* (Notre Dame, IN: University of Notre Dame Press, 1991).

Royle, E., 'Administrative changes in Local Government, 1600–1900' in Butlin, R. A. (ed.), *Historical Atlas of North Yorkshire* (Otley: Westbury, 2003).

Rugg, J. 'Defining the place of burial: what makes a cemetery a cemetery?', *Mortality*, 5:3 (2000), 238–59.

—— 'Lawn cemeteries: the emergence of a new landscape of death', *Urban History*, 33:2 (2006), 213–33.

—— 'Managing "Civilian Deaths due to War Operations": Yorkshire experiences during World War II', *Twentieth Century British History*, 15:2 (2004), 152–73.

—— 'A new burial form and its meanings: cemetery establishment in the first half of the nineteenth century' in Cox, M. (ed.), *Grave Concerns: Death and Burial in England, 1700–1850* (York: Council for British Archaeology, 1998).

Rushton, J., *The History of Ryedale: From the Earliest Times to the Year 2000* (Trowbridge: Blackthorn Press, 2003).

Russell, A., *The Country Parish* (London: SPCK, 1986).

Scotland, N., *Methodism and the Revolt of the Field* (Gloucester: Alan Sutton, 1981).

Shiels, W., 'Roman Catholic recusancy 1580–1792' in Butlin, R. A. (ed.), *Historical Atlas of North Yorkshire* (Otley: Westbury, 2003).

Shiels, W. and Lawton, R., 'The Religious Census of 1851', in Butlin, R. A. (ed.), *Historical Atlas of North Yorkshire* (Otley: Westbury, 2003).

Simon, J., *English Sanitary Institutions* (London: Cassell and Co., 1970 [1890]).

Sington, A., *The Interment of the Dead* (Manchester: John Heywood, 1888).

Sloane, D. C., *The Last Great Necessity: Cemeteries in American History* (Baltimore MD: Johns Hopkins University Press, 1991).

Smale, D., *Davies' Law of Burial, Cremation and Exhumation* (Crayford: Shaw and Sons, 1993, 6th edn).

Smith, M., 'The Church of Scotland and the funeral industry in nineteenth-century Edinburgh', *The Scottish Historical Review*, 88:1 (2009), 108–33.

Snell, K. D. M. and Ell, P. S., *Rival Jerusalems: The Geography of Victorian Religion* (Cambridge: Cambridge University Press, 2000).

Speight, H., *Kirkby Overblow and District* (London: Eliot Stock, 1903).

Spicer, A. '"God will have a house": sacred space and rites of consecration in early seventeenth-century England' in Hamilton, S. and Spicer, A. (eds), *Defining the Holy: Sacred Space in Medieval and Modern Europe* (Aldershot: Ashgate, 2005).

Stock, G., 'Quaker burial: doctrine and practice' in Cox, M. (ed.), *Grave Concerns: Death and Burial in England, 1700–1850* (York: Council for British Archaeology, 1998).

Strange, J.-M., *Death, Grief and Poverty in Britain, 1870–1914* (Cambridge: Cambridge University Press, 2005).

Sykes, N. (ed.), *The Position of the Laity in the Church, being the Report of the Joint Committee of the Convocation of Canterbury, 1902* (London: Church Information Board, 1952 [1902]).

Tarlow, S., *Bereavement and Commemoration: An Archaeology of Mortality* (Oxford: Blackwell, 1999).

—— 'Each slow dusk a drawing-down of blinds', *Archaeological Review from Cambridge*, 11:1 (1992), 125–40.

—— *Ritual, Belief and the Dead in Early Modern Britain and Ireland* (Cambridge: Cambridge University Press, 2011).

—— 'Wormie clay and blessed sleep: death and disgust in later historic Britain' in Tarlow, S. and West, S. (eds), *The Familiar Past? Archaeologies of Later Historical Britain* (London: Routledge, 1999).

Thompson, F. M. L., *English Landed Society in the Nineteenth Century* (London: Routledge and Kegan Paul, 1963).

Thompson, K. A., *Bureaucracy and Church Reform: The Organisational Response of the Church of England to Social Change, 1800–1965* (Oxford: Clarendon Press, 1970).

Thompson, V., *Dying and Death in Later Anglo-Saxon England* (Woodbridge: The Boydell Press, 2004).

Tyson, N., 'Candie Cemetery and its monuments: death and self-presentation in 19th century St Peter Port, Guernsey', *Societé Guernestaine Report and Transactions*, 23:3 (1993), 599–626.

Walker, G., *Gatherings from Graveyards* (London: Longman's and Co., 1839).

Walter, T., *The Revival of Death* (London: Routledge, 1994).

Ware, F., *The Immortal Heritage* (Cambridge: Cambridge University Press, 1937).

Waterson, E., 'The development of the country house', in Butlin, R. A. (ed.), *Historical Atlas of North Yorkshire* (Otley: Wesbury: 2003).

Watts, M. R., *The Dissenters Volume II: The Expansion of Evangelical Nonconformity* (Oxford: Clarendon Press, 1995).

Webb, S. and B., *British Local Government from the Revolution to the Municipal Corporations Act* (London: Longmans, Green and Co., 1924).

Welch, P. J., 'Bishop Blomfield and church extension in London', *Journal of Ecclesiastical History*, 4 (1953), 203–15.

West, K., *A Guide to Woodland Burial* (London: Shaw and Sons, 2010).

Whistler, L., *The Imagination of Vanburgh and His Fellow Artists* (London: B. T. Batsford, 1954).

Whitehead, T., *Illustrated Guide to Nidderdale and a History of Its Congregational Churches* (Keighley: Feather Books, 1932).

Wiggins, D., 'The Burial Act of 1880, The Liberation Society and George Osborne Morgan', *Parliamentary History*, 15:2 (1996), 173–89.

Wilson, A. and Levy, H., *Burial Reform and Funeral Costs* (Oxford: Oxford University Press, 1938).

Wolffe, J., *The Religious Census of 1851 in Yorkshire* (York: Borthwick Paper 108, 2005).

Wrigley, F., *The History of the Yorkshire Congregational Union, 1873–1923* (London: James Clarke and Co., 1923).

York, Diocese of, *The Care of Churchyards* (London: SPCK, 1936).

Newspapers and periodicals

Easingwold Advertiser and Weekly News
Lancet
London Gazette
Malton Gazette
Northern Echo
The Times
York Herald
Yorkshire Gazette

Unpublished Sources

Matthews, S., 'Representations of the grave in nineteenth-century English poetry: a selected commentary' (PhD dissertation, University College, London, 1997).

Rugg, J., 'The rise of cemetery companies in Britain, 1820–53' (PhD dissertation, University of Stirling, 1992).

Sellers, I., 'Liverpool Nonconformity' (PhD dissertation, University of Keele, 1969).

Stirling, F., 'Grave re-use: a feasibility study' (PhD dissertation, University of Sheffield, 2009).

Wiggins, D., 'The Burial Acts: cemetery reform in Great Britain, 1815–1914' (PhD dissertation, Texas Tech University, 1991).

Internet Sources

'Cimitière', in *Encyclopédie, ou Dictionnaire Raisonné des Sciences, des Arts et des Métiers*, accessed June 2005, humanities.uchicago.edul/ARTFL/projects/encyc/

english-heritage.org.uk/publications/list-cemeteries/, pages accessed October 2011

justice.gov.uk/downloads/burials-and-coroners/natural-burial-grounds-guidance.pdf, pages accessed June 2012

Index

Note: page numbers in *italics* refer to illustrations

Index

CPSIA information can be obtained at www.ICGtesting.com
Printed in the USA
BVOW04s1742121015

421814BV00004B/16/P

9 780719 097355